CHILDHOODS

CHILDHOODS

CHILDHOODS
Growing up in Aotearoa
New Zealand

EDITED BY

Nancy Higgins
& Claire Freeman

First published 2013
Text copyright © the authors as named
Volume copyright © Otago University Press

The moral rights of the author have been asserted.
ISBN 978-1-877578-49-6

A catalogue record for this book is available from the National Library of New Zealand.
This book is copyright. Except for the purpose of fair review, no part may be
stored or transmitted in any form or by any means, electronic or mechanical, including
recording or storage in any information retrieval system, without permission in writing
from the publishers. No reproduction may be made, whether by photocopying or by any
other means, unless a licence has been obtained from the publisher.

Publisher: Rachel Scott
Editor: Vanessa Manhire
Design/layout: Fiona Moffat
Index: Diane Lowther

Printed in New Zealand by PrintStop Ltd, Wellington
Front cover: Children enjoying the playground at Dansey's Pass Holiday Park.

Contents

	Foreword / *Keith Ballard*	7
	PART ONE: THE CONTEXT	
Chapter 1	Introduction: Children in Aotearoa New Zealand – an overview / *Claire Freeman & Nancy Higgins*	13
Chapter 2	A theoretical framework for childhood / *Anne B. Smith*	29
Chapter 3	Children and vulnerability / *Nicola Atwool*	44
Chapter 4	The changing environmental worlds of Aotearoa New Zealand children / *Claire Freeman*	59
Chapter 5	Ethics in research with children / *Jude MacArthur & Margaret McKenzie*	77
	PART TWO: EXPERIENCING DIVERSE CHILDHOODS	
Chapter 6	Recollecting childhood at school in the early twentieth century / *Helen May*	95
Chapter 7	Managed childhoods: A social history of urban children's play / *Christina R. Ergler, Robin Kearns & Karen Witten*	110
Chapter 8	Growing up Māori and disabled in Aotearoa New Zealand / *Hazel Phillips & Nancy Higgins*	126
Chapter 9	Multicultural childhoods in a globalised world / *Karen Guo*	141
Chapter 10	Children and young people's participation in family law decision-making / *Nicola Taylor & Megan Gollop*	153
Chapter 11	The needs of adopted and fostered children / *Anita Gibbs*	167
Chapter 12	Being young and working / *Ruth Gasson & James Calder*	180

Chapter 13 Technology occupies us: Children, media and Aotearoa
New Zealand society / *Martha Bell & Victoria Farmer*   192

PART THREE: CHILDREN'S AND YOUNG PEOPLE'S VOICES

Chapter 14 Children's participation and voice in early childhood
education / *Lyn Foote, Fiona Elllis & Ruth Gasson*   207

Chapter 15 Children of prisoners / *Julie Lawrence*   220

Chapter 16 Children's understandings of success / *Judith Sligo &
Karen Nairn*   235

Chapter 17 Disrupting heteronormativity: A high-school
queer–straight alliance? / *Kathleen Quinlivan*   249

Chapter 18 Stories from the margins: Rangatahi Māori experiences of
transition to work / *Moana Mitchell & Hazel Phillips*   262

Chapter 19 Conclusion: Where are we going? / *Nancy Higgins &
Claire Freeman*   274

About the contributors   281
References   287
Index   317

Foreword

This is a book about children. It will be of value to parents, family, whānau, professionals and any combination of these. The editors, Nancy Higgins and Claire Freeman, together with the researchers who have written with them, ask what it is that we know about children's lives in Aotearoa New Zealand and what it is that children know of us and of a world they are active in forming.

Some chapters closely examine the sociopolitical contexts in which children's lives are embedded. Others give us access to how children experience their homes, classrooms and communities, how they read and interpret their relationships with adults and with one another, and what is good and not so good in their interactions with people and places. What the children have to say is insightful and sometimes deeply moving. It suggests that what we think we know about children may not represent the perceptions and experiences that children themselves live, enjoy, fear, share and keep secret each and every day.

There are a range of professional groups – law, health, social services, education – that would see understanding children and the worlds in which they live as an essential basis for the theory and practice of their field. In education, for example, the notion of pedagogy embraces a concern for the well-being of children. It means that in order to teach, we should – as best we can – strive to relate to children and to understand 'the world in which [our] students live' (Freire, 1998, p. 72). This is not to frame the teacher as a social worker or political activist, although some may choose aspects of those roles as part of the teaching role. They will understand that classroom interactions are imbued with the power differentials of the wider society and so can involve experiences of both justice and injustice. A contextual model of pedagogy, therefore, requires that we take children and research about children seriously, which is what this very good book does.

The researchers in this collection of studies have examined the environments that adults create for children: environments determined by sociocultural beliefs regarding how children are to be thought of, supported and constrained. For example, we are reminded that in the early days of schooling in Aotearoa New Zealand the classrooms were often highly regimented and included the use of a strap or cane to beat children. This seems a limited and unkind world for the child. Yet quite recently many people marched in our streets to oppose a 2007 law that regulated against hitting children and against other violent acts that some adults use to control and constrain younger people.

These protests were not successful and this law has not been changed. In this and in other ways we now acknowledge that, in words at least, children are citizens with autonomy and rights identified by international agencies and United Nations conventions. However, as we can read in this book, it is often the case that these rights are not readily enforceable and that in Aotearoa New Zealand we have some of the worst levels of child poverty and child health in the OECD (Organisation for Economic Cooperation and Development) countries, along with exceptionally high rates of child suicide. So how much has changed since children were held silent in classrooms and physically abused for poor spelling or for speaking Māori? As this book records, a childhood of hardship and deprivation in a context of high levels of inequality is not an environment of social justice for more than a quarter of our children, who are denied the economic and social resources necessary for health and enjoyment and for a fair chance in the world of adulthood.

Māori children face particular challenges in this regard. In 2004, the then leader of the National Party, Don Brash, gave a speech at Orewa in which he described Māori concerns over stolen land as the 'Treaty grievance industry'; claimed that Māori gained special privileges from government funding based on 'race'; and suggested that there were no 'full blooded Māori', a reference to the idea of blood purity that forms a basis for eugenics. In an editorial, the *Sydney Morning Herald* said that this speech 'was playing the race card' and that the 'liberation of racist ... views ... is not always easy to reverse' (Editorial, 2004, p. 12). That would seem to be the case, and such views, which have proven highly popular, are now present in mainstream print and broadcast media. What must it be like for Māori children to hear their identity and culture dismissed day after day? What are the implications for all children when the expression of such views is normalised?

In his book based on documents from within the National party, Nicky Hager (2006) shows that those writing the Don Brash speech knew that their claim of 'Māori privilege' could not be sustained because, as one said, 'Māori are generally at the bottom of the heap' (p. 93). Just how serious the overall situation for Māori has become under both Labour- and National-led governments as they pursue their neo-liberal agenda is evident in research by the Ministry of Health and the University of Otago (2006). A basic measure of the well-being of a group of people is their mortality, that is, how long they live. The Ministry of Health and University of Otago research covering the years 1981 to 1999 shows that in this period, which they describe as the 'decades of disparity,' Māori showed a decline in life expectancy in comparison with non-Māori. At the beginning of the period (1981), Māori were living six to seven years less than non-Māori. By 1999 the difference was eight to nine years. The data showed that neither socio-economic status nor lifestyle factors, such as diet and smoking, could account for this discrepancy. The researchers concluded that the serious decline in Māori well-being over these years reflected a 'racialised social order' of economic and health inequality (p. 4).

In terms of our ideas about childhood and support for families, this research holds significant implications for Māori children whose lives in our settler society are the focus of several chapters in the present book. But there are also implications in this data for all of our futures in terms of the kind of society that we wish to be.

The kind of society we are now is made evident throughout this book but particularly in chapters that discuss the experiences of children who are seen as not conforming to a white, able-bodied heterosexual norm. These accounts show that our responses to cultural differences, to disability and to different sexualities may either value or reject some children, engendering either pride in their identity or distress over their oppression. In these areas in particular – but also a feature throughout this book – the writers show the power of theory for analysing and interpreting how we choose to know and name the world and the implications for children's lives of the constructions and discourses that we use to shape policy and practice.

The research reported in this book identifies areas of policy and practice that are failing many children and in their concluding chapter, the editors outline some economic, social and environmental issues that need urgent attention. In this regard our failure to develop effective ways to address climate change is surely one area that will have the most profound implications for our children and grandchildren. Climate scientist James Hansen (2011), Director of NASA space studies, says that our failure to protect future generations from 'climate catastrophe' is a 'gross case of intergenerational injustice' (p. 258) and an issue in which we are all implicated.

From this book we can see that there are adults and children who do care about fairness and justice and, from the stories told here, we might identify ways in which all of our lives could be better. Progress toward a better world for children would involve rejecting the neo-liberal values of selfishness, inequality and consumerism and supporting more cooperative ideas and actions for the social good.

We will clearly need to act cooperatively on global warming if we are to ensure any kind of sustainable future – or any kind of future at all – for the world's children. Thinking seriously about children, as this book does, could encourage us to act from a sense of responsibility and interdependency in our lives. We might then accept that humans are irrevocably linked to one another and to the various and complex non-human life forms and natural systems of our planet.

Keith Ballard
Emeritus Professor of Education
University of Otago

PART ONE

The Context: Children in Aotearoa New Zealand

PART ONE

The Care of Children in Aotearoa New Zealand

INTRODUCTION

Children in Aotearoa New Zealand – an overview

Claire Freeman & Nancy Higgins

A book on childhood

Currently around a quarter of New Zealanders are experiencing childhood, and one-third of all households include children, yet we know little about how childhood is experienced by children. We know some key statistics: the number of children as a proportion of the population decreased from one in three in 1971 to one in four in 2001; over half of children, at the time of the census, had lived overseas or elsewhere in Aotearoa New Zealand; and only 5% did not have at-home access to telecommunications (Statistics New Zealand, 2002). Children in Aotearoa New Zealand are living in a changing world and planet; they are becoming a smaller proportion of our society; they reflect the increasingly diverse nature of Aotearoa New Zealand's population; and they are more physically mobile in regards to where they live. They are more connected to the global network than their parents were, and some children are becoming increasingly involved in decisions about their own lives. Children growing up in Aotearoa New Zealand today are experiencing a very different world and a very different childhood from that experienced by previous generations.

Is it a better or worse childhood, or both? Children today have access to a wide choice of excellent well-resourced schools. In rural areas, however, many schools, which are so important for small communities, have closed or are threatened with closure. Many children have increasing access to a vast range of activities, from swimming, kapa haka, BMX riding, surfing, chess and robotics clubs to that ever-present rugby club, but they are also under pressure to succeed academically, culturally and socially in ways that leave some children with little time for childhood.

The environments that Aotearoa New Zealand children live in and visit can be stunning. There are long golden beaches, swimming lakes, mountains and forests; but rivers here are polluted, and children are the most likely population sector to live in overcrowded homes and experience respiratory disease associated with cold, uninsulated housing. Aotearoa New Zealand also has one of the fastest-growing income gaps between the rich and the poor. In 1986 an estimated 11% of children lived in poverty; by 2011, that figure had risen to 25%, or about 270,000 children (Child Poverty Action Group, 2012).

Socially, Aotearoa New Zealand is diverse. It is a bicultural nation in which Māori (the indigenous people) and other New Zealanders experience two cultures, Māori and the European (Pākehā) culture that predominates. There seem to be 'two worlds' in Aotearoa New Zealand as well, in that Māori are more likely to experience poverty, violence, and difficulty at school. Within the main Pākehā world, there are also a multitude of New Zealanders of different cultures and ethnicities. Children in Aotearoa New Zealand live in a variety of whānau or family structures. There is no universal Aotearoa New Zealand childhood, but a multiplicity of childhoods that reflect the many ways that the country provides or fails to provide for its children. In this book we explore, and contemplate, the nature of childhood in Aotearoa New Zealand today.

Updating childhood

Our book, we hope, will fill a gap in the literature about childhood in Aotearoa New Zealand, and also provide an enjoyable and informative read. Few books have addressed the overarching nature of Aotearoa New Zealand childhoods. By contrast, there is a wealth of stories written for children,[1] as well as a good number of academic books about specific aspects of Aotearoa New Zealand childhood, such as child development (Smith, 2005), inclusive and 'special' education (Carrington & MacArthur, 2012; Frazer, Motzen & Ryba, 2005), early childhood and schooling (Duncan, 2012; May, 2011), disability and whānau (Ballard, 1998), children and young people's rights (Smith, 2000), transitions from school (Nairn, Higgins & Sligo, 2012), play (Sutton Smith, 1981), and most recently, children and democracy (Hayward, 2012). The last study to tackle Aotearoa New Zealand childhood as a whole was Ritchie and Ritchie's 1978 book *Growing up in New Zealand*, and as we have identified, much has changed since the children of 1978 became the parents of today.

This book aims to better understand what it means to be a child in Aotearoa New Zealand today. It presents current issues and research about diverse childhoods and 'growing up' in Aotearoa New Zealand, focusing on

---

1 Aotearoa New Zealand has some very well-known children's authors, such as Margaret Mahy and Lynley Dodd (author of the Hairy Maclary series).

issues such as social justice, children's voices and rights, identity, societal change and the experience of different childhoods in Aotearoa New Zealand. The first part sets the framework for this book and the context for the study of childhood in Aotearoa New Zealand, looking at Childhood Studies, vulnerability, children's environments, and considerations around researching with children. In Chapter 2, Anne Smith further discusses the chapters in this book in relation to Childhood Studies theory. Part Two explores diversity in childhood and key issues affecting Aotearoa New Zealand's children in the past and in the present, including school, play, the law, work and the media as well as the context for different childhood experiences, such as being Māori and disabled, being adopted or fostered, and experiencing other cultures. The final part of the book presents children's and young people's voices in diverse settings and with reference to a range of issues, including early childhood, parents in prison, ideas of success, gay–straight alliances in secondary schools, and Māori youth's transitions to work and adulthood.

The book was initiated by the University of Otago's Children and Young People as Social Actors Research Cluster. The researchers in this Cluster come from a diverse range of academic disciplines, such as education, Māori studies, health, law, social policy, planning, disability, geography, social work and anthropology. However, despite this wealth of expertise, this is not a book written by the Cluster alone: it also includes contributions from researchers from elsewhere in Aotearoa New Zealand whose work was too important to leave out.

We intend that families, students, policymakers, researchers and academics will use this book as a general resource when exploring what it means to be a child in Aotearoa New Zealand. It will be of interest to social work, sociology, education, and youth work practitioners and students, as well as to a range of childhood-related professions and general readership. This book will inform our community about the diverse nature of childhoods in Aotearoa New Zealand and the issues that need to be addressed so that children can positively participate and be included in a society that takes account of all children's needs, voices and perspectives.

To set the scene, we now look at the physical, social and economic character of Aotearoa New Zealand, its way of life and the state of children in general. However, Aotearoa New Zealand in the twenty-first century is a connected place, part of a wider global context whose influence on children's lives we ignore at our peril. It is no longer only Aotearoa New Zealand's young people, by way of that stalwart institution called the great 'OE' (overseas experience), who are connecting internationally, but all of its children and youth.

Aotearoa New Zealand: A good place to grow up?

Aotearoa New Zealand is a small country, with a population of four and a half million people (Statistics NZ, 2011), half a million of whom are Māori. It has a stable population in terms of growth. The population is unevenly distributed, with three-quarters living in the North Island and one-third concentrated in Auckland; around 87% of Māori live in the North Island, though only 24% in Auckland. Significant are the number of New Zealanders living abroad, estimated at around 600,000 (477,000 in Australia). Many of these are young New Zealanders, who after completing high school or tertiary education, go abroad for their OE, a common 'rite of passage' for the previous generation as well. While most young New Zealanders do return, not all do, and some return later bringing with them children and partners. A common rationale for returning is the desire to enable their children to have an Aotearoa New Zealand childhood, which brings us to the primary question addressed in this book: *is Aotearoa New Zealand a good place to grow up?*

According to the United Nations Human Development Report 2013, Aotearoa New Zealand was among the countries in the 'very high human development' category, ranking sixth (United Nations, 2013). In the 13th State of the World's Mothers report (Save the Children, 2012), which ranks the best countries in which to be a mother, Aotearoa New Zealand came fourth behind Norway, Iceland and Sweden. In contrast, the report *Measuring Child Poverty* ranked New Zealand twentieth out of 35 OECD countries in regards to the percentage of children living in relative poverty (OECD, 2009). Aotearoa New Zealand was in the bottom half for most measures in this report, except literacy. Our suicide rate was the worst, more than twice the OECD average, and our teenage birth rate was also high, surpassed only by Mexico, the United States, Turkey and Britain. These findings accord with the situation identified in *The children's social health monitor 2011 update*, which highlighted rising inequity and high levels of deprivation for children, especially those living in families dependent on benefits. These issues are also expected to worsen in the future with the economic downturn. There are currently large disparities in child health status, 'with Māori and Pacific children and those living in more deprived areas experiencing a disproportionate burden of morbidity and mortality' (*Children's Social Health Monitor*, 2011, p. 7). So do these point to an answer to the question of whether Aotearoa New Zealand is a good place to raise children? And does this question need to be qualified by, and depend upon, resiliency and the cultural, social and economic setting in which the child grows up?

Receiving Aotearoa New Zealand citizenship can be an important day in some children's lives.

On the positive side, Aotearoa New Zealand is a 'wonder filled' country of great natural wealth. Generally, it is well resourced and it benefits from magnificent natural environments – albeit environments under stress from factors as varied as the exploitation of natural and agricultural resources, pollution, rising CO_2 emissions, pest invasions, offshore oil exploration and rising levels of traffic. However, for most New Zealanders, to some extent, regardless of social class and income level, the possibility of raising a family in a single-storey detached house with a garden, of having holidays at the beach, of going fishing in rivers or lakes, picnics in parks and of walking in mountains and forest still exists. It is this possibility that is immensely valued by returnee New Zealanders, who want to raise their children here; but in reality 'growing up' is more than this. It is equally about the life chances that children experience, including the life opportunities offered. It is about Aotearoa New Zealand's commitment to ensuring equitable access to these opportunities and to providing children with the nurturing, social, economic, educational, and environmental resources that they need to fulfil their potential. As we will demonstrate, in this regard, Aotearoa New Zealand falls well short of the ideal.

A different and changing country – global children

Situated in the south-western Pacific Ocean, Aotearoa New Zealand's land mass is 268,021km². It is a small country by international standards, but in spite of its geographic location far from the global centres of Europe, the US and Asia, it is closely connected to them and affected by what occurs there. The global economic downturn, for example, has impacted on the job prospects and the take-home pay of Aotearoa New Zealand families; yet in a double-edged twist, the 2010 and 2011 earthquakes, which caused human, housing, infrastructural, and commercial disasters in Christchurch, have offset the downturn in Aotearoa New Zealand because of the investment, albeit slower than expected, that is now beginning with Christchurch's rebuild.

Children live in a globally connected world, and Aotearoa New Zealand's children are competing on the global stage. This was demonstrated in 2012 by a group of children from Awakeri School, a primary school near Whakatane, who beat teams from Australia, Canada, Scotland, South Africa and the United States to win the World Kids' Literature Quiz competition. On a daily basis, children at schools around Aotearoa New Zealand join the online Mathletics site, where they meet and compete against children from different cultures from around the world.

Ethnic and cultural diversity is also encountered here in Aotearoa New Zealand, where 24% of children identify as Māori, 11% as Pacific peoples and 7% as Asian, with children being ethnically more diverse than their parents and also more likely to have been born here (Statistics New Zealand, 2002). Particularly relevant is the move towards a more multicultural society, as indicated by the increasing percentage figures for diverse population groups. The six largest Asian groups between 2001 and 2006 recorded the following growth rates: Chinese 40.5%, Indian 68%, Korean 61.8%, Filipino/a 52.7%, Sri Lankan 18.8%, and Cambodian 31.3%. These figures point clearly toward a more diverse population in the future (Statistics New Zealand, 2006).

Despite its colonial heritage as part of the British Empire and Commonwealth, Aotearoa New Zealand is a Pacific country in location and increasingly in orientation, with its majority population looking increasingly towards the Pacific rather than Britain for its identity. Indeed Auckland is commonly described as the Pacific's first city given its large Pasifika population (approximately 178,000 in 2006). For several Pacific groups, more people live in Aotearoa New Zealand than the 'home country' (see Table 1.1). The population make-up is important because there is a younger demographic for Pacific and Māori residents (Figure 1.1), who have higher fertility rates than the general population: this results in more families and children, and a higher rate of population increase when compared to other ethnicities in Aotearoa New Zealand.

Auckland is Aotearoa New Zealand's most diverse city, with 40% of its population having been born overseas and China the most common birthplace. It is home to people from 188 different ethnicities (Auckland Council, 2010),

Table 1.1: Size of main Pacific ethnic groups in Aotearoa New Zealand compared to home country 2006

Country	Usual resident population in NZ	Estimated resident population in home country	Ratio of Pacific population in NZ compared to home country
Samoa	131,103	176,908	0.74
Cook Islands	58,008	21,388	2.71
Tonga	50,481	114,689	0.44
Niue	22,476	2166	10.38
Fiji	9861	905,949	0.01
Tokelau	6822	1392	4.90

Source: http://www.stats.govt.nz/browse_for_stats/people_and_communities/pacific_peoples/pacific-progress-demography/population-growth.aspx

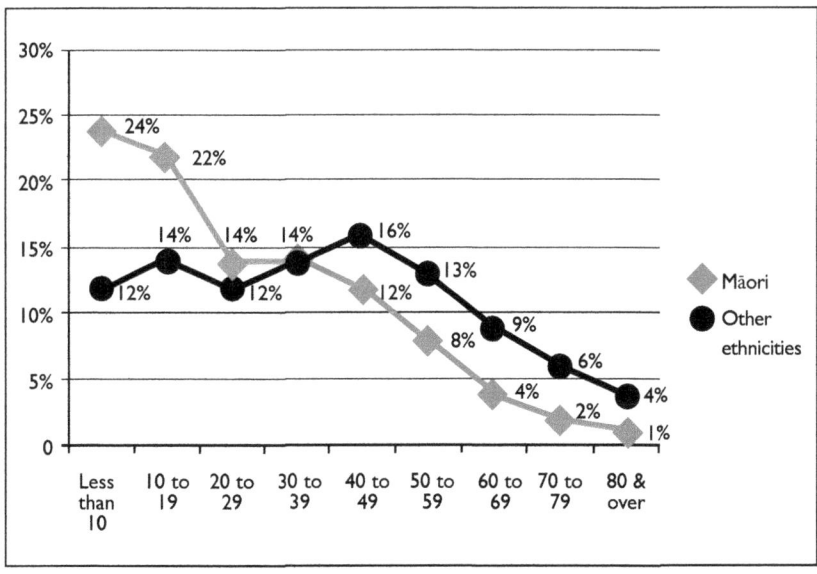

Figure 1.1: Proportion of Māori population and of non-Māori population by age, 2006 NZ Census

INTRODUCTION 19

one-third of whom speak more than one language, with Samoan the second most commonly spoken language after English. Generally this diversity is seen positively: half of Auckland city residents (49.3%) believe greater cultural diversity makes Aotearoa New Zealand a better place to live. Moreover, the majority of residents believe that different cultures are valued and respected, and that new people who move to the city are made to feel welcome (p. 74).

While Aotearoa New Zealand is increasingly multicultural, with a large Pasifika population and identity, the country's biculturalism is of particular importance. The bicultural mandate for Aotearoa New Zealand was set down in the Treaty of Waitangi in 1840. The Treaty, signed by representatives of the Crown and some 500 Māori from around Aotearoa New Zealand, was an 'agreement in which Māori gave the Crown rights to govern and to develop British settlement, while the Crown guaranteed Māori full protection of their interests and status, and full citizenship rights' (Waitangi Tribunal, n.d). The bicultural nature of Aotearoa New Zealand is therefore of central importance in what it means to be a New Zealander. At all levels, from preschool to high school, children learn songs and some vocabulary in Te Reo (Māori language), observe or take part in cultural performances, and go on visits to marae (centres of Māori community life). For other children, complete Māori cultural immersion is more significant as they attend Māori preschools (Kōhanga Reo), bilingual units at regular schools, or Kura Kaupapa (Māori immersion schools). Around one quarter of all Māori (24%, or 131,600 people) reported in the 2006 Census that they could hold a conversation in Māori about everyday things while 14% of Māori aged 15 years and over could speak Māori 'well' or 'very well'. This was an increase from 9% in 2001 (New Zealand Government, 2010). Māori, English and New Zealand Sign Language make up Aotearoa New Zealand's three official languages.

Few children anywhere in Aotearoa New Zealand live only in a monocultural or a bicultural environment. For example, in 2010, of the 357 children attending Awakeri, the large rural school which won the worldwide literature quiz, 75% were Pākehā, 22% Māori and 3% Indian. Aotearoa New Zealand's diverse population means children experience a range of festivals, cultural and religious events such as Ramadan, Chinese New Year, Matariki (the Māori New Year) and Christmas. Children are increasingly connected to a global society through telecommunications, the internet, television and the media (see Chapter 12). They eat curry, pizza, wontons, and sushi as readily as fish and chips: even their diet reflects international influences. Aotearoa New Zealand's children are not just New Zealanders, but are global citizens.

Children take part in a street protest against the closure of their school with a haka (traditional Māori challenge).

Not only are children increasingly reflective of global society but their lives are enhanced and supported by global initiatives. Aotearoa New Zealand is part of a global human rights network, and signatory to a number of United Nations Conventions. The following four are of particular importance for children:

1. *The United Nations Convention on the Rights of the Child* (signed by Aotearoa New Zealand in 1993) requires the state to act in the best interests of the child and uphold children's own rights to (among others) life, identity, privacy, parental relationships, play, leisure, protection and the right to have and express their own opinions. As a signatory Aotearoa New Zealand has to make reports to the United Nations on its progress: three have been submitted to date.
2. *The Convention on the Rights of Persons with Disabilities* (signed by Aotearoa New Zealand in 2007) requires signatory states to accord children with disabilities full equality with other children and an inclusive education. Accommodation of a student's impairments should also be made so that the young person receives appropriate support. Their education should maximise their potential and identity, and their academic and social development. (Higgins, Phillips, Cowan, Tikao, & Wakefield, 2010)

3. *The United Nations Convention on the Status of Refugees* (the Refugee Convention). Aotearoa New Zealand acceded to the UNHCR Convention in 1960. Under the refugee quota programme some 750 UNHCR priority refugee cases enter Aotearoa New Zealand each year. Many are children, usually with family members but not always. Recent arrivals have come from Afghanistan, Ethiopia, Iraq, Myanmar, Somalia and Sudan.
4. *The United Nations Declaration of the Rights of Indigenous People* (2007) was endorsed by Aotearoa New Zealand in 2010. This declaration acknowledges indigenous people's rights to determine their own future and identity. It gives them the right to be involved in government decisions that affect them. Interestingly, it has been reported that Aotearoa New Zealand's support for this declaration was not unconditional in that Prime Minister John Key stated that the declaration was 'aspirational' and will only be implemented within the current legislative and constitutional frameworks (Survival for tribal peoples, 2010).

While global influence and internationalisation are important considerations, it is now important to identify what children experience when growing up in Aotearoa New Zealand itself.

Services for children

Aotearoa New Zealand is well served by an array of organisations and agencies whose focus is the welfare and well-being of children. Foremost amongst these is the government's child protection organisation, Child, Youth and Family (CYF). Child, Youth and Family works to 'protect, support, and care for' children so that they can 'be safe, strong, and thrive'. CYF's website states that in 2012 it received 152,800 notifications (reports of concern). Of these, 62,678 were family violence referrals made when police attend a family violence case and find a child present, 61,074 required further action and 21,525 were found to have substantiated child abuse or neglect. CYF supports over 5000 children who live with caregivers or extended families/whānau, and houses 100 youth in youth justice residences. It also operates four residences for children who need care and protection, as well as supporting children to live in respite or foster care. (CYF, 2013)

Two other organisations that provide vital advocacy services to children are the Office of the Children's Commissioner and the Families Commission. The former was established under the Children, Young Persons and their Families Act 1989. Acting under the Children's Commissioner Act 2003, the Children's

Commissioner's mandate is to promote the rights, health, welfare, and well-being of children and young people up to the age of 18 and to implement the United Nations Convention on the Rights of the Child (1989). The office also monitors the activities of CYF, advocates on behalf of children, investigates child-related matters and promotes good practice, especially for children's participation (Office of the Children's Commissioner, 2012). The Children's Commissioner is independent of government.

The Families Commission is an autonomous Crown entity established under the Families Commission Act 2003. The Families Commission reports to the Minister for Social Development and thus works closely with government. Its declared remit is as follows: 'The Families Commission is New Zealand's centre of excellence for knowledge about families and whānau. We are a dedicated research, evaluation and knowledge organisation' (Families Commission, 2012, unpaginated). In 2012, a major governmental shake-up of the organisation was announced, in which its funding was to be halved and the number of commissioners cut from seven to one. It remains to be seen what the effects of these changes will be. Also important is the work that the Human Rights Commission, the Disability Commissioner, and the Office of Disability Issues do for children, and there are a number of charitable agencies and Trusts, such as Plunket, Barnardos, the Child Poverty Action Group, Anglican Family Care, Presbyterian Support, and the Inclusive Education Action Group, who provide vital services.

In regard to education, the Education Act 1877 established national, compulsory, secular, and free primary schooling. Today, this schooling for children aged 5 to 18 is still called 'free' (from age 6 to 16, attendance is compulsory) but there are a number of associated and required costs: books and stationery, school uniforms, activities such as school camps and field trips, and exam fees. Schools also ask for a 'voluntary' donation from families/whānau. Most children attend government schools, but there is also a well-developed network of private fee-paying schools. Children aged three to five are entitled to 20 hours a week from an early childhood education provider, commonly preschools and early childhood centres. The quality of education in Aotearoa New Zealand is high, with the country scoring well on international rankings for educational achievement. However, achievement levels within Aotearoa New Zealand are varied, with Māori students, Pasifika students, and disabled students having generally lower levels of educational achievement. Disabled children have the right to attend their local school and the government's goal is to have a fully inclusive education system by 2014 (Ministry of Education, 2012). Currently, there are a few 'special' schools and some regular schools have dedicated units designed to cater for special needs children, who may switch between time in the unit and time in a regular class setting. The quality of and ease of access to inclusive education services can be variable, especially for children with complex needs or who do not meet thresholds required for resource allocation (Higgins, MacArthur & Morton, 2008).

Health care is also 'free' – but children over the age of six generally have to pay for doctors' visits and prescriptions, though there is no cost for hospital care. A number of support agencies exist, the most important for young children being Plunket, who provide support services for those under the age of five. Maternity care under the hospital system is free, as are follow-up health checks for children, such as eye and hearing checks and immunisations. New mothers are entitled to up to 14 continuous weeks of paid maternity leave and a further 38 weeks unpaid, provided that they have been working for 10 or more hours per week for the previous six months. Children get free basic dental care until they are aged 18.

Health services for disabled children are provided by the government but coverage and access can be inconsistent and hard to access (see Chapter 8). There are a number of agencies whose focus is on Māori health. Ngāti Kāpo O Aotearoa Inc. (www.kapomaori.com) was founded in 1983 by and for kāpo (blind) Māori, in order to improve the quality of life of kāpo Māori and their whānau. Te Roopu Waiora Trust, founded in 2001, is a unique kaupapa Māori organisation founded and governed by whānau with physical, sensory and intellectual disabilities. In addition to providing disability information and advice, Te Roopu Waiora also assists whānau to access Māori communities and service providers, including government agencies (www.teroopuwaiora.org.nz/12/contact). Service initiatives targeting Pasifika families are also available in areas with high Pasifika populations.

Government financial assistance, known as 'benefits', is available for families whose adults are unemployed or who receive low incomes. Additional benefits are offered for families who are experiencing financial hardship, for example to assist with accommodation, exam fees, car seats and access to health care services. Government-supported accommodation is also available, but accessing this housing is becoming increasingly difficult because successive governments have reduced investment in the government's housing stock and much has been sold to private occupiers. Although these and other benefits do exist, the well-being of children whose families are dependent on benefits can be severely compromised.

Aotearoa New Zealand's neo-liberal economy is not conducive to maintaining support for the most vulnerable children in society, given its emphasis on individualism and economic matters rather than on social welfare.

In their study on child poverty and well-being, Hodgson and O'Brien (2010) return us to our starting question: *Is Aotearoa New Zealand a good place to grow up?* They assert that it could be a good place, but to make it so requires further government commitment and support:

> ... policy decisions can be taken which will reduce children's poverty, if there is the will to do so. 'If' is the critical word here. Child poverty and improving the position of all New Zealand children is possible, but this can only occur through active policy commitments to do so and by prioritising the needs of all children ... Then we could more seriously make the claim that 'New Zealand is a great place to bring up children' and apply that to all children (Hodgson and O'Brien, 2010, p. 37).

What then is the likelihood of such government support being forthcoming? And would this support, if forthcoming, provide for a better future for children and young people?

Future challenges

There is little doubt that the economic challenges and transformations highlighted by Nairn et al. (2012) as central determinants of the life experiences of the young people interviewed in their study, *Children of Rogernomics,* are not going to go away. The likelihood is that economic change, the impact of a neo-liberal economy, and its associated uncertainty will continue to be part of the lived reality for children and their families in Aotearoa New Zealand in the coming decades. In her book on democratic citizenship, Bronwyn Hayward identified four difficult and intersecting challenges: dangerous environmental change, weakening democracies, growing social inequality, and a global economy marked by unprecedented youth unemployment and unsustainable resource extraction (2012). Some of these challenges are those that we have already mentioned in this chapter and that are recurrent themes of this book: for example, growing inequality and difficulties relating to employment for young people and their families.

A significant challenge for New Zealanders is that of environmental change. Children today are growing up in an era of environmental uncertainty. They are bombarded with environmental and health messages, which provide warnings about their future, including real messages about climate change; environmental catastrophes; rapidly increasing air, land and water pollution; chemicals in food; food shortages; and the unsustainable use of resources leading to shortages, for example of fish, water and oil. As children and young

'Car free day' rally provides a rare opportunity for children to safely cycle on city streets that have become more dangerous as a result of increasing traffic volumes and vehicular emissions.

people grow up in an era of readily available media, they have a steady diet of images of environmental (and political) disasters from around the world, including oil leaks with pictures of dying birds and the impacts and loss of human life from extreme weather events and natural disasters such as floods, droughts, hurricanes, cyclones, tsunamis and landslides. At home, we have the experience of the *Rena* oil spill off the coast of Tauranga; the unrest over enhanced oil prospecting around the coasts; regular flooding incidences in communities across the country, and volcanic eruptions, as Tongariro erupted in 2012 for the first time in 105 years.

Aotearoa New Zealand has an unstable environment and this instability is part of the subconscious reality with which New Zealanders live. This subconscious reality, however, became very real for Christchurch children after the first major earthquake on 4 September 2010 and the devastating earthquake of 22 February 2011. They saw their schools, homes, streets, shopping centres and communities devastated; knew of lives being taken; lost access to facilities that formed important parts of their lives, like swimming pools, sports pitches and beaches; became cut off from their city centre; and in many cases, left the

Cleaning up liquefaction after the February 2011 Christchurch earthquake was a common activity for children living in some Christchurch suburbs.

city and saw their families separated and struggling. Yet this crisis also showed the strength and creativity children and young people bring to Aotearoa New Zealand.

In the immediate aftermath of the February 2011 earthquake the student army rallied, with 10,000 young people gathering through social networking sites to help those suffering as a result of the earthquakes. All across affected communities students could be seen shovelling liquefaction deposits, transporting food and helping in a multitude of ways. Children also set to, helping their families, neighbours and friends. The tragedy of the earthquake has revealed both the vulnerability and the strength of children and young people in Aotearoa New Zealand as they and their families get on with rebuilding their lives, a process in which the innate optimism of the children has shone. In a study of children following the earthquake, 81% of the children interviewed said that they still wanted to live in Christchurch (Gollop, 2012). What also came through in this research was the importance of family in the lives of children. Family at the centre of children's lives is a theme encapsulated in the following Māori proverb based on the harakeke (flax) plant whose very structure represents the way the family or whānau protects and nurtures its children or tamariki:

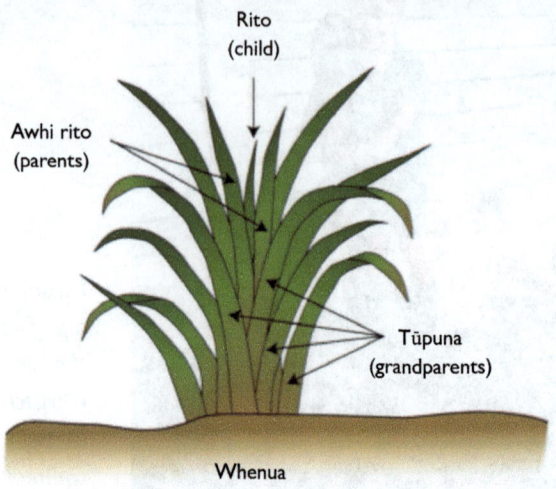

Hutia te rito o te harakeke
Kei whea te Kōmaki e kō?
Kī mai ki ahau:
He aha te mea nui o te Ao?
Māku e kī atu,
he tāngata, he tāngata, he tāngata.

If the heart of the harakeke was removed, where would the bellbird sing?
If I was asked what was the most important thing in the world:
I would be compelled to reply: It is people, it is people, it is people.

(www.paharakeke.co.nz/index.php/about/harakeke-folklore-rituals/)

(Flax graphic redrawn by Tracy Connolly)

Aotearoa New Zealand faces many political, environmental, and social challenges that compromise it as a good place for children to grow up. We now leave you, the reader, to delve further into the many and varied possible answers to our question as you explore this book.

CHAPTER 2

A theoretical framework for childhood

Anne B. Smith

With a commitment to interdisciplinarity at its core, and drawing on sociology, anthropology, psychology, history, geography, and law, what united this field of concern was a concern for the socially constructed character of childhood that involves the twin research foci of childhood as a sociocultural space and children's own perspectives as social actors. (James, 2007, p. 263)

Childhood Studies is a relatively recent and still evolving paradigm for the study of children and childhood that provides a theoretical framework for this book. This paradigm aims not just to produce better knowledge about childhood and children's experiences, but to contribute to social justice for children, and children's empowerment (Alanen, 2011). Childhood studies evolved from a critique of traditional academic discourses, such as developmental psychology, 'the essentialism endemic to traditional theorizing' (Woodhead, 2004, p.x), and narrow views of children as the objects of socialisation and acculturation. It challenges assumptions that children lack independence, rationality, intelligence, autonomy and confidence (Oakley, 1994) and are on a prescribed pathway towards acquiring these characteristics in adulthood (Bluebond-Laugner & Korbin, 2007). Childhood Studies is concerned with the historical, cultural, social and political contexts that influence childhood, and the different ways we think and talk about (or socially construct) them. Childhood Studies emphasises that children are social actors and agents, with their own perspectives, who make important contributions to their own development and actively participate in society. They are not just adults in the making, but people *now*.

Constructions of childhood

A predominant feature of Childhood Studies theory is that childhood is understood as a social construction rather than a natural state: it 'is neither a natural nor a universal feature of human groups but appears as a specific structural and cultural component of many societies' (Prout & James, 1997, p. 8). In other words, childhood has different meanings and interpretations at different points in history, and in different cultures and societies.

This book as a whole helps to highlight the changing historical and cultural meanings and experiences of childhood in Aotearoa. Claire Freeman and Nancy Higgins' initial chapter gives us an overview of the historical and contemporary contexts of childhood. Helen May recounts stories of early twentieth-century school life, characterised by strict discipline and children's fear, even amidst progressive educational ideas (Chapter 6). Children's environmental worlds have shrunk over time, providing fewer opportunities for them to explore and be independent, according to Claire Freeman (Chapter 4). Christina Ergler, Robin Kearns and Karen Witten explain how childhood play has always been managed (though with changing rationales), and how it has moved from the streets into the private domain (Chapter 7). How social welfare policies of adoption and fostering have changed over the years is documented by Anita Gibbs (Chapter 11). Children's embedding in a technologically structured world in the twenty-first century with instant interconnection and immediate access to peers and to information is highlighted by Martha Bell and Victoria Farmer (Chapter 13).

Different cultural ways of knowing, being and doing are highlighted in several chapters, and a particularly moving and powerful account of growing up in Māori and Pākeha worlds is given by Moana Mitchell and Hazel Phillips in Chapter 18. Chapters 8 (Hazel Phillips and Nancy Higgins) and 9 (Karen Guo) and give further insights into the pervasive impact of culture on constructions of childhood and children's experiences. They show how culturally different ways of doing and understanding things are not easily accommodated by dominant practices and meanings.

Our constructions of childhood are shaped by discourses. A discourse is defined as 'a whole set of interconnected ideas that work together in a self-contained way, ideas that are held together by a particular ideology or view of the world' (Stainton-Rogers, 2004, p. 126). These persistent ideas about childhood, that seem to be self-evident truths, shape the way that we treat children within families, schools and society. Different beliefs about children – what is in their best interests, how they should behave, and what should be expected of them – have a powerful effect on their value and position in society, and influence social policies, parenting styles, professional practices and institutional arrangements for children's education, care and welfare. Examples of powerful discourses influencing childhood can be seen throughout this book. Jude Sligo and Karen Nairn (Chapter 16) describe the powerful neo-liberal discourse of individual responsibility for achieving success that permeates our education system, thereby constraining the range of activities where children can easily experience success. Kathleen Quinlivan (Chapter 17) explains how heteronormative discourses create dominant and oppressive regimes of identity and social practices, but also how young people have successfully resisted this marginalisation. Ruth Gasson and James Calder (Chapter 12) show how the prevailing ideology in Aotearoa New Zealand, which says that children are meant to play and go to school rather than work, conflicts with the reality that many children work.

The government's recent Green Paper for Vulnerable Children (especially the title of the document) is an example of a discourse of child concern (Stainton-Rogers, 2004) that positions children as vulnerable to neglect, abuse and other risks. According to the Minister of Social Development, 'my first priority is the protection of vulnerable children. Every hour two children in this country are physically, emotionally or sexually abused. It has to stop. We have to make a concerted effort to protect children from the lifetime of harm abuse can cause' (Bennett, 2011, p. v).

Discourses of concern, according to Stainton-Rogers (2004), do not merely describe; they carry moral imperatives that require action. She argued that social welfare services for children in Britain and other parts of the English-speaking world are dominated by concerns to protect children from abuse, and that there are unintended dangerous consequences which 'can lead to a very partial and distorted concern – to protect a child from abuse at virtually any cost. This renders invisible all other concern about other "needs" the child may have (such as access to information) and, indeed, about their fundamental human rights' (Stainton-Rogers, 2004, p. 131).

Such discourses of risk and vulnerability have been referred to as 'moral panics' that create the impression of a breakdown in social order and create a climate of fear (Kennedy, 2010). Kennedy (2010) believed that in the UK there have been negative effects of the pervasive risk discourse, citing Furedi's argument that 'it is difficult to retain a sense of perspective when the safety of children becomes a permanent item of news' (2001, pp. 9–10, cited in Kennedy, 2010, p. 80). Other negative effects of risk and vulnerability discourses include the loss of privacy through sharing of data about children and families, restriction of children's play, suppression of affectionate contact between adults and children, de-skilling children as unable to look after their own safety, and diversion of attention from serious risks. Nicola Atwool (Chapter 3) outlines some of the problems with identifying and defining vulnerability, and recommends an entirely new approach to this issue involving a commitment to reducing inequality, more coordinated delivery by professionals, and the active involvement of children.

The dangers and problems associated with a deficit-based understanding of childhood are highlighted in several chapters (see Phillips & Higgins, Chapter 8; Quinlivan, Chapter 17; Mitchell & Phillips, Chapter 18). Deficit constructions are inherent in the medical model that characterises disabled people as having abnormalities that need to be fixed; 'at risk' discourses view queer youths as abnormal; and educational policies of testing, streaming and tracking result in marginalisation, silencing, and discrimination of Māori rangatahi. These deficit approaches are embedded in institutional practice within schools, social welfare agencies and the legal and health systems in Aotearoa New Zealand, but they can be challenged.

Many Childhood Studies scholars are critical of the dominant discourse established by developmental psychology, which has influenced many generations of teachers, social workers, and other professionals towards viewing children primarily in terms of their pathway towards adulthood. Western discourses in developmental psychology around a particular concept of childhood, assuming a universal experience for all children, have been exported and globalised as standards by which other childhoods are judged (James & Prout, 1997; Woodhead, 2009): 'Discourses about ages and stages offer a particularly telling example. Thinking about childhood in terms of developmental norms linked to children's age is taken for granted – encoded in everyday talk about milestones and developmental delay, and institutionalized in age-graded classrooms, and groups organized solely or mainly around their birth dates, and their progress tracked according to predefined key stages' (Woodhead, 2009, p. 21).

Another example of constructions of children that are embedded in developmental psychology is in the area of physical punishment. Although the empirical evidence in this field does provide compelling evidence that there are harmful long-term effects of the use of parental physical punishment on children's development, the research is predominantly framed by a particular construct of childhood: 'From this perspective [Childhood Studies], the very nature of research on physical punishment is called into question. We begin to recognize that this research is driven, conceptualized, conducted and interpreted by adults whose histories and values shape their definition of the issue. For example, one of the main debates in this area focuses on whether physical punishment can induce children to comply with parental commands. (Durrant, 2011, p. 51)

In such research, children are viewed as the passive objects of adults' power and control and they are expected to obey immediately and unquestioningly, without expressing their own views. Childhood Studies, instead, views children as social actors with their own perspectives on fairness, justice, punishment and rules. It provokes research to explore the child's perspectives and insights, such as that of Terry Dobbs, who reported children's experiences of being hit with spatulas, tennis rackets, spoons, belts and canes, and their feelings of being scared, sad, ashamed and unloved (Dobbs, Smith & Taylor, 2006).

Most research in developmental psychology has been carried out in North America and Europe, despite these areas only having 12% of the world's population, so there is a huge gap in our knowledge about the childhoods of most of the world's children (Woodhead, 2009). This book is one small contribution towards addressing that imbalance and providing some understanding of childhood in Aotearoa New Zealand.

Agency and voice

Another key feature of the paradigm of Childhood Studies is the recognition of children's agency and voice: 'Children must be seen as active in the construction of their own social lives, the lives of those around them and of the societies within which they live. They can no longer be regarded as simply the passive subjects of structural determinations' (Prout & James, 1997, p. 4).

The ascription of agency to children suggests that children are active meaning makers within the context of social relationships with others (Bluebond-Langner & Korbin, 2007). Children are not just objects of concern in need of protection and moulding but competent social actors, with voice and agency (Pufall & Unsworth, 2004). 'Voice' refers to children's unique point of view – their interests, hopes, worries and expectations. 'Agency' involves 'children's capacity to understand and act upon their world' (Waller, 2009, p. 8). Viewing children as agents means that they are seen as people who can make a difference through their actions 'to a relationship, a decision, to the workings of a set of social assumptions or constraints' (Mayall, 2002, p. 21). Viewing children as agents does not mean that the care and nurturance adults provide for them are unimportant. Children's agency must be balanced by their dependency, and the two are not incompatible (Alderson, 2001). Whether or not children express their capacity for agency is heavily influenced by their social and cultural contexts, and the extent to which there is a space for them to express their views and to exercise responsibility.

Childhood Studies opens our eyes to a different way of thinking about children, which suggests that adults should be sensitive to children's perspectives about their lives, learning and experiences. If adults make an effort to listen to children's voices and figure out what the world looks like from children's point of view, there is a much better chance that they will cater for children's wellbeing and provide a supportive context for their learning and development.

In the past, research about children was mainly from the perspective of parents, teachers or other adults, or through measurements of children's performance (such as structured observations or assessments), that do not allow children to express their own viewpoints (Smith & Taylor, 2000). We argued in 2000 that the voices of children have been 'a missing piece of the puzzle in understanding childhood'. Today, most researchers are much more sensitive in trying to understand children's standpoints in the context of their everyday lives, and there is now a body of literature, to which this book adds, that helps us understand the world from children's perspectives (James, 2007). It is still the case, however, that in many government policy documents (such as the current Green Paper for Vulnerable Children), lip service only is given to children's agency, while their vulnerability and need for protection is given much more prominence.

This book provides a window into the worlds of Aotearoa New Zealand's children and young people by documenting their voices and recognising their agency and participation rights. Jude MacArthur and Margaret McKenzie (Chapter 5) show how recognition of children's voice and agency has transformed research ethics towards positioning children as knowledgeable participating subjects and using 'children-friendly' and respectful methods. Nicola Taylor and Megan Gollop (Chapter 10) show how family law in Aotearoa New Zealand has been transformed to become a world leader through its recognition that children are not just the objects of law, but active and competent participants in decision-making that affects their lives.

It is heartening to see that recognition of children's perspectives has made a difference in approaches to some policy issues in the last few years, and a good example of this is family law policy and legislation. Parental separation, divorce, and re-partnering had previously resulted in children's voices being muted or ignored when decisions were made about them in Aotearoa New Zealand (as in many other countries). Research highlighting children's perspectives on parental separation (Flowerdew & Neale, 2003; Smith, Taylor

Positive fun interactions with adults support children's well-being.

& Tapp, 2003) has shown that children are experiencing individuals, and that they have their own active coping strategies and viewpoints in relation to these issues. Hence the Care of Children Act 2004 has given increased recognition to the importance of ascertaining children's views and taking them into account. A clause about ascertaining children's views, near the beginning of the Act, states that 'the welfare and best interests of the *particular* child in his or her *particular* circumstances must be considered' (Clause 4(2)). The use of the word 'particular' is intended to ensure a focus on each individual child and to avoid generalised assumptions being applied to children whose parents are disputing aspects of their care. The Act provides recognition of the critical importance of children's views within the family, and the need for their views to be ascertained when decisions are being made – whether by parents, other family members or Family Court professionals.

Turning to early childhood education, the recognition of children's agency and voice in the early childhood curriculum, *Te Whāriki,* is described in this book by Lyn Foote, Fiona Ellis and Ruth Gasson (Chapter 14). They found though that the recognition of children's agency in early childhood education centres was more at the level of listening and responding rather than allowing children to participate in decision-making. Julie Lawrence (Chapter 15) compensates for the previous invisibility and voicelessness of the children and families of prisoners by presenting children's moving accounts of their relationships (or lack of these) with their fathers. Her research highlights the importance of practical, emotional and financial support for these children and families, and the damaging effects of stigmatisation on them.

Children's rights

> Rights are claims that are justifiable on legal or moral grounds to have or obtain something, or to act in a certain way. (James & James, 2008, p. 109)

There is a congruence of vision between the Children's Rights movement and Childhood Studies, since both paradigms recognise the importance of listening to children's perspectives, encouraging their participation in social processes, constructing children as persons not property, and understanding that they constitute multiple voices rather than a collective and undifferentiated class (Freeman, 1998; MacNaughton & Smith, 2009; Smith, 2007).

The introduction of the United Nations Convention on the Rights of the Child (UNCRC) in 1989 helped change the dominant image of childhood and bring about a new culture in relation to children's rights and interests in many parts of the world (Karp, 2008). Aotearoa New Zealand ratified the UNCRC in 1993, and it has proved to be a useful instrument for reminding politicians and lawmakers of the inalienable and universal rights of children to human dignity, respect and fairness. The UNCRC provides an important focus on social justice and empowerment for children, and relies on moral pressure, dialogue and cooperation rather than strong enforcement mechanisms. It helps make children visible, challenges governments and others to question their assumptions, and values children as people in their own right today, rather than what they will become tomorrow. Respect for rights also promotes a climate of caring and reciprocity, as 'consciousness of one's own rights is related to tolerance of expression of rights by others' (Melton, 2008, p. 910).

There are three main types of rights in the 54 articles of the UNCRC: provision rights (to health, education, social security, physical care, play etc.), protection rights (to be safe from abuse, discrimination and injustice) and participation rights (to have a say in matters which affect you, to have access to information and to be able to express an opinion) (Lansdown, 1994). That children have a right to participate – to receive and give information, and to take part in decisions in matters that affect them – is one of the more controversial aspects of the convention, and one that threatens the predominant construction of children as the objects of socialisation and adult control, and as incompetent.[1] Yet the actual wording of the article, that 'the child who is capable of forming his or her own views' has a right to be heard, is, as Gary Melton pointed out, a very low standard, because 'children who express their views are *ipso facto* capable of doing so' (Melton, 2008, p. 909).

Woodhead (2005) argued that the image of a child in need is associated with protection rights, while an image of a competent child is associated with participation rights. Both protection and participation rights are important elements of how children should be treated (Melton, 2008), but as illustrated in my previous discussion of the Green Paper for Vulnerable Children, our society is more comfortable with an image of children as vulnerable rather than resilient. Melton (2008) asked us to '[c]onsider, for example, how daily life would change if public officials (not only politicians but also teachers, recreation leaders, pediatric health workers, and social workers) took seriously the requirement to at least have a conversation with children before taking actions affecting them' (p. 915).

The involvement of the United Nations Committee on the Rights of the Child in monitoring the implementation of the UNCRC keeps state agencies on their toes, and helps child advocates to press their case. It also provides useful independent feedback to countries on their policies and practice for children and promotes the visibility of childhood in law and society. In its most recent report, the UN Committee made particular critical mention of Aotearoa New Zealand's lack of attention to mechanisms promoting children's participation rights: 'The Committee notes with regret that the views of children are not adequately respected within the family, in schools and in the community. The Committee also regrets there is no means by which children can express their views in the public domain, that the State does not systematically take into consideration children's view when formulating laws and policies that affect them' (UNCRC, 2011, para 26).

The implications of a respect for children's rights is reflected in this book in the authors' concerns for how their research is used to improve children's situations and address children's rights and interests in Aotearoa New Zealand, as well as their commitment to conduct the research ethically and ensure that children's voice is heard. Using a children's rights focus helps to remind us that Childhood Studies is about contributing to social justice for children, and this

---

1 State Parties shall assure to the child who is capable of forming his or her own views the right to express those views freely in all matters affecting the child, the views of the child being given due weight in accordance with the age and maturity of the child. (#1, Article 12, United Nations Convention on the Rights of the Child)

The right to play is enshrined in the United Nations Convention on the Rights of the Child.

is reflected in this book's many chapters that highlight the many social contexts in which Aotearoa New Zealand children participate and the ways in which their rights are respected or denied in these contexts. Children's participation rights are discussed in chapters on ethics, disability, family law, children's work, technology, early childhood education, and sexuality. Cultural and language rights are emphasised in chapters on indigenous experience and multicultural settings. Rights to be protected from harm, violence and discrimination are important aspects in chapters on adoption, incarceration, children's work and school environments. Lack of provision rights for children to access basic services and facilities like social welfare, education, recreation, health, legal advice, good housing and healthy urban environments, is another theme that runs through many chapters.

Guided participation

Sociocultural theory suggests that participation in cultural processes and communicating with others in close and trusting relationships are the means through which we come to know our worlds. Guided participation is a process through which adults or peers provide 'bridges from known to new' to support children to acquire skills and knowledge (Rogoff, 1990). If children are to have a voice, then there has to be time, space, recognition and support for them to gain expertise and to formulate and express their views. I have argued (Smith, 2002) that it is necessary to integrate Childhood Studies with sociocultural theory, to highlight that there are multiple possible pathways to learning in the contexts of social relationships with other people, culture and the tools of culture, rather than a single pathway. 'Funds of knowledge' within families and communities provide rich resources for children's learning and a repertoire of knowledge that can be passed on through generations and adapted to suit contemporary society (Gonzales, Moll & Amanti, 2005; Rogoff, 2000). Children receive guidance within social contexts that communicate information effectively to them, are receptive to hearing their voices, and are supportive of their efforts to formulate their views. Hence the relationships that children have with adults and peers, and how they are positioned as participants (and viewed by others) in families, institutions and communities, are elements that support their pathway towards agency.

Although Childhood Studies recognises children's agency, this does not mean that children are individuals who come to understand the world and act on it as lone individuals. Children's social environments are the source of their agency, from early infancy when infants' vocalisations and smiles are responded to by their parents: 'The spark of agency is simply the perception that the environment is responsive to our actions' (Johnston, 2004, p. 29). Johnston (2004) described how teachers can invite children to take an agentive role by embedding them in narratives that put them in the role of agents. Narratives of agency help children to believe that their actions can affect the environment, and that they have what it takes to change things. Sociocultural theory suggests that reciprocal and responsive relationships, which put children in authoritative roles, nurture children's agency and help them to stay motivated in tasks in spite of setbacks (Carr, Smith, Duncan et al., 2011). An example of a responsive classroom environment that embeds a child within a narrative of agency is described by Carr et al. (p. 94). Five-year-old new entrant David is engaged in a writing task and for the first time 'writes' a story. He tells the teacher that he has written a story about going on a boat, his teacher recognises that 'something clicked for David that day', and she tells him that he is a 'very very clever writer'.

Adults are a responsive audience to children within early childhood settings and by listening and taking into account children's interests they can provide useful scaffolding for children's learning (see Chapter 14). Yet interactions with children need to move beyond responding and listening, towards children having a greater degree of control and initiation, and this is less common. Before children can have a meaningful input into decisions about their lives, however, it is important that they are provided with relevant information and support (see Chapter 10). To enhance children's ability to participate, both family and professionals play an important role in supporting children's knowledge and understanding. In order to do this effectively, professionals have to focus on developing a relationship with children and gaining their trust. Julie Lawrence (see Chapter 15) has also shown that children's knowledge and understanding of why their fathers were incarcerated were critical in helping them to come to terms with their situation, and they were dependent on adult honesty and support to enable them to gain this knowledge.

Key individuals are sometimes important in empowering young people, as illustrated by Mitchell and Phillips (see Chapter 18). Support and empowerment does not necessarily have to come from adults, as illustrated by Kathleen Quinlivan's inspirational account (see Chapter 17) of how the Yes! Alliance students supported each other to challenge a climate of homophobia and heteronormativity and show that it was all right to be different.

Being and becoming

Childhood has commonly been viewed as a period of social apprenticeship where children are on a pathway to becoming future adults. This idea of 'futurity' (Jenks, 1996, cited by James & James, 2008, p. 63) where children are seen in terms of 'becoming' rather than 'being' has been criticised by many Childhood Studies theorists (James & Prout, 1997; Mayall, 2002; Prout, 2005; Qvortrup, Corsaro & Honig, 2009). At some point in a futurity perspective, children are expected to arrive and achieve adult status (including rights and citizenship). Childhood is viewed entirely in terms of its being a journey towards an end point of adulthood, and children as representatives of a category of incomplete beings (James, 2009). This draws attention away from what children are experiencing and feeling now, and their rights and perspectives as children. It also portrays them as incompetent and immature, a construction that has often led to their current experiences being unimportant and invisible, and their concerns and interests ignored. Alison James (2009) argued that the focus on agency and children's perspectives has had a dramatic effect on researchers, leading to a reconceptualisation of what childhood is and how children are understood. A Childhood Studies perspective on the issue of being and becoming suggests:

Children have an innate sense of adventure and challenge.

> Children are not merely or first of all to become adults, though, of course, we all expect and hope that they will become adults. However, this expectation and hope had, in lore and science, gained so much attention and conveyed so much significance that it was more or less forgotten that children also have a life when they are children. To insist that this life has a worth in its own right amounts to saying that it should not necessarily be formed according to criteria for a successful later adult life. (Qvortrup et al., 2009, p. 5)

How young people are limited by futurity and the demands of achieving well to take their place in adult society is well illustrated by Jude Sligo and Karen Nairn's study of children's understanding of success (Chapter 16). The limited focus on academic achievement for future success constrained children's opportunities to experience the richness of other activities in which they could develop their skills, interests and abilities.

Challenges and debates

There is a strong sense that Childhood Studies is a critical social science that can use scholarship to actually make a difference in the world, by challenging the way that children's lives are organised and regulated, and by challenging the undervaluing of childhood in modern societies (Alanen, 2011). Another part of being critical is for researchers to take a reflexive role, and to ensure that they are ethical in their research procedures: 'Critical Childhood Studies implies being critical not only of our own research but the very practices and social arrangements that we study in the "real" world of children and childhood' (Alanen, 2011, p. 150).

Childhood Studies has made enormous progress in stimulating research on children as social agents and revealing the voices of children. The number of studies in this vein has proliferated almost to the point where the call for attention to children's voices has become 'a pervasive mantra for activists and policymakers worldwide' (James, 2007, p. 261). James took a somewhat critical stance on children's voice research, arguing that, in itself, listening to children's voices and views is not sufficient to ensure that these views are heard and actually make a difference. She outlined the risk of glossing over the diversity of children's lives and experiences through focusing on individuals, and the danger that authentic children's voices may not be heard because of adult control over selection and interpretation of interview material. She also suggested that it is still vital to examine the structural conditions that shape childhood.

There is a debate within Childhood Studies between advocates of plurality and 'multiple voices', and singularity (the commonalities that cut through class, ethnicity and gender) (James, 2010). Qvortrup (2005, 2009) argued that the emphasis on plurality draws attention away from the structural constraints and oppression that children suffer, the significance of generation and intergenerational relationships, and the way children's marginalisation and invisibility are brought about by social and economic policies. Adrian James (2010) believed that the pluralistic and singularistic perspectives can be brought together, like the warp and weft in a piece of cloth, to strengthen Childhood Studies theory and research. Similarly Martin Woodhead (2009, p. 56), while critical of some developmental psychology perspectives and ready to assign them to the 'dustbin of history', believed that it would be a mistake to discard the diversity of developmental research, which he compares to throwing out the baby with the bathwater.

A theoretical framework for thinking about childhood is always a work in progress, and it continuously finds new iterations. There is no reason why Childhood Studies cannot encompass a more joined-up perspective on the diversity of children's experiences; the embeddedness of this in different contexts; the inclusion of children's own perspectives; and the injustices and oppression that structure their lives. I believe that research on the macro as well as the micro level of children's experiences is absolutely crucial if Childhood

Studies is to remain critical and, at the same time, be relevant to social justice and human rights for children. This book is concerned with both macro and micro levels of experience, with structural issues of poverty, availability of housing, statutory legal frameworks, schooling procedures (like streaming and competitive assessment), and access to health and education support (especially for disabled students or children of prisoners). Yet it is through the micro-level recording of the diverse voices and experiences of children, within these constraining or supportive structures, that we develop a rounded picture of the nature of childhood, and can look for strategies to improve children's well-being. Childhood Studies should accept a pluralist approach and multiple methods to move forward, as is suggested by Allison James:

> One way forward toward sustainable childhood research would be to set the by-now commonplace qualitative studies of children's own perspectives, voices, and agency alongside other work that explores the structural conditions that shape childhood as a generational space. Such an integration would help ensure that we do not lose sight of the different impacts that societal forces such as the market, neoliberalism, the state, urbanization, and so on have on childhood as a generational unit (James, 2007, p. 270)

CHAPTER 3

Children and vulnerability

Nicola Atwool

Most New Zealanders are aware of our appalling child abuse statistics and there is an increasing awareness of the number of children whose lives are compromised by poverty. The Green Paper for Vulnerable Children (2011) consultation document is an acknowledgement by the government that we need to be doing more for our children. The 'aspirational' vision within that document is 'Every child thrives, belongs, achieves' (New Zealand Government, 2011, p. 1). The document's primary goal is to improve the situation of 'vulnerable' children. Unfortunately, that term is never defined, despite the statement that an estimated 15% of children fit within this category (New Zealand Government, 2011). In this chapter I begin with an exploration of what the term 'vulnerable' means when applied to children. I then address the issue of prevalence, using Aotearoa New Zealand data to arrive at an estimate of how many children might be considered vulnerable, before moving into an exploration of what makes a difference for children in vulnerable circumstances. I finish with a discussion of barriers to change and the policy implications.

Who are 'vulnerable children'?

The revised third edition of the Collins dictionary (1995) defined 'vulnerable' as 'capable of being physically or emotionally wounded or hurt', 'open to temptation, censure, etc.', 'exposed to attack' (p. 1515). All children and young people meet this definition. Humans have the most protracted period of development of any species and it is the price we pay for the degree of physical, emotional and cognitive sophistication that we have achieved. It is, however, widely acknowledged that while we arrive in the world with genetic potential, the outcome of that protracted development is determined by gene-environment interaction (Fonagy, 2003; Centre on the Developing Child, 2007). At the very beginning of life the infant is completely dependent on adults for survival. We now know that shaking an infant can cause severe brain damage and death, and there can be no more profound reminder of the extreme vulnerability of very small children. But we are not just talking about survival.

Our understanding of vulnerability has been expanded by research on psychopathology and resilience. Initially the focus was on understanding why some children have very poor outcomes, often evident by the time they reached adolescence (Cichetti & Toth, 1995). More recently, motivated by a desire to understand why not all children who are born into adverse circumstances do badly, researchers have turned their attention to what makes a difference. Both bodies of research have identified risk factors and have reformulated our understanding of vulnerability to mean susceptibility to poor outcomes (Sroufe, Cooper, De Hart & Marshall, 1992). Resilience literature has extended our understanding by paying attention to protective factors and it is agreed that it is the balance of protective and risk factors in children's lives that largely determines outcomes in adulthood (Boyden & Mann, 2005; Fraser, 2004; Kalil, 2003; O'Dougherty Wright & Masten, 2006). Such an understanding does not change the assertion made earlier that all children are vulnerable; it does allow us, however, to have a better understanding of which children may be rendered more vulnerable by the circumstances of their lives.

There is an extensive list of risk factors and very few of these originate in the child. Disability and chronic health difficulties may increase children's risk of vulnerability (Hibbard & Desch, 2007) but almost all risk factors emanate from the environment. At the societal level they include poverty, poor housing, violent neighbourhoods, and marginalisation. At the family level they include isolation, family violence, abuse and neglect, compromised parenting due to mental health issues, alcohol and substance abuse and gambling; second-hand smoke exposure; parent(s) with a criminal record; low level of parental educational attainment; early parenthood; high mobility; and changing family structures (Connolly & Doolan, 2007; Duncanson, Smith & Davies, 2009; MSD, 2011a). As a result of exposure to these factors, by the time a child is entering school they may have acquired behaviours that are also labelled as risk factors: behavioural difficulties; compromised health; and lack of preparation for participation in a formal learning environment. Children exposed to only one risk factor will fare better than children with exposure to multiple risk factors but even one risk factor can compromise development, particularly if endured over time (Masten & Coatsworth, 1998).

The protective factors include the individual attributes of the child. Characteristics such as a sense of self-worth, competence, and positive attitude have been identified as contributing to resilience (Brown & Rhodes, 1991; Compas, 1987). These are, however, acquired in the context of stable, consistent parenting and it is dangerous to overlook this (Masten & Coatsworth, 1998). The other three factors – family support (Fraser, 2004; Wyman et al., 1999); a supportive relationship with a person or agency in the community (Yates et al., 2003); and positive cultural belonging (Ungar, 2003; 2005) – are dependent on relationships. It is therefore important, when considering the question of vulnerability, to pay attention both to the physical and emotional space adults have available to invest time and energy in parenting and to other child-related activities in the community, such as education and delivery of health and social services.

Vulnerability can be defined as a characteristic of childhood because of dependence on adults to provide positive, growth-promoting environments in the home, education settings, and the community. Some children, however, are rendered more vulnerable because the number of risk factors in their lives outweighs the protective factors available. In the most dangerous circumstances there may be an absence of protective factors. The question then remains: how many children fall into this category and how should the situation be addressed?

Prevalence

Māori and Pasifika families are over-represented in many of the negative statistics discussed in relation to risk factors. This can lead to a simplistic equating of ethnicity and risk (see for example Duncanson et al., 2009). Over-representation is largely a feature of socio-economic positioning and the role of colonisation and immigration in determining this. Equating ethnicity with risk overlooks the interrelated nature of risk factors. This may distort perceptions leading to the underestimation of risk in the dominant population. It may also inadvertently deny children access to the protective influence of positive cultural connection when their ethnicity is perceived as evidence of risk.

The Green Paper estimates 15% of Aotearoa New Zealand children are vulnerable and this appears to be based on the data available from the two longitudinal studies that have been undertaken here. The children in the Christchurch study were born in 1977 and the Dunedin cohort were born even earlier in 1972 or 1973. This was a period of low unemployment and higher social cohesion. The dramatic changes that came with the social and political changes of the 1980s did not impact on the early years of these children's lives. The rapid rise in poverty rates did not come until the late 1980s (Perry, 2011). As the Chief Science Advisor (2011) has noted, the social environment has also undergone significant change, with the impact of electronically connected networks changing the nature of peer pressure and exposure to role models at a time when young people have greater freedom engendered by more ready access to funds.

If resources are to be targeted at vulnerable children, we need to know who they are. Ten per cent of children up to the age of 15 are identified in the Green Paper as having a disability or significant health problem. It is unclear whether this includes children with learning disabilities, who are at much greater risk of joining what the Chief Science Advisor (2011, p. 2) has referred to as 'the "long tail" of educational underachievement and social disengagement.' There is also evidence of children exhibiting the effects of risk exposure during childhood and adolescence. An estimated 6000 children are reported to have a significant behavioural problem by the time they go to school, and 8 to 12% of children under the age of 16 are truanting. The Christchurch longitudinal study indicated that despite the more favourable social context in the 1970s, 5 to 10% of children aged between three and 17 developed conduct problems (Fergusson, Boden & Hayne, 2011); Moffit (1993), using the same data for children, provided a similar estimate for those who developed life-course-persistent conduct problems associated with adult offending. Between 10 and 15% of young people between the ages of 12 and 19 are reported to engage in heavy and abusive cannabis use (New Zealand Government, 2011), and a third of young New Zealanders are at risk of alcohol-related problems (Fergusson & Boden, 2011). The Green Paper also reported that 7% of adolescent males and 3% of females have attempted suicide.

The proportion of children living in poverty was estimated to be 20% in the Green Paper (2011). The Child Poverty Action Group (CPAG, 2011) provided a slightly higher figure of 26% (after housing costs). It is possible that some children living in poverty are not exposed to other risk factors and have access to protective factors in their homes and communities. The research evidence, however, demonstrates that poverty is associated with a range of negative outcomes, partly due to the increased exposure to other risk factors (CPAG, 2011; McLoyd, 1998). In particular, poverty is associated with educational underachievement (McLoyd, 1998; Quilgars, 2001). Poverty is not just about lack of money. In the 2008 *Living Standards Survey*, 51% of Pacific families, 39% of Māori families, 23% of ethnic groups classified as 'other', 15% of New

Zealand European families, and 59% of benefit-dependent families scored four or more on the composite deprivation score (Perry, 2009). Hardship extends into all aspects of children's lives, including poor housing, inadequate clothing, and limited access to school trips, medical treatment and recreational activities (Perry, 2009). Hardship limits children's access to social capital, which is the key to attaining success in adulthood. The impact is particularly severe in the context of the marked inequality that characterises Aotearoa New Zealand (O'Brien, Dale & St John, 2011).

The Children's Social Health Monitor (2011) provides evidence that children in the two lowest socio-economic deciles are 5.6 times more likely to be admitted to hospital as a result of assault, neglect or maltreatment than children in the least deprived two deciles. In 2010, 20 children per 100,000 were admitted to hospital with intentional injuries. The rate per 100,000 is 4.2 for the highest decile compared with 42.2 for the lowest. This data also provides overwhelming evidence of a range of medical conditions that are sensitive to social gradient, some of which have long-term effects on health.

The risk of violence is associated with socio-economic status and significant numbers of children have their lives compromised by exposure to violence. In the Dunedin study, a quarter of young adults reported exposure to acts or threats of violence carried out by one parent against another and, of these, 80% had been exposed to violence before the age of 11 years. This is similar to the proportion surveyed by Carroll-Lind (2011) in a more contemporary study. New Zealand Police statistics recorded 74,785 incidents attended by police where children were present (MSD, 2011a).

In 2009–10 there were 124,921 reports of concern to Child, Youth and Family. Of these 55,494 required further action and 26,169 were substantiated (MSD, 2011b). Neglect is the most common finding among cases reported and Mardani (2010) reported that 45% of cases came from the most deprived areas of Aotearoa New Zealand. Sixty per cent of findings came after one or two reports of concern, but on average, 3.1 notifications were made prior to a substantiated finding and 211 children had between 10 and 19 notifications before a substantiated finding: these figures indicate that some children are living in compromised circumstances for considerable periods of time before action is taken.

Further evidence of the co-occurrence of risk factors can be found in a study of the case records of 171 infants for whom Child, Youth and Family Services were notified over the course of a year (1 July 2005 to 30 June 1996). Forty-nine per cent of the mothers and 41% of fathers had been involved with Child

Youth and Family as children or young people. In 82% of these situations, the adult relationships predominantly involved conflict or violence. Adults were also found to have alcohol or drug problems, antisocial behaviour and mental health issues (Connolly, Wells & Field, 2007).

The Green Paper reported that 20% of parents of children in the early years have a mental health issue and that 3.5% have an alcohol and drug issue (p. 5). The latter figure would appear to be a significant underestimate, given the high prevalence among mothers with children coming into government care before the age of two. Harmful parental drinking has a negative impact on children's physical health and is associated with behavioural issues, poor educational performance, and early onset of – and heavy – alcohol use in adolescence (Girling, Huakau, Caswell & Conway, 2006). In the new *Growing Up in New Zealand* longitudinal study involving nearly 7000 children born in 2009, it was found that although the majority of the 6882 mothers stopped drinking during pregnancy, one-third of those with an unplanned pregnancy consumed four or more drinks of alcohol a week during the first trimester (Morton et al., 2010). The estimated prevalence of Foetal Alcohol Spectrum Disorder is 1% of live births (MSD, 2011a), and a survey of midwives reported that 80% of pregnant teenagers consume alcohol during pregnancy (ALAC, 2001 cited in MSD, 2011a).

Parental separation has been identified as a risk factor for children (Harold, 2011). Many children will experience at least one change in family structure during their childhood and some will experience multiple changes (Families Commission, 2008; Poland, Cameron, Wong & Fletcher, nd). These changes may or may not be associated with other risk factors such as exposure to conflict and violence. In even the most benign circumstances, however, children may have to move house, change school, and at the very least, get used to a different pattern of relationships with the most important adults in their lives.

Considering this evidence as a whole, it would seem that the figure of 15% underestimates the number of children living in circumstances that increase their vulnerability, particularly when we take into account the children affected by the Christchurch earthquake. The co-occurrence of risk factors would suggest that 20% is a more realistic estimate: this is supported by the Prime Minister's Chief Science Advisor, who noted that '[a]dolescents in New Zealand relative to those in other developed countries have a high rate of social morbidity. While most adolescents are resilient to the complexities of the social milieu in which they live, at least 20% of young New Zealanders will exhibit behaviour and emotions or have experiences that lead to long-term consequences affecting the rest of their lives' (2011, p. 1).

Within this group there is likely to be a group of 5 to 10% who are exceptionally vulnerable, and not all of them will survive to adulthood. The estimated financial cost of our collective failure to protect children from adversity has been estimated at approximately $6 billion (Infometrics, 2011). What then is needed to turn the tide?

Making a difference

Across the English-speaking world there is universal agreement that the key to making a difference lies with early intervention (Allen & Smith, 2008; Centre on the Developing Child, 2007; Early Years Commission, 2008; NSW Commission for Children and Young People, 2004). Tasked with investigating what it would take to reduce social and psychological morbidity in adolescence, the Chief Science Advisor to the Prime Minister and the 22 other contributors to the taskforce came to the conclusion that a primary prevention or 'life-course' approach is needed and recommended that '[s]ocial investment in New Zealand should take more account of the growing evidence that prevention and intervention strategies applied early in life are more effective in altering outcomes and reap more economic returns over the life course than do prevention and intervention (or punitive) strategies applied later' (2011, pp. 15–16).

If the key is early intervention, then how do we put this into operation? Most social service delivery is reactive and after the event. Statutory services only come into play when someone makes a report of concern. The threshold for Child, Youth and Family intervention is high and may not occur until children have been exposed to multiple risks over time. Nevertheless, the Partnered Response initiative, which allows families not meeting this threshold to be referred to community-based organisations, relies on their agreement to engage with services (CYF, 2009). The pathway to services via a report of concern to CYF may, in itself, also be a barrier to effective engagement (Scott, 2006).

Traditionally, services have operated in silos and professionals within those silos define their roles in ways that may limit their responsiveness to children who are vulnerable (Scott, 2009). Teachers and health professionals may only feel comfortable making a report of concern when they see evidence of abuse. They may not know what to do when they have concerns but there is no concrete evidence of abuse and no disclosure by the child. Such ambivalence is likely to underpin the failure to act when children are being neglected (Mardani, 2010).

Many of our services are adult focused and the impact of adult behaviour on the children in their care may be overlooked as long as parents appear to be making an effort (Smith, 2011). In some services the adult is defined as the client and there may be limited attention to the impact of their behaviour on other members of their family, including any children (Scott, 2009). Many families have multiple needs, and despite the rhetoric of coordinated service delivery, coordination is proving difficult to achieve (Atwool, 2003). The government's Whānau Ora initiative is a significant step in this direction,[1] but it remains to be seen whether mainstream services will be willing to work in different ways in order to achieve the goals of such an approach.

An investment approach is needed if we are to be proactive about reducing vulnerability. Given the current concentration of resources in remedial services, this investment will have to be made while we are still paying the price for earlier failures to ensure that every child has the opportunity to thrive, belong and achieve. The current economic climate does not provide many opportunities for additional expenditure and a long-term view is needed if we are not to perpetuate the negative cycles that characterise the current situation (Infometrics, 2011).

Both the Chief Science Advisor's report and the Green Paper make reference to targeting services, thereby ensuring that these more intensive services are delivered in a cost-effective manner to those who most need them. Although this makes sense, it is not easy to achieve. Access to targeted services is determined by eligibility criteria. This may mean that families who fall on the wrong side may find themselves worse off than those who are eligible (Gilbert et al., 2009; Scott, 2006). It may also result in perverse behaviour such as manipulative gaming of the system (Infometrics, 2011).

Alternatively, families may be damaged by spreading the net too widely and identifying some as being 'at risk' when this is not the case (Scott, 2006). Such collateral damage may be considered unavoidable and justified by the greater good. What this view fails to take into account is that families may become reluctant to come forward when they need help for fear of what may happen. This only serves to increase the isolation and marginalisation of families and children (Infometrics, 2011).

The alternative to targeting is usually perceived to be universalism. The major objections to this approach are high cost, wasted resources in providing services to families who may not need them and the disproportionate advantage to middle-class families (Infometrics, 2011). There are, however, other disadvantages. Universality does not guarantee that all families will

---

1 Whānau Ora is an inclusive inter-agency approach to providing health and social services to build the capacity of all Aotearoa New Zealand families in need. It is targeted at the whānau (family) as a whole rather than focusing on individual family members and their problems. (Te Puni Kōkiri, www.tpk.govt.nz/en/in-focus/)

engage with the services that are provided and there is a risk that the families who are most in need are the most likely to be under-represented (Buchanan, 2007; Cortis, Katz & Paulny, 2009; Infometrics, 2011). Partly this may be 'accounted for' by the failure of universal services to cater for different needs. For example, Māori and Pasifika children are under-represented in early childhood education despite subsidies being available (Infometrics, 2011).

There are clearly no one-size-fits-all answers and the challenge is to provide cost-effective early intervention to those with greatest need. In a comprehensive review of issues related to the recognition of and response to child maltreatment, Gilbert et al. (2009, p. 177) concluded that 'international comparisons emphasise the need for an approach that combines a focus on child safety with the broader benefits of a focus on child and family welfare'. A public health model has the potential to ensure adequate provision of universal services as the entry point for access to more intensive services when needed (Reading et al., 2009; Whitaker, Lutzker & Shelley, 2005). Such an approach allows for progressive universalism.

Health and education are universal services that have a role in the life of every child in this country and it makes sense to utilise these front-line services to address the needs of children in vulnerable circumstances. Ensuring that every pregnant woman has a midwife, and that all children are enrolled with a Well Child or Tamariki Ora Service and a primary health provider, is a good place to start. Most parents want the very best for their children and are more likely to be open to engaging with support services when a child is born. Availability of services to all families reduces the risk of stigmatisation that creates barriers to engagement. Funding contracts for such services will need to allow for the active outreach that may be needed to engage those parents who, due to current life circumstances or previous negative experiences, may be resistant to receiving such supports (Buchanan, 2007; Cortis et al., 2009; Gray, nd). The make-up of the workforce providing front-line services for children and families will need to reflect the cultural diversity of our population and it will be important that part of the workforce is located within culturally based services such as Whānau Ora (Gray, nd).

As children grow they move into the world of education. Traditionally, the education sphere has focused on teaching and learning, with varying degrees of engagement with families. Children who come into the education environment with behaviours that impede learning are a source of frustration and may be perceived as somebody else's responsibility. Early childhood education is not compulsory and children with very difficult behaviour may be excluded on the grounds that they pose an unacceptable risk to other children. Education environments, however, have considerable potential to contribute to the identification of children in vulnerable circumstances and to provide active outreach to their families (Gilbert et al., 2009). The recent increase in the number of social workers in low-decile schools (Bennett, 2012) and the active engagement of some early childhood centres with families and community resources (Duncan, 2006) are evidence that this potential is recognised. There are also examples of more comprehensive approaches such as Victory Village,[2] which demonstrate what is possible when schools seek active engagement with their communities (Stuart, 2010).

To ensure that universal services function as entry points to other supports, it will be imperative that people working in these services have the knowledge and skill required to engage effectively with families; ask the hard questions that need to be addressed when there is a possibility of issues that may adversely impact on parenting; and have the ability to connect families with appropriate services when such issues are identified. The Green Paper (2011) has made reference to the workforce for children including those in health, education and the social services. It will be important that professionals in these fields recognise that they are part of this workforce, if they are to be proactive and engage in the additional training and development that is needed to improve children's access to timely intervention.

Barriers

Cost is the most obvious barrier, but it is not the only one. Social attitudes and values have shaped the delivery of services to children and their families. The family has traditionally been held sacrosanct with uninvited intervention reserved for the most serious situations. The debate over the repeal of Section 59 of the Crimes Act revealed very strong resistance to the notion of interference in 'ordinary' families (Wood, Hassall, & Hook, 2008).[3] There has been a tendency to assume that most families are doing a good job and should be left to do so. Parenting, by and large, is something we take for granted and it is assumed that most people are capable of fulfilling this responsibility. People who abuse and

---

2   Victory Village is a community development initiative involving a partnership between a low-decile school and a health centre in Nelson. The initiative has increased parent engagement, improved student achievement and attendance, and reduced mobility. An evaluation is available from the Families Commission website: www.familiescommission.org.nz
3   Section 59 of the Crimes Act allowed adults accused of assaulting a child to defend themselves on the grounds that the force used was reasonable. A private member's bill sought to repeal this section, fuelling widespread public debate and very strong opposition from some quarters. Section 59 was not repealed but was replaced by the Crimes (Substituted Section 59) Amendment Act 2007.

neglect their children are assumed to be fundamentally different from 'good parents'. Underlying these assumptions has been a great deal of uncertainty and few parents feel fully confident. This combination makes it difficult to acknowledge problems and ask for help.

Despite the widespread agreement that family is the building block of society, family is located in the private sphere. This has allowed adults to exert enormous control within the family and has allowed parental responsibility to be largely ignored by policymakers. For example, the recent claims that the solution to poverty is paid employment completely overlook the fact that 15% of all children who experienced four or more items in a measurement of deprivation came from non-benefit-dependent households (Perry, 2009). The drive to get sole parents into the workforce so that they are not dependent on financial assistance from the government fails to address the possibility that this will simply increase the stress of daily life without necessarily improving the financial situation. Employed parents incur additional costs in the form of transport, suitable clothing, after-school and early childhood care, and additional tax if holding down more than one part-time job. Despite this, we appear to be comfortable with the rhetoric that in addition to improved financial circumstances, work makes a positive contribution to parental well-being.

New Zealanders work some of the longest hours in the world. A Families Commission report (2009) based on 2006 census data revealed that 23% of the total workforce (29% of those employed full-time) worked 50 or more hours per week. Among couples with children, 29% of dual-earner couples worked 80 or more combined hours and 8% worked more than 100 combined hours. Men were more likely to work longer hours than women and those in the 40–54 age group were slightly over-represented. In terms of education, two groups emerged as more likely to work long hours: those with the highest qualifications (masters' degrees and doctorates) and those who had no qualifications. Those with Level 2 NCEA or lower (including no qualifications) made up 40% of those working long hours. Although long hours workers were more likely to have higher incomes relative to the total workforce, slightly more than half earned less than $50,000 and 22% of these earned $30,000 or less. Qualitative interviews revealed a number of adverse impacts, including having less time and energy to spend with their families (Families Commission, 2009).

Not surprisingly, when children in Years 7 and 8 were asked about what makes a good childhood as part of the Green Paper consultation process, many identified the importance of family time and parents being available to listen and to support them (Office of the Children's Commissioner, 2011a).

Camp games at a holiday park. Holidays are important in providing social time for children and family time but even camping holidays are beyond the budget of many families.

Another group of young people aged 12–18 reiterated these themes (OCC, 2011b), indicating that the commonly held assumption that teenagers have less need of their parents is not necessarily valid. When asked how they thought government should help families, many commented on the hours worked by their parents and the low minimum wage. That children are aware of such issues demonstrates the impact parental employment has on their lives.

Another potential barrier is government emphasis on evidence-based approaches (New Zealand Government, 2011; Prime Minister's Chief Science Advisor, 2011). While it is important that there is accountability and evidence of effectiveness, there are questions about what constitutes evidence. The Incredible Years and the Triple P programmes[4] are frequently cited examples of being evidenced-based because they have been subjected to rigorous evaluation, including the use of randomised control methodologies. These are focused parenting programmes and, unfortunately, many social work interventions do not readily fit into such methodological strategies. When families face multiple

---

4   For more information see www.incredibleyears.com and www.triplep.net

issues requiring coordinated service delivery across more than one agency, it becomes very difficult to isolate the many variables that have a bearing on outcomes.

Evaluative tools are available but these do not always fit established definitions of evidence. In a recent review of international evidence about improving outcomes for children and families, emphasis was placed on the importance of choosing the right paradigm from the range available and ensuring consistency between programme philosophy and evaluation strategy (Maluccio, Canali, Vecchiato, Lightburn, Aldgate & Rose, 2011). The need for comprehensive approaches that allow for continual input for programme improvement and include collaboration and participation of all stakeholders is also emphasised. Such approaches require resources and we do not have a tradition of investment in evaluation. If, however, we are to capitalise on our history of innovation and ensure culturally appropriate service delivery, as envisaged in the Green Paper, this issue must be addressed.

Where to from here?

The current pattern of service delivery allows far too many children and families to fall through the cracks. Tinkering with the existing arrangements is not going to produce the fundamental shift that is needed. Any policy initiatives have to be based on a whole child / whole family approach, incorporating all of the government agencies that have direct and indirect impacts on family life. This includes policies related to the economy, employment, taxation, housing, and justice, as well as the more obvious domains of health, education and social services. The United Nations Convention on the Rights of the Child provides a framework for such an approach and is compatible with a public health strategy (Reading et al., 2009). The starting point needs to be an assumption that all families may need additional support at times. It is in the nature of family life that difficulties are encountered and our capacity to manage these is largely determined by positive experiences of overcoming challenges. Not all families start from the same baseline in terms of risk and protective factors. It makes sense to ensure that families with the greatest need are prioritised, but in order to identify those families, there have to be points of contact and these are most accessible in health and education settings.

Each community is likely to have different patterns of need and New Zealand has a strong tradition of responsive community-based initiatives (New Zealand Government, 2011). Services need to be where people are. A key factor in families' ability to achieve positive outcomes in the face of adversity is the cohesiveness of the communities in which they are located (Jack, 2000). Local approaches are needed to capitalise on this phenomenon.

We have a long way to go; but if we fail to begin the journey, we are condemned to continued high expenditure on negative outcomes that threaten to destabilise our society. As a signatory to the UN Convention on the Rights of the Child, the government has an obligation to ensure that the rights of all children are honoured, and this includes ensuring that families have the resources that they need to fulfil their responsibilities. If we are to respond effectively to children made vulnerable by their circumstances, we need an approach that incorporates:

- government leadership, preferably endorsed by an agreement across all political parties to set national priorities and provide the infrastructure needed to facilitate an investment approach that focuses on early intervention in the life of the child and in the life of any problem that a child or family may encounter;
- a commitment to reduce inequality and eliminate child poverty in order to ensure that no child is denied access to the social capital needed to achieve positive outcomes;
- the development of shared knowledge, skills and values among professionals working with children and young people to facilitate communication and effective service delivery;
- local government leadership to ensure coordinated service delivery within communities and the identification of gaps or emerging issues that require a response;
- the active involvement of children, young people and families in the design and delivery of local initiatives to ensure relevance to, and buy-in from, the intended recipients;
- consultation and flexibility when developing new services to ensure that these are tailored to the needs of the diverse groups within our communities;
- funding packages that are facilitative, sustain service delivery over time, and support wrap-around services; and
- evaluation strategies that address the complexity of service delivery and are outcomes focused.

As a nation we are facing a stark choice. We can continue to tinker with an old system based on the idea that children and families needing help can be identified and targeted for service delivery. Or we can build a new approach starting from the assumption that all children are vulnerable and any family may need additional support at particular points in time. The old approach incurs considerable financial, emotional, and social cost over time. The alternative will require investment to set up but will save money and accrue exponential benefits through the development of stronger and more supportive communities that ensure that every child thrives, belongs and achieves.

CHAPTER 4

The changing environmental worlds of Aotearoa New Zealand children

Claire Freeman

Aotearoa New Zealand has often been called 'Godzone' (God's own country), reflecting the notion that it is a special place whose inhabitants are blessed by their good fortune in living there. If we look at what people generally envisage when they use the term 'Godzone', most would refer to the Aotearoa New Zealand environment: the mountains, the green hills, the bush, white beaches, wild surf, untamed rivers, sheep, the kiwi and the vast skies. Indeed Māori named the country Aotearoa (land of the long white cloud) for its environment,[1] and named the South Island Te Wai Pounamu (the waters of greenstone).[2] Both names capture the essence of the land where New Zealanders still live. Likewise, Australia is referred to as the 'lucky country' and on occasion also 'Godzone', though not as widely as in Aotearoa New Zealand. In 2005 Fiona Stanley, co-author of the book *Children of the Lucky Country*, argued that Australia had turned its back on children, that this view of Australia as a country blessed with good fortune was a myth and that for many Australian children their lives were ones blighted by abuse, poverty and inequality. Similar challenges can perhaps be laid at Aotearoa New Zealand's door, challenges in many ways directly related to poor living environments.

In this chapter, while recognising Aotearoa New Zealand's special environment, I explore whether this environment really does make Aotearoa New Zealand a 'Godzone' for children today, or whether it is rather the case that Stanley makes for Australia – that it is perception and myth rather than reality. The first part of the chapter looks at the changing domestic and outdoor environments that provide the stage on which children's lives are played out.

---

1 In pre-colonial times this reference was for the North Island only.
2 Originally *wāhi pounamu* ('place of greenstone'), later replaced by Te Wai Pounamu.

The next part looks at changing childhoods and the contrasting themes of shrinking and expanding activity spheres. In particular, I look at the shrinking realm of outdoor play and wider use of the environment, as access to private transport leads children into more mobile lives. The final part looks at a study of Aotearoa New Zealand children and their relationships to their local environment, because for children it is the locally accessible daily environment that can be especially important.

The changing domestic environment

The rural–urban shift

In 1881 a report on urban and rural populations in Aotearoa New Zealand reported that 'New Zealand was firmly a rural country, with just under 60% of the population living in a rural area' (Statistics New Zealand, 2010, p. 10). The belief in Aotearoa New Zealand as a rural nation was so strong that in 1923, the prominent educationalist, Professor James Shelley, wrote that children 'should not be educated in the town ... I do not think you realise how destructive it is' (p. 10). However, Aotearoa New Zealand was changing: 'Between 1881 and 2001 the balance of the population moved from rural to urban areas. During this period, the population of urban New Zealand increased by over 1,500% compared with an increase in rural areas of only 83%' (p. 11). Aotearoa New Zealand is now a predominantly urban country where some 86% of New Zealanders are urban dwellers (Statistics New Zealand, 2010a). The population of Aotearoa New Zealand is not evenly distributed. Auckland, Hamilton, Wellington and Christchurch are home to 54% of Aotearoa New Zealand residents, with Auckland on its own being home to about a third of New Zealanders with 1,459,700 residents (Statistics New Zealand, 2010a). Most Aotearoa New Zealand children today, therefore, will be brought up in towns and cities. Outside of the cities, there are smaller urban centres, often only a few thousand in number, that in most other countries would still be classed as rural villages. However, the main centres (i.e. the 16 centres with populations of 30,000 plus) remain dominant, making up 72% of the total Aotearoa New Zealand population (Statistics New Zealand, 2006).

From quarter acre to compact city

Aotearoa New Zealand has characteristically been seen as a low-density environment, favouring single standalone houses on large plots, colloquially termed the 'quarter-acre section'. Despite the centrality of the quarter-acre section concept in the Aotearoa New Zealand consciousness, the reality is that most homes are in fact on sections much smaller than a quarter acre. Few Aotearoa New Zealand children outside of rural areas and small towns now experience the quarter-acre section with its standalone home. In urban areas section sizes are decreasing, while the size of new homes is increasing. Exact figures for section size are hard to come by, but Hall's study in Australia carefully documents these changes for Australia, where average house size is increasing. From an average floor size of 162.2m^2 in 1984–85, by 2003–2004 the comparable figure was 227.6m^2, an increase of 40%. Houses now cover increasingly large proportions of the sections, whilst sections are becoming smaller, decreasing from an average size of 800m^2 or more to sections on new estates commonly being just 400 to 500m^2 (Hall, 2010, p. 424). The trend identified by Hall is also occurring here in Aotearoa New Zealand, especially in the larger urban centres. Another trend is described by the popularised term 'McMansions'. These are large, usually ostentatious new 'family' homes, ironically possessing minimal play space because most of the section (or land) is covered by the house. There is also usually little street connectivity in that access is typically though automated garage entrances and the property is surrounded by high walls or fences, limiting children's ability to connect to the street or neighbourhood.

Medium-density housing in Auckland with good communal play space.

The urban environment itself is becoming denser. One contributory factor is the process of infill development. Infill is where second or subsequent homes are built on existing sections, usually behind, or in front of, the existing family home and new homes are built on 'leftover' spaces in residential areas. A second factor is the building of higher-density housing. Single family one- to two-storey linked housing is especially common in Auckland, following efforts to promote more compact cities (Dixon and DuPuis, 2003; Auckland Regional Council, 2009). Compact dwellings in themselves are not problematic, as long as there is adequate indoor and outdoor play space. They can in fact be a good environment for children, who may find it easier to meet other children living in the complex or development than in lower-density single housing suburbs.

Inner-city living

There is a trend towards children in traditionally low-density housing countries, such as Australia and Aotearoa New Zealand, moving from low-density separate single housing units into higher-density housing, notably flats or apartments. In Melbourne, Australia, where this phenomenon has been the subject of a recent study, it is estimated that by 2021 some 10,000 children under 15 will reside in the City of Melbourne, many of whom will be accommodated in high-rise housing (Mizrachi and Whitzman 2009). Recent studies of central Auckland detect similar trends. Between 1991 and 2006, there was a 92% increase in the child population and between 2001 and 2006 an annual 12% increase in the number of children under 15 was noted. A study by Carroll et al. (2011) of the experiences of families living in central Auckland apartments concluded that '[w]hile apartments in the inner city are clearly providing convenient housing for an increasing number of families, they fall short of meeting the specific needs of families and children' (2011, p. 365). The problem is not that inner-city living itself is problematic, but more that the apartments in which the families are living were generally not designed with families in mind. It is apparent that the trend towards increasing numbers of families living in the inner city, already well established in cities such as Melbourne, is likely to continue here in Aotearoa New Zealand.

Not only are increasing numbers of city children living in homes not designed for children but increasing numbers of children are living in inadequate homes. In a longitudinal study of Pacific families in South Auckland, 37% of mothers reported housing dampness or mould and 53.8% reported cold housing (Families Commission, 2008, p. 88). A study of infectious disease and inequality in Aotearoa New Zealand noted clear ethnic and social inequalities in infectious disease risk (Baker et al., 2012). They found inequalities have increased substantially in the past 20 years, particularly for Māori and Pacific people in the most deprived groups. Other studies report a decreasing affordability of housing for many lower-income and even middle-income families (Ministry of Social Development, 2010; New Zealand Productivity Commission, 2012). This is problematic because in Aotearoa New Zealand home ownership has traditionally been seen as providing a stable base for the family to grow and develop; the opportunity for better health and education outcomes; a sense of belonging to a community; and an opportunity for children to achieve social mobility (Families Commission, 2008, p. 101). In Aotearoa New Zealand the physical quality of the home environment is highly variable: too many children still grow up in cold, damp, overcrowded houses, while conversely, for others, the sheer quantity of space can be isolating. If the domestic environment is changing – and not always in a positive direction – so too is the outdoor environment.

The changing outdoor environment

Aotearoa New Zealand childhoods – the arcadian image

Tourism New Zealand has as its catchphrase '100% Pure New Zealand' and markets Aotearoa New Zealand as 'clean and green'. The marketing is supported by evocative natural images that include unfurling ferns still in their koru shape, wild mountain peaks, long sandy beaches, tussock grasslands, various adventurers getting a thrill from the Aotearoa New Zealand environment, and children in a mountain stream. How real is this natural, invariably rural environment, though, in terms of the lives of the 'real' environmental experiences of Aotearoa New Zealand children? Do they live in pristine natural environments where climbing mountains and swimming in bright, clear rivers is part of their lived experience?

The rural outdoors has played an important role in New Zealanders' childhood consciousness. One of the earliest written examples of Aotearoa New Zealand's image as a good place to raise children comes from a letter written in 1850. New Plymouth settler Hannah Stephenson wrote, 'What a glorious place this is for children. They wander about in the woods and fields and sun. I, who am of a rather anxious nature, know they can get into no danger' (Te Ara: The Encyclopedia of New Zealand, online). Much later, in 1988, 20 prominent New Zealanders were asked to reflect on their childhood (Gifkins, 1988). The following extracts from their reflections indicate the continuing importance of the natural environment for New Zealanders growing up in the twentieth century. Andrew Fagan (b.1962) described taking off from his Wellington home: 'On a two- or three-hour morning excursion I would usually clamber up and down the sides of the southern half of the gully ... On a full day's excursion I would enter the almost impenetrable Maori bush and flounder about for hours in dim dense thickets of intrigue and fascination' (p. 64). Shonagh Koea (b.1943) described how her excursions provided relief from domestic turmoil: 'I went rowing about in a little boat I found. It was made of two sheets of corrugated iron nailed roughly together over some sort of wooden frame and sank in no time. It was many years later that I realised I could have drowned but learned instead to swim quite suddenly ... In the school holidays if I wished to save the bus fare to the next town I would cycle there. It was, I think about twelve miles' (p. 70).

In a more recent study on Aotearoa New Zealand families, Kevin Prime described his whānaungatanga,[3] a family life close to nature:

> For our children, being part of our family was: walking four kilometres each way daily to catch the school bus; being part of the weekly cooking roster from age eight; being part of planting, weeding and harvesting the garden crops; shooting or catching game; preparing it for eating, like plucking and gutting birds; gutting and drying eels; killing and dressing a pig; killing and dressing mutton plus treating the skins for use as mats or as a cushion for horseback riding; killing and dressing beef, corning surplus meat, treating the skin to make leather products; breaking in new horses; cutting and chopping firewood for the wood stove; doing the laundry by hand; lighting the kerosene lanterns. (Families Commission, 2009, p. 7)

These recollections, evoking a sense of freedom, adventure and connection to the land even for city children, resonate for many New Zealanders of all ages: the natural environment seems to provide positive and fondly recalled memories of times devoid of responsibility yet full of promise, and a life with few boundaries in which adults feature only at the margins.

In their seminal text *Growing up in New Zealand*, Ritchie and Ritchie (1978) wrote of both the benefits and problems associated with Aotearoa New Zealand's natural environment:

> When New Zealanders think of the phrase 'quality of life,' it is not the absence of opera, ballet or art galleries that they have in mind but ever more crowded beaches at the weekend, long queues of cars clogging the homeward road

---

[3] The principle of whānau, like Tino Rangatiratanga, sits at the heart of Kaupapa Māori. The whānau and the practice of whānaungatanga form an integral part of Māori identity and culture. The cultural values, customs and practices organised around the whānau and 'collective responsibility' are a necessary part of Māori survival and educational achievement (Tuhiwai Smith, 2000, p. 10).

on Sunday evenings, the destruction of forests, threats to breeding grounds, the pollution of trout streams ... The family holiday to the tent cities of the seaside, to camp in caravans, and to seaside cottages and baches is a national institution. (p. 176)

Despite the problems that they identified, they concluded '[w]e think that most New Zealanders would agree that this is a good place to bring up children' (p. 179). The intention here is not to see the past through golden spectacles, because in many ways life for children in Aotearoa New Zealand today is more secure and less traumatic, and children have access to a huge range of sporting, educational, cultural and other experiences. The next question in this chapter, though, is how the play, adventure and opportunities to be independent recalled above resonate in the lives of children today.

Environments today

Childhood environments in the developed world today have been pronounced as debilitating and hostile to their well-being. Sue Palmer's book *Toxic Childhood* pointed to a range of growing childhood ills, including behavioural, developmental and health disorders. She suggested that raising children today is like negotiating a minefield (2006, p. 12). In a similar vein, Brendan Gleeson (2006) referred to what he calls modernity's paradox, where children in Australia, despite a general overall rising wealth, are 'fatter, sicker and sadder'. In 2000, David Buckingham wrote his book *The death of childhood* about growing up in an electronic age. However, the negative title notwithstanding, he argued that despite popular psychology promulgating a doom and gloom view of childhood, life is far more complex than this simple, conservative, and pessimistic view would suggest. Is different necessarily worse? And are we doing our children an injustice by continual use of negative terminology when talking of children's lives, such as 'bubble-wrapped kids', 'cotton-wool kids', 'couch potatoes', 'backseat kids' and 'junk food addicts'? A whole range of 'experts' evidently feel free to pontificate on children's lives, with even the Archbishop of Canterbury wading in and talking of a crisis in modern childhood. Richard Louv (2005) in the US wrote that children today are suffering from 'nature deficit disorder'. While this negativity has generally been targeted at children growing up in the US, Britain and Australia, increasingly Aotearoa New Zealand too is picking up on these notions.

There are a number of identifiable and significant changes occurring in the environments that children experience, some of which have led to the production of the pessimistic views indicated above. Two changes that we look at here are changes in transport and changes in access to outdoor environments.

Transport and independence

Children's lives, globally, are becoming increasingly car dependent. Aotearoa New Zealand ranks fourth in the world in terms of car ownership per capita, a ratio of 620 cars per 1000 people. This is seven times the ratio in 1960 and an estimated 92% of journeys are by car, with one-third of journeys being less than two kilometres (Ministry for the Environment, 2006). This rising car use has implications for children in a number of ways. As traffic increases there are more accidents: between 2000 and 2005, there were 6004 pedestrian injuries and 259 fatalities (Ministry of Transport, 2005). Children were disproportionately highly represented amongst these figures, with peak figures being associated with school travel times (Ministry of Transport, 2005). Further, accidents peak around school locations. In a study of 345 recorded injury locations for children aged five to 15 in Dunedin between 1980 and 2002, 48.1% occurred within 250 metres of a school (McGee & Ketchel, 2003). The congregation of cars around schools creates what Paul Tranter calls a social trap (2006). As more parents drop children off at school by car, the school environment becomes congested and increasingly dangerous for the remaining child pedestrians, whose parents then in turn start to chauffeur their children, thereby further increasing traffic. In addition, children's smaller size makes them particularly vulnerable to diseases related to car emissions. For example, the risk of leukaemia is higher if a child lives in a place where more than 10,000 cars a day pass compared to 100 cars a day (European Commission, 2002, p. 14).

As children become more car-dependent, a decrease in independent mobility and outdoor play occurs, a trend identified across a number of developed countries, including Australia, the UK, the Netherlands, and the US (Valentine 1996; Karsten and van Vliet, 2006; Pooley et al., 2006; McDonald, 2012). Increased traffic levels contribute to children's withdrawal from the street and neighbourhood. Yet a study in Zurich found that children who play out in the street have a wider circle of friends and their parents also know more people (European Commission, 2002; ESRC, 2007). Increased traffic and rising car dependence results in a loss of children's own autonomous decision-making, as they are dependent on parents to get around. The *New Zealand Health Survey 2006/07* found one in 12 children (aged two to 14 years) were obese, and other studies in Aotearoa New Zealand have found international trends of decreased independence and outdoor play (Tranter and Pawson, 2001; Collins, Kearns and Neuwelt, 2003; Freeman and Quigg, 2009; Freeman, 2010).

If children are losing access to the local environment as their independent mobility decreases, many are concurrently increasing their access to a much wider spatial area for schooling, cultural and other activities, sports, and

Walking to school is becoming less common as car travel takes precedence.

visiting friends and relatives. This accessibility creates – for children whose parents have income and vehicular access – the possibility of socially and culturally richer lives. Saturday morning sport, a significant part of Aotearoa New Zealand social life, is testament to this. However, this access creates its own pressures, of time compression and trip chaining. Time compression is where more activities are fitted into each day, usually associated with 'trip chaining', where collecting or taking children is combined with journeys to other locations (Johansson, 2006; McMillan, 2007; Pooley et al., 2005). One consequence of such pressure is reduced time for free play.

Outdoor environmental experience

The causes of reduced independence and outdoor play relate not only to rising car use but also to social factors, notably rising fear, commonly referred to as 'stranger danger'. The concerns over safety accentuate the myth of child vulnerability. In the foreword to the *Milo state of play report* (2011), author Grant Schofield wrote: 'The state of play in our country has reached such a critical point that [it] has to be addressed today, not tomorrow. Plugged playtime has become the default activity, displacing active unstructured play with friends and family.' Three key findings from the study were:

- Almost one in two (46%) kids are not playing every day. Further, parents (64%) and grandparents (74%) agree that children don't create their own play or games as much as they used to in their own childhoods.
- Two in five (40%) Kiwi kids are saying they want more play time outside and almost two thirds of children (63%) want more time playing with their parents.
- Parents and children face similar barriers when it comes to play: finding the time, sourcing inspiration and over-reliance on technology (Milo Team, 2011, p. 10).

Parents in developed countries, including Aotearoa New Zealand, have become increasingly risk averse (Valentine, 2004; Gill, 2007; Cook, 2011), and that aversion is carried over into schools. A 2010 study for SPARC reports that Aotearoa New Zealand society is becoming less tolerant of risk and parents more risk averse, as evidenced in the wake of the Le Race 2000 incident,[4] which resulted in the Auckland Primary Principals' Association threatening to cease all EOTC (education outside the classroom) in members' schools unless the Ministry of Education indemnified principals from liability (NZTRI, p. 33). Providers were also observed to be reducing access to 'higher-risk' activities, especially those involving water. Nonetheless, findings from this study were generally positive, with most teachers and parents willing to tolerate some degree of risk in activities (see Table 4.1), thus going some way towards challenging the notion of the paranoid parent in Aotearoa New Zealand. An overall trend of increased involvement in outdoor education programmes was noted; however, the types of activities are changing, with schools increasingly opting for lower-risk activities.[5]

Many New Zealanders remain committed to providing outdoor experiences for their children. Holidays continue to be an important part of many New Zealanders' lives. Some 80% of New Zealanders have been camping at some point in their lives. Most campers began camping as children and the vast majority of New Zealanders (91%) consider access to places to go camping to be either 'extremely important' (60%) or 'important' (31%) (Mobius, 2006, cited in DoC, 2006). In a study of Aotearoa New Zealand families camping at

---

4 After the 2001 Le Race, during which a 31-year-old female cyclist collided with an oncoming car and was fatally injured, the event organiser was convicted of criminal nuisance and fined $10,000. This was seen as indicating that anyone involved in organising an event could be liable in the case of an accident.
5 My own children, when in Year 6 and aged 10, did the Tongariro Crossing as a class outing. After the retirement of the then principal the outing ceased due to rising concerns about risk, and it is no longer available to children attending the school today.

Table 4.1: Contingency Table for outdoor activities that parents and teachers see as 'Acceptable' or 'Unacceptable' (NZTRI, 2010)

	Acceptable to Parent			Acceptable to teacher		
	Yes	No	Unsure	Yes	No	Unsure
Day hike	456	4	5	267	1	1
Residential school camp	457	7	4	263	3	2
Trips to remote places (2+ hours walk to vehicle access)	365	55	42	183	60	26
Overnight tenting on a trip	426	25	12	238	21	11
Canoeing/kayaking in a pool	447	8	7	254	8	3
Canoeing/kayaking in sheltered waters	406	32	22	247	13	9
Canoeing/kayaking on a river	201	170	78	108	126	33
Science field trip to the bush or natural water feature	457	5	4	264	2	1
Artificial wall climbing or abseiling	453	8	5	262	4	2
Rock climbing or abseiling on a natural cliff-face	319	83	59	173	71	25
Cooking with an open fire	423	26	15	639	57	36
Activity involving cookers	434	17	12	250	9	10
Skiing	411	30	22	195	36	35
Rope course activities	447	7	9	258	4	7

five campsites in the South Island during the 2011/2012 summer season, the 69 families interviewed revealed a strong commitment to providing outdoor experiences for their children.[6] Most families chose campsites with relatively low-key facilities (usually toilets, taps, possibly showers and a camp kitchen) that were close to rivers or the sea; children roamed freely across the site, and in many cases beyond. For all families, camping was a positive choice, providing a time for togetherness and relaxation from the pressures in their lives. It gave opportunities for a whole raft of activities, including swimming, cycling, hunting, kayaking, jet skiing, motor biking, fishing, spotlight (hide and seek with torches at night) and walking. The rules that were in place at home about where children could go and with whom were reduced and children particularly enjoyed the relaxed eating and sleeping arrangements. Some 81% of respondents were concerned about the decline in children's outdoor play experiences, seeing camping as a means to offset this loss.

The final part of this chapter summarises the findings from research on children's lives undertaken in Dunedin. This study provided information on children's use of, and own views on, the environment. The relatively constrained levels of freedom present in children's lives contrasts with the freedom exhibited in the camping study.

The Dunedin experience: Case study

The study

Between 2006 and 2009 we carried out a study with 163 children from 10 schools in Dunedin. They were aged nine to 11 and in their last two years of primary school education, i.e. Years 5 and 6 (Freeman, 2010; Freeman and Vass, 2010; Freeman and Quigg, 2009). The aim of the study was to explore children's relationship to the city and, in particular, to their home neighbourhoods. The children were recruited from schools that were from different geographical areas of the city and different socio-economic groups. Some were schools recruiting mainly from the local neighbourhood, and others were schools that attracted children from across the city. Karsten and van Vliet (2006) identified evidence of a wider spatiality for children living in the city: mainly due to increased access to private transport, children are accessing larger areas of the city as part of their daily lives. We wanted to see if the trend they observed in the Netherlands was happening here in Aotearoa New Zealand, and if so, what it means for children's sense of connection to community. Data for the study was

---

6   This research was conducted by C. Freeman and R. Kearns through the University of Otago and is currently unpublished.

Going down the rapids at Dansey's Pass Holiday Park.

Children wait their turn to jump off the cliff into the swimming hole at Dansey's Pass Holiday Park.

collected in four ways. This included a class exercise where students drew a map of their neighbourhood on which they were asked to include their own home and the homes of people and places that matter to them. Some children drew maps that covered the whole city but most drew neighbourhood maps. Children then talked about their maps and their lives in a one-on-one interview. They were asked about their family, the school and why they attended it, their travel and play patterns and about their neighbourhood. In the 2009 study, children also completed a computer exercise in which they looked at an aerial photo of their home and neighbourhood and were asked to point to the homes of people they knew and to places that mattered to them. This was then recorded using a geographical information system (GIS).

School attendance, travel and independence

The findings were very interesting. Local schools, normally seen as the heart of the community, were often bypassed by children attending a more distant school. Some 35% of children did not attend their closest school. Schools showed substantial variation in regard to local attendance, ranging from one school having all its children living in the neighbourhood to two schools having only 17% and 21% of their children living locally. Where children attended the local school, most walked; conversely, most travelled by car to more distant schools. Attending a more distant school invariably means a car-dependent life as they go by car to access cultural, sporting and educational activities, to play with friends, and to access sport, shopping, health facilities etc. Levels of independent mobility, that is the degree to which they could access places independently of adults, varied significantly between individual children and between schools, ranging from children who could go nowhere unaccompanied to children who had free range across their neighbourhood. Children were only allowed to access places outside their neighbourhood if it was on a specific journey, such as catching the bus to ballet class or travelling to a parent's workplace. A surprising number of children could go 'nowhere' without adults and it was reasonably common for adults to accompany children to play places such as parks (see Figure 4.1). However, general figures hide the fact that there were substantial variations. Levels of independence were highest where children attended the local school, the school was less than one kilometre away and the children lived in a neighbourhood with a clear identity and boundary. The highest levels of independence were in two very different neighbourhoods. One was a small, self-contained, high socio-economic suburb a few kilometres outside the city and bounded by the sea and rural land. The other was a low-income suburb bounded by rural land on two sides but which

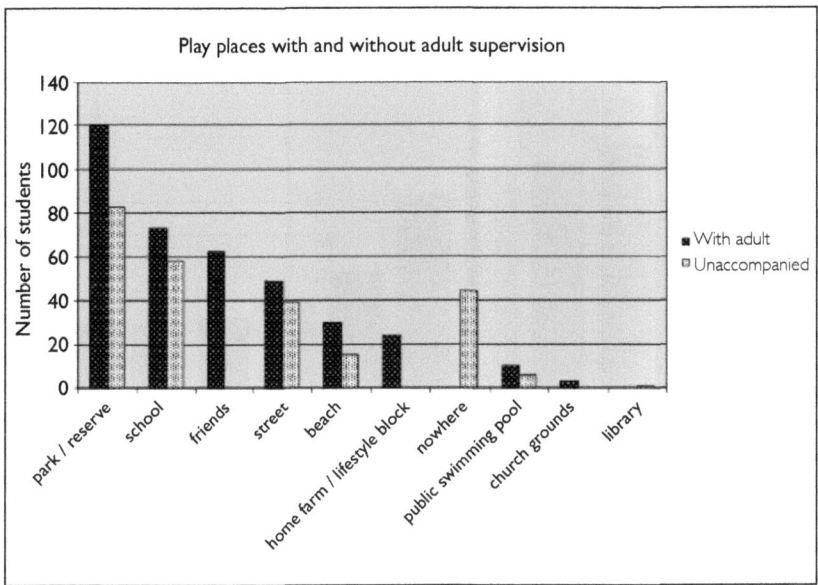

Figure 4.1: Play places with and without adult accompaniment.

required a climb up a steep hill to be accessed from the main city. Both had high attendance at the local school and a strong community ethos.

The neighbourhood

In our study we were interested to see if children were socially connected to the neighbourhood. As well as being asked to put the homes of people they knew on their hand-drawn maps, children in the 2009 study were asked to look at an aerial photo and identify all the homes of people they knew. For the six schools in the 2009 study, the average number of people/homes identified ranged from 9.53 down to 3.44. The school with the highest scores had all children living locally and attending their local school. Children from this school also identified the most places, an average of 16.87 places. Because the interview was time limited, some more socially connected children didn't necessarily have time to record all their people and places. Children from the lowest-scoring school, where only 17% lived locally, also scored lowest on identifying neighbourhood places at 7.72 places per child.

We were interested to find out whether children could attend a non-local school but could still connect to their neighbourhood. Our findings suggested that such connection is difficult. This was illustrated in one of our rural villages, where children attending the local school generally had high scores for the

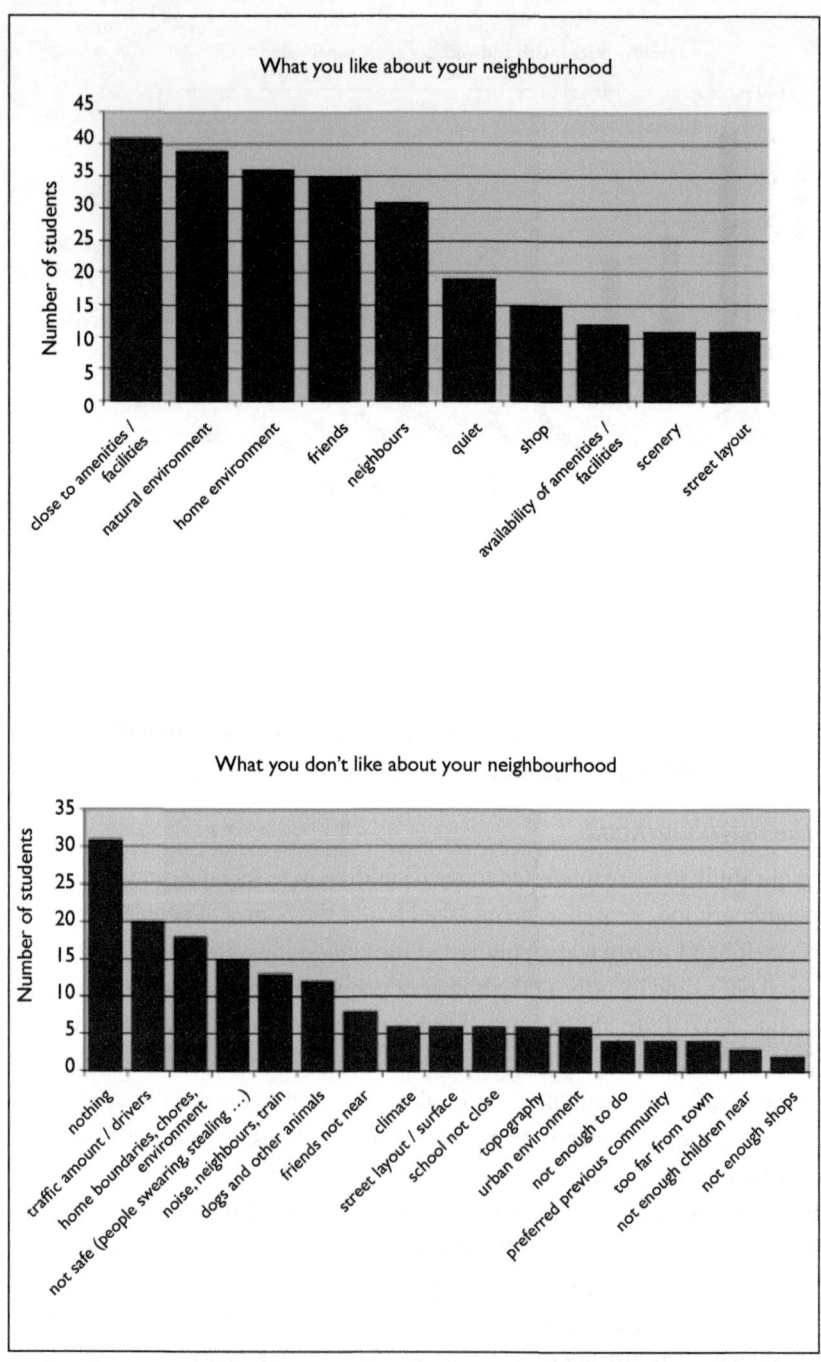

Figure 4.2: What children like and don't like about their neighbourhoods.

number of people and places identified, but a child in the same village, who commuted to a distant school, had difficulty in recognising even adjacent neighbours and labelled his neighbours 'anonymous' on his map. There clearly are some neighbourhoods that support independence better than others, despite individual differences between children. Low traffic densities, a clear sense of neighbourhood boundaries and a locally attended school all help.

We also asked children about their neighbourhoods. Children universally liked where they lived; they thought it was friendly (86%) and safe (84%), and knew someone they could go to for help if necessary (84%); around half had visited a neighbour in the past week and a similar number helped their neighbours (57%), most commonly by feeding animals. In their neighbourhoods they liked (in order of most frequently mentioned) the facilities and amenities present (e.g. parks, shops, sports pitches), the natural environment, their homes, and friends and neighbours. Interestingly children found it far more difficult to talk about what they didn't like and the commonest response was 'nothing', followed by traffic (Figure 4.2).

The children in the study were leading varied and full lives. They accessed the wider city on a regular, often daily, basis for school, activities, or as part of their parents' working lives. They have diminishing independence levels, with some children having no independence, but levels varied across individuals and neighbourhoods. Nonetheless, children retained an affinity to their neighbourhoods and immediate home environment, even if they didn't access it independently, and most of all, they had a very positive attitude to the places they live in.

Environmental challenges for New Zealand children

Aotearoa New Zealand offers a potentially excellent environment for children and has been portrayed as a clean green outdoor environment in which children can play and run free. The reality is that fewer children, outside of their holidays, are indeed running free. Yet the changing environment also offers opportunities: despite their problems, private vehicles offer easier access to activities and places and to distant friends and families. The challenge is to use this advantage wisely and not let excessive use of vehicles restrict children's play, mobility or opportunities to know the people and places where they live. It is important to reclaim the street so that children are a visible, acknowledged and protected part of our environment; we should see children out and about, and see them enjoying pristine rivers in '100% pure' Aotearoa New Zealand. We must refute pronouncements about 'toxic childhood' (Palmer, 2006), 'fatter, sicker, and sadder' children (Gleeson, 2006) and 'nature deficit disorder'; and we must resist the negative trends identified as increasingly dominant in childhoods, such as pressured lives, lack of independent mobility and freedom, and limited outdoor play. The New Zealanders we interviewed in our camping study are committed to doing just that.

CHAPTER 5

Ethics in research with children

Jude MacArthur & Margaret McKenzie

The Children and Young People as Social Actors Research Cluster (referred to in this paper as 'the Cluster') is a group of 24 researchers at the University of Otago, Dunedin, Aotearoa New Zealand, with a shared interest in research that includes children. Such research is ethically and methodologically challenging, and questions around ethical issues have frequently entered into Cluster discussions. Despite the mandate of Childhood Studies and children's rights for ethical research that includes children and young people, we had all experienced barriers and pitfalls when it came to conducting such research. Shared areas of concern included gaining ethics approval for proposed methods and methodologies; recruitment and access to children; children's 'vulnerability' and 'capacity' to be informed and give consent; and preventing harm. This chapter reports on issues discussed in a series of dedicated meetings by Cluster members on research methodologies and ethics in research with children and young people. Issues raised in our own projects were problematised in order to develop some guiding principles that support ethically sound research.[1]

Emerging questions about ethics

The Cluster initially identified a common set of concerns. First, there is a need for research that is focused on the recognition of children as the basis for improving policy and practice (Frankel, 2007). Second, despite the emphasis on

---

1 This paper is based on the following presentation: McKenzie, M. & MacArthur, J. (2009, November). *Ethical principles in research with children: Developing guidelines through critical collegial collaboration*. Paper presented at Children as Experts in their Own Lives: Child Inclusive Research Symposium of the International Conference of the International Society of Child Indicators Counting Children in Child Indicators Research Theory, Policy and Practice, Sydney, Australia.

children's rights and the United Nations Convention on the Rights of the Child (UNCRC), there is a low level of theorising in research on children's rights; few studies ask children for their views; and there is widespread uncertainty about the relative prioritising of children's rights on the one hand, and the rights of parents and adults on the other (Quennerstedt, 2011).

A third point related to processes of ethical review, with some Cluster members experiencing difficulties at the point of submitting their research proposals to institutional ethics committees. While there was an appreciation that gatekeeping was usually done in the name of protection for children and young people, researchers' theoretical positions about childhood, children's rights, and the implications for children and young people's place in research were not always well understood. Ironically, ethics committees could impede important research with children through the regulation and blocking of children's involvement; through an insensitivity to children's participation rights (Powell & Smith, 2009; Powell, Fitzgerald, Taylor & Graham, 2012); and through assumptions about childhood that emphasise children's vulnerability and lack of competence, rather than their willingness and capacity to be involved in research (McGuire, 2005; Powell & Smith, 2006; 2009). Other researchers internationally have shared the Cluster's concern that sound research of value and benefit to children could be disrupted, slowed down, or even halted (see for example, Campbell, 2008; Centre for Children and Young People, 2005; Skellett, 2008).

The importance of research including children

While research has not ignored children and young people, their involvement in the past has been largely determined by adults, and their lives have been observed from an adult point of view and through a power imbalance favouring adult agendas (Smith, 2011). Greene and Hill (2005) conclude from extant research that 'the emphasis has been on children as subjects, on child-related outcomes rather than child-related processes, and on child variables, rather than children as persons' (p. 1). Thinking about childhood has been strongly influenced by adult assumptions about what children do and don't know, what they think and why: consequently, child-related policy has typically emerged out of adult-dominated thinking (Frankel, 2007).

Advances in Childhood Studies have led to an improved understanding of the way in which children themselves experience their childhoods, as opposed to understandings evolving out of adult interpretations. Ideas about the socially constructed nature of childhood, and the salience of relationships and settings in children's lives, have also promoted an understanding of the diversity of childhoods, as opposed to the idea of 'one universal child'. Children know more than anyone else about their own lives and cultures, and in this regard, can be considered as experts (James et al, 1998). Involving children more directly in research respects their participation as subjects rather than objects, who can 'speak' in their own right, and it can 'rescue them from silence and exclusion, and from being represented, by default, as passive objects' (Alderson, 2001, p. 142). Undertaken with thought, care and attention to ethical processes, research that models children's participation in its own design can enhance children's participation rights and become transformative of their relationships with their communities (Beazley et al., 2009; Cheney, 2011). Researchers can be guided by the principle that if the research matters for children and young people, there is a mandate to consider how children and young people can be involved. The wide-ranging research projects represented within the Cluster, and in this book, heighten our awareness of the different ways in which children experience their worlds, and of the impact of variables such as gender, ethnicity, disability, and social and economic circumstances. To reflect this diversity of experience, it behoves researchers to commit to ethical and methodological approaches that take greater account of children's views, and not simply to 'hear children's voices', but to assure children of their rights (Clavering & McLaughlin, 2010; Harcourt & Sargeant, 2011).

The UNCRC (United Nations, 1989) has drawn attention to the rights of children and young people to have greater involvement in decisions that affect them; to have opportunities to express their views; and have their views heard by the people who matter in the places that are relevant to them. It vindicates children's rights to be considered as people in their own right, so the nature of their experiential life should be of central interest to the researcher (Greene & Hill, 2005; Powell et al., 2012; Powell & Smith, 2009; Smith, 2011). Children's participation in research has been shown to enhance children's skills and self-esteem, support better decision-making and protection of children, and improve policies and practices for children (Powell & Smith, 2009).

Research with children and young people provides opportunities for practitioners and policymakers to learn how to support children's lives in ways that are contextually sensitive and responsive to their lived experience. In our own work, we have observed situations where children and young people have articulated a perspective unique to themselves that is beyond the expectations and/or contradictory to the interests, views and perspectives of adults. For example, in a study of the school experiences of students with physical disabilities, 10-year-old Alan explained that he disliked having to leave class to go to physiotherapy:

Alan: I go somewhere else for therapy. In the spare room.

Interviewer: Do you mind going to the spare room?

Alan: I have to put up with it.

Interviewer: What would you rather do?

Alan: Stay in the classroom.

Interviewer: If you were doing something fun in the classroom and you didn't really want to leave, would you say that?

Alan: Yes – but I would just have to do it.

In contrast, Alan's teacher said 'He's quite happy to go out of class ... the only time he complains ... is [when] something exciting is happening, he's reluctant to leave ... he understands he has to do things' (Clark, MacArthur et al., 2007, p. 246). This example illustrates how Alan's understanding of his situation is at odds with that of his teacher, but it also raises questions about children's rights to express their views and to have them responded to – in this case, at school. Alan spent time on his own at break times, wanted to have friends, and felt it was important to be in class with his peers, but adults at school prioritised his physical needs over his social needs. As McGuire (2005) points out, children have good social radar for assessing the situations and contexts in which they find themselves, their perspectives and voices are important signifiers of what is important to them.

Including children and young people in research is one thing, but researchers can also contribute to a better understanding of what constitutes effective child and youth participation. Some Cluster members have undertaken research with young people as researchers themselves, and have reflected back on the successes and limitations of a peer research methodology using the concepts of cultural and subcultural capital (Nairn, Higgins, & Sligo, 2007). Emerging out of their projects are observations of the assets brought by young people to the research endeavour, including a capacity to quickly establish rapport with interviewees 'on the street', and an understanding of how subcultural capital could create ease between interviewer and interviewee. Nairn et al. conclude that 'diverse faces on a research team could increase the likelihood that participants might find someone to connect with' (p. 7). They suggest that researchers need to take seriously young people's desires to be involved in research that connects more closely to *their* interests, making it more likely that young people are able to use their subcultural capital well throughout the research process.

The multiple ways in which children can participate in research

It should be possible for children and youth to participate across a wide range of research initiatives, from small-scale qualitative projects through to grand-scale projects. Equally, it should be possible to consider how children and young people can be involved across a range of methods, including, for example, experimental, survey, observation, interview, ethnographic, indirect gathering of information, focus group, online, medical, and visual methods such as photographs and film. Particular methods are associated with particular ethical issues, concerns, and dilemmas, so it is important for researchers to know their methods well and ensure that children's participation and protection rights are considered and addressed (Cheney, 2011; Fargas-Malet, McSherry, Larkin & Robinson, 2010; Skelton, 2008). This process involves the careful analysis of related methodological and ethical concerns at all levels, and throughout the natural life of a project.

Children as social actors

Childhood Studies has fostered an understanding of children as social beings, active in the construction and determination of their own lives, the lives of others around them, and the societies in which they live (James et al., 1997). Relationships and interactions with others are viewed as significant features in children's lives, with attention turned to the quality and nature of the settings in which children participate. Within a research context, these ideas have led to an understanding of the particular significance of ethics and research settings. Children's relationships with researchers; the research they participate in; how they are positioned as research participants; and how they are assessed are all keys to advancing authentic knowledge of children and childhood (Smith, 2011).

Researchers need to be constantly aware of the power differentials in research with children (Clavering & McLaughlin, 2010). While we may consider that having been a child allows us to be an 'insider', the power of being an adult does not dissolve away in a research context. Our own childhoods were different from those of the children in our research today, so the differential exists in both age and time (Skelton, 2008). If adults are genuinely concerned about seeking children's perspectives 'then children have to be positioned as participating subjects, "knowers" and social actors, rather than objects of the researcher's gaze' (ibid). This establishes children and young people as active participants with valued opinions and insights on their own childhoods, capable of making decisions about their involvement in research, and able to express their own views.

Primary accountability to the child

The UNCRC upholds children's rights as paramount, and the Cluster's position is that the responsibility and primary accountability of the researcher is first and foremost to the children and young people in their project. This becomes a key principle guiding the researcher's role and behaviour, and as a starting point, research is justified through the potential benefit to children and young people themselves, and not to our own curiosity. If we are unable to justify the research in terms of its contribution to knowledge and to the greater good for children, young people and communities, then it is unlikely that our research will be ethical.

The notion of primary accountability to the child can deliver 'sticking points', however. Accountability and responsibility depend on the development of a positive and trusting relationship between children and young people and researchers, and research funders do not always appreciate that this can take time. Those of us who have enjoyed the luxury of longitudinal funding have been able to use the time available productively to focus on this critical part of the research process. As researchers, our capability to work productively and effectively with children and young people is enhanced by funding regimes that respect this point.

Parental interest can also raise questions about children's rights to confidentiality. For example, will consenting adults expect to receive information from an interview with their child? According to Munford and Sanders (2001) primary accountability to the child means that children are *assured* confidentiality, reseachers will not pass on any information unless it concerns the child's safety, and children are clearly informed about how their information will appear in research documents. In the case of challenging issues such as disclosure of abuse, guidance for researchers can come from research protocols developed in advance (for example, encouraging the child to talk to appropriate adults, or agreeing to the researcher doing this).

While advance preparation is always desirable, the nature of the research we undertake with children and young people means that we can never predict every situation that will arise. Cluster members have discussed the need to make instant decisions in response to unexpected situations that arise. One member recalled a situation where a young secondary school student in her research project was upset by impairment-focused bullying prior to entering class. He was subsequently unable to focus on his classwork, became noisy and was eventually asked by the teacher to leave the class. When the researcher later asked him whether he wanted to report the bullying, he was concerned about retaliation and did not wish to report it. After some discussion, he agreed that it would help if the researcher informed the teacher of that class in a general way, and without naming names, that bullying often happened in the hallway and it made it hard for some students to learn. The researcher's role in this situation is in a state of flux, shifting between researcher and advocate for the young person. Where does primary accountability to the child begin? Should the researcher intervene when the bullying occurs outside class? Should she advise the teacher about the circumstances leading up to the student's eviction from class? Or was it appropriate to follow up with the student after the event and discuss possible solutions with him?

Another member described an unanticipated situation where simply working through the information sheet resulted in a child participant becoming upset in response to an example that was used. These experiences illustrate the need for researchers to maintain a flexible position, including being prepared at any time to suspend the research process in the interests of participants, even if this means losing data, or perhaps even losing participants.

Issues of age and competence

The variety of disciplines and research interests represented within the Cluster means that, as a group, we have been involved in projects that include a wide range of children and young people. Some researchers have worked with children as young as two years, while others have undertaken projects in which adolescents have taken on the role of researcher themselves. Others have undertaken research with children and young people with disabilities, including those who use alternative communication methods or who find direct conversation difficult.

The UNCRC is written for all children, and age or perceived 'competence' or 'capacity' should not be used to justify excluding children and young people from decision-making around their participation in research. All children and young people can be viewed as competent, as able to participate, as having a perspective that can and should be heard (Alderson, 2008; Clavering & McLaughlin, 2010; Frankel, 2007). A child's age is an arbitrary factor and the Cluster considered the notion of children's *experience* to be a far more important variable for researchers to consider.

Nonetheless, it is our experience that gatekeeping can occur at various levels of a research project, preventing the participation of some children perceived by others to be 'vulnerable' and therefore at risk in a research context (see for example Powell & Smith, 2009; Powell et al., 2012). Vulnerability is determined either on the basis of children's age (too young) or their perceived 'capacity' to understand about research and give their consent to be involved (e.g. disabled children or children living in care). Barriers to children's participation can occur at ethics committee level; when gaining consent; and when conducting research in particular settings such as hospitals or schools. We have taken the position that it is possible for researchers to attend to children's participation *and* to their protection rights by adopting a careful and sensitive approach to ethical issues throughout the life of a research project. As Skelton (2008) argues, ethical research practice can evolve out of child-centric perspectives and a social sciences framework that opens up possibilities for children and young people's participation rather than closing them down.

A socioculturally based view of childhood suggests that children construct their own understanding through relationships with, and guidance from, other children and adults (Smith, 2011). Within a research context, the implication is that children's capacity to talk about their experiences and express their opinions can be enhanced through supportive relationships with researchers and others. It is up to researchers themselves, to find ways to include young children (Birbeck & Drummond, 2007), or diverse groups of children and young people in their research (see, for example, Beazley et al., 2009; Cameron & Murphy, 2006; Clavering & McLaughlin, 2010; Kelly, 2006; McGuire, 2005; Wright, 2008). Researchers then have a responsibility to ensure that children are fully informed and understand what the research is about and how they will be involved; are able to give their consent; remain happy to be involved throughout the project; and have ways to express their views and perspectives (Powell et al., 2012).

In some of our work with disabled children and young people, for example, we have found it important to take the time needed to get to know children well, to build trusting relationships, to understand when, where and how they are comfortable to speak with us, and to know what can and cannot be talked about (MacArthur, Sharp, Kelly, & Gaffney, 2007). This included the unique ways in which some children would communicate their views to us. Two 11-year-olds in our study enjoyed communicating their views through an interactive digital Asterix and Obelix book, while a 12-year-old who disliked face-to-face communication told his own story through drawings that were interpreted through his caregiver.

Respect and consideration for children

Respect and consideration for children is another principle valued by the Cluster (Alderson, 1995; 2008). In practice, this means acknowledging the contribution that children and young people make to our understanding of childhoods; respecting their willingness and ability to participate; and respecting their perspectives – what children say and how they say it. The difference in social status between adults and children cannot be ignored, and there needs to be an awareness of the influence of these power relations to ensure that children are not vulnerable to persuasion, adverse influence or harm (Hill, 2005).

In the process of conducting research, we sometimes collect children's drawings and written work as illustrations of experiences that are important to them, or of issues they wish to highlight for us. This approach provides alternative ways for children in our research to voice their opinions. Within the Cluster we have raised questions about consideration for children in relation to ownership of this material. Is this 'data' to be stored in a locked place commensurate with the dictates of the ethics committee? Or does it belong to the child in our study? Some of us have also been asked by children to have their real names (as opposed to a pseudonym) used in research publications. Sometimes this request comes with a sense of ownership and pride in their writing or drawing, or in their own opinions, perspectives and status as a knowledgeable contributor. But these requests are rarely consistent with ethics requirements to protect confidentiality. We do not yet have answers to these questions, although Skelton (2008) asks whether ethical practice in research (as demanded by ethics committees especially) might be an adult construction, and whether young people as competent social actors might write different guidelines about their participation in research processes.

Because we work across a very wide range of contexts and settings, we have also discussed the importance of having respect for the age of the children and young people in our research, and for the various contexts in which we undertake research (at home, in families, at school, in early childhood services, in hospitals, on the street, and so on). Each setting brings its own freedoms, constraints, and demands, and we have found it necessary to be open and responsive to these. For example, when working in schools our presence as researchers needs to be carefully explained to other children, but without identifying or drawing attention to particular children who may be the focus of our research. It has also been important to clarify with teachers our role in classrooms, particularly in relation to the children and young people participating in our project.

Ethics as a process

A final key principle influencing our own work as researchers is the idea of 'ethics as a process'. Addressing ethical issues is not a single task undertaken at the outset of a project. Nor are ethical issues and principles fully addressed once a project has successfully made its way through an ethical review. As already discussed, unanticipated ethical issues will always arise, both 'in the field' and throughout the duration of a research project. It is important that researchers approach and understand ethics as a *process* (Alderson, 1995, Powell & Smith, 2009; Powell et al., 2012).

The notion of ethics as a process means there are implications for continuous adult reflexivity, and this includes reflexivity by researchers involved in student supervision. Because ethical approval is not a 'one-off' matter, provision needs to be made for an ongoing review process that allows for the discussion of:

- ethical issues as they arise;
- the subsequent decisions that need to be made (was the right decision made, are there further issues arising out of earlier ethics decisions?;
- the effectiveness of those decisions; and
- the opportunities for children to opt out.

We like the idea of an 'ethical radar' promoted by Skanvors (2009), emerging out of her research with two- to five-year-old children. Skanvors describes how children readily bought into the research project, but later expressed their resistance to being observed or interviewed. This is, she suggests, an example of child agency (not necessarily of a desire to withdraw from the project), and at these times, researchers need to 'unfold and take note of what I would like to label their "ethical radar", which entails being attentive to the children's actions and reactions towards the researcher' (p. 15).

Skanvors's example is familiar. Many of us have been in situations where we decided to leave the setting in which we were observing, not to follow behind a group of students at secondary school, or to sit in a place where our presence was less conspicuous. While these decisions could mean losing opportunities to gather valuable data, the notion of respect and consideration for the children and young people in our projects is paramount. While we always tell children and young people in our research that they can 'tell us to go away' if they do not want us to be around at any particular time, it is really up to the researcher to be sensitive and responsive to the comfort level and body language of their participants at all times. This requires an alertness to the moments when children and young people reject the status of research participant in order to be alone, to be a family member, to be a student at school, or to simply be with their peers.

Informed consent

There are particular considerations in relation to consent and choice to participate that are unique to research with children and young people. The key ethical issue is maintaining a balance between preventing harm on the one hand, and the risk of silencing children's views and experiences and preventing their participation on the other (Alderson and Morrow, 2004; Clavering & McLaughlin, 2010; Skelton, 2008; Powell et al., 2012). Obtaining informed consent entails the consideration of several key concerns. One is children's 'capability' to consent. Yet, we could argue that this consideration is more appropriately reframed as the *researchers' competence* to obtain consent from children. Other considerations are the need for parental or guardian consent; and ensuring ongoing informed consent.

Two overarching themes have emerged from our discussions about informed consent. First, informed consent relies firmly on the principles of the UNCRC, which is written for *all* children. In this regard *all* children are seen as competent and able to consent to their involvement and participation in research. The second and associated theme is the researcher's responsibility to find ways to fully inform children, to provide information and seek consent by building and maintaining supportive relationships between researchers and children who are research participants.

The presumption of children's competence to consent

The starting point is the *presumption of competence* to consent for all children and young people. Assessing children's ability or competence to consent is not simply an age and stage and/or 'ability' judgement. These factors alone are not good indicators of competence; children need to be assessed individually and with regard to experience. In contrast, we acknowledge that while the capacity to consent is presumed, and children and young people need to be seen as *having experience* worthy of our research attention, children and young people need to be recognised as *inexperienced in the research context*. It is a researcher's responsibility to carefully consider this point so that consent is given from a *fully* informed position (Thomas and O'Hare, 1998).

Researcher competence to gain informed consent

The presumption of including all children in research, and obtaining informed consent, places responsibility on the researcher to find ways to fully inform children. As mentioned earlier, particular attention needs to be paid to the power and status differentials between adults and children and to the ways in which these can be redressed or minimised (Morrow & Richards, 1996). Recognising our roles as researchers, not as teachers, counsellors, social workers, advocates or friends, is critical, while acknowledging that our responsibility to do sound ethical research is embedded in participatory processes which seek children's own views.

Within the Cluster we have talked about how we work to achieve these productive relationships. No single approach emerges as the best way to proceed, and it is apparent that researchers bring to their role their own background, experience, skills, and preferences. In one study conducted in schools, for example, two researchers who were also trained teachers negotiated an active, 'hands-on' approach with class teachers and children in the classroom. A third researcher with a different professional background took a more detached, 'fly-on-the-wall' approach to her classroom work. Both approaches worked for the researchers, teachers and children involved. This example illustrates the benefits that can accrue from having a range of disciplines represented on research teams.

Concerns for researcher competence extend into several other areas, including, for example, what to say to children and young people at the start and end of a project; how to check consent to use verbatim and other material; how to convey information to children about project findings; and whether or not to give gifts/koha. The provision of payment is as contentious for child participants as adults (Alderson & Morrow, 2004). In our own work it is not unusual to give children a token of our thanks at the end of the project in recognition of their valued contribution. We are aware of the need to exercise caution, however, so that children do not interpret such gifts or payments as an inducement rather than due recompense for their time and contribution (Hill, 2005).

Information and consent processes relevant to age, ability, experience and culture

The question of what it *means* to be informed has also arisen in our Cluster meetings. Informed consent means that children will understand the nature of the research and their participation in it. This includes why we are undertaking the research; who the research is likely to benefit; exactly what they will be asked to do; that they can withdraw or decline participation without harm; who is funding it; and what will happen to their information.

Information provision and consent processes should be relevant to the experience, age, ability, culture, language and mode of communication of participants, with due recognition given to the capacity of children to communicate and participate in a variety of ways. Sometimes it is simply a matter of exploring 'what works'. Some children in our research projects have, for example, chosen to draw pictures about what they 'like' and 'hate' about school, rather than directly talking about these things. The focus needs to be on 'user-friendly' materials and mechanisms. Munford & Saunders (2001), for example, used a video mock-up of an interview with their own children to illustrate and explain to children what is involved in being in an interview study.

How is consent sought and who can give consent?

Our view is that *active and informed* consent is needed and must be gained from children themselves (Smith, 2009; Powell et al., 2012.). Parental/guardian consent is not sufficient to replace this, even where legal and institutional requirements are that parental consent is obtained. Active and informed consent contrasts with passive consent which involves the acquiescence or agreement of a parent or guardian on behalf of the child (Thomas and Kane, 1998).

'Assent' is also very different from informed consent. Its use has been justified in the past in situations where children were considered 'incompetent' to give their consent. However, it should not be assumed that children 'assent' simply because their parents agree for them to be part of a study. Several members of the Cluster had been in situations where parents or caregivers had expressed the view that it was unnecessary to ask their children for consent because they 'say it's fine'. We have pointed out that it is the researcher's responsibility to ensure children can be informed and that consent can be sought, and on that basis, assent is not acceptable to us. Any decision to use assent might only be sustained when applied to research with very young children (Munford & Sanders, 2001).

Researchers need to ensure children themselves choose freely to participate, and that recruitment procedures do not make them feel pressured to join in. Our 'ethical radar' can be alert to children's body language and lead us to use our better judgement when children say 'yes', but their body language says 'no'. Fundamentally, children need to know *they are in a research project*. This means informing children to ensure they understand what is happening and why, and how research can be used to change and improve things for children.

Consent is active and genuinely informed over time

Obtaining and giving consent is not a 'one-off event', and researchers need to be ready and able to manage continued consent, providing children with choices to opt out and in again if and when consent is under question. This requires researcher awareness of children's levels of comfort or discomfort, involvement or otherwise, and a preparedness to respond in a supportive way. Practical mechanisms can be put in place to provide children with opportunities to review their participation throughout the research process.

Sensitive issues and vulnerabilities are defined as those experienced by the individual child participant and not by the imposed criteria of the researcher. Despite our best protocols, we can never fully anticipate what might be a sensitive issue as any issue can be 'sensitive' for a child at any stage. The earlier example of the child who became upset while going through an information sheet illustrates this. Researchers are wise to expect the unexpected; appreciate that there will be unexpected moments requiring instant decisions; and be skilled in responding to such events.

We have also discussed the parameters that determine when and where consent ends. For example, what safeguards are there for ensuring that material such as children's drawings, or photographs taken in a research project, are not used in later publications and for a different purpose than the original? In response to these questions we have identified the need to provide for consent processes that are time and context specific.

Informed consent – privacy and confidentiality

A key aspect of informed consent is the guarantee of privacy and confidentiality that is assured when obtaining consent. Primary responsibility to the child means children must be afforded the same rights to confidentiality as adults. When ethical issues arise, the rights of the child are paramount and this becomes a guiding principle in seeking solutions where limits to confidentiality must be made. The disclosure of abuse, neglect or harm are examples of situations where rights to confidentiality cannot be promised and such limits need to be spelled out when seeking informed consent. It is the researcher's responsibility to ensure that these matters are conveyed in an accessible manner relevant to the children and young people involved.

Finally, it is important for researchers to understand the relevant national and international legal requirements around consent and context. This includes legal issues relating to privacy, ethics and rights, and in relation to specific contexts such as schools, hospitals, and institutional care settings.

Conclusion

This chapter has highlighted some of the ethical issues faced by researchers in the University of Otago Children and Young People as Social Actors Research Cluster. Over 20 years have passed since the adoption, by the General Assembly of the United Nations, of the Convention on the Rights of the Child (United Nations, 1989). The Convention prompted a research agenda that attends to the human rights of children at a time when governments are required to report on progress towards children's rights objectives (Beazley et al., 2009). While progress has been made in this time towards rights-based research with children, this chapter illustrates some of the ethical challenges faced by researchers as we explore ways to conduct research that values and enhances children's participation and supports them to express their views. Our Cluster discussions have lead us to agree with the conclusion drawn by Powell et al. (2012), that ethics cannot simply be reduced to codified principles, but rather are a vehicle for promoting the exploration and examination of dilemmas. In this regard, the questions we raise are a productive part of the discussion that is needed to advance a better research agenda for children: one that positions them as knowledgeable participating subjects and social actors and uses children-friendly and respectful methods, while also addressing the complex factors that impact on their lives.

PART TWO

Experiencing Diverse Childhoods

CHAPTER 6

Recollecting childhood at school in the early twentieth century

Helen May

I arrived in standard one hardly able to add or read. I was a left-hander who couldn't write as the teacher required. I had been battered to utter misery and exhaustion, bashed with straps, held hostage in front of the class, or made to stand up for ridicule on the desk top. Somehow I had moved onto standard one, where a lady floated like a waterlily into the room and into my life. She was as lovely as she looked. She came I think from Lumsden, and was named Miss Loudon. She worked hard. She got me going. I fell in love and, for my loved one, worked well. I was happy at last and thankful for her care and attention. (McCahon, 1981, p. 32)

Colin McCahon's recollection of leaving the misery of the infant classroom in 1926 contrasts a teacher who punished cruelly with a teacher he could love and learn from. The harshness or kindness of teachers is a recurring theme in children's remembrances of their schooling.[1] Such memories from this period are also indicative of the influence of new education ideas concerning learning and teaching, underpinned too by new psychological and sociological understandings of childhood (Boyd & Rawson, 1965). Such ideas and understandings originated in Europe, Britain and the United States in the early twentieth century but were rapidly appraised by policymakers in Aotearoa New Zealand, and variously considered, ignored, rejected and trialled by teachers (Middleton & May, 1997). The infiltration of the ideals of new education into classroom practice was slow, with a mismatch of the rhetoric and the reality stretching across decades. McCahon experienced this mismatch. The mantra

---

1 Some quotations and comments in this chapter also appear in the author's book '*I am five and I go to school': Early years schooling in New Zealand 1900–2010*, Dunedin, Otago University Press, 2011.

of new education concerned understandings of children as individuals, as creators of knowledge and active participants in their schooling, and according to John Dewey as citizens of the school community (Dewey 1900a, 1916). The modern field of Childhood Studies is a rather delayed consequence of such understandings. The extent to which Miss Loudon allowed the young McCahon's creativity to burst forth is not evident, but she did at least understand him as a child.

Since the nineteenth century, childhood has been significantly constructed around notions of the schooled child, a process that, in Aotearoa New Zealand, starts at the age of five years. Aotearoa New Zealand studies of schooling and education have been mainly framed around policy, history and curriculum implementation, but more recently shaped by agendas around researching children's learning at school. There has been little critical appraisal of childhood and schooling, although education researchers influenced by Childhood Studies are including the perspectives of children in a range of insightful ways. New education and the burgeoning field of empirical education research were much entwined; it was Stanley Hall's research on children that began the notion of 'Childhood Studies' and gave impetus to the new education movement (Hall, 1901, 1907). Pioneering ventures of new education often began as laboratory experiments (Mayhew & Edwards, 1936). However, it has taken almost a century for research on childhood to embrace the ideals of new education concerning children's agency in their learning and development. This chapter is not an analysis of childhood and schooling, but rather illustrates possibilities for rethinking the history of education and schooling by considering the child participants as agents in the construction of history. Childhood Studies embraces the quest to understand childhoods in both the past and the present. Each informs the other.

Remembrances by adults of their experiences of primary schooling are not extensively documented and are also selective, usually shaped by the extraordinary occurrence and focused on their years as older pupils. This posed challenges for me in compiling data that was inclusive of the perspectives of children for the book *'I am five and I go to school': Early years schooling in New Zealand 1900-2010* (May, 2011), particularly for accounts of the early years of the twentieth century that excluded the possibility of interview prompts. Nevertheless, fleeting comments and recollections – on starting school, getting to school, changing schools; teachers and children at school; classroom or playground activities; or the apparatus of schooling – yield surprising information, corroboration and insight. In this chapter, several vignettes from the early 1900s are illustrative of the cusp of change in the pedagogy and practice of early years schooling in the variously called infants, primers or preparatory classes. The comments themselves might be a few phrases, rarely more than a short paragraph, and originate in autobiographies (and the occasional biography) whose authors or subject started school between 1900 and the 1920s. Their insights were often a passing introduction to more momentous memories of the higher levels of school and the conduit to the life that came to deserve recording.

The data of early years schooling

It has taken many fragments to piece together a history of early years schooling, the existence of which is mainly absent from histories of education that generally emphasise a policy story compiled from archival documents. An exception is *Teachers talk teaching: Early childhood, schools, teachers' colleges 1915–1995* (1997), which I co-authored with Sue Middleton: in this book we charted the tides of educational ideas as described by 150 teachers across the early childhood and school sectors. '*I am five and I go to school*' is not an oral history of childhood, but sought to include the perspective and work of children. Of course, much of what children produce during their first years at school is ephemeral: the content of the slates, copybooks, sand trays and blackboards was short-lived.

Hard copies of children's first reading books have survived. Booklets recording the histories of individual schools abound in libraries, but they give

'Free period' in Dorothy Edward's classroom at Te Aro School, Wellington, 1921. *(Alexander Turnbull Library, ABHO W4399 Box 1.)*

Unidentified crowded primer room, 1919. (Alexander Turnbull Library, MNZ 2816)

only passing mention to the infant classes. Some individual school records have survived the school clean-outs but the records make little mention of the youngest children. Government records of education have been useful in documenting the changing policy interest, or lack of interest, in early years schooling. The reports of school inspectors do give clues about what might have been happening in the infant classroom.

Other accounts of life in the infant room have been harder to source. Few teachers deemed their time teaching infants as worth recording or their resources worth saving. Fortunately, there have been exceptions. Interviews with teachers provide an invaluable insight into life in the infants–juniors but generally cover the latter half of the century. Some of the richest records are photographic. Assisted by technology, school images of the young shifted from infants lined up outside the school to include more informality. Visual evidence of the cusp of change can be seen in these school settings photographed between 1916 and 1919.

New Education

'I am five and I go to school' starts at the beginning of a century. The methods of 'new education' were deemed progressive. Since understanding the young child was at the heart of progressive thinking, many of society's ills were attributed to the consequences of misunderstanding. As a confluence of ideas emerging in Europe, Britain and the US, progressive education underpinned education reforms across many Western countries. Curriculum and practice were reshaped through a combination of new insights, such as John Dewey's (1900a, 1900b) understandings of the social context of education, and the drive of reformist kindergarten practitioners. From Italy, the work of Maria Montessori (1915) was for a few years heralded as the cure-all recipe for early years education. The radical theoretical insights of Sigmund Freud (1905) created the field of child psychology, and educators such as Susan Isaacs (1929) promoted self-expression in childhood as a foundation for psychological well-being. At the same time, Jean Piaget (1926) was formulating his theories on the development of rational thinking in young children, which he postulated grew out of the child's spontaneous play. Cumulatively, the impact was dramatic. New education, with the possibilities of both individual (psychological, intellectual and behavioural) and collective (sociological and political) transformation, promised a pathway to various new social orders in which, ideally, the child was an active participant, not only in constructing their learning, but also in the sites of learning. Teachers always struggled, and still do, with the realities of realising such ideals, particularly with very young children, who it was thought had to be trained to learn and behave in acceptable ways.

'I am five and I go to school' is the twentieth-century sequel to *School beginnings: A nineteenth-century colonial story* (May, 2005) and traces new education ideas emerging at the start of the new century as they slowly transformed life in the classroom for young children. There was a long tail to this transformation that stretched into the post-war years of the 1950s, before it was possible to say that most infant classrooms, to some degree, organised their programme around principles of learning through play and hands-on activity.

Evidence of new educational ideas was the increase in activity and practical work, and the provision of lessons that were both stimulating and cognisant of children's interests, creativity and abilities (Ewing, 1970). That new education had the support of some school inspectors is evident in the 1900 report from Southland inspectors James Hendry and George Braik, who stated that there was 'hardly a school in the district in which kindergarten methods, or at least some of the principles of teaching given to the world by Pestalozzi and Froebel, have not been introduced.'[2] They looked forward to the possibility of a child being 'solaced by an occasional hour's "learning by doing" during which his natural tastes may freely manifest themselves' (Hendry & Braik, 1900, p. 42).

The new century rethink in education policy was made possible by new leadership. George Hogben, appointed Inspector-General in 1899, was interested in progressive methods and reforming the primary school syllabus was a priority. At a conference of inspectors in 1904 to launch a new syllabus, Hogben acknowledged the challenge: 'All the best teachers have, step by step, been led to change their point of view, and have altered their methods accordingly. To you, therefore, the change, though rapid, has been an evolution in educational ideas and methods, to *others* who have followed it less closely, or have allowed themselves to fall behind, the change appears as a sudden and complete revolution' (Hogben, 1904, p. 2).

The 'others' comprised a significant number of teachers. Hogben claimed that 'change was inevitable unless New Zealand was to be content to be left behind in the educational contest' (ibid.). His priorities were clear:

> The important thing … is not the amount of things that are taught, but the spirit, character, and method of teaching in relation to its purpose of developing the child's powers … We must believe with Froebel and others of the most enlightened of the world's educators, that the child will learn best, not so much by reading about things in books as by doing: that is exercising his natural activities by making things, by observing and testing things for himself; and then afterwards by reasoning about them and expressing thoughts about them. (ibid.)

There are inklings of the participant child in this statement, but few clues for teachers regarding what this might mean in practice. Hogben's syllabus soon encountered criticism, as teachers were in the main professionally ill-equipped, in terms of both confidence and competence, to implement such new approaches. The vignette recollections presented in this chapter are revealing of the mismatch between the policy rhetoric and aspirations of education leaders, such as Hogben, and the classroom realities experienced by the children who later reported their experience. Yet amid the generally grim tales, glimpses of the 'new education' are apparent.

---

[2] In the early years of the nineteenth century, the Swiss educator Johann Pestalozzi practised schooling methods premised on affection and engagement between teachers and children; his student Friedrich Froebel coined the term 'kindergarten' and his recognition of children's unique needs and capabilities influenced the development of modern education.

The painting class

At the turn of the new century in 1900, few of the five- to seven-year-old children in schools would have discerned, and even less recalled, any change in their classroom life. In his recollection of starting at Amberley School in 1901, Rewi Alley captures the likely grimness of the experience:

> I well remember the day I turned five, running up a pile of bags of chaff before my golden curls were cut off, shouting, 'I'm a man now' ... In the primer classes we had a mistress who was determined that every one of her charges without exception should learn. More than two mistakes in spelling or more than two sums wrong brought the strap. Coming into school with dirty knees brought the strap ... I do not think I escaped the strap on a single day in those early years. I do not think the mistress was particularly successful in teaching me to spell ... There was one day when I was strapped five times, the last offence being when I pulled my short pants high and painted my designs on my legs instead of the paper during a painting class. (Alley, 1986, p. 15)

Punishment was institutionalised in European and colonial schooling traditions and its demise was slow. But the fact that Alley had a 'painting class' was a clue to changes in the focus and fabric of schooling that were slowly infiltrating classroom practice. Policy documents of the period suggest a more kindly regimen and considerably more innovation. Poorly trained teachers, too many children, ill-equipped and unhealthy classrooms, and stern standard examination requirements were realities that frustrated endeavours to introduce new methods intended to provide a more understanding, interesting and creative environment for the youngest children at school.

Thirteen years later, in 1914, Alley's sister Gwen Alley (later Somerset) began her training as a pupil-teacher in the infant room at Elmwood School:

> On my first morning I found two rows of new entrants of five years seated on two forms facing each other beneath a blackboard. The room was deathly quiet except for the occasional squeak of a pencil slate. The two rows of new children sat quivering in fear of the strange world into which they had just been deposited. The Infant Mistress loomed above them. She announced, 'The first one who cries will get this,' and showed her strap. (Somerset, 1988, p. 105)

Fredric Alley, the father of Rewi and Gwen, was the head teacher of the school where Rewi got a daily strapping. While a stern disciplinarian of his children, Fredric was also known for his progressive methods and his love of literature, music and the natural environment. Recalling his fear that the inspectors would fault his focus on 'children rather than results', he told his daughter that 'Father Pestalozzi might never have existed' (Somerset, 1988, p. 256).

Gendered classroom

> The infant room was a small hall with a partition down the middle separating the girls from the boys, and with a classroom at either end ... The girls seldom saw the boys on the other side of the partition as infants spent most of the day immobile, wedged into little seats with wide shelves on the right for slates ... At roll call we listened to the names of the invisible creatures on the other side of the partition. (May, 1973, p. 14)

Muriel May started attending High Street School in Dunedin at age six years around 1905. Her recollection of this gendered classroom was sharpened by the contrast between the infant room and the nearby kindergarten that she had previously attended, and where she recalled paper folding, weaving, music, games and plants. Photographs of High Street Kindergarten in which May is most likely present illustrate the accuracy of her memory and provide corroboration of the stark contrast of life in the infant classroom.

High Street Kindergarten, Dunedin, 1902. (Hocken Collections, University of Otago Library, S12-525a)

Infant boys, North East Valley School, 1913. (Hocken Collections, University of Otago Library, S09234f)

May also recalled that the infant mistress tucked pansies into her hair. She recorded few other memories until standard one with a teacher May describes as being 'an enthusiast, interested, warm-hearted, humane but one of her generation.' On one occasion during those 'barbarous days' the children were warned they would be strapped if they failed to spell 'squirrel' correctly. Although a competent speller, May was so concerned by the prospect she had written 'spuirrel.' For others, classroom life was more brutal. Jessie, 'a girl from an unorganised home,' for instance, 'was strapped daily for being late even in winter when her chilblains were broken' (May, 1973, p. 16). It was the contrast in experiences on the same school site, a personal fear of the strap and a remembered injustice that shaped May's early school remembrances. While sketchy, there are rich insights of interest to the historian, yielding evidence of parallel paradigms of learning in the kindergarten and the school, the disciplinary tools of curtains and later the strap, and teachers who were both warm-hearted and cruel.

Playground land wars

A gradual lessening of violence within the classroom did not necessarily mean peace in the playground. John Money recalled that his first day at school in 1923 was 'abominable' to a five-year-old 'enthralled by the prospect of learning.' He described his first day at Morrinsville School to Michael King, who wrote that he felt like a stranger among the Lord of the Flies. He was utterly unprepared for the manner in which the Pakeha children fought with Māori children in the playground, replaying, as he saw it, the Waikato Wars of sixty years earlier. (There were at the school grandchildren and great-grandchildren of men who had fought on both sides of that conflict). Local Māori members of the Ngati Haua tribe were still smarting from the confiscation of much of their land as punishment for their rebellion against the Crown. (King, 2006, pp. 24–25)

Money sought help from his older cousin in the girls' play shed. However, he found: 'The girls would have nothing to do with a boy in their sanctuary [and] abandoned me to the attacking warriors. Catastrophe!' (Money cited in King, 2006, p. 25). At lunchtime John ran home, on the pretext that school had finished, but was promptly returned by his mother to the classroom. He learned to absent himself from the parts of the playground 'where combat seemed to erupt every playtime and lunchtime.' Money's mother did not demand that the school protect younger children. Such protection was only for girls and in the 'sanctuary' of their shed. The vignette also serves as a reminder of the short time span of our schooling and colonial history. Money died in 2006, yet his first experiences at school re-enact the central events of nineteenth-

Ohuru railway camp school built by settlers in a forest clearing, Whanganui district, 1909. (Whanganui Regional Museum, scs/misc/94)

century colonial history. While encounters between Māori and Pakeha became less cataclysmic, both races used schooling to transform and contain the turn-of-the-century demarcations in power, politics, land and language. The many images of schools in forest clearings might be heroic stories of endeavour for Pakeha settlers but these same forested lands were the subject of loss by Māori.

Māori Primers

Government involvement in the education of Māori children became increasingly pervasive from 1894, when attendance at their local Native School, if there was one, was made compulsory for Māori children. From 1903 they were otherwise required to attend their local Board school. Successive governments instituted policies in the Native Schools designed specifically for Māori children around speaking and teaching in English.

In conversation with Anne Salmond, Māori elder Eruera Stirling recalled his first days at Raukokore School at the beginning of the twentieth century when he was seven years old. Prior to starting school, Eruera had spent several years being inducted into the sacred knowledge of the Whānau-a-Apanui tribe, living with his grandparents in a secluded whare nīkau (nīkau palm hut):

> The trouble was I could not speak anything else [but Māori] and school life was not very happy for me at the start. I kept away from other children, I wasn't interested in playmates and I got worse and worse, my mind kept going back to that other life ... Pretty nearly every day I'd get a hiding, and one morning I got so wild I refused to come into the classroom, I stayed outside talking Māori to the birds. They had to come and get me, and the master gave me a very strong thrashing. The marks showed on my hands and feet, and I cried and cried and cried. (Stirling & Salmond, 1980, p. 94)

Eruera's punishment for speaking Māori was something many Māori children endured throughout the twentieth century. Eruera was more fortunate than many of the other Māori children in his school. His parents became so 'wild' that they confronted the headmaster, Mr Mulhern:

> Don't you ever give my son the strap again, you bloody Irishman. If you touch him again I'll give you a hiding – you leave him alone ... This son of mine is the only one in the whole school who has been through the channel with the old people, in the real Māori custom way. You've got to give him time to pick up, I don't want you to punish him again ... you have to help him and be good to him. (ibid.)

Children weaving baskets, Waikouati School, 1902. (Archives New Zealand, Auckland R14899)

Mr Mulhern did in fact offer help by arranging special lessons for Eruera with his own daughter, Kathleen. Soon Eruera was progressing well at school and surpassing the other children in tests. He was of a generation of Māori whose knowledge and education was steeped in both the Māori and European traditions from a young age.

Eruera's experiences coincided with shifts in policy, perspective and personnel relating to Native Schools. In 1904, William W. Bird was appointed the Inspector of Native Schools. Like Hogben, Bird was interested in the new educational methods and had worked on the 1904 syllabus. For the first time, the new syllabus and its 'modern methods' also applied to the Native Schools – although 'not too rigidly' (Barrington & Beaglehole, 1974, p. 145). Bird was intent on raising the standard of teaching in Native Schools; but despite the ideals of a gentler 'new education', the new educational methods tended to have the opposite effect for many Māori children.

Bird made competency in English paramount for Māori children and introduced an immersion approach. This 'direct or natural method' of teaching created a harsher learning environment for young children than the earlier more gradual introduction to English had allowed. While Bird's approach undoubtedly hastened the acquisition of English, punishment inevitably became a tool of enforcement. For the youngest children, who arrived into the

Preparatory classes at drill, Whirinaki Native School, 1905. (Archives New Zealand, Auckland, R14899j)

primers speaking only Māori, the cruelty of the experience became embedded into the psyche of successive generations (Simon & Tuhiwai Smith, 2001). Accordingly, there is an irony to Bird's accounts of the benefits that Māori children gained from the introduction of the 'modern methods'. At Waimea School in 1906, he reported: 'With regards to the work of the children I am pleased to note an improvement, and this is due to the fact that at last the teachers have broken away from their old methods. Special mention is due in the case of the preparatory classes at Waimea School where the infants receive a careful training on modern methods and are in consequence well advanced' (Bird, 1906, p. 7).

Slow pace of change

Such small snippets recording the experience of very young children at school can be rich in insight. In particular, they remind us that the study of policy and curriculum documents and texts of the period, accompanied too by the remembrances of teachers and the photographic records, usually portray the examples of classrooms where new education methods were practised. These stories of 'against the odds' endeavours by teachers to implement new education ideas have sometimes been recorded, and feature in *'I am five and I go to school'*. However, the evidence from children, and to some extent from inspectors' reports, suggests that there were many more teachers who lacked confidence, training or any belief in new education pedagogy. The infrastructure of schooling was not conducive to new education, though. Cyril Bradwell recalled 'wonderfully kind teachers' in a galleried classroom at Phillipstown School in 1921, as well as a 'range of activities – certainly sand trays and things like that. You weren't regimented in those tiered seats all the time' (May, 2011, p. 32). Miss Menzies, who would have taught the young Cyril, recalled that 'the school consisted of two very large classrooms and two very small rooms, and I taught huge classes under very adverse conditions. I will never forget a primer one, well over 100 pupils at one stage, packed like sardines in the gallery of the infants' room … The school was overcrowded and understaffed with monthly changes of temporary staff' (Menzies, 1952, p. 21).

The gallery was dismantled in 1922. By linking the small fragments recalled by Cyril alongside that of his teacher, a fuller understanding of the mismatch between aspirations concerning new education and classroom realities is reached. Without Cyril's fragment of information, gallery lessons might have been deemed as always grim, but at Phillipstown School the teachers tried hard to overcome the constraints.

Top education officials were disappointed in the pace of change in the classroom. In 1923, the Chief Inspector of Primary Schools, T.B. Strong, was concerned about the 'stagnant educational thought' he perceived in 'some quarters'. Strong placed the blame on certain head teachers, who had 'grown out of touch with modern methods' and were 'damping' the 'enthusiasm' of new teachers from the training colleges. Strong claimed he would be 'inclined to welcome rather than to quell the revolutionary, who with his "mad theories" at least stimulates thought and challenges contradiction. Anything is better than smug content with the "is" or the "has been" ' (Strong, 1923, p. iii).

Comparing the qualities of the older and newer teaching methods, he stated: 'The former made the child the passive recipient, and in most cases the unwilling storehouse of as much information as the teacher could induce him, or alas! force him to hold. The new methods of teaching aim at securing the co-operation of the child, mainly through the interest that certain subjects possess in themselves, or through the satisfaction gained in acquiring knowledge by self effort' (ibid.). New methods required a teacher who would 'point the way and, as it were, … accompany the child in his search for truth. He and the child become co-workers' (ibid.). Such remembrances of children of their schooling during these years, while selected and limited, give no impression of ever considering themselves as co-workers. Such sentiments are at the crux of new education thinking and express a view of the child that has affinity with the ideals of modern Childhood Studies.

Clarence (C.E.) Beeby became the architect of hastening so-called 'playway' learning into the mainstream upon his appointment as Director of Education in 1939. He recalled the experience of starting school, at aged six years, at Christchurch East in 1908 where he was placed high in the gallery and along a row that made it impossible to get to the toilet (Beeby, 1991). Beeby shifted to New Brighton School:

> I was ushered into a vast roomful of children (500 in memory, probably sixty in fact), ranged on benches rising in tiers to almost half the height of the room. They were chanting in unison ... It was assumed I had been initiated into the ritual at Christchurch East School and, seated in the front row [this time], I had no option but to open and shut my lips in unison and let no sound escape. The headmistress, a stern but kindly figure, lace collar of a long black dress held high to her throat by celluloid strips, and only face, and fingers of her mittened hands, giving sight of human flesh, seemed satisfied. I got away with it for two or three days until I realised that the chant was 'twice one is two, twice two is four ...' or one of its wretched variants. In one day I had been introduced to both arithmetic and guile ... At New Brighton I led a double life, both halves happily. There was, as yet, no talk of 'educating the whole child' (Beeby, 1992, pp. 4–5)

Beeby the child may not have heard such talk, but policymakers and some teachers had, and they set about the slow transformation of new education ideas into practice.

Summary

The field of Childhood Studies emphasises the participant child whose perspectives and contributions are valued; new education similarly heralded the child whose individuality, opinions and creativity were valued as a contribution to classroom knowledge. Providing a supportive environment where children had opportunities to be an active participant was deemed a function of new styles of schooling for new education. Realising such ideals in the early twentieth century was challenging and often resisted by teachers. This chapter has provided some glimpses of the 'new' and the 'old' school practices for young children in Aotearoa New Zealand. In the spirit of Childhood Studies and new education ideals, it includes the perspectives of children in the construction of this historical story. It is illustrative too of the potential of Childhood Studies for enriching our understandings of childhood in both the past and the present.

CHAPTER 7

Managed childhoods: A social history of urban children's play

Christina R. Ergler, Robin Kearns & Karen Witten

[...] Let's all play Polar bears;
And crawl about with doormats on,
And growl and howl and squeak,
Then in the garden let us fly
And play at hide and seek;

And 'Here we gather Nuts and May',
'I wrote a Letter' too,
'Here we go round the Mulberry Bush',
'The Child who lost its shoe'

And every game we ever played.

from 'A Joyful Song of Five', Katherine Mansfield (1923)

Although children might not be aware of the economic and political context in which they develop their play, they are nevertheless affected by it. The values and accomplishment that a society sees in various forms of children's play help shape, and in turn are shaped by, local and national policies, market forces, and the natural and built environment. Social realities of contemporary children's play practices are a product of how norms and rules around 'play' have evolved over recent history. To explore contemporary 'play' in Aotearoa New Zealand we adopt the position that it is necessary to understand how 'play' has been developed and transformed over the course of history: it has involved a twofold change – in philosophy of play (what play *means*) and in how play is practised (what play *is*). In other words, 'play' needs to be understood in relation to a particular time and place (Schwartzman, 1980). Our argument in this chapter is that as the context changes, so does play.

Free play has long been recognised as important for children's health and well-being.

We survey five historical periods, starting in the early colonial period, to illustrate how urban children's play has been shaped by changing societal beliefs and norms and the country's economic fortunes. We argue that children in Aotearoa New Zealand have always experienced a largely managed childhood and question whether notions of 'free ranging' children are more nostalgic than factual accounts of earlier childhoods. Reflecting on the influences of compulsory schooling, the introduction of organised sports, suburbanisation, the feminist movement and neo-liberal reforms, we briefly survey the changes in Aotearoa New Zealand children's play, paying particular attention to experience in the largest city, Auckland. Although we acknowledge urban children's play experiences have always been diverse, this chapter documents common norms and major trends defining Pākehā children's play. In doing so, we provide a summary of 'universal' play practices which have dominated public views of children and childhood.

Shanghais and tea parties: Paradoxes of the (un)managed childhood of the early days

Aotearoa New Zealand was largely settled by English and Scottish colonists during the industrial age. New settlers left behind poverty and pauperism, as well as disease and degeneration, in the slums of flourishing but polluted British cities. Migrants were promised a land of abundance, 'God's own country', which augured a paradise 'of apple orchards and vineyards, of children playing in thick leaved trees and singing mothers' (Fairburn, 1975, p. 3). A communally tinted rural myth was thus created – a myth still evident in the spatial forms of this late-colonised country where there was a widespread desire by many to live in detached houses with big backyards where children could easily play.

Most children did not live the fairy-tale life painted by Fairburn. Despite the glorification of children's independent mobility in these early days, children's lives were managed by teachers, parents and employers. Affluent children's days were ordered by piano, painting and school lessons interspersed with time to play both in school and at home (in which they could create imaginary worlds of shops, tea parties, Cowboys and Indians) (Sutton-Smith, 1981). In the central city slums the air was filled with children's noises as they wandered and played in the streets (Bush, 1971). Toys and extracurricular activities were unattainable for impoverished children and this led to imaginary play and self-made equipment. For boys and girls alike, contributing to the family's income was invariably combined with play. Wharves, timber yards, the backs of factories and rubbish dumps were adventure playgrounds for poorer children. Scavenging was a lucrative pastime as scrap metals, used bottles or pieces of timber could be brought home and used or cashed in. Such play was possible for two reasons. Free materials provided opportunities for imaginative play and large families meant playmates were plentiful. Although children were mostly unsupervised and allowed to roam freely in the city from a very young age, their lives were managed by other means. Older boys and girls made a crucial contribution to the family income as factory workers, tailors or delivery boys. Younger ones handled errands, ran messages or sold flowers and newspapers on the street (Husbands, 1992).

Aiming to avoid the demoralising slums and hordes of ungoverned and ungovernable children wandering the streets as in Britain, educated immigrants convinced political leaders to introduce compulsory schooling in 1877 (Beagle, 1975; Stephenson, 2009). Educational philosophies at that time were based on the Appollonian premise that childhood is a stage of purity and innocence. Therefore, children of the educated needed to be protected from such evils of society as the licentiousness of the lower classes. The path to heavenly salvation was seen to involve obedience, moral citizenship and a proper piety that was best bestowed on children through the right sort of schooling (Frost, 2009; May, 1997). This Victorian educational philosophy also found its way into children's play practices.

With the advent of public schooling, folk games gained popularity as children needed a way to entertain themselves in an orderly, obedient manner. Children often played under supervision in confined areas such as the schoolyard or community picnic spaces and sporting grounds, which gained popularity during this time. Children learned from an early age to obey rules around outdoor play, as institutional constraints were placed on their play practices. The Victorian educational philosophy had benefits, although often not as anticipated by its advocates. There were also downsides of demanding obedience through discipline because children often internalised practices copied from teachers. Rituals like dares or bullying were common (Sutton-Smith, 1981).

With the introduction of compulsory schooling, the lives of poor and rich children converged in space and time, with school in the morning and time to 'play' in the afternoon. Although the play practices were distinct in each social class and many working class children still needed to adapt their play practices around their chores, the idea that all children should be permitted 'free' time to play gained currency, albeit tinged with the Victorian obligation to spend this time in a meaningful way. This responsibility has durably inscribed itself into notions of appropriate children's activities.

Meaningful pastimes: Supervising children's free time in the beginning of modernity and war times

Between the 1900s and the 1940s, children's lives became more structured in response to the militaristic and economic needs of the new colony. Social Darwinist ideas gained currency, consistent with nationalist movements worldwide (Byrnes, 2009). According to these ideologies, moral and economic progress could only be achieved through a healthy society. Children's value was in their future roles (Labrum, 2000). Hence, investing in children's moral, physical and school education (e.g. open air schools, health camps) was viewed as an investment in the prosperous (economic) future of this young state (Dalley, 1998; Kearns & Collins, 2000; Tennant, 1994). Physical education was particularly valued for moral purposes and daily classes were compulsory for boys and girls. This instruction was designed to teach children the virtues of regular physical activity in order to counteract the purported weaknesses of an urban lifestyle. By promoting physical education, political leaders also aimed to form healthy bodies, which were strong enough for childbirth and physically demanding labour in factories. To have an efficient future workforce, it was important to develop physically robust children who spent their time wisely, cultivating their fitness and health (Bryder, 1991). Consequently children were taught not only the virtues of teamwork and self-control in victory and defeat but also standards of behaviour and time-keeping (Daley, 2003; Sullivan, 2009).

The demarcation of adults' time into work and free time was an outcome of industrialisation. Likewise, children's attendance at school divided their week into learning and leisure time. The Turner movement of the early twentieth century advocated sport – 'rational recreation' – and meaningful use of free time to build strong bodies and guard against delinquency (Daley, 2009, p. 426). Individuals who held influential positions in local politics and business were instrumental in setting up clubs (e.g. the Auckland branch of YMCA), and many children remain enrolled in these today. Moreover, spending time outside being physically active in a natural setting, especially during the summer months, was believed to build healthy bodies, strong character and, ultimately, good citizenship. Engaging in active free play was deemed to be an obligation of good citizens. James Parr, Mayor of Auckland 1911–15, asserted: 'I have seen on a summer afternoon at Point Erin Park [close to the central city], in Auckland, over one hundred mothers and their little families picnicking in the park and enjoying the beach which bounds it. I am sure these people go home in the evening feeling refreshed in body and spirit, and consequently are more contented and better citizens' (Parr, 1919, p. 237).

Since the time of Parr, the positive contribution to well-being of being 'out and about' and exposed to fresh air and sunshine, especially during the summer months, has been inscribed into the sensibility of the Aotearoa New Zealand population (although contemporary practices have been adjusted to the risks of sun exposure (Collins & Kearns, 2007)). Swimming during the summer months has become a popular pastime for children and families. Urban beaches gained popularity on weekends through an improved and affordable public transport system. Lifesaving patrols were established, pools provided arenas for physical activity and drowning prevention, and during the depression sports fields were built by relief workers, further structuring children's play opportunities (Daley, 2003). The legacy of this development is still visible in the physical infrastructure of neighbourhoods. While extracurricular activities were not as common then as now, the idea of a healthy population underpinning the economic well-being of the country still structures and transforms children's play. 'Play', then and now, often has an underlying meaning of *playing sports*.

Whereas early twentieth-century society's concerns centred on the physical health of children and military preparedness, by the twenty-first century rising obesity rates concerned the nation. We now find public health messages directed at active play rather than simply the act of playing (Bell, 2011; Burrows, 2010).

Beach scene at Shelly Beach (Auckland Central) around 1914. (Photo courtesy of the Alexander Turnbull Library)

The growth of public pools. (Photo courtesy of John Allsop)

While there is a renewed attention to the outdoors, this attention is focused on the type of play in which children should engage. For example, a recent campaign *only* promotes unstructured sport and ball games as play (MILO, 2012). This focus potentially contributes to influencing, if not limiting, future children's associations with play and confining children within certain play spaces often designed for them by adults.

The intensification of Auckland due to economic growth before and after World War I reduced the number of 'natural' playgrounds. The idea that special settings should be introduced for children evolved out of the American Playground Movement (Cavallo, 1981). Playgrounds (e.g. featuring 'jungle gyms') provided venues for building healthy strong bodies while at the same time children were easier to control, given that they were confined in a small area rather than playing at large across the city. Again, in the words of the former Mayor of Auckland:

> The conditions of thirty or forty years ago are rapidly passing. In those far-away days before our cities became crowded you and I had no difficulty in finding a playground. The vacant paddock adjoining the school or one's father's house was nearly always available. But these spaces have all been built upon, and there is nowhere for the child of to-day [sic] to run about and play his [sic] games. [Therefore playgrounds] should be provided in all residential areas within half a mile of all houses. (Parr, 1919, p. 240)

While parks had been established in the early days of Auckland, providing recreational possibilities for all ages, the advent of playgrounds to stimulate and entertain growing children marked a clear divide between adults' and children's worlds. The state became a de facto social parent, asserting its power through urban design. The playground was seen as a nursery in which good citizenship was cultivated through organised play, protecting children from questionable amusements that would otherwise have tempted them on the streets. Ideas around play were enmeshed with physical and moral improvement, nationalistic, imperialistic and militaristic ideas: playing with educative toys was common, as were sports, marching, filing and flag salutes (Cusins-Lewer & Gatley, 2008; Daley, 2003). Volunteers or paid children's game supervisors (e.g. Gertrude Armstrong for Myers Park) monitored and organised children's play, ostensibly in the interests of safety; however, the aim was less to avoid accidents than to prevent damage through children's (mis)behaviour. On the playground, children learned to obey rules and authorities. Despite the promotion of physical activity, Auckland's officials locked up children's play areas (e.g. tied up swings) to maintain Sundays as days of rest until 1934 (Bush, 1971).

Economic growth and modernism influenced playground construction, but also impacted on how children carried out their play activities on the streets. Children needed to align their outdoor play to new developments in Auckland (e.g. electrification of trams) fuelled by economic prosperity (Sutton-Smith, 1981). When muddy and dusty streets were replaced by asphalt, which was, for example, too smooth for playing marbles, children quickly adapted their

Orderly playing in Myers Park around 1910. (Photo courtesy of the Alexander Turnbull Library)

Playground in Wanaka: Aotearoa New Zealand now has a wide range of formal play spaces with multiple play opportunities available for children's play.

games to the new settings and surfaces (Sutton-Smith, 1953; Trewby, 1995). Similarly, newly installed power lines interfered with kite flying. The most important change, however, was the increased number of private automobiles in the city. In response, from the 1920s, children were taught about road safety by the Automobile Association in school. Political acknowledgement of the incompatibility of children and cars on streets was apparent in 1936 when the Minister of Transport highlighted the dangers of playing on the footpaths or highways. However, it has been suggested that the safety of children was less at the heart of this comment than the possible damage children could cause to vehicles (Sullivan, 2009; Sutton-Smith, 1981).

Structuring children's time with meaningful pastimes to position them for their future life gained currency around the turn of the twentieth century. Ideas that took hold during this time live on and continue to influence the lives of contemporary children. Adults had (and still have) a clear idea of 'appropriate' pastimes for children. They have not only interfered on the macro level in children's lives through legal acts (e.g. compulsory schooling or the Child Welfare Bill of 1925) and play advisers (e.g. as in Myers Park), but also on the micro level by establishing certain norms and 'rules of play', as the aforementioned comment by the Minister of Transport showed. Less knowingly, adults also have structured children's play through the design of cities and new technologies. Children have needed to adjust their play to the changing circumstances of modernity.

Play and well-being in the post-war period: The suburban nuclear family

Positioning children for their future role as responsible and educated citizens remained an implicit societal goal. Four major developments transformed children's play after World War II, initiating a shift from the streets towards the home environment.

First, from the 1950s, families started moving into newly built 'dormitory suburbs' and children adjusted their play to the possibilities offered by larger indoor spaces and private gardens. The nuclear family became the dominant household type in these newly established neighbourhoods. In Auckland, the opening of the Harbour Bridge in 1959, the rural to urban migration of Māori and the immigration of Pacific people hastened the pace of suburbanisation (Bush, 1971; Macpherson, Spoonley & Anae, 2001).

Second, the buoyant post-war economy impacted positively on the financial situation of families. The growing middle class increasingly shaped the nature of children's play and childhood. Families began to invest in purchased (rather

Growing affluence and car ownership.

than home-made) toys, thereby changing the nature of children's play. Street games were slowly replaced by activities involving equipment, such as built-for-children bicycles, and a greater range of balls became essential play equipment for both genders. Overall, static pursuits were displaced by more physically active games (Sutton-Smith, 1981). Moreover, informed by the increasing scientific knowledge of children's psychological development, adults began to design toys that stimulated children's intellectual and physical development (May, 1992; Shallcrass, 1973). The quest to increase children's skills in order to position them better for the workforce became an important goal in itself. The value of intellectual 'fitness', like bodily fitness in an earlier era, was slowly adopted by all classes and promoted through puzzles and science kits.

Schools of music teaching violin, piano and singing also began to flourish in the 1950s and 1960s. Many parents saved for investment in developing such accomplishments (Trewby, 1995). However, the most influential change in children's play began with the arrival of television in 1960. The critical implication of television broadcasting was its promotion of passive recreation: essentially television viewing confined children to the home. The arrival of television arguably supported the ideal of the nuclear family, privatisation of leisure and the use of leisure time for educational ends. However, concerns about its possible negative side effects (e.g. societal stultification and diminishing social and physical activity) began to emerge when televisions became the focal point in living rooms (NZNCIYC, Lewis & Lockhart, 1980).

Third, the role of mothers in children's upbringing changed. Motherhood became a full-time job, with well-behaved, well-adjusted children being the expected outcome (May, 1992; Ritchie & Ritchie, 1970). The role of schools was primarily to teach children literacy and numeracy, while mothers were responsible for children's physical and emotional well-being. The cruelty of the war and the tacit understanding in society that such misery must never happen again underpinned these changing mores. It was believed that the key to a more humanitarian world should be found in raising a generation of healthy, emotionally stable and happy children (Byrnes, 2009). The Play Centre movement embodied these ideals, providing opportunities for learning and bonding between mother and child. Meeting in community halls, the movement also advanced the notion that even early childhood education could be a valuable stimulant for children and an opportunity to intervene positively in young lives and to better position children for their future (May, 1997). Children's play, and to an extent the home environment itself, became managed more systematically through the influence of such organisations. Closely related to this idea were implications of enhanced safety as a consequence of the attention children enjoyed from their mothers.

Last, the need to protect children from bodily harm as well as building healthy bodies began to gain a foothold by the mid-1960s, coinciding with the founding of the National Safety Association at the workplace (Sullivan, 2009). Parents as well as representatives of the state began to raise awareness about possible accidents around independent play (Lynch, 2006; McDonald, 1978). The playground safety movement of the 1970s was prompted by recognition that the materials used for playgrounds had not changed since their original construction. Surfacing, materials and equipment started to be assessed according to possible injuries and harm instead of being recognised, in the first instance, for their learning and bodily fitness possibilities. This increasing concern with safety foreshadows the later identification of the so-called 'bubble-wrap' generation (Collins, Kearns & Mitchell, 2006; Malone, 2007; May, 1992).

Children's play and the feminist movement

The 'baby boomer' children moved into parenthood in the 1970s better educated and with a stronger awareness of risks than any previous generation. Children's play began to be managed further and more systematically as it became acceptable for educated women to have careers and leisure time. Servicing young children's needs increasingly became a collaborative exercise involving not only mothers but also fathers and non-governmental organisations, such as

Free Kindergartens (Kindergartens Inc., 2009; Phillips, 1983). Sending children to preschools became the norm. Children who were not attending kindergarten were seen as disadvantaged, missing out on essential education. It was believed that kindergartens taught children the necessary discipline to learn in groups under the premise that they would be better prepared for school. Researchers claim that the majority of children adjusted to ready-made entertainment (e.g. drawing time) during this era (Duhn, 2009; Stover & New Zealand Playcentre Federation, 1998). They had to conform to entertainment presented to them, which in turn influenced their own perceptions of 'appropriate' play.

In the afternoons, the norm was still to play outside independently, but the idea of the necessity of extracurricular activities began to structure children's afternoons more systematically than in previous generations. For children in more affluent families, scheduled pastimes left little time for free play. The perception of physical activity as something which stimulated intellectual performance as well as bodily fitness became widely accepted and enrolment in sport clubs increased as a result (Wills, 1973). Structured pastimes increased, based on the belief that these activities fortify learning better than independent outdoor play. This increase was despite the fact that Somerset (1976), an instrumental figure in the Play Centre movement, stressed that all types of play improve children's skills.

In time, some parents began to question the contention that children should only be taught facts and skills and began to promote the idea (following Somerset and the liberalising Play Centre movement) that children can create their own learning by explorational play. Subsequently, alternative kindergartens and schools were founded (Morris, 2005), institutionalising an ideological divide concerning the purpose of play.

Curiously, while children's time began to be managed more systematically, the focus on 'under-represented' views influenced by the feminist movement brought to the fore a new understanding of children as capable social actors. Children's rights began to be questioned and addressed more openly. Supported by the Plunket Society, and as a result of the International Year of the Child (IYC) in 1979, the government funded a committee for children which acted as a voice for children and their concerns (NZNCIYC et al., 1980). For example, the IYC report recommended the review of by-laws and existing legislation to incorporate children's and teenagers' leisure needs in town planning (NZNCIYC et al., 1980, p. 28). This development indicated a new shift. Children as a user group of city space had been widely neglected in urban planning since the establishment of playgrounds in the 1920s (see for example Bush & Scott, 1977). Legally, children began to gain more rights and became more visible. The

Commissioner for Children, first appointed in 1989, promoted child-friendly policies and children's legal rights, for example in cases of parental separation or in the controversial 'non-smacking law' passed in 2007 (Barrington, 2004; Taylor & Smith, 2008). However, and paradoxically, in everyday situations children's competencies became curtailed more and more. As their legal rights were extended, authorities and parents began to question children's abilities to negotiate the risks of playing outdoors independently.

Pluralism or individualisation of play? Neo-liberal tolls on children's play

Three distinct developments have influenced children's play from the mid-1980s onwards. These developments arose out of the discrepancies between acknowledging children as capable actors and the need for their protection

Commercialised play equipment is increasingly available.

Snow days when schools are closed provide welcome opportunities for children in colder parts of Aotearoa New Zealand to be out and about. Children 'sledging' on body boards which in summer are used in the sea.

in uncertain economic times (e.g. environments of neo-liberal reforms, recessions) in light of the downsides of increasingly urbanised lifestyles.

First, the feminist movement and the 'Māori renaissance' led to heightened awareness of the influence that class, gender, ethnicity, culture, family composition and place can have on childhood experiences. As a consequence, there were challenges to an otherwise universal (Pākehā) understanding of childhood involving structural norms of play. Simultaneously, the universalising effects of globalisation on children's play (e.g. toys) gained more recognition (Jenks, 1996). Play (especially toys) became more individualised to cater for children's tastes, but play also became globally commodified. Since the 1980s, companies have begun to target children specifically with their advertisements, shaping children's toy consumption (e.g. computer games). Shopping has become institutionalised and a form of leisure even for children (Buckingham, 2011; Gregory, 1997). Synergies between different types of consumption appeared from the 1980s when, for instance, fast food outlets offered giveaway toys that were branded with television or movie characters. An extreme expression of this trend occurred at the Starship Children's Hospital in Auckland where an 'in-house' McDonald's restaurant included both company and hospital-branded iconography (Kearns & Barnett, 2000).

Second, parents and institutions have become increasingly mistrustful of children's ability to negotiate risks and dangers in their local environments.

Parents who themselves grew up in a time in which safety played a more important role now began to raise children. Growing up in what Beck (1992) has called a 'risk society' can affect how parents raise their children. Tangible risks in children's lives are removed as much as possible while they grow up in a culture of fear (e.g. abduction, injury) (Collins & Kearns, 2010; Sullivan, 2009).

For many children, outdoor play, much like walking to and from school, has become a supervised event that occurs in alignment with parental schedules or in the context of after-school, or institutional, care (Kearns, Collins & Neuwelt, 2003). As a consequence children are living increasingly sedentary lives (Public Health Advisory Committee, 2010). Children's freedoms are curtailed when their lives are spent in environments entirely controlled by adults and childhood experiences are determined by procedures and guidelines (Freeman & Tranter, 2011). However, this development is still based on the premise that learning in institutional settings is valued more highly than independent outdoor play for gaining the necessary skills for a successful future.

Conclusion

This historical account of common norms and trends of 'play', albeit from a predominantly Pākehā perspective, has assisted in understanding the origins of our children's contemporary play practices. The dominant themes running through the historical periods involve children's need for protection and preparation for their roles as adult citizens. At first, it was rhetoric about the threat of moral decline and public health exhortations in Victorian times that led to compulsory schooling to 'correctly' supervise and discipline children. Later the idea of meaningful pastimes designed to create fit bodies and minds was instrumental in the introduction of spaces designed *for* children (e.g. playgrounds) and fuelled the development of sport clubs. The automobile, and the suburbanisation of cities which rapidly followed, substantially altered children's play, moving children off the streets and into the private domain. At the same time, child-rearing became scientifically evaluated and psychological theories began to highlight the importance of structuring children's play so as to foster a healthy mental, physical and social development. Educational toys and the Play Centre movement were influences enhancing children's development. Through Victorian attitudes aimed at structuring children's free time for the sake of society, children's free time became structured for children's own sake: they should be able to reach their own potential. Parents began to introduce extracurricular activities into their children's weekly schedules. By the end of the twentieth century, this rescheduling of children's lives led to a situation in middle-class households in which free play was displaced by an array of sports, music or language classes. Children's independent mobility and physical activity has declined in recent decades, in unison with an increase in time spent engaged in sedentary indoor activities.

Our review allows us to conclude that urban children, especially, in Aotearoa New Zealand have always experienced elements of a managed childhood, and that the contemporary discourse about the loss of childhood needs to be seen in the context of its historical development. Children's lived experiences embody this legacy of the past as it has influenced and is influenced by the family cultures, changing local and national policies, market forces, and the natural and built environments that shape their everyday worlds. Promoting a less managed childhood, and appropriate spaces to enable 'free' play, is enriched by this deepened understanding of temporal and contextual influences on play practices and the values and norms bestowed on 'play'.

CHAPTER 8

Growing up Māori and disabled in Aotearoa New Zealand

Hazel Phillips & Nancy Higgins

Little has been written about Māori with disability in Aotearoa New Zealand, even less about tamariki and rangatahi Māori (Māori children and youth). Further, tamariki and rangatahi are usually viewed through deficit lenses by Aotearoa New Zealand social systems and institutions. When accessing public health and education services their youth, ethnicity and abilities are rarely considered in a holistic way.[1] This results in tamariki and rangatahi, and their whānau, experiencing considerable marginalisation in education and health environments where their differences are constructed as inferior. Under such conditions, it is often difficult for children and their whānau to access culturally appropriate public health and education services that positively take into account their multiple identities.

The historical and contemporary contexts of tamariki and rangatahi with a disability are central to understanding their lived experiences, their identities, and the ways that they are marginalised. These contexts have multiple layers and include traditional knowledge and practices, colonial discourse and its impact on the Māori world, disability paradigms, and the way young people are disenfranchised. This, in turn, occurs within a particular sociopolitical framework that has imposed particular modes of thinking and acting, in which relationships of power and subordination have been marked out.

In this chapter, the authors will discuss the childhoods of kāpo (blind or vision impaired) Māori, specifically the issues that revolve around 'growing up' as Māori with a disability in Aotearoa New Zealand. These issues are drawn from the findings of a large research project about 'growing up kāpo Māori' and accessing health and education services. Given that 81% of those who

---

1 We recognise that other identities are also marginalised in Aotearoa New Zealand (i.e. gender, sexual orientation), but the focus on our research projects was specific to these three identities.

participated in the research had other impairments and health conditions, we suggest our findings are not exclusive to the experience of being kāpo. They may also have relevance to the experiences of tamariki and rangatahi with multiple impairments. We begin with a brief overview of the multiple contexts in which kāpo tamariki and rangatahi grow up and are constructed. The second half of this chapter discusses the issues that kāpo tamariki and rangatahi and their whānau face through the unpublished stories that they shared with us in the research project.

Māori traditional world view

Little is known about the way in which old time Māori viewed and understood impairments in general, and blindness and vision impairment in particular. However, by reviewing traditional literature and whakapapa (genealogical descent) a sense of traditional discourses can be determined. Some accounts from the traditional Māori anthology directly refer to kāpo atua (blind Māori gods/goddesses) (Tikao, Higgins, Phillips & Cowan, 2009). In these accounts, being kāpo was considered a sign of greatness rather than a disability. For example, Maui, a well-known hero and trickster in Aotearoa and Polynesian myth, had a grandmother Muri-ranga-whenua who was blind.[2] In this account, Muri-ranga-whenua gifted her jawbone to Maui so that he could create a fish hook and fish up Te Ika a Maui (the North Island of Aotearoa). For tūpuna (ancestors), knowledge resided in the jawbone: thus it was through knowledge that the Māori world was brought into existence. Given that knowledge was pivotal to the world coming into being, knowledge also provided the location for, and shaping of, a specifically Māori identity.

This narrative exemplifies that being kāpo is not a stigma or a disability; rather, people who are kāpo have the capacity to lead productive lives, contributing to society and being exemplary leaders. They serve as counternarratives to the medical and social models of disability and the stigmatism and marginalisation that arise from them. The account above shows disability was seen as part of the natural fabric of traditional life. Similarly today whānau members who are kāpo are seen to be very much part of the fabric of whānau, hapū and iwi (Higgins, Phillips et al., 2010).

Colonial discourse

While whakapapa remains an important marker of identity today, colonial settlement processes have meant that new and diverse ways of identifying as

---

2 Note that in some accounts Muri-ranga-whenua was Maui's grandfather.

Māori have emerged (Durie, 1997). According to Moeke-Pickering (1996) there are two frameworks for conceptualising Māori identity in contemporary society. One is whakapapa and the other is based on cultural practices such as language, customs, kinship obligations and traditions in which shared understandings are constructed and maintained. It is within these 'nests of identity' (Macfarlane, 2003) that the whānau is central to understanding individual and collective Māori identity and Māori life worlds. This has become increasingly important today as many Māori, for a range of reasons, such as urbanisation, have at best tenuous connections to their hapū and iwi. It is in this complex identity context that the primary marker of identity for many Māori, including those who are kāpo, is whānau (Higgins et al., 2010).

Despite Aotearoa New Zealand's increasing ethnic diversity and articulations of biculturalism – and in more recent times, of multiculturalism (Singham, 2006) – it remains a largely monocultural society. This impacts on Māori aspirations to live as Māori, precisely because social structures and institutions reflect Pākehā ideologies. Thus, the issues, concerns and needs of Māori and, specifically Māori with a disability, have largely been constructed and defined by Pākehā.

One of the imposed characterisations that have sustained the marginalisation of Māori in Aotearoa New Zealand is their perceived inferiority. This belief in the inferiority of Māori was a key rationale in the colonisation of Aotearoa that resulted in Māori being dispossessed of their land, language, and culture. In turn, this has not only led to Māori being culturally dislocated, but also to ongoing disparities across the social indices including health, education and income. Cornell and Hartmann (1998) argued that the belief in the inferiority of some people designated or stereotyped as certain 'races' has been handed down from generation to generation and in the process has structured the way people perceive others. While such a view is a remnant of colonialism it is, they argued, given fresh relevance by changing social conditions. In other words, the ways in which 'deficit thinking' manifests itself at a given time reflects the social and political contexts of that time.

In Aotearoa New Zealand, one area where this is most clearly seen is in education. For example, until the 1960s, limited expectations of Māori intellectual capacity meant that Māori students were primarily educated for manual work. Since the 1960s, cultural deficit explanations have been used to understand the educational underachievement of Māori (Phillips, 2005). Deficit thinking results in teachers not recognising or challenging perceptions of the superiority of dominant knowledge codes and the inferiority of Māori cultural experience and home background. It can also result in overt expressions of racism. Deficit thinking remains embedded in institutional and individual practices and continues to have a negative impact on Māori in terms of both identity and educational outcomes (Bishop, 2002). For example, focusing on individual needs 'flies in the face' of Māori values of collaboration, collectivity, and accountability of the community. Rather, Māori value an educational focus on all people who are in the learning environment, and who can work together to address the problems that an individual is experiencing (Berryman, 2008).

Disability paradigms

It is not surprising, therefore, that Kingi and Bray (2000) have argued that colonisation, land alienation, the loss of te reo Māori, poverty and the imposition of Pākehā ideas and values are disabling for all Māori. Kliewer and Fitzgerald (2001) traced the origin of contemporary thinking on disability to the beginning of Western colonialism, arguing that the oppression of people with disability is enmeshed in a symbiotic relationship with cultural and racial oppression that colours the lenses through which people view the world.

The predominant ways in which disabled people are viewed and understood are through the medical and social models of disability. In these models the disabled person is viewed as an individual. In the social model or paradigm, for example, individuals have impairment and are disabled by a society that takes no account of the individual's impairments. In the medical model of disability, disabled people are defined as individuals who have 'abnormalities' that need to be fixed or cured. The professionalisation of services has grown from the medical model of disability and has worked in ways to maintain the oppression of people with impairments. Barnes and Mercer (2003) argue that professionals are disabling and self-serving, precisely because of their increased involvement in disabled people's lives. Oppression, they argued, is not just about tyrannical power; it is also 'effected through apparently liberal and "humane" practices, that include medicine, education, and leisure. Thus people in their everyday lives act and think in ways that are "oppressive" to disabled people, but do not always recognise their actions as having this effect' (2003, p. 21).

Contemporary Māori views and ways of defining disability challenge both the social and medical model views. Wilkie (2000) has written that in education the term 'special education (and special needs)' makes no sense to Māori because Māori make no distinction between people on the basis of their abilities or disabilities because everyone is special – regarded unique in their own right. Similarly, there is no Māori equivalent word for the term 'intellectual disability' (Bevan-Brown, 1994).

Higgins, Phillips, & Cowan (2011), who found that kāpo Māori have been marginalised through culturally dissonant education and health services, pointed out that kāpo Māori view their lived realties as disabled people in relationship to being Māori and to their identity within their whānau. In a 'whānaucentric' paradigm of disability, the whānau is defined very widely to also include unrelated individuals who are connected with each other by having ongoing interests and interactions (Collins & Hickey, 2006). In this paradigm whānau are collectively living the experience of disability and are working together to positively change this experience and society's disabling social and public systems (Higgins et al., 2009).

In conclusion, there is tension between Māori paradigms of disability and Eurocentric paradigms from which education and health services have developed. Thus, tamariki and rangatahi and their whānau may encounter difficulties when accessing such services.

Poverty and tamariki and rangatahi Māori disenfranchisement

Tamariki and rangatahi face ongoing struggles in accessing the benefits of education and health services (Dale, Obrien & St John, 2011). The Ministry of Social Development's *2010 Social Report* painted a bleak picture of disparities across the social indices for Māori. For example, life expectancy for Māori is lower than non-Māori, and the suicide rate for Māori youth is twice as high as for non-Māori. Education statistics for Māori are also of concern. Over half of Māori are leaving school earlier and with fewer qualifications. (Ministry of Social Development, 2010)

While disability paradigms and ethnicity have played major roles in educational and health disparities, socio-economic positioning and poverty are equally problematic. Ridge & Wright wrote in 2008 that poverty 'is not just about material, social and economic resource, it is also about social relationships, social process and the control and exercise of power' (cited in O'Brien, Dale & St John, 2011, p. 13). According to Dale, O'Brien, and St. John (2011), Aotearoa New Zealand's income inequalities are high in comparison with other Organisation for Economic Cooperation and Development (OECD) countries and have a significant ethnic dimension. Ethnicity and poverty combine to multiply the health risks to whānau and tamariki and rangatahi in particular (Baker, Barnard et al., 2012).

It is tamariki and rangatahi who are bearing the brunt of socio-economic disparity. For example, St John and Wynd (2008) wrote that Māori children were twice as likely to be living in poverty than Pākehā children, in households where the income was 60% below the median household income. They argued that Māori children were most at risk of poor health and that lack of disposable whānau income, substandard housing, inadequate nutrition and inequitable access to health care all played their part. They also found that access to early childhood education was limited for low-income whānau because of the difficulty they had paying fees and donations.

It is clear that whānau continue to experience significant inequalities, despite the various national and international mechanisms to address the rights and inequalities of children, Māori, and people with a disability. Coupled with policies such as *The New Zealand Disability Strategy* (2001) and its Māori counterpart, *He Korowai Oranga* (2002), there are plenty of legislative requirements intended to ensure a range of social, cultural, political, health and educational rights for Māori, and especially Māori whānau with a disability. However, in practice, this is not the case (United Nations Committee on Economic, Social and Cultural Rights, 2012). While all New Zealanders enjoy a set of basic human rights through the Bill of Rights 1990 that guarantees civil and political rights for all New Zealanders, and the Human Rights Act 1993, that guarantees the right to non-discrimination on the basis of race, there is little evidence that these safeguard Māori, children's, and disabled people's rights (Anaya, 2011).

Nor do the United Nations (UN) conventions that Aotearoa New Zealand is a signatory to, such as the Rights of Persons with Disabilities (2008) and the Rights of the Child (1990), as well as the Declaration of the Rights of Indigenous People (2007), provide protection for Māori. Despite the obligations that the Aotearoa New Zealand government has to uphold the rights contained within the UN conventions because they are legally binding documents, the implementation of them is limited. As Rodriguez-Piñero Royo (2009) argued: 'International monitoring of human rights is one thing but translating human rights into people's real lives is a different thing altogether. Decades of developing the standards and practice of international mechanisms has shown the sad, well-known reality that the impact of the human rights regime in the field is, at best, limited ... and that violations of human rights continue to be widespread no matter how sophisticated the means to protect them' (p. 329).

Part of the problem at the level of the 'real lives' of Māori is that most of these national and international measures are framed as individual rights. This is problematic for Māori because their cultural, social and political orientation is collective in nature. On this basis the most important mechanism through which the rights of Māori can be advanced is the Treaty of Waitangi. Indeed the Treaty, despite the fact it has no legal teeth, remains the most significant aspirational document and leverage for Māori to redress historical wrongs and advance Māori aspirations to be Māori and to be self-determining.

Multiple identities and oppressions: Stories of kāpo Māori and their whānau

Health and education services, which are delivered to tamariki and rangatahi with a disability, impact directly upon their and their whānau's health and identity (Bevan Brown, 1989; Collins & Hickey, 2006). Culturally appropriate educational services foster emotional and psychological well-being, raise self-esteem, and facilitate learning (Bevan-Brown, 2000). Macfarlane (2005) argued that the reason so many Māori fail in both mainstream and special education settings is because the links between culture and education are missing, in particular an understanding of Māori cultural practices and values. Overseas, researchers have argued that disabled people who are black or of an ethnic minority experience racism and 'disablism', and note that the impact of multiple oppression needs to be researched and recognised so that culturally competent services can be delivered (Johnson & Morjaria-Keval, 2007; Miles, 2002).

Within this theoretical and research context, our recent research project, 'Growing up kāpo Māori: Accessing paediatric ophthalmology services', explored the demographics of kāpo Māori and their whānau and the barriers that they faced when interacting with educational and health services (Higgins, Phillips et al., 2012). One hundred and fifty whānau with a kāpo tamariki and rangatahi completed a demographic questionnaire, and 37 whānau participated in in-depth qualitative whānau interviews. Within the context of a whānaucentric paradigm of disability, whānau voices were central to understanding the experiences of kāpo tamariki and rangatahi. The project was hosted and managed by Ngāti Kāpo O Aotearoa Inc., a service organisation 'for and by' kāpo Māori. It was funded by the Health Research Council. All quoted material hereafter is from this study.

Some of our demographic findings indicated that the social, health and educational well-being of kāpo Māori whānau, like Māori in general, is of concern. We found that:

- the average number of people living in the household was 4.7 people compared to 2.6 people in the 2006 general population (Statistics New Zealand, 2006, 2010);
- $40,690 was the participants' average household income compared with $79,300 in the general population (Statistics New Zealand, 2010);
- the average age of a kāpo child receiving their first vision service was three years and seven months and this was almost two years after the average age

when their vision impairment was first noticed;
- 70% of the time whānau noticed their child's vision impairment, and not their GP or community nurse, despite indications that they were regularly seeing their GP; and
- 60% of all participants wanted initial or additional referrals to Ngāti Kāpo O Aotearoa while 55% wanted referrals to unspecified Māori Health Services.

The demographic data clearly highlighted disadvantages faced by kāpo Māori. The stories that they told were about encountering exclusionary discourses and practices when attempting to access health and education services.

Discrimination and stereotyping practices

A recurring theme for many of the participants was the discrimination they experienced because of their ethnicity. For example, one young single mother noticed that her Pākehā friend, who also had a disabled child, was being offered more comprehensive health and education services: 'The difference between what John got and what [my friend's] child got was quite obvious. She got better treatment … We weren't offered as many things as she was offered … She'd sort of go, "Hey I got this. Why can't John have that?" … There was a bit of discrimination going on'.

One whānau encountered professionals that believed that their child had been abused because of their age and 'their looks':

> We had to grow up very fast … We understood his condition and everything, but they still treat you like you're stupid and don't know anything … Yeah, I remember that they did check over Kahu once for child abuse when he went in for eczema … Like the specialist knew that this was eczema and everything … But me and Tim (my husband) were there with him, and I must admit the nurse did check him over, thinking it was child abuse. I don't know if that was because we were young and the look of us as well.

Another whānau refused to stay in hospital and receive services because of the manner in which they were being stereotyped: 'Just because we're Polynesian Māori we're seen as being inbred … We left [hospital] thinking that "You guys must think we're dumb horis or Rarotongans" … In a way it stopped us from accessing services because we didn't want to go back to that situation again. Because it wasn't very good sitting there and they're saying "interbred" … There were certain things that I didn't like and that's why I had to leave … cultural things, yeah.'

Deficit thinking

Whānau also encountered professionals who viewed not only their children, but also being Māori and being young, through deficit eyes. The outcomes of deficit thinking were varied. One whānau opted out of services because of the way their child was seen as a complex array of conditions, rather than as a whole child. The mother said: 'I tell you what really got up my nose was the geneticists – yeah it was kind of "your daughter's fingers are too long, her ears are too big, her toes are too long" ... I know what they were doing, they were trying to find specific areas of her body that might have been related through to some sort of genetic ... I couldn't take that.' Another whānau encountered a social worker who had very low expectations of the intellectual capacity of their baby, as the mother explained:

> And then the Social Worker from the Hospital ... said not to expect Chris to achieve anything. 'He's not going to reach normal milestones like a normal child, and we had to prepare ourselves for the worst,' is what she told us. ... Yeah, on the day he was born! ... [My partner] and I were just flabbergasted, and we haven't liked her since ... I mean being told not to expect your child to achieve anything, horrible, when you've just been told his condition.

One mother noted that despite four visits to her GP, her worries seemed not to be taken seriously by her doctor because of her age. It was only when her older aunty, a nurse, intervened that he addressed her concern. She said, 'If my aunty hadn't stepped in, we probably would have gone back to him again, and – nothing.'

Cultural ignorance

Whānau also spoke about encountering culturally unresponsive services. One whānau, for example, described a struggle that they had with deciding to have a skin tag removed from their daughter. Not only was this part of who their daughter was, but also the removed skin was still a part of her. It was important for this whānau that her skin tag be cared for, and buried along with her placenta. Huia's parents explained:

> When Huia was born, she had a skin tag on her ear, and when she was three she was on the plastic surgery list [to have it removed]. Anyway Hemi and I really struggled. This is a part of her body, do we get it removed, what do we do? In the end we decided to get it [removed], you know because her body's young. It'll heal better. She'll never have to go through any of the emotional trauma of being teased. But then when they took it off we had to ask for it back.

Hemi was like, 'well that's her, that's her body, we don't want that to go in the medical waste bin, or wherever that goes.' We had to specifically ask, and the nurses were like, 'Oh, you want it? What?' But they got it and put it in a little bit of saline solution. We brought it home and buried it. Huia made a little pot for it, we put it in the pot, put it in the ground, and she planted a tree on top.

Socio-economic issues

A number of whānau noted that the cost of accessing services was at times beyond their means and that consequently they were not able to receive all of the care and services that may have been available to them and their tamariki and rangatahi. One father reported:

We've noticed, if we know some people that have money that they were getting services. It seemed like [the hospital] paid them more attention. There were times when I couldn't make it up to the hospital and they would come down here. But, they were like, 'Oh this is costing the hospital money'. And it was like, 'Well I can't get up there [because] it costs too much.' Now we have to get dropped off because we've got to pay for parking.

One mother reflected on the experiences of whānau accessing funding from WINZ (Work and Income New Zealand), the government agency that manages the various disability benefits and allowances, for financial support of their kāpo tamariki and rangatahi. In her experience as a whānau support person, many whānau were not accessing appropriate funding because of the negative experiences they had, not only because they were Māori but also because they had a child with a disability. She stated, 'A lot of families will not go to WINZ to get financial support because they've had bad experiences from there. They're

Support and strength is given by whānau.

looked down upon, you walk in there with a special needs child and you're looked down upon twice.'

Exclusionary practices based on impairment and/or age

A number of whānau talked about encountering health and education services that excluded them because their services did not attend to their child's impairment or age. Whānau recounted how they had few options when it came to schooling. For example some whānau sent their children to special schools because specialist itinerant services or teacher aide support weren't available in their area for them to attend a mainstream school. One mother told of how her daughter could only attend school on a half-time basis. The school said that it couldn't guarantee their daughter's safety at school without one-to-one support, which wasn't available on a full-time basis:

> There's no more funding to allow Alice to attend school full time any more … She used to have full time [teacher aide] hours at school … Um, well Alice is very high needs. So she needs the one on one. And it's dangerous not to have the one on one for Alice, mainly … because of the [risk of] eye haemorrhage … She can attend, but it'll be at our own risk [according to the school]. And for safety reasons, that's just unwise, and so Alice has to come home.

In health services, a whānau described how their daughter was refused a referral to an optometrist, because the ophthalmologist did not consider she would benefit from prescription glasses because of her intellectual impairment. The mother reported: 'The ophthalmologist stated that because we didn't know what the brain was doing, it didn't matter whether we put glasses on her face, it wouldn't make any difference to her vision. Because of her intellectual impairment there was no point to her wearing glasses.'

One whānau spoke about early childhood education centres not being able to adequately include their son, Hemi. The father stated:

> Hemi is not mobile. He spends a lot of time on the floor. He was forever getting collected on the floor and they [kindergarten] just couldn't provide a safe enough place. So … we moved him to playcentre. I kind of regret it now. I didn't actually realise how good I had it at kindergarten. Going to playcentre, we were totally outcasted [because of his impairments]. We weren't involved in anything and it got to the point where I thought 'Well bugger you'.

A few whānau indicated that their children were excluded from services because they demonstrated their competence. For example, one whānau said their kāpo child, who used a wheelchair, was not seen as being kāpo and was denied access to a reader for his National Certificate of Educational Achievement (NCEA) tests because he was adept at getting around.

Sometimes kāpo tamariki were excluded because there was no wheelchair access to, or throughout, the school. Wheelchair access was also of concern in hospitals where the vision assessment equipment didn't allow space for wheelchairs. One whānau was unable to have their son's eyes checked: 'It's not just about the eyes, it's about different bits and pieces and you know their machines don't fit in his wheelchair. They didn't do the check.'

At hospitals, whānau were more likely to feel excluded because of their child's age. Hospital appointments and waiting rooms were organised for adults, and not for children. Many whānau spoke about how their children became impatient at the long waits without anything to do, which in turn affected their ability to participate in the doctor's examinations. One whānau said, 'Going in with a four-year-old and they have just sat in a waiting room for two hours and then they go in and the doctors rushing them to do the test … And it didn't matter what amount of bribes I took, we could never get Maia to sit. Fair enough. She is fed up. She doesn't want to be there any more and then they are putting drops that sting her eyes.'

Whānau resistance and agency

Within our research, there were also narratives about love, hope and transformation. In all instances, and often as a result of their negative experiences, the parents of kāpo tamariki and rangatahi wanted more for their children. They wanted their children to be seen as children rather than their disability and have the same opportunities that sighted children had. One mother said about her kāpo son: 'Sometimes people think that because he has a vision impairment, that he's limited in what he can do. He'll do anything. He'll attempt anything and everything, and it's not until he'll have an accident or something that he'll realise, "Oh well I won't do that again" (chuckle) … He's got to go and explore … and test the water. And [we will] always be there to love and support [him] when things don't go [right].'

In challenging and resisting the services that their tamariki and rangatahi received, parents in the process also changed their own lives as well as the lives of other whānau in their communities. Take for example one father, the primary caregiver in his whānau, who had become a 'Google master' to learn as much as he could about his son's condition. His knowledge about his son and his condition, along with his frustration with the services that his son received, led him to take charge of the situation and call a meeting with all the people involved in his son's care. He reflected on how difficult it was to access appropriate services and how he used his knowledge to support and advocate for other whānau. He explained: 'All the people that we had involved – teaching, learning, hospital, occupational therapist and the Royal Foundation for the Blind – they were all pulling in their own directions, and chasing what they thought to be right, so I called a big meeting and I got everybody there. I said, "Look, as a parent, I think I've got the right to decide what's right and what's wrong for my son."'

Another parent, reflecting on her own experiences as a mother of a teenager with multiple disabilities, including vision impairment, proposed two ideas that would benefit whānau. One idea was to establish a 'passport system' so that whānau with children with complex needs would only need to fill in one form about their child, that they took with them when they went to specialist services. The other was to establish a 'navigator' service to support and benefit whānau. She said:

> If I could get another family, newly diagnosed, up to where I am now, up to 13 years, it's going to benefit a lot of people. You know, so they don't have to go through all that bullshit, and red tape, and so they have someone to walk along beside them, until they feel secure enough to handle that themselves. Don't take the power away from them, support them. Support them to a point where they're able to stand on their own. And just touch base now and again.

Not only were whānau resisting discriminatory and culturally irrelevant practices, they were realising their desire to be self-determining or agents of change for themselves and for their communities.

Conclusion

Our research has shown that young kāpo Māori and their whānau are seen through deficit lenses. Whānau experienced marginalisation in multiple ways, despite a raft of policies and legislation that have been put in place to eradicate discrimination and inequalities. While being young, Māori, kāpo and poor were viewed, primarily, as discrete identities and discrete issues in education and health services, within the context of contemporary Aotearoa New Zealand, they are, nevertheless, 'interconnected parts of a whole way of looking at the world in which difference is considered inferior and in which unequal relationships are demarcated' (Phillips, 2005, p. 88). Exclusionary discourses and practices went on to limit what services whānau were offered on the one hand, and to influence whether and how whānau engaged with them on the other. Certainly, health and education services need to provide culturally

The whānau is central.

relevant and appropriate services so that whānau will not only access them, but also in the process maintain a strong identity as Māori. While whānau resisted and rejected services that they saw as demeaning and marginalising, some went on to support other whānau, while others became advocates and activists in their communities.

Kāpo Māori and their whānau who participated in this research were highly resilient and resourceful in their everyday lives. Kāpo Māori resilience is exemplified in the artwork below by two young brothers, Waka and Anaru Te Tai, one of whom is kāpo. Their artwork tells the story of what it means to grow up Māori and kāpo. At the heart of kāpo Māori childhood is whānau and the associated practice of whanaungatanga (whānau relationships and connections, obligations and responsibilities, both past and present), to ensure physical and cultural survival and well-being.

Specifically, their artwork expresses the nested nature of Māori identity and kāpo Māori life worlds. Within the centre circle, framed by three koru, is a triangle that represents kāpo Māori and their whānau. The three koru that form the corners of the triangle represent the generations of kāpo Māori and their whānau who have passed away and now watch over the new generations of kāpo Māori and their whānau, linking each generation together. The threads that flow from the outer circle represent the knowledge that has been passed down

through the generations of kāpo Māori and their whānau. As expressed by the artists, '[t]he theme of the painting reflects that the future is uncertain but the experiences, knowledge and teachings handed down through the generations of kāpo Māori and their whānau give encouragement and confidence and although the future cannot be seen clearly there is a path to follow and it can still be great' (Waka and Anaru Te Tai, cited in Higgins et al., 2010, p. iv).

In conclusion, growing up kāpo Māori in Aotearoa New Zealand is not only about the struggle for equality and inclusion, it is also about possibility and transformation as evidenced by whānau who expressed, in a variety of ways, their desire and right to be self-determining, and their ability to live life being true to themselves. The challenge is for the health and education sectors to provide culturally responsive services to kāpo tamariki and rangatahi that better reflect kāpo Māori realities and aspirations.

CHAPTER 9

Multicultural childhoods in a globalised world

Karen Guo

> Western nations, including ... New Zealand, have experienced immigration and various movements of racial [and cultural] awareness that have forced them to confront questions concerning the ways they define themselves. (Kincheloe & Steinberg, 1997, p. 1)

It is now 40 years since what was probably one of the first publications on multiculturalism in Aotearoa New Zealand. Sutherland (1973) noted the trend of increasing immigration in Aotearoa New Zealand and predicted the growth of a multicultural society. Sutherland's point has proved remarkably prescient. As we move into the twenty-first century, we can easily see that Aotearoa New Zealand has become a country of many cultural and ethnic groups. In this chapter, I will argue that childhood in Aotearoa New Zealand is also affected by these demographic changes. Traditional ways of representing childhood as the product of a distinct culture no longer seem adequate, and learning cannot be considered as a monocultural construct any more. The assumption that multiculturalism refers to cultural relationships is made explicit by Penn (2005), who argued that 'culture is forever being amalgamated and reshaped as people from different communities come into contact with one another' (p. 93).

In this chapter, I will examine contemporary childhood in Aotearoa New Zealand within its multicultural context. The chapter begins with a brief overview of the multicultural background in Aotearoa New Zealand, before defining culture and multiculture more fully. I then discuss a range of multicultural situations, outlining some issues that impact on the current relationships between cultures. There is a connection between cultural relations and children's multicultural experiences: multicultural childhood is the product of the country's multicultural relations, including their incorporation into the policies and practices of early childhood education. In the concluding section, I explore ways in which childhood in Aotearoa New Zealand can be recontexualised into a multicultural context. The main force in this exploration is the idea that a multicultural childhood benefits children in their present life, as well as preparing them to become global citizens in the future.

The making of New Zealanders

Aotearoa New Zealand is a nation of culturally diverse settlers. The first settlers, ancestors of the indigenous people or Māori, arrived in the thirteenth century. 1769 was another significant year in history, when Captain James Cook, a British explorer, sailed to Aotearoa New Zealand: this led to a surge in arrivals of explorers, traders and missionaries from Europe and North America and created a range of remarkable cultural changes. In 1840, with the increasing inflow of new settlers, the national founding document, the Treaty of Waitangi, was signed. This document gave rise to the country's bicultural context, namely Māori and Pākehā (European New Zealander). There was also extensive European and Asian settlement throughout the rest of the nineteenth century. The 1950s in Aotearoa New Zealand were marked by regular arrivals of Dutch, English and Scottish people, and in the 1960s, people from the Pacific Islands increasingly moved to Aotearoa New Zealand for work opportunities. The last 30 years have witnessed a rapid influx of immigrants from Asia and Africa as a result of the introduction of the Immigration Act 1987 that aimed at enabling skilled and business migration (Smith, 2012).

Aotearoa New Zealand is made up of multi-ethnic and multicultural groups. Census statistics (Statistics New Zealand, 2009) show that continued immigration has contributed to the increasing ethnic diversity of Aotearoa New Zealand's population. It seems an inescapable conclusion from this kind of evidence that the cultural structure of Aotearoa New Zealand has evolved towards a cosmopolitan nature (Duhn, 2008). Its cultural structure was initially constructed in the form of the Māori tradition, but was then reconstructed by European and Polynesian heritage, and later by the characteristics of many other cultures and norms.

The multi-ethnic and multicultural make-up of Aotearoa New Zealand is no doubt reflected in the population of children. As Anne Grey (2010), an Aotearoa New Zealand early childhood academic, points out, 'Aotearoa New Zealand has become increasingly multicultural as many families from other countries come to settle and form communities here. For this reason, more children are born into, and develop and learn within, a multicultural setting that contains multiple cultures and contexts' (p. 50).

The construction of the Chinese gardens in Dunedin represented a joint initiative between the Chinese community and the city and provides a superb facility for children and their families to explore.

Culture and multiculture in New Zealand terms

Culture is defined by Grey (2010) as 'the broad patterns of behaviour that are determined by beliefs and values of groups of people that are shaped and reshaped over time, and passed from one generation to the next' (p. 49). Her position is that culture has particularity, meaning that each culture is unique. Anne Smith (1998) takes a similar view, stating that different cultures provide children with different experiences for learning.

This matter of the particularity of culture brings me to a point raised in an earlier study about multiculture. Multiculture means many ways of knowing, being and doing that are respectively inherited from diverse traditions (Yang, 2008). This is a significant point. In considering how a multicultural environment in Aotearoa New Zealand might play a role in children's lives, it is important to recognise the many and different dimensions of cultural identities, knowledge, and practices.

The idea of cultural particularity is necessary but not sufficient. It also must be acknowledged that another important feature about culture is its generalisability, referring to 'aspects of culture that may link some cultures together into groupings' (Sanders, 2004, p. 56). My own study on Chinese immigrant children's learning experiences in multicultural settings in Aotearoa New Zealand early childhood centres reported a range of intercultural relations between the children's home culture and the cultures of the centres (Guo, 2010). In that research, 'the [Chinese immigrant] children were looking for ways to negotiate the coexistence of different sets of cultural tools to function, learn and develop in intercultural learning contexts. The children entered into a culture–culture relation through which they created their own repertoires of practice' (p. 224).

To illustrate cultural relations as a human experience in multicultural situations, this chapter presents key findings of my research with Chinese immigrant children. The research identified three types of cultural relationships which appeared to have contributed to children's learning experiences in multicultural early childhood settings. The first type of cultural relationship is cultural bridging. Children's home and cultural tools, primarily the Chinese language, acted as a bridge for their learning in the new cultural context of the centre. Examples of cultural bridging included when children approached their Chinese-speaking teachers and communicated with them in Chinese to find out what was happening within the centres.

The second type of cultural relationship is cultural converging. Cultural converging was identified when the children interchangeably used Chinese and English in the same learning encounter. This is illustrated by an example from Jim, a three-year-old child: 'Jim is playing in the water trough on his own. He sprinkles water onto the ground. As he plays, Jim laughs: "water, water jiao di di" [water, water the ground]' (Guo, 2010, p.144).

The third type of cultural relationship is cultural togetherness. Cultural togetherness was shown in this study through Chinese immigrant children's close interactions with Chinese-speaking peers. It was observed that all the Chinese immigrant children had lengthy and engaged interactions with one or more Chinese peer, and they explained this as follows: 'We are Chinese. We can speak Chinese. We are friends' (Xiaohan, a four-year-old Chinese child). I learned in this study that Chinese immigrant children naturally and consistently related their home cultural tools with those of the early childhood centres, and that these intercultural and multicultural tools positively mediated their learning experiences.

In Aotearoa New Zealand, the primary foundation for the national culture and the bicultural mandate is grounded in the relationship between Māori and later settlers (Smith, 1998). However, the dynamics of cultural relations and interactions in Aotearoa New Zealand also characterise it as a multicultural nation, as demonstrated in my study with Chinese immigrant children. This idea is at the very centre of my deliberations in this chapter. The relationship between cultures in Aotearoa New Zealand is an influential contextual framework that gives rise to children's experiences in this multicultural society. The significance of cultural relations lies primarily in its impact upon children's development as multicultural citizens, but also upon what children learn about the society and about themselves in, and through, these relations in the society.

Positioning multicultural childhood within discourses of multicultural relations

Cultural diversity

The view that cultural diversity is an important issue for Aotearoa New Zealand's multicultural society has been discussed by Stephen May (1999). He stated that 'the prevailing conception of multiculturalism focuses on a struggle for the recognition of diversity within existing social structures' (p. 114). From this perspective of multicultural relations, the primary issue is the struggle for recognition.

Cultural diversity provides many different ways of doing things, which existing social structures may find difficult to accommodate. For children and their families from different cultures, Aotearoa New Zealand's monocultural structures, such as education, may be difficult to traverse. In the early childhood years, these issues can include, for example, diverse child-rearing beliefs and practices, or ideas about learning and play. In my research, I found that Aotearoa New Zealand early childhood teachers saw play and child-initiated experiences as important parts of young children's learning and development, while Chinese parents believed that the capacity to learn was imposed on children by adult instruction and teaching (Guo, 2010). The presence of diverse child-rearing beliefs and practices has also been noted in previous studies (Chan, 2006; Genish & Goodwin, 2008; Robinson & Diaz, 2006).

The complexity involved in the meaning of 'culture' goes some way to explain the difficulty of establishing educational practice that attends to diversity. According to William (1958) ' "culture" is one of the ... most complicated words in the English language' (cited in Ryan, 1999, p. 55). For many, ' "culture" is a state of being or something that is seen' (Goodwin, Gheruvu & Genishi, 2008, p. 6). Rhedding-Jones (2005) also raised an important point about the range of meanings given to the word 'diversity', noting that 'people will have multiple interpretations of the concept of diversity' (p. 134).

Gonzalez-Mena (2003) has reminded us that cultures can be broadly organised into two distinct themes: individualism and collectivism. If many different cultures exist in Aotearoa New Zealand, then it follows that there will be cultures based on individualism in this country. For individuals within these cultures, what people do with their lives is largely a matter of their own concern. This belief has consequences for multicultural educational practice, because some people will then remain indifferent to what differs from them, regardless of how culturally and ethnically diverse Aotearoa New Zealand becomes.

Cultural boundary

Cultural boundary is an approach to addressing cultural diversity. This approach divides cultures into their own space and territory. This division defines cultural groups in a restricted way by drawing up a boundary line between them. Yang (2008) also pointed out that 'where there is a division, there is a boundary' (p. 81). The conception associated with the idea of cultural boundary is that 'traditional cultural values and practices ... exert considerable influence ... and may accordingly be slow to change' (May, 1999, p. 33). In some sense, cultural boundary seeks to organise and limit multicultural relations. We can, therefore, find reasons why 'minority ethnic groups have often come to be represented as being contained within their culture and the discursive practices associated with them' (May, 1999, p. 33). The optimistic view of cultural boundary is that it helps cultures conserve their differences, and assists a country to sustain 'belongingness'.

Such a division of cultures is too simple and arbitrary, and the idea that cultural boundaries keep people in a defined cultural position can be easily challenged, as demonstrated in the findings from my study with Chinese immigrant young children (Guo, 2010). These children operated within a convergence of their home culture and those of the early childhood centres. In my study, one example of this was that the children invented their own language that resembled both English and Chinese. It illustrates that in an environment where different cultures meet, boundary lines between them can be crossed.

One reason why people prefer a cultural boundary is the fear of losing their own traditions, which, for them, are normal and appropriate. Ritchie (2010) presented an example from her study that 'teachers in early childhood education focus on other ethnicities as having a culture ... Cultural processes are not recognised as reflecting their (Western) "culture" because they are seen as merely "normal"' (p. 3). It is likely that the teachers were seeking to control unfamiliar disturbances to the norms and values of their own culture. For this to happen, they kept their own culture away from the others, thereby creating a boundary between that and those of others. This division was legitimised by the belief of the teachers that they were 'normal'. Implicit in this belief was the idea that others were deviant.

Within a multicultural context, distinctions between cultures have cloudy borders and cultural boundaries tend to get blurred. In fact, 'boundaries are constantly negotiated and transgressed as individuals engage the forces and discourses that shape them' (Kincheloe & Steinberg, 1997, p. 215). This does not mean, however, that people lose the integrity of their original cultures. Hall (1992) pointed out that in a multicultural setting, 'all speak from a particular place, out of a particular history, out of a particular existence, a particular culture' (p. 258).

Multicultural pluralism

The concept of multicultural pluralism means that different types of cultural values and practices are realised in a common place. As people live within the framework of multicultural pluralism, their diverse cultures and traditions are maintained during their cross-cultural interactions with others.

The idea of multicultural pluralism is a political response to the multicultural characteristics of Aotearoa New Zealand society. Singham (2006) noted that the key focus of multicultural practice for the Aotearoa New Zealand government 'has been ensuring equality and reducing disparities between minority and majority communities' (p. 35). The general principle of multicultural pluralism, that aims to attain equality in cultural relations and maintain social cohesion (Robinson & Diaz, 2005), is accepted to be the basis of work with multiculturalism.

There are, however, difficulties inherent in the implementation of multicultural pluralism. Given that the multicultural context in Aotearoa New Zealand coexists with many other aspects of the country, such as its historical and political dimensions, any attempts to move towards multicultural pluralism cannot be made easily. These difficulties can be broadly arranged under two themes: European superiority and power relationships.

The entrenched tradition of Pākehā/European domination in Aotearoa New Zealand sets expectations and constrains the actions of multicultural pluralism. These expectations and constraints are manifested in both policies and practical realms, and in most cases, are linked 'to the expansion of capitalism in the sense that whiteness signifies the production and consumption of commodities under capitalism' (McLaren & Torres, 1999, p. 55). According to May (1999), the dominant white cultural group rejects attempts to bring other cultures into their group for fear of losing the legitimacy of identity and social systems. For them, a single culture is 'necessary', 'fundamental' and 'immutable' (p. 34). Therefore, the ideology of multicultural pluralism can be a difficult practice in

Aotearoa New Zealand. Practical evidence about European privilege is found in other Aotearoa New Zealand studies (Ritchie, 2010; May & Sleeter, 2010).

A second, closely related difficulty for multicultural pluralism is the power struggles between cultural groups. Power is the operational mechanism of 'complex discursive sites of identity formation' (Sharma, 2010, p. 115). Within the Aotearoa New Zealand context, a long-held assumption is that the predominant culture is all-important (May & Sleeter, 2010). This has been influenced, in part, by the realisation that cultural convergence usually heads towards a single framework of the prevailing norms, which is believed to create social harmony and unity (Dijkstra, Geuijen & de Ruijter, 2001). This 'harmonious' aspiration, therefore, becomes an ideological arena in which the predominant culture subtly upholds its power and status.

For this reason, Robinson and Diaz (2006) were concerned that cultural pluralism has limitations in terms of its commitment to equality of opportunities and its challenges to the social, institutional and legal status of multicultural countries. If the focus of multicultural pluralism remains on differences, it could not contribute to effective changes to multicultural relationships because differences could mean inequalities. The ideology of multicultural pluralism is thus hampered in practice by the ideology of social harmony on the grounds that any attempts to focus on differences would threaten the harmony of the social system.

Globalisation

Globalisation has an impact on multicultural childhoods in Aotearoa New Zealand. The shift towards globalisation, and its interconnected effects on the many facets of Aotearoa New Zealand society, has brought about changes in a multicultural dimension (Larner, Le Heron & Lewis, 2008). According to Banerjee and Linstead (2001) globalisation is one of the most important influences on multiculturalism.

Children's lives in Aotearoa New Zealand are influenced by the way in which cultures are expanded, transformed and relate to each other in this globalised multicultural society. There are more cultural variables and diversities as a result of the globalising economy and the changing composition of international migration flows. Larner (2006) argued that a significant effect of globalisation on Aotearoa New Zealand society is the broadening of its bicultural foundation to include a complex framework of diverse cultures.

The particular relevance of globalisation to multiculturalism is that it extends cultural diversities. It is precisely the influence of globalisation on cultural dynamics which explains why many writings on globalisation focus on interpersonal relationships, providing a way to speak about a range of notions, such as universalisation, sustainability, continuity, equity, justice, and power distribution (Moss 2008; Scholte 2008). In many ways, globalisation essentially means connections between people. Scholte (2008), for example, argued that the vital point is that globalisation 'involves reductions in barriers to social contacts. People become more able ... to engage with each other' (p. 1478). Blackmore (1999) saw globalisation as inherently a matter of convergence of people and their cultures.

It would seem, then, that the influence of globalisation on people and cultural relationships is important in multiculturalism. In a useful discussion of globalisation and multiculturalism, Yang (2008) pointed out that 'the relationships of various cultures and civilizations are becoming fundamental in the human society of the era of globalization' (p. 79). Thus multiculturalism, which has been an apparent feature of Aotearoa New Zealand society, will become more visible in the context of globalisation as well. The need for Aotearoa New Zealand children to cultivate a multicultural awareness and develop multicultural knowledge, therefore, seems meaningful and understandable.

However, within the context of globalisation, multiculturalism in the present is different from the past (Pieterse, 2007). The past has been characterised by managing cultural relationships within a nation. In the current situation, the advancement of information technologies and the ease of travel help create cross-national multicultural relationships. In my study, many Chinese immigrant fathers worked in China or other overseas countries. They communicated with their children in Aotearoa New Zealand on a frequent basis, and reunited with them either in Aotearoa New Zealand or sometimes overseas. There is little doubt that such 'astronaut family' arrangements can have a considerable influence on the cultural dimension of Chinese immigrant children's lives. The children experienced not only the cultures in Aotearoa New Zealand and those of China, but also cultures from their fathers' and their own overseas travels. It is these transnational experiences that give globalisation a particular significance for multicultural childhoods.

Another factor of globalisation that influences multicultural childhoods is its emphasis on Western culture. The notion of globalisation as a strong force to re-drive and re-expand the diffusion of Western culture was encapsulated in the influential paper by Banerjee and Linstead (2001). They spelt out that Western cultural knowledge is commonly presented as the most useful source of learning. This can result in Western cultural capital being willingly, if not blindly, embraced by people of minority cultures. Evidence of this process was seen in my work with Chinese immigrant parents (Guo, 2010). Participating parents' perceptions of their minority status and the value that they gave to the dominant culture caused them to prefer a monocultural/mainstream/western way of learning for their children in multicultural early childhood settings. These parents' attitudes not only stem from many experiences in their personal lives, but could also have been the result of the worldwide prioritising of the Western culture. Globalisation also enables this to happen because there is a focus on wealth, economic development, and global competition (Kassimeris & Veyonides, 2012).

Globalisation enriches children's cultural exposures because they encounter differences, but it also limits their multicultural experiences because of the emphasis placed on the value of the dominant culture. While globalisation further diversifies the cultures of the country, the importance it gives to the dominant knowledge can impede children's engagement with many non-dominant cultures. In other words, in this global era, children in Aotearoa New Zealand still learn mainly about and through the dominant culture.

Multicultural early childhood education

One thing we can be sure of is that multicultural educational practice is encouraged in Aotearoa New Zealand early childhood education centres. The national early childhood curriculum, *Te Whāriki*, supports the integration of minority cultural aspects in early childhood programmes and calls for an early childhood pedagogy that is responsive and sensitive to different cultures (Ministry of Education, 1996). However, early childhood programmes have limited multicultural components. Issues have been identified, including tokenistic teaching practice regarding other cultures, implementation of only celebratory aspects, and use of a one-for-all model to deal with differences (Guo, 2010).

The explanations for the limited multicultural early childhood educational practice in Aotearoa New Zealand is the strong role that *Te Whāriki* takes in upholding the bicultural nature of the curriculum. Duhn (2008) indicated that *Te Whāriki* is a bicultural document and despite its well-intentioned multicultural orientation, the document is unlikely to lead to multicultural practice. For her, the philosophies and beliefs in *Te Whāriki* are derived from the bicultural heritage of the country, rather than its multicultural situation: '*Te Whāriki* shies away from addressing the complexities of multiculturalism in favour of outlining biculturalism' (p. 90); 'discourses of multiculturalism are overlaid by bicultural issues' (p. 90); and 'diversity and multiplicity are reduced to manageable sameness' (p. 88). Rhedding-Jones's (2002) impression of *Te*

Whāriki has been that while there is a strong emphasis in the document on the integration of minority cultures, it has not explicitly suggested multicultural educational practice in a widely inclusive way, and it considers minority culture to be mainly that of Māori: 'There is no mention ... of the children ... whose families migrated from Asia, Africa, or Eastern Europe ... Constructing a double difference and a double resource, as in bilingualism, is thus done well in New Zealand. But moving toward fluid multiplicities, where people belong to a range of simultaneously operating categories, beyond a binary, remains a challenge' (p. 94).

It is my contention that while *Te Whāriki* defines a broad agenda for diverse cultural practice, it does not specifically help with multicultural practice in the early childhood sector. Alongside others (Chan, 2009; Duhn, 2008), I see the document as making its contribution to children's development in a bicultural, but not a multicultural manner. *Te Whāriki's* focus on the bicultural dimension of Aotearoa New Zealand is strong and does not necessarily propel efforts of early childhood education towards multiculturalism.

Reconceptualising multiculturalism in childhood

The ideas raised in this chapter point towards a single message: that children in Aotearoa New Zealand are developing in a country that consists of multicultures, but the prospect for a multicultural childhood in this multicultural country is weak. In the current situation, Aotearoa New Zealand children live alongside multicultures but not with them.

Throughout many years of demographic changes, Aotearoa New Zealand has been made up of multicultures. New Zealanders have created a society characterised by the coexistence of many cultures. Global development in recent years has produced a new cultural dynamic. There seems little doubt that the demographic situation in Aotearoa New Zealand society demands a greater degree of responses to its many cultures.

Children in Aotearoa New Zealand have limited experience of multicultural childhoods. Cultural relations in Aotearoa New Zealand do not mirror its multicultural structures. A set of historical, cultural, value and practical constraints limit the experience of a multicultural childhood for children in this country. Eurocentric superiority, globalisation, and difficulties in implementing culturally diverse practice all imply the presence of a boundary line between the dominant culture and other cultures: alongside the strong bicultural orientation of *Te Whāriki*, they create a monocultural or bicultural childhood within a multicultural context. It is certainly the case in Aotearoa

New Zealand that 'certain cultural knowledge can become marginalised and misrepresented by more privileged discourses' (Locke, 2010, p. 89).

The question which we must answer in order to find a satisfactory way to handle the issues of multicultural childhood is this: How are we to imagine Aotearoa New Zealand participating in a global system in which all children have full and equal rights to have their cultures, and there is genuine appreciation and respect of others? Sarsona et al. (2008) stated that we need 'a healthy, evolving community that immerses children in the richness of their heritage culture as the basis for preparing them to participate successfully in the educational, social, and economic opportunities offered by a modern, global society' (p. 15). This, at best, provides the answer to this question.

In a multicultural childhood, the meaning of the term 'culture' needs to change. A multicultural childhood does not resemble the childhood of any particular culture. All children of all cultures need to be given the opportunity to actively interact and relate in equal and valued ways. This idea suggests that there need to be relational rather than linear contacts between cultures.

In this chapter, I have argued that a multicultural childhood for all Aotearoa New Zealand children will enable them to experience different cultures instead of simply being exposed to them, so that they can become full members of the global community with full rights and responsibilities. Viewed simply from the demographic condition of the country, we can say that it is no longer appropriate to think of Aotearoa New Zealand as a country in which minority cultures are an unimportant and insignificant characteristic. More importantly, given that the multicultural trend is going to continue in this global era, thinking about multicultural childhood is essentially 'forward looking' and serves an important purpose for preparing children for the future.

My interest here is also in the ideas that might be used to assist the educational practice of early childhood professionals in this country. An effective way to prepare Aotearoa New Zealand children for the future is to match responsive educational pedagogy to the cultures that are available in Aotearoa New Zealand children's lives (Brown, 2010). In Aotearoa New Zealand, education for young children is correctly aligned with a bicultural orientation; in addition, I argue, Aotearoa New Zealand's culturally diverse society justifies similar work on multicultural education.

CHAPTER 10

Children and young people's participation in family law decision-making

Nicola Taylor & Megan Gollop

Children's participation in decision-making processes following their parents' separation has been an under-researched issue internationally (Taylor, 2006). However, ascertaining children's views and providing opportunities for their direct engagement with lawyers and judges is increasingly of interest within the courts of many common and civil law jurisdictions (Taylor, Fitzgerald, Morag, Bajpai & Graham, 2012). The significant body of research and commentary highlighting the benefits of children's participation (Lansdown, 2010; Parkinson & Cashmore, 2008; Percy-Smith & Thomas, 2010; Smith, 2002; Tisdall, Bray, Marshall & Cleland, 2004), together with the United Nations Convention on the Rights of the Child (UNCRC) and theoretical developments in the field of Childhood Studies, has helped to transform the way children contribute to the resolution of family law disputes between parents over post-separation care arrangements (Taylor, 2005, 2006). Aotearoa New Zealand has been particularly innovative in encouraging children's participation in Family Court proceedings and is at the forefront of developments in the Western world in this regard. This chapter outlines the socio-legal research programme ascertaining children's perspectives undertaken at the Children's Issues Centre[1] since 1996 and traces its influence on legal policy and professional practice within the New Zealand Family Court. The world-leading provisions of the Care of Children Act 2004, regarding children's views and the role of lawyers appointed to represent children, are considered within the context of private law proceedings following parental separation and divorce.

---

1 Now known as the University of Otago Centre for Research on Children and Families.

Influences on child participation in family law proceedings

No longer just objects of the law, children are increasingly considered as subjects in the determination of decisions made on their behalf. While children's participation rights are therefore generally understood as an important principle of contemporary family law decision-making, the debate continues over the mechanisms by which this is best achieved. Two key influences at the heart of efforts to develop more child-inclusive styles of practice within the legal system are the UNCRC and the findings from the child-centred research undertaken by Childhood Studies scholars.

The UNCRC

Children's right to express their views is specifically emphasised in Article 12 of the UNCRC. Article 13, freedom of expression, also manifests children's participation rights through the right of the child to seek, receive and impart information. Article 9(2), which relates to children separated from their parents, provides that 'all interested parties shall be given an opportunity to participate in the proceedings and make their views known' – a provision that Melton (2006) has suggested must surely include children themselves caught up in legal proceedings over their post-separation care. While the term 'right to participate' does not appear in Article 12, there is direct reference to it in the General Comment on Article 12 by the UNCRC (2009). This recognises the obligation to implement the right of participation in the context of divorce proceedings: 'all legislation on separation and divorce has to include the right of the child to be heard by decision makers and in mediation processes' (para 52).

Participation is also enunciated as one of the four General Principles for interpreting all other provisions within the Convention (UNICEF, undated). This reflects the UNCRC's intention to place special emphasis on a child's participation rights so they might 'guide the way each individual right is ensured and respected; a criterion to assess progress in the implementation process of children's rights; and an additional dimension to the universally recognized freedom of expression, implying the right of the child to be heard and to have his or her views or opinions taken into account' (UNICEF, 2008, p. 1). Participation is thus conceptualised within the Convention as 'a procedural right through which children can act to protect and promote the realisation of other rights' (Lansdown, 2005, p. 17). Furthermore, governments who have ratified the Convention (as Aotearoa New Zealand did in 1993) have a responsibility, under Article 4, to take all available measures to ensure children's rights are respected, protected and fulfilled.

Childhood Studies

Research asking children directly about their experiences of family transitions, including separation and divorce, has flourished over the past two decades and significantly challenged our thinking about children and childhood (Cashmore & Parkinson, 2008; Smart, Neale & Wade, 2001; Taylor, 2005, 2006). Childhood Studies explores the social relations and practices, cultural contexts and political processes through which childhood is constructed and regulated (Honig, 2009; James, 2010; Monk, 2009; Smith, 2002). Its three key features include 1) the many ways in which childhood is socially constructed and culturally situated; 2) recognition of children's status, agency and rights as a starting point for research, policy and practice; and 3) being unable to understand childhood without consideration of the influence of intergenerational relationships (Woodhead, 2009). This conceptual framework, and the research it has generated, emphasises children's own accounts and perspectives, the aim of which has been to 'do research *with* children rather than *on* or *about* them and in the process, to give their views legitimacy' (Smart, Neale & Wade, 2001, p. 14).

This contemporary approach to the theorisation of childhood initiated a fundamental rethink within the legal system as children came to be regarded as social actors with their own views and strategies, rather than passive and uninformed victims of family change and parental dispute (Fitzgerald, 2009; Henaghan, 2012; Taylor, 2006). Family law became keenly aware that gaining a deeper understanding of children's perspectives on their post-separation lives, and what was important to them, would likely lead to better-informed decision-making *and* assist the child to benefit from feeling heard and to more readily understand/accept the outcome.[2] The law, of course, plays an important role in constructing and legitimating new understandings, assumptions and practices concerning children. It is not simply a set of rules, but a 'shifting cultural and social text' (Monk, 2009, p. 178) that has long privileged children's protection and provision rights and has, more recently, also begun to embrace and respect their participation rights.

The statutory context in Aotearoa New Zealand

The Family Court was introduced in Aotearoa New Zealand in 1981 and provides a range of dispute resolution processes including counselling, mediation and defended hearings for parents in dispute over their children's

---

[2] Not all children want to express their views in family law proceedings and this must be respected. Most children who do express their views do not want to decide the outcome (as they appreciate this responsibility rests with the parents or ultimately the judge), but they do want to have their say and to know that this has been taken into account.

care (Boshier, Taylor & Seymour, 2011). Most private family law disputes are resolved by the parents themselves reaching agreement or through legal negotiation, counselling or mediation. Only 6% of applications to the Family Court are determined by a judge, and they are assisted in this task through the appointment of lawyers to represent children and the availability of specialist psychological, social work, medical and cultural reports.

The Guardianship Act 1968 was the key statute setting out the legal provisions governing the resolution of disputes between parents until 1 July 2005. It was thus this law that was in effect during the period of time we were conducting many of our studies on children's perspectives on socio-legal issues (see next section). Under section 23 (2) of the Guardianship Act the Family Court was required to ascertain the wishes of the child if the child was able to express them. These wishes were to be taken into account to such extent as the Court thought fit, 'having regard to the age and maturity of the child'. In practice this meant that young children, particularly those under the age of 10, could have their wishes ignored purely on the basis that they were not of sufficient age and maturity (Robinson & Henaghan, 2011). Counsel for the child was often appointed in cases likely to proceed to a hearing,[3] but these lawyers were not required to meet with the child and their hybrid role encompassed advocating both the child's wishes and best interests – thus fuelling the possibility of tension or conflict arising in their representation of the child when these clashed. During this era it was also most uncommon for a judge to talk with a child whose parents were unable to agree on the post-separation care arrangements for their child.

However, the influence of the UNCRC and the growing body of research and theory on children's participation (Gollop, Taylor & Smith, 2000; Smith, Taylor & Gollop, 2000; Smith, Taylor & Tapp, 2003; Taylor, 1998, 2005; Taylor, Tapp & Henaghan, 2007), has led to children's views being accorded much greater prominence when the Care of Children Act 2004 replaced the Guardianship Act on 1 July 2005 (Boshier, 2005). We discuss the contribution of our socio-legal research to this reform in the next two sections and then review the amendments to the law and the professional practices of lawyers for the child and Family Court judges in the penultimate section of this chapter.

Socio-legal research programme

Over the past 16 years the authors' programme of socio-legal research has encompassed eight studies addressing children and young people's perspectives

---

3 Renamed as Lawyer for the child in the Care of Children Act 2004.

(and at times, also those of their parents/caregivers and professionals including lawyers, judges, psychologists, social workers, counsellors and social service agency staff). These studies occurred in such sensitive family contexts as separation and divorce, care and protection, out-of-home care, supervised contact and relocation. They specifically examined:

- Access and post-separation issues – 1996–1997 (Gollop et al., 2000; Smith et al., 1997);
- Children in kinship and foster care – 1997 (Smith, Gollop & Taylor, 2000; Smith, Gollop, Taylor & Atwool, 1999a, 1999b);
- Access arrangements following parental separation – 1997–1998 (Gollop, Smith & Taylor, 2000; Smith & Gollop, 2001a, 2001b);
- The role of Counsel for the Child – 1998 (Taylor, Gollop & Smith, 2000; Taylor, Gollop, Smith & Tapp, 1999);
- Children's rights in New Zealand family law judgments – 1999 (Taylor et al., 2000);
- Dispute resolution in the Family Court – 2000-2003 (Taylor, 2005, 2006);
- Supervised contact centres – 2005 (Gollop & Taylor, 2005);
- Relocation following parental separation – 2007–2009 (Gollop & Taylor, 2012; Taylor, Gollop & Henaghan, 2010a, 2010b).

This research programme was designed to explore the experiences of children and young people using a children's rights approach, primarily based on Articles 3, 9, 12 and 13 of the UNCRC, and the theoretical framework offered by Childhood Studies that constructs children as active, competent participants rather than the passive recipients of family transitions and family law processes. The studies have mainly been qualitative in nature, ascertaining children and young people's perspectives through the use of open-ended, semi-structured interviews.

The major emphasis of this research has been to highlight the visibility and voices of children and young people, to identify the experiences and challenges they face during family law disputes between their parents over their care, and to document the factors that help them cope during these difficult family times. Much of the research in the parental separation/divorce field focuses on the risks to children and the negative impact of family transitions on their lives. Our research has taken a more strengths-based approach to identify factors that promote the rights, well-being, welfare and best interests of children. The findings have been used to promote more child-friendly and child-inclusive practices and policies to support children and parents facing family transitions.

Three of our studies most directly related to children's and young people's voices and participation in family law disputes following their parents' separation/divorce. We briefly outline each study and then draw on their findings to present key themes that emerged across all three studies.

1. Access arrangements following parental separation

The focus of this study was on the perspectives of 107 children and young people, from 73 families who had experienced parental separation, about the contact they had with the parent they did not live with.

2. The role of Counsel for the Child – perspectives of children, young people and their lawyers

This research investigated children's perceptions of the role of Counsel for the child, particularly their understanding and experience of their contact with the lawyer appointed to represent them in care and protection and guardianship issues. Twenty children and 12 lawyers were interviewed in two Family Court districts.

3. Relocation after parental separation: The welfare and best interests of children

This three-year study focused on ascertaining the experiences of 114 parents and 44 children and young people (from 100 families across Aotearoa New Zealand) who had experienced a relocation dispute. Such disputes arise when a separated parent wishes to relocate within Aotearoa New Zealand or internationally with their children, and the other parent objects to this move (usually on the basis that the proposed relocation will detrimentally affect the contact or shared care arrangements already in place).

Key themes across the three studies

We now turn to explore some of the key themes that have emerged across the three studies and influenced family law policy and practice. These relate to consultation with children and young people within their family, their knowledge and understanding of family and legal processes, and their experiences with family law professionals.

Consultation within the family

One of the strongest themes to emerge from our research was children's desire to have their views heard, both within their family and within the court. When the children in our study on access arrangements were asked what advice they would give to parents who were separating, the most common response (mentioned by half of the children and young people) related to the importance of consulting children. This included listening to children, asking children for their views and letting them have a say, giving children a choice and respecting those choices. The young people thought that parents should not assume that they knew what their children were thinking or feeling. For example:

> Talk to your kids definitely and let them have an input and let them have a say and regard them around the matters. I know that it's between the two of them but you've got to have your kids in mind here. You can't just push them aside cos the kids are the ones that get hurt a lot. (Petra, 17, Access study)[4]

> Parents, listen to your kids. Just make sure that you're listening to them and not having any preconceptions about what you think they want and make sure you tell them what's going on. (Kayla, 16, Access study)

> I don't really like being told what to do. I like being given the option type thing … As long as kids get a good say in what happens and it's taken into account, they should be quite happy. Try and take into account the kids' views because the kids know what they want more than the parents do, because they're them. (Grant, 15, Access study)

> Listen to your kids … instead of having to go through all the Courts and spend all their money on lawyers. (Louise, 13, Relocation study)

The children varied in how much they were consulted and their roles in decisions about their living arrangements and their contact with the parent(s) they did not live with. Generally, those who were given a say valued and appreciated this opportunity, whereas those who had limited input into decisions that affected them, yet wanted to, were the most dissatisfied with their arrangements. This was particularly so when children were forced to have contact with a parent they did not want to spend time with or, conversely, a parent reduced or ceased contact altogether when the children wanted to have a meaningful relationship with their non-resident parent. Some children expressed a desire to change how much they saw of their contact parent, but had little ability to achieve this:

> Like I wish we could say that I'm sick or something and say I really don't feel like going and like do a sickie on the phone. (Melissa, 10, Access study)

> Well, to be honest, I kind of think Mum's kind of like the big meanie. She arranges that I can only see my Dad for so and so. Mum kind of [is] the one who pulls the strings which I hate … She's kind of in control about how much [contact] I get I think … I don't really like it how adults always control the world, what's going to happen. (Julian, 10, Access study)

---

4 All names used are pseudonyms.

Children who were unhappy about their contact arrangements sometimes took matters into their own hands, particularly as they grew older:

> When I was little I was just sort of told, 'Oh, you're going to see your Dad on Sunday' and now I can just say, 'I'm not going to come this Sunday, cos I've got other things to do'. *(Tamara, 16, Access study)*

Children do not necessarily want to be making the decision about who they live with, even though they value being informed and consulted about their family situation. Many children in our research spoke about how it would be 'too hard' or 'too messy' to have to choose between their parents. This was particularly problematic if they felt pressured by one or both parents to make a choice about who to live with:

> I just said, I don't care, I just want to be with one of my parents ... [if you say I want to go with Dad] that would be mean to Mum, or I wanna go to Mum, and that'd be mean to Dad. And, like, I wanted to be with both of them. (Chloe, 11, Relocation study)

> [Dad] sort of put it on me quite harsh whether I wanted to live with him, and I sort of didn't really know. Just sort of said, yes, and then sort of changed my mind in the end ... I'd probably have preferred he just didn't bother asking really. (Carl, 16, Access study)

> One of them wanted me to say one thing and the other one wanted me to say the other thing, so I shut up and just didn't say anything ... Mum moaned about some things. Dad moaned about some things. 'Oh, why did you say that?' Then it would all come back on me. (Dean, 13, Access study)

Other children were very accepting of not being consulted or asked their views about their living situation. Sometimes the lack of consultation was due to the unavailability of alternative options.

Children's knowledge and understanding

Another strong theme to emerge from our research was the variation in children's knowledge and understanding about their family situations, the associated family law issues and the professionals who came to be involved in their lives. Children need the relevant information in order for them to be able to formulate and express their views. Furthermore, even if they cannot participate in decision-making processes, they are still entitled to know why and how the outcome was decided. Children's understanding may also develop over time and so ongoing age-appropriate discussion is important. Sometimes children can unfortunately reach inaccurate and upsetting understandings of their family situation if their parents do not discuss matters with them:

> Well, I think some kids, like their parents won't tell them why they're separating and that sort of thing and they're like, 'My father ... he doesn't love me any more.' I think that would be hard. I think they're better to tell that they're separating, but not for a trial, because I never actually got over that. I was like waiting ... when's he going to come back. (Jodie, 15, Access study)

> Make sure they know what's going on or else it gets really confusing for a kid. And so if they know what's going on, then they can feel like they've at least got some control over the situation. (Kayla, 16, Access study)

Role of professionals

Many of the children involved in our research had had contact with various professionals, for example, lawyer for the child, psychologists and judges. Children were often confused about the roles of the different professionals they encountered. They could remember talking with someone, but were not sure who or what their role was. Some children who had multiple professionals involved in their lives found the experience difficult and intrusive: 'I wanted to live a normal life instead of continually going to see a lawyer and a psychiatrist and a psychologist and a social worker ... All I wanted [was] a normal life'. (Nina, 13, Relocation study)

Children who had a lawyer appointed to represent them were clearer in their understanding of this professional's role. They understood that their lawyer would speak on their behalf and stand up for them. Some children believed that having an adult presenting their views gave these more weight:

> They're sort of like me in court. They're just like me, except I'm not there. They're stand-ins ... I'd say he had made a difference. It's sort of opened up a whole new thing for the Judge ... There was Dad's views and Mum's views, but you need a third party to bring the Judge's eyes round to the side ... He needs a third party in the middle to be me. (Craig, 13, Counsel for the Child study)

> Basically, just to speak on behalf of you ... You need someone that's kind of adultish, kind of older to put it across. (Kate, 14, Counsel for the Child study)

> Like the thing that she really helps us with is usually I don't have the guts to say things to others, to stand up for myself and say what I would really like. (Justine, 14, Counsel for the Child study)

Children have emphasised the importance of professionals establishing positive relationships with them. For example, one child described his lawyer as being 'just like a really good friend.' Children liked lawyers who were friendly, trustworthy, respectful and child-centred:

> She's always really kind and listens really hard and she's really good at what she does. We get everything out and we can trust her so it makes it easier ... She's really good at her job I reckon cos she like explains it all. Like some people say it briefly, but she sits us down and tells us about it really slowly and goes over it so we know what's going on. (Michelle, 10, Counsel for the Child study)

> It feels like he understands you when he's talking to you and he doesn't hurry you into answering. (Chloe, 11, Relocation study)

Those children who spoke negatively about their lawyer often described having a poor or minimal relationship with them. They did not like talking with strangers about family matters, did not like or trust their lawyer, or found the encounter 'boring':

> It's sad you have to speak to a stranger. I don't like talking about Mum and Dad breaking up to a stranger. (Connor, 11, Relocation study)

> He was a stinker! I didn't like him cos I just don't trust him. (Charlie, 8, Relocation study)

> I don't think she understood that my future was resting on her shoulders, and I don't think she took the time to understand just what she was doing ... How important her role is and I don't think she took it seriously ... She's getting paid to do what she's doing and she wasn't taking responsibility for it, cos she had a lot of power over what would happen to me and with that power comes great responsibility. I don't think she was being responsible enough with what she was doing. (Nina, 13, Relocation study)

Children's concerns

Some of the children in our studies raised concerns about their engagement with professionals, such as feeling pressured, parental alignment, breaches of confidentiality, having their views misrepresented, or not being informed of, or understanding, the court's decision:

> They were pretty tough questions. Like what parent do you like best? What parent do you want to live with? I didn't answer any of them. I said 'Dunno'. I got pretty annoyed. I think they were just lining up, who can crack the code, who can make me say 'I want to live at that house.' (Adam, 11, Relocation study)

> [The lawyer] seemed a bit one-sided. She sort of said it was our fault that we didn't want to see him and that we should want to see him because he was our

father. We said that we didn't really want to see him and she said, 'Oh, well, I suppose that's your opinion, but maybe you should go and see him and see what it's like.' [I] sort of thought that she shouldn't butt in. (Daniel, 15, Counsel for the Child study)

She didn't say to the Courts what we wanted. She didn't tell them. She decided for us. She said the total opposite thing I wanted to do. I said I didn't want to go see my Dad and she said to the Court she does want to see her Dad. (Charlotte, 10, Relocation study)

They just got things muddled up. Like the way that I worded it and they wrote it a different way. Sort of the real sort of high way that I can't understand and it sounded different. It meant the opposite thing to what I meant. (Dean, 13, Counsel for the Child study)

The lawyer didn't tell me what was decided or anything – I think that they could do that ... Even if he just told me what was decided in court. (Julie, 9, Counsel for the Child study)

I didn't quite get what she was talking about ... Well, she could have come and talked to us more often and seen us. And she could have told us what was going on, because I never knew what was going on. (Rebecca, 13, Counsel for the Child study)

Reform of the law

Many of the issues raised by the children participating in our studies were subsequently addressed when the Care of Children Act 2004 took effect on 1 July 2005. This significantly modernised the law governing guardianship, day-to-day care (formerly 'custody') and contact (formerly 'access') and placed much greater emphasis on respecting children's right to participate. Section 6 considerably widened the requirement for the Family Court to provide reasonable opportunities for children to express their views and for these views to be taken into account by the court: 'In proceedings involving the guardianship of, or the role of providing day-to-day care for, or contact with, a child; ... a child must be given reasonable opportunities to express views on matters affecting the child; and any views the child expresses (either directly or through a representative) must be taken into account' (section 6, Care of Children Act 2004).

This new world-leading statutory provision dispensed with the traditional 'age and maturity' criteria in section 23 (2) of the Guardianship Act 1968, changed 'wishes' to the broader concept of 'views', and now requires the Court to take any of the child's expressed views into account regardless of the age of the child. However, the child's views are not determinative, but rather contribute to the weight of evidence considered by the judge. The Principal Family Court Judge considered that the Care of Children Act 2004 'represents an unmistakeable shift towards the recognition of greater rights for children and allows for their greater input into decision-making processes' (Boshier, 2009, p. 1).

Section 7 of the Act provides for the appointment of a Lawyer for the Child in private law proceedings. When appointed, that lawyer must meet with the child unless there are exceptional circumstances (section 7(3)). The lawyer's primary role now is to provide independent representation and advice to the child. He or she has a duty to put before the Court the views of the child (usually via a written report) and can call and cross-examine the parties and any witnesses. Following the Court decision, the lawyer must explain the effect of any parenting order to the child in a way that the child can understand (section 55(4)). The child also has a right of appeal (section 143(3)). It is pleasing that these provisions, and the Practice Notes issued by the Principal Family Court Judge, have taken account of many of the issues raised by the children we interviewed in our various studies.

Since the Care of Children Act took effect, judicial interviews with children have become increasingly more common (Henaghan, 2012; Mill, 2008; Robinson & Henaghan, 2011) and 'an invaluable part' of the judge's 'toolbox' (Boshier, 2009, p. 6). Some judges engage in a 'meet and greet' role with the child, while most others use the opportunity to directly hear the child's views and to better understand the child as a person. The child's lawyer will usually also be present. Judges have received skills-based training in child interviewing techniques and report very positively about their experiences of meeting with children (Boshier, 2009; Mill, 2008; Robinson & Henaghan, 2011).

Despite Aotearoa New Zealand's progressive statutory provisions, the fact that old judicial habits linger was confirmed in a recent analysis of 120 cases (involving 203 children) decided in the Family Court from 2005 to 2010 (Robinson & Henaghan, 2011). A lawyer for the child was appointed in 99% of the cases, and a judicial interview occurred in 33% of the cases. However, Robinson and Henaghan (2011) discovered that age still counts for children – it was the children aged 11 or older, who had strongly and consistently held views, whose views were most likely to be followed. Young children under seven years old, and any child considered to have been influenced, coached or aligned, tended to have their views ignored. In 33% of the cases the judge still mistakenly referred to the child's 'wishes' (not 'views') and just over a third (39%) of the 203 children had their views followed or partly followed. Robinson and Henaghan (2011) concluded that their study demonstrated 'there has not been a significant shift in how judges deal with children's views since the Guardianship Act 1968, despite the significant legislative changes, thus indicating judges have not internalised the rationale behind the legislative change to s 6' (p. 46).

Children's participation in Alternative Dispute Resolution (ADR) processes still remains relatively uncommon in Aotearoa New Zealand, despite its more widespread use overseas (McIntosh, Long & Wells, 2009). Yet child-inclusive ADR processes have the potential to benefit so many more children whose parents are in dispute over their post-separation care. Just one child-inclusive mediation model has been empirically piloted here (Goldson, 2006). However, consequential amendments to the Care of Children Act 2004, as a result of the 2008 passage of the Family Court Matters Bill, do now allow for the inclusion of children in counselling and mediation (Goldson & Taylor, 2009). Regrettably, their implementation has been stalled due to the lack of resourcing during the economic recession. The current reform of the Family Court, however, has foreshadowed interest in child-inclusive and family-facilitated dispute resolution processes as a means of better assisting parents to reach agreement without the need for litigation over their children.

Conclusion

The findings from our programme of socio-legal research undertaken since 1996 have clearly demonstrated children's ability to formulate and express their views about sensitive family matters. This can be even further enhanced when children's knowledge and understanding is scaffolded by family members and court professionals. The insights from our research have influenced some of the most significant reforms to family law, policy and professional practice that Aotearoa New Zealand has witnessed over the past decade. The applied nature of our studies, and the government consultations to which we have contributed, have helped to shape the progressive nature of those provisions in the Care of Children Act 2004 relating to the ascertainment of children's views and the role of the lawyer for the child. Our research on children and young people's perspectives on family transitions, and on their parents' associated legal proceedings, has also influenced the increasingly common use of judicial interviews and the more child-inclusive styles of practice opening up in the ADR (counselling and mediation) field.

In the Aotearoa New Zealand context, Childhood Studies and the UNCRC have come to intersect with family law developments in ways that are far more respectful and inclusive of children. The challenge now is to ensure that the gap between legislative commitment and opportunities for children to express their views *and* to have these taken seriously is further closed so that children are not just 'heard', but are also 'listened to' within the Family Court (Robinson & Henaghan, 2011; Taylor et al., 2012): 'Entitlement to participation has to be embedded in legislation, policy and practice as the right of every child' (Lansdown, 2010, p. 21). Aotearoa New Zealand has travelled a considerable way down this path – further than many other jurisdictions – yet the complexity of translating children's participation rights into practice, even within a legislative context that allows for it, remains challenging. While it is pleasing that our socio-legal research programme has contributed to the reforms thus far, we are very mindful of the need to continue refining child-participatory practices within the Family Court and to ensure these are appropriately evaluated.

CHAPTER 11

The needs of adopted and fostered children

Anita Gibbs

To begin with a short story ...

Once upon a time, three little children, Mary (aged 9), Morris (aged 5) and Mini (aged 2½), lived with two lovely parents, Doreen and Dirk (both in their 40s), in a nice part of a nice city. Dirk ran his own decorating business and Doreen was a part-time kindergarten teacher. Mary was born to Doreen and Dirk, and they decided to adopt after several years of unsuccessful and distressing fertility treatments. After a rigorous assessment by social workers and police, and medical checks, Doreen and Dirk were approved to adopt, and after a relatively short wait of six months they were chosen by Morris's birth mother to become parents to Morris. They received Morris into their home when he was three months old. Initially, all went well with Morris; but over time it became apparent that there were some delays in his speech and hearing abilities. He had input from speech therapists when he was three and several related minor operations to remove tonsils and add grommets, which helped a little. Morris and his family had little contact with Morris's birth mum but Doreen and Dirk sent photos and letters two to three times a year, which kept her informed of his progress. His birth mum did not reciprocate. Shortly before Morris started 'all day' kindergarten Doreen and Dirk felt they could parent another child but this time they decided that long-term fostering might be a better option for them. They attended a training course and underwent further assessment and were approved to foster. Mini arrived when she was 18 months old after a difficult start in life involving severe neglect at the hands of her birth parents. Doreen and Dirk gained shared custody of Mini with Child, Youth and Family and planned to apply to the courts to gain a Parenting Order, which would allow them to offer Mini a 'home for life' without the need for shared custody. Mini came with only the clothes she wore, and limited financial support was given to help the family get the essentials for her. Mini had supervised contact with her birth father once a month. Mini showed signs of distress after each contact visit but her foster parents felt unable to prevent this because the contact was court ordered. Mini's birth mother died of a drug overdose shortly after Mini was removed from her care. Doreen and Dirk loved their family very much and were doing their best to provide love and security for all of their children.

You have just read a not untypical story of the life of some Aotearoa New Zealand families. In this chapter, I aim to consider the needs of families such as these and children like Mary, Morris and Mini, and how they might be better supported, within the varying contexts that operate around adoption and long-term fostering. The chapter will briefly overview the development of adoption and fostering, including comment on the trends in the number of children either adopted or fostered over time. It will go on to discuss the main legal aspects and key practice frameworks that have influenced how fostering and adoption practices are undertaken in the varying communities of Aotearoa New Zealand. It will then consider social work practice with regard to adoption and fostering, including how children are 'selected' for either fostering or adoption; how they are prepared and supported in their alternative families; and how 'would-be parents' are selected, prepared, and supported. We will then focus on the needs of adopted and fostered children, as well as on how these are met within their 'new' families and through other avenues of support. The chapter will end with some reflections on the future support of fostered and adopted children in Aotearoa New Zealand. In writing this chapter I have drawn on extensive literature, and informal and focused conversations with networks of adoptive and foster parents in Aotearoa New Zealand and Britain.

Historical, legal and practice perspectives

In Aotearoa New Zealand adoption is rare and it is more likely that children, who cannot be cared for by birth parents, will be looked after by kin or foster carers. By *adoption* I mean the full legal transfer of parental rights and responsibilities, including the child receiving a new name and new birth certificate (Shannon, 2001). By *long-term fostering* I mean that children are looked after on a day-to-day basis, often permanently, by relatives or non-relatives, when they are no longer able to be cared for by their birth parents, and often because they have been abused or neglected by people who are caring for them, including their birth parents (Ludbrook, 1990).

In 2009–10 there were 199 adoptions recorded in Aotearoa New Zealand (Child, Youth and Family, 2010): 136 of these were by carers with a prior connection to the children, and 63 were by non-relatives, known as 'stranger-based' adoptions. The stranger-based adoptions involved around 40 Aotearoa New Zealand born infant adoptions and about 20 intercountry adoptions (known as ICAs). The countries from which most current intercountry adoptions originate are Russia, China, Lithuania, Thailand and India. Annually, about 300 other ICAs occur: these are relative-based with children coming from Samoa and other Pacific nations to join kin in Aotearoa New Zealand (Selman, personal communication, 2010).

Historically, Aotearoa New Zealand's adoption rates have been much higher. While there has been somewhat inaccurate statistical information available, estimates are such that between 1955 and 1974 adoption numbers averaged around 2800 per annum (Else, 1991). After that, the figures drop off. The *New Zealand official yearbook* recorded adoptions as being around 744 in 2000 to 640 in 2008 (*New Zealand official yearbook*, 2010). Goldson (2003), however, recorded adoptions in 2000 to 2001 as being around the 382 mark, which differs from the yearbook figures. Also, the Hague Convention on Private International Law (HCCH, 2011) receive data on intercountry and domestic adoptions specifically from Aotearoa New Zealand government departments, and they showed that in 2008 adoptions in Aotearoa New Zealand totalled 271, compared to the yearbook figure of 640 for the same year (*New Zealand official yearbook*, 2010). The yearbook included the Pacific nation kin but the HCCH did not. Accurate data on adoptions is difficult to obtain and differs according to the publication, and is, therefore, extremely difficult to interpret; and the picture for long-term fostering is even more obscured. What can be said with confidence is that adoptions have decreased dramatically since the 1970s and ICAs occur as often as do domestic Aotearoa New Zealand adoptions for stranger-based adoptions.

Aotearoa New Zealand's legal system around adoption has a long history. Aotearoa New Zealand was the first country in the British Empire in 1881 to legalise adoption (Goldson, 2003; Ludbrook, 1990). Pre-1881 adoption was informal and unenforceable in court, rather like much kin care today. Ironically, Aotearoa New Zealand now lags behind most OECD countries, relying on the outdated and discriminatory Adoption Act 1955 (Ludbrook, 1990; Walker, 2001). The 1950s to late 1970s saw adoption as closed, secretive and final, with little opportunity for birth parents and birth children who had been adopted to stay in touch (Else, 1991). With the introduction of the Adult Information Act 1985, adult adoptees and their birth parents could trace each other. By the

1980s, European Aotearoa New Zealand society was more favourable to the idea that it was in many children's interests to know about their past and be able to have ongoing relationships with their birth relatives.

Fostering has always occurred in some form in Aotearoa New Zealand and while trends in figures are not available, there have been notable periods. For example, pre-1881 all out-of-birth-family care was fostering in nature, albeit informal and, for many children, permanent. During the late 1940s to 1954, 549 child migrants arrived from the UK to pre-arranged foster homes (Select Committee on Health Third Report, 1998). More recently, with legislation like the Children and Young Person's Act 1989 and the Care of Children Act 2004, fostering arrangements have enabled more formal and permanent arrangements for foster children. According to the latest data from Child, Youth and Family (2010) for the year 2009–10, there were 5500 children in the custody of Child, Youth and Family, with about 1000 of these living in group homes or group-based residences; about 1000 living with their parents or independently but supported by Child, Youth and Family; and around 3300 children living with extended kin or foster carers. Of this latter group, 1730 were Māori and 1540 non-Māori, and of the same group, around 1500 were living with non-kin foster families. In addition, in the two years ending in 2010, 389 children who were being fostered long-term were given a 'home for life', which meant they were no longer in the care of the state but had permanent homes with guardianship and custody, or a parenting order, granted to the new carers, whether kin or non-kin (Child, Youth and Family, 2010).

Māori had their own customary system of adoption known as Maatua Whangai ('feeding parent') long before Europeans arrived in Aotearoa New Zealand (Shannon, 2001; Walker, 2001). This system was more akin to fostering, because children were cared for by members of the whānau (family), hāpu (subtribe) and iwi (tribe), with openness about birth origins and connections to birth family being vital. With the advent of various adoption-related legislation in the twentieth century, and especially the 1955 Act, which promoted an era of closed and legally finalised adoptions, many Māori children lost their family roots and whākapapa (ancestry) ties (Else, 1991; Goldson, 2003; Walker, 2001). It was not until the mid-1980s that Māori practices were recognised again alongside European/Pākehā practices (Walker, 2001). In the year 2009–10, there were 1730 Māori children living with extended kin or foster carers (Child, Youth and Family, 2010). Few Māori are adopted at all.

The few adoptions and much larger numbers of children in foster or kin care reflect policy at all levels – government, organisational and familial policy – that it is in the best interests for a child to remain with, or in close contact with, their birth families, and that care outside of this is for their protection and well-being. Aotearoa New Zealand's current framework on adoption to strangers is focused on baby-only adoption at the domestic level and ensuring that Hague Convention procedures are followed to prevent abuse of children coming to Aotearoa New Zealand through ICAs (Gibbs, 2011). The main focus of Aotearoa New Zealand's alternative care arrangements is on protecting vulnerable children by using short-term and long-term foster carers to take care of children who cannot live with birth relatives, although extended family kin-based care is used more often than stranger-based foster care (Frengley, 2007). Connolly has discussed the Aotearoa New Zealand approach to caring for vulnerable and troubled children as having both a child protection orientation and a family support orientation, evidenced in the way family group conferences promote safety and wider family inclusion (Connolly, 2004). More recently, the new 'home for life' scheme promoted by Child, Youth and Family is attempting both to protect children at risk for their duration of childhood, and to provide intermediate fostering support services to the families who offer children a home for life (Child, Youth and Family, 2010).

Selection, preparation and training

Adoptive and foster parents undergo rigorous selection and training procedures in Aotearoa New Zealand before they can be approved as adoptive or foster parents. Doreen and Dirk, in the story above, would have visited their local Child, Youth and Family office and filled in an application form expressing an interest in adoption, and then attended two to three days of adoption-related training (Parent Education Courses, as they are known: see Goldson, 2003). After that, they would have experienced many interviews with social workers, including having police and medical checks, and would have provided references. Following these, the social worker would have written a report, and Doreen and Dirk, being found suitable, would have been approved to adopt. If they had chosen to adopt from overseas, they would have completed one extra day of training focused on adopting from overseas. They would have completed their parent education with other prospective adoptive parents. As part of their training they would have met families who had been formed through adoption. On their courses they would have learnt about the needs of adoptive babies and older children, the adoption process in Aotearoa New Zealand and some overseas countries, open adoption and how to keep in contact, preparing a portfolio for birth parents to view, preparing a home study to send overseas, dealing with loss for the child, birth parents and adoptive parents, and parenting issues generally. When Doreen and Dirk decided to become foster parents they may have completed another two to three days of training or similar over a period of evening sessions. The focus of foster training would have been on meeting the needs of foster children and exploring the range of fostering options; answering the question, 'Is fostering for me?'; learning about caregiving rules and procedures; getting support; and keeping in contact with birth families or other birth relatives. More recently, education for adoption or fostering has become merged, so that would-be parents complete two days of generic education, followed by one day of specialist training.

I have spoken to a number of parents who have completed the foster and adoption training programmes over the years, and while most appreciated the input, there were areas which they felt were lacking. These included not enough attention to the legal aspects of alternative care and to the kinds of ongoing parenting issues that families might face once children stayed long-term. Parents who had attended adoption training felt that the social worker's presentation of ICA was particularly negative. This has been confirmed by a recent study of ICA parents in Aotearoa New Zealand (Johnstone & Gibbs, 2012).

As far as the children are concerned, the idea of systematic, rigorous, well-planned adoption or long-term fostering is somewhat of an ideal but not always a reality. For the 40 or so domestic adoptions to non-kin each year, the birth parent(s) choose from a selection of portfolios presented to them by social workers (Goldson, 2003). The interests of the infant may come into it but the birth parent makes the decision with support from social workers and others of importance to them. The process of adoption thereafter is usually comprehensive and systematic, with specific rules and procedures in place for legal assistance, obtaining the Adoption Order, and maintaining contact with birth parents. For ICAs, the process allows some matching of children to parents by a sending country, and then approval of the matches by the New Zealand Central Authority. ICA children may receive some preparation from their caregivers, but usually they come to Aotearoa New Zealand in a state of stress and requiring additional support. Much of this distress is likely to be related to the anxiety of being with new caregivers and language barriers precluding explanation or reassurance about what is happening to them.

When it comes to fostering, protecting and safeguarding children are often the first priorities, which means that some children are removed immediately from the care of their birth parents and placed in emergency short-term foster care while the family situation and needs of the child are assessed (Connolly, 2004). Mini would have come to Dirk and Doreen via this process and, as suggested above, arrived with only the clothes she had on and little else. Doreen and Dirk might have had little or no warning of her imminent arrival as well, so they would have had to quickly get the basics for Mini. Other (older) children, however, may have a better chance of being prepared for long-term foster care, especially if it becomes apparent that a short-term placement will turn into a permanent one and that there is no likelihood of a return to the birth family. Here, a child's social worker and indeed the foster parents can spend time preparing and helping the child express their desires and ensuring that the child is aware (as far as their understanding allows them) of the parenting arrangements being made for them.

The role of the social worker in setting up long-term alternative care options is critical (Connolly, 2004; Dance et al., 2010). At each stage social workers are making key decisions about if, and where, a child should be placed; giving advice to potential adoptive or foster parents; advising them about children available; writing approval or home study reports; writing care and protection reports and presenting information in courts; organising contact; providing or arranging ongoing support for families – the list is endless and the influence of the social worker is substantial. Parents to whom I have spoken are both positive and negative about the varying social work interventions that they have experienced. Some concerns include: not having enough information about the child's birth family situation and potential problems being passed to them; the lack of communication on a regular basis between, and from, the various social workers involved; having supportive workers who allow foster parents to freely discuss the difficulties they are facing without overreacting and removing the child; and taking the long-term perspective – that these kinds of families will require help throughout the duration of their lives together (Johnstone & Gibbs, 2012).

Research on selection and matching (Dance et al., 2010; Sellick, Thoburn & Philpot, 2004; Sinclair, 2005) has suggested that where social workers provide honest and factual information, as well as being reliable, efficient and supportive, then carers will be more satisfied, and problems in the new family may be reduced. Furthermore, in relation to meeting the needs of children likely to be placed in long-term care, it is crucial that social workers act quickly, and are actively seeking out potential long-term carers and giving them the right training and support (Biehal, et al., 2010; Dance et al., 2010).

The needs of children and their families

Adoption and long-term fostering are examples of special and distinct parenting and family expressions, yet at the same time also express normal family rearing practices (Luckock & Hart, 2005). Adopted and fostered children over the age of six months, who have been placed in long-term family arrangements, often present similar profiles and requirements (Biehal et al., 2010; Connolly, 2004; Sinclair, 2005). The similarities include a likely background of poverty, neglect, or abuse unless adopted as a very young baby; challenges presented by being rejected and alienated from birth families; being vulnerable to educational, behavioural and mental health problems as they grow up; attachment issues; and a capacity for remarkable resilience, survival and self-determination (Biehal et al., 2010; Connolly, 2004; Johnstone & Gibbs, 2012; Shannon, 2001). However, foster children are more disadvantaged because they often have had more placements prior to a permanent home, and they have had less security with their sense of belonging to a 'forever family'. These factors – alongside significant behavioural or emotional issues – can then impact upon their carers, who may find it difficult to attach to them and may worry that a child may not be able to stay with them (Selwyn & Quinton, 2004; Sinclair, 2005).

The needs of fostered and adopted children fall into many categories and mirror the normal developmental stages of most children (Scherman, 2010). Hence, there is a need for nurture, love, stability, consistency, their physical and health needs being met, good attachments, positive relationships, support, gaining skills for life, having good educational opportunities, their cultural and spiritual needs being met, identity being acknowledged, and having enough money to get by (Connolly, 2004; Pringle, 1986; Scherman, 2010; Sinclair, 2005). Where these children may differ is that if they have experienced adverse early experiences, the effects of these may last for the entirety of their childhood and beyond. Scherman (2010) identified particular issues that adopted children will face: these include coming to terms with pre-adoption trauma, including living in institutions or temporary care situations; building attachments with new adults several times over; feeling or looking different to birth children or their adoptive parents; searching for answers about their birth families or birth countries; coping with adoption-related loss; managing the adoptive identity; and coping with contact arrangements.

The issue of contact between birth families and adopted or fostered children, and for managing it well so that children are protected from further harm or distress, is crucial (Sinclair, 2005; Biehal et al., 2010). Careful planning is required. There must be good consultation between foster parents, adoptive parents, social workers, other agencies (if the contact is to be supervised), and birth relatives, and flexibility in arrangements (Neil et al., 2011). Contact can be fraught with extreme tension if it involves distress for the child, and if caregivers feel they are not protecting the child, as in the case of Mini in our scenario.

However, it can also be positive and each case must be carefully assessed. In Morris's situation above, the only contact with his birth mother is that the adoptive family sends her letters and photos and she does not reciprocate. At this stage it is too early to conclude as to whether this situation will change and whether, as Morris asks questions and begins to try and communicate his needs as well, the birth mother may respond. Mini's contact, on the other hand, may have to be reviewed by the social workers and courts in the light of her obvious distress after seeing her birth father.

Mary also has needs. She is the biological child of Doreen and Dirk and did not suffer neglect or disadvantage in her early years, but her whole world has been upturned at different times: first when Morris arrived and then when Mini arrived. The energy expended in helping Morris with his health problems and Mini with her emotional issues will affect Mary. Having to get used to sharing her parents' attention and developing relationships with her siblings will present ongoing challenges – some of which are normal childhood experiences, and some of which are less normal, for example coping with Mini's distress around contact with her birth father.

Children who are adopted or fostered often have significant health and educational challenges, which require extra intervention from services (Berridge, 2007; Connolly, 2004). Morris, for example, requires speech therapy, and at school he needs a teacher aide to assist him in class for one hour a day. Many children like Morris and Mini will have had poor early health care, especially children from overseas orphanages but also those from neglected backgrounds in Aotearoa New Zealand. Delays to early health care can result in long-term issues with behavioural problems and educational attainment. The earlier children can be seen by specialists and can get treatment, the better the outcomes. Stable placements are associated with better educational outcomes (Berridge, 2007). Protecting children from harm means less emotional, psychological and neurodevelopmental damage, and doing this early increases a child's chances of better school performance (Berridge, 2007). In Mini's case, she has experienced a range of neglect and trauma, and the fact that she has been in her new 'forever family' since she was 18 months old gives her a much better chance than if she had been three or four years old. However, her parents and social workers and other professionals will still have to be alert to the fact that she may need additional educational support as she develops.

It is crucial that culture, racial identity and background be acknowledged and met (Connolly, 2004; Scherman, 2010). This is especially important where the cultural and/or ethnic group of the child differs from the 'new' family. Sometimes families do not have to do much – for example, they can speak positively about the child's cultural background; they can take the child to visit their birthplace; they can celebrate events associated with a particular country or culture and just generally be open about the child's difference and what this means to them. As Morris and Mini grow up, their desires to connect with their families of origin and to have knowledge about their background may increase; and they may require additional counselling and support over and above what their parents provide, in order to deal with feelings of loss, rejection, and confusion about their identities.

Sinclair (2005) discussed studies of foster children, summarising their wishes as follows: foster children want normality; not to feel different; to belong to a family; to have their origins respected; to be listened to; to have self-determination and control over their lives; and to have opportunity for growth, for example, using their potential, gaining independence, and finding employment. In a recent study of foster care, Selwyn, Saunders and Farmer (2010) added that foster children really want to be able to have friends and that when they do not have stable family lives their chances of friendship are significantly reduced.

Sinclair noted that 'it matters less who meets the child's needs than that somebody does' (Sinclair, 2005, p. 50). Parents and professionals attempt to meet the needs of adopted and fostered children within the available resources and time, and inevitably there are limits to these. It is frustrating for parents when they do everything they can, but still a child seems not to thrive or settle; often they request help from a range of professionals and support groups. Adoptive and foster parents are very adept at networking and accessing resources to help the children in their care but sometimes they cannot get those services when the child most needs them. Delays for services are common: parents often talk of how it takes months and years to get educational, psychological or health assistance for their adopted and fostered children and when they do, they find that professionals, such as paediatricians or teachers, are poorly informed about the needs of adopted or fostered children, and thereby often unable to provide the kind of services the child might benefit from.

Families require different kinds of support and there are many excellent examples of post-adoption and long-term fostering support available – mostly, however, in overseas settings. In the UK, post-adoption support is 'legislated for' and specialist adoption social workers are active in providing a range of supports including finance, access to counselling, help with contact of birth relatives, and organising for adoptive families to meet other adoptive families (Gibbs, 2010). Other services to adopters from independent organisations include individual family support and group-based adoptive parenting programmes, which have been positively evaluated (Gibbs, 2010). In Europe and the USA, there are many well-researched interventions helping families be the best they can be. In Aotearoa New Zealand, we lag behind our international counterparts. Statutory post-adoption support is usually limited to advice about contact, as well as helping adult adoptees gain information about their birth relatives or background (Shannon, 2001). It also involves social workers and families complying with post-adoption reporting requirements to overseas countries. Some post-adoption support is provided by Intercountry Adoption New Zealand (ICANZ), the agency that helps most families achieve ICAs in Aotearoa New Zealand, and by other small NGOs. Most post-adoption support is in the form of adoptive parents supporting each other and their children through coffee mornings, camps and internet chat groups. There can always be more services and Barth and Miller (2000) have outlined an excellent framework of educational, material, and clinical services from which families who have adopted could benefit.

In Aotearoa New Zealand, support for long-term fostering is slightly more extensive than that for adoptive families. The 'home for life' scheme provided by Child, Youth and Family (2010) provides initial financial assistance of $2,500 and advice about gaining the Unsupported Child's Benefit, help with meeting legal costs, and ensuring access to respite care, counselling or other assistance for a period of three years. Social workers or a 'home for life' specialist worker will also assist with ongoing contact between birth relatives and the foster family. In addition to this, Child, Youth and Family provide ongoing support to all foster carers who look after children in the care of CYFs, including visiting children every two months, providing a dedicated telephone service for foster carers to call for assistance, and a foster care allowance. But while appreciative of what is available, foster carers still feel there are gaps, especially when it comes to financial support, too many social workers being involved with the case, and communication between professionals and caregivers. Doreen and Dirk, for example, would have seen between one and three social workers for their adoption case, several more social workers when undertaking fostering training and approval, and still more social workers for Mini's caregiving and supervised contact. Many parents would prefer to be able to turn to the same one or two social workers for help; but sadly, with high staff turnover rates, high workloads, and high stress rates among social workers, this is unlikely to happen (Connolly, 2004). The overseas model of 'therapeutic team parenting' comes to mind here (Staines, Farmer and Selwyn, 2011). This model views foster carers, social workers and other key people, such as teachers, as a team: it emphasises the therapeutic function of fostering and directs positive efforts at the environment in which children grow up in order to ensure it helps them learn and develop (Staines, Farmer and Selwyn, 2011). The approach to fostering is systemic and means that foster families are less isolated, and that their views for the child's well-being are accepted as being as important as that of the professionals.

Another promising intervention is 'treatment foster care' (Connolly, 2004; Macdonald & Turner, 2008) which provides foster families with a tailor-made programme to help bring positive change to the lives of children with significant behavioural, emotional and psychological needs. Treatment foster care, however, does rely upon well-trained and well-supported foster carers, including greater access to specialist support and increased financial packages (Connolly, 2004).

Key messages from research

It is clear that most long-term foster placements and the majority of adoptions stay intact, with 80% of adoptees and adopters in Britain, the US and European countries expressing satisfaction with their relationships (Sellick, Thoburn & Philpot, 2004). About 80% of permanent arrangements remain intact in Britain and the US, but no data is available in Aotearoa New Zealand. The quality of the placement and relationships are critical to success (Biehal et al., 2010). Disruption rates are higher for foster care arrangements, and it seems that adoption provides a greater sense of permanence and stability than fostering (Biehal et al., 2010; Sinclair, 2005). The age at placement is always key too: the younger age at placement, the more favourable the outcomes, whether fostered or adopted (Sellick, Thoburn & Philpot, 2004). But if children also have high needs and have been previously institutionalised or abused, then less favourable outcomes are likely (Biehal et al., 2010). Parents who adopt or foster can make a difference to a successful placement by having realistic expectations; accepting the child's dual identity, including the significance of the birth family for the child; giving quality time; being committed; being authoritative but not authoritarian; and having a conscious child-centred parenting model (Johnstone & Gibbs, 2012; Sellick, Thoburn & Philpot, 2004).

Conclusion: Supporting adopted and fostered children in the future

The issue of long-term support for adopted and fostered children and their 'forever families' is largely ignored in Aotearoa New Zealand. It is assumed that once children are in permanent settled care, little statutory assistance will be required. While this can be true for many adopted and long-term fostered children, the research suggests that significant numbers will require a whole range of supports for different periods in their lives, whether relational, cultural, health, psychological, practical, financial, or educational. Children must be able to access help, whether it is of an individual or counselling/mentoring nature or as part of a group, as in peer supported education. Crucially, they should not have to wait until their situation has reached a crisis or is posing a high risk of harmful behaviours. Parents usually know when things are going wrong, but they often do not know where or how to access the right help. It would be good if agencies like Child, Youth and Family could offer a long-term support option which gave adoptive and long-term foster parents access to a support worker who could advocate on behalf of the needs of children in addition to what the parents already do. Parents of adopted and long-term fostered children want to promote trust and security in their children, and in the majority of cases they achieve this. But in order to meet the needs of their children fully, a whole range of dedicated resources must be available to families, and agencies must work in partnership with families and communities to protect adopted and long-term fostered children beyond the initial few years.

CHAPTER 12

Being young and working

Ruth Gasson & James Calder

This chapter investigates issues around young people and work. Four relevant international agreements relating to children's rights are outlined, and their views of childhood and child employment are identified and discussed.¹ A questionable aspect of three of these agreements is the requirement for blanket minimum working age legislation. This requirement ignores positive aspects of youth employment, and arguably contradicts other requirements, including the right of children to participate in decisions that affect their lives and the promotion of children's best interests. We examine youth employment in Aotearoa New Zealand by outlining the findings of research that investigates the work children do, their employment conditions, and other relevant data. The findings reveal that employees under 16 years of age in Aotearoa New Zealand are often unfairly treated and have little understanding of their workplace rights. However, they also suggest that many young people in Aotearoa New Zealand benefit from work, and most do not want to legislate themselves out of employment. We argue that any action undertaken in the problem-solving process must include young employees and their families, and provide ongoing support to apply, revise, and sustain any proposed solutions.

Aotearoa New Zealand is a signatory to a number of international agreements that are intended to address the rights and interests of children. This chapter discusses four relevant international agreements: the Universal Declaration of Human Rights (UDHR) which was adopted in 1948, The International Labour Organization (ILO) C138 Minimum Age Convention (MAC) of

---

1   The United Nations Convention on the Rights of the Child of 1989 defines a child as anyone under the age of 18 years unless national laws recognise majority earlier. This definition is used in this chapter, unless stated otherwise. The terms 'young people' and 'children' are used interchangeably.

1973, the United Nations Convention on the Rights of the Child (UNCRC) of 1989, and the ILO C182 Worst Forms of Child Labour Convention (WFCLC) of 1999. It examines how each agreement addresses the rights and interests of young employees. There are tensions within – and conflicts among – the agreements, and an unintended consequence is that they provide space for countries to interpret international guidelines in ways that best suit local social and economic circumstances. States can validly argue against the merit of implementing some provisions if this would violate others.

Research suggests that young people like to be involved in decisions that concern their lives (Taylor, Smith, & Nairn, 2001), and that policies developed in collaboration with them are more likely to improve their lives than policies imposed without consultation (Bourdillon, Levison, Myers, & White, 2010; Boyden, 1997). When given the opportunity, young employees have used their knowledge and experience to identify practical ways of addressing workplace pitfalls. Their solutions tend to favour policies that protect young people *in* work above policies that protect them *from* work. As Leonard (2004) stated, 'when children's own perspectives are taken into account they move beyond the limits of protecting them from the world of work to suggesting frameworks whereby they can be empowered in the labour market' (p. 59). Conversely, policies that are developed without input from young workers can harm the people they are intended to protect. For example, in 1993, an international boycott of goods made by children led to children being banned from the garment industry in Bangladesh: 'A follow-up study carried out by the ILO/UNICEF found this well-intentioned action fundamentally increased the vulnerability of the children affected by the boycott. Rather than returning to school or other positive activities, the children ended up in more hazardous and exploitative occupations and experienced increased economic insecurity' (White, 1996 cited in Leonard, 2004, p. 58). Had the ILO and UNICEF initially consulted with the children and taken their views seriously, it is likely that they would not have lobbied for children to be dismissed from regulated employment, thereby forcing children into unregulated work, including prostitution. In this light, international conventions such as the MAC, which aim to restrict children below a certain age from entering any form of paid work, may do more harm than good.

Furthermore, while the issue of children and work is more serious in developing economies, young people in many developed nations also commonly engage in regulated work, and it is appropriate to consider their views, and possible impacts on them, when making decisions concerning their lives.

Aotearoa New Zealand has a tradition of children working (New Zealand Government, 2003, para 24), which continues to the present. A nationally representative study in 2007 found that most secondary school students in Aotearoa New Zealand had worked for pay during the year, and around 39% had regular part-time work (Adolescent Health Research Group, 2008). Children in Aotearoa New Zealand are employed in a variety of roles, including delivery work, babysitting, cleaning, gardening, retail and hospitality (O'Neill, 2010). In light of Aotearoa New Zealand's history of working youth, the New Zealand government has not instituted blanket minimum age legislation, although there are minimum ages for work and workplaces considered potentially hazardous, and restrictions on the times that children can work. The government's 2008 report to the Committee on the Rights of the Child maintains that 'New Zealand's consistent approach is that our existing policy and legislative framework already provides effective age thresholds for entry into work in general, and for safe work', and lists a range of relevant legislation (New Zealand Government, 2008, para 33). Nonetheless, Aotearoa New Zealand is considering ratifying the MAC (New Zealand Government, 2008, para 39).

Young people in Aotearoa New Zealand often have to cope with inadequate working conditions (Pugh, 2007), some receive poor remuneration (Caritas New Zealand, 2006; Shuttleworth, 2010), and many have little understanding of their rights as workers (Gasson et al., 2003; Pugh, 2007). To examine the issues, this chapter addresses those aspects of the Universal Declaration of Human Rights and the three previously identified conventions that are most pertinent to children's rights in relation to work, and their rights to participate in decision-making processes that affect them. Data from local studies of children's experiences are presented. These studies show that the majority of children in Aotearoa New Zealand do not want to legislate themselves out of employment (Gasson, Linsell, Gasson, & Mundy-McPherson, 2003); that most enjoy their work (Caritas New Zealand, 2006); that they generally experience light work as beneficial (Shuttleworth, 2010); and that children from high socio-economic catchment areas are more likely to work than students from low socio-economic catchment areas (Gasson et al., 2003; Adolescent Health Research Group, 2008 cited in O'Neill, 2010). Given that children's paid employment is common in Aotearoa New Zealand, and the likelihood that a blanket minimum age would exclude from employment tens of thousands of children who want to work, many of whom benefit from it, we argue that it is appropriate to consult children and families before implementing a blanket minimum age, and to consider instead whether it might be more appropriate to protect the rights of young people *in* work.

Relevant international agreements

The UDHR, adopted by the United Nations General Assembly in 1948, stated that all human beings are born equal in dignity and rights. Paragraph 2 of Article 23 stated that 'everyone, without any discrimination, has the right to equal pay for equal work.' These provisions do not exclude young people. However, later in the document, mothers and children are identified as being in need of special protection (Article 25 (2)), and parents are specifically provided with a right to choose the kind of education given to their children (Article 26 (3)). When Aotearoa New Zealand voted in favour of the UDHR, children were conceived of as 'developing' or 'becoming people' who were in need of special protection. Accordingly, children were effectively excluded from the realm of rights holders.

The MAC is arguably the most influential and the most controversial convention pertaining to young workers. In 1998 it was declared one of seven core ILO conventions (Bourdillon, White, & Myers, 2009). It has not been ratified by Aotearoa New Zealand, but the ILO Declaration requires that the principles of core conventions be respected and promoted by all member states, 'even the member States that have not yet ratified [them]' (ILO, n.d.).

Whereas the UDHR arguably provides the same rights to all citizens, the MAC specifically excludes young people under 15 years old, or under the minimum school-leaving age, from the right to work, and subsequently the right to equal pay for equal work. The MAC allows states to negotiate exceptions in the form of 'light work' for a specified number of hours for children aged 13 years and over in richer countries, or 12 years and over in poorer countries. It also requires states to determine exactly what qualifies as 'light work' for children, specifying only that in addition to not being harmful to children's health, safety, or morals, it must also not interfere with their development or education (ILO, 1973, article 7).

Broadly speaking, the MAC identifies children (people under 18 years of age) as needing special protection. Those under 15 are portrayed as potential victims who need to be protected *from* employment to ensure their proper development. Furthermore, the MAC suggests that young people under the age of 15 have a right to be excluded from employment (Myers, 2001). In particular, the MAC assumes that:

- Children under 15 years of age are not competent to be involved in decisions affecting their employment.
- Employment is bad for children under 15 years of age, schooling is good, and employment and schooling are incompatible.

- People younger than 15 years of age primarily enter employment because of poverty, and the only justifiable reason for them to enter employment is to relieve poverty.

Between the adoption of the UDHR in 1948 and of the MAC in 1973, the prevailing ideology in Western societies was that adults worked and cared for children, and children played and attended school (Morrow, 1994; Punch, 2003). Schooling was viewed as a means of helping young people develop into rational and independent adults able to make choices on their own behalf. Children's needs were to be met by adults who directed their lives. Children were perceived as simply not capable of real work, and any paid work young people engaged in was seen as insignificant, akin to play, and not contributing to the economy.

This ideology did not, and does not, reflect reality for many children. In many non-Western countries, the distinction between adulthood and childhood is blurred, as young people move in and out of so-called adult/child roles. Young people in non-Western countries commonly act as caregivers to younger siblings and contribute to the economic unit of the family while also being involved in some form of schooling (Rogoff, 2003). The unemployed, dependent, and cared for child, who is primarily engaged in school work and play, is thus revealed as a cultural construction. More specifically, the dependent child is a historically situated Western ethnocentric ideal that has achieved universal status via international conventions such as the MAC. This ideal devalues the beliefs and experiences of young people and families in non-Western countries (Boyden, 1997; Gasson & Linsell, 2011; Myers, 2001; Punch, 2003; White, 1996), and does not reflect the reality of lives for many children in Western countries.

The assumptions that employment is bad for young people and that employment and education are mutually exclusive are questionable (Bourdillon et al., 2010). Some young people do engage in harmful work and some are exploited in their workplaces (Caritas New Zealand, 2006). However, the relationship between children's employment and their well-being is complex (Bourdillon et al., 2010; Woodhead, 2004). The nature of the work that children do and the time they spend doing it affect their well-being, but there are also consequences for young people being denied work. For instance, this may result in fewer opportunities for young people, or the work undertaken may have been a source of self-esteem. Furthermore, while workplace relationships can be degrading for young workers, they can also be positive and affirming (Bourdillon et al., 2010; White, 1996; Woodhead, 2004).

The relationship between work and schooling is similarly complex. For some children in poor communities, their work facilitates their schooling. Alternatively, the quality of schooling may be poor or it may not be regarded as an attractive option. Moreover, in circumstances where children's well-being would improve if they worked less and spent more time at school, economic incentives and improved access to quality schooling are more effective than simply prohibiting young people from paid work (Bourdillon et al., 2009). In wealthier societies, paid work and schooling are often not in direct competition, and despite many children being subjected to poor working conditions, most young people do not want to leave their jobs. Most succeed at school while in paid employment, while disadvantages are more commonly associated with young people working longer hours, that is, more than 10-20 hours a week (Hobbs, McKechnie, & Anderson, 2007; Leonard, 2002; O'Neill, 2010).

In poor countries, many young people work to provide themselves and their families with the basic necessities of life, and some in wealthier countries also work to relieve family poverty. However, most research shows no direct link between family poverty and child employment in developed countries (Bourdillon et al., 2010; Frederiksen, 1999; Gasson & Linsell, 2011; Gasson, Linsell, Gasson, & Mundy-McPherson, 2003; Leonard, 2002, 2004; Morrow, 1994). Young people enter employment for a multitude of reasons, including independence and *relative* poverty. Relative poverty can have a powerful effect on psychological well-being. As Wilkinson & Pickett (2009) stated, 'Inequality … is a powerful social divider …. We tend to choose our friends from among our near equals and have little to do with those much richer or much poorer' (p. 51). It follows then that when children choose to work in order to purchase goods or take part in activities like, and with, their peers, depriving them of that opportunity will harm them.

Although the MAC has the status of a core convention, Myers (2001) described it as 'anachronistic', and Bourdillon et al. (2009) argued that it is an ineffective legacy of history. This raises the question of whether countries are morally bound by a convention that does not always appear to promote the best interests of children (Bourdillon et al., 2009) – a question especially pertinent in light of the dilemma posed when the MAC is looked at in conjunction with the UNCRC, which requires states to implement policies that promote the best interests of children.

The UNCRC was adopted in 1989 and is markedly different from the UDHR and the MAC in that it portrays children as subjects and as rights holders, independently of parents, although with adult support (Article 12). The UNCRC also requires 'the best interests of the child … to be a primary consideration' (Article 3), and specifically addresses the issue of child workers by stipulating measures to protect them from hazardous and harmful work, and from work that would interfere with their education. More controversially, however, like the MAC, the UNCRC requires states to legislate a minimum age for employment (Article 32). When the Aotearoa New Zealand government ratified the UNCRC in 1993 it placed a reservation against Article 32, which it continues to uphold.

Significantly, the UNCRC affords children the right to be involved in decisions that affect their lives 'in accordance with the age and maturity of the child' (Article 12). This is important because the majority of young workers enjoy their work (Caritas New Zealand, 2006), and do not want to be excluded from employment (Gasson et al., 2003).

The four international agreements span more than 50 years, and over this time, ideas concerning rights entitlements have changed. The participation rights accorded to children in the UNCRC are a relatively recent development. Previously, children were excluded from involvement in decisions affecting their lives on the same basis used to exclude women from the public and economic spheres about two generations ago. Women were regarded as less rational and needier than men, and therefore requiring protection rather than the right to participation. It is still common for adults to underestimate the capacities of children; to make decisions on behalf of young people without consulting them; and to justify this by arguing that children need protection (Morrow, 1994).

Should the Aotearoa New Zealand government legislate a minimum age for employment to comply with UNCRC Article 32 and the MAC, supposedly to protect young people, when this is against their wishes, and therefore appears in conflict with Article 12 of the UNCRC? Given that research shows that such legislation may not promote the best interests of children (Bourdillon et al., 2009; Morrow, 1994; Woodhead, 1998), this would also seem to go against Article 3. Furthermore, the idea that young people are rights holders rather than 'becoming adults' has attracted a great deal of support from young people and child advocates internationally. It has empowered young people to lobby on their own behalf for better conditions, and it has encouraged local groups to support them (Myers, 2001).

When the Aotearoa New Zealand government placed the reservation against UNCRC Article 32 in 1993, it maintained that Aotearoa New Zealand had legislation in place that protected children from hazardous and harmful work (United Nations, n.d.). While international evidence supports the stance against legislating a blanket minimum age, research in Aotearoa New Zealand shows that some rights and protections, which children have in theory, are not evident in practice (Gasson, Diorio, & Stigter, 2009; Gasson & Linsell, 2011; Gasson et al., 2003; Shuttleworth, 2010). The intent of the UNCRC requires that this situation is addressed, and that young people should be involved in the process.

The fourth agreement, the WFCLC, was introduced in 1999, and was intended to complement the MAC, becoming the eighth core convention (ILO, n.d.). Aotearoa New Zealand ratified the WFCLC in 2001. Unlike the MAC and the UNCRC, the WFCLC does not require a legislated minimum age for employment. Its focus is on eliminating work that is 'likely to harm the health, safety or morals of children', and as Bourdillon et al. (2009) pointed out, this leaves, 'only harmless work covered by 138 [MAC] and not 182 [WFCLC]' (p. 108).

The WFCLC requires states to identify harmful work, promoting national negotiation of international guidelines. Workers' organisations and employers are to be involved in identifying harmful forms of work and monitoring and revising procedures for their elimination. The Convention promotes a proactive stance by identifying possible causes of harmful work, seeking support from the international community, and advocating 'social and economic development, poverty eradication programmes and universal education' (ILO, 1999, article 8). The WFCLC can be interpreted as respecting the participation rights of young workers as long as the 'workers' organisations' include young workers who will be affected by subsequent policies. This has implications for countries like Aotearoa New Zealand where there is little support for young workers to form or join workers' organisations. Moreover, Bourdillon et al. (2009) argued that the WFCLC renders the MAC unnecessary, as the WFCLC addressed the issue of harmful work and there is no sound reason to exclude children from work that is not harmful. Being more inclusive of diversity, the WFCLC is an improvement and alternative to the MAC and can be interpreted as portraying children as rights holders. However, its narrow focus means that it still needs to be read in conjunction with the UDHR and the UNCRC.

A local profile of young workers

To gain an understanding of young people's positions on work in accordance with the spirit of the UNCRC, in 2003 about 1500 students aged between 11 and 15 years from randomly selected Auckland schools were surveyed about their working lives and opinions on work (Gasson et al., 2003). The findings provided a general profile of attitudes and working lives of young people in

Aotearoa New Zealand, which has since been complemented and affirmed by other data (O'Neill, 2010).

When asked why they worked and/or why they didn't think there should be a minimum age for employment, the most common response was for monetary reasons, though other reasons included experience, independence, and fun. Typical replies of the children included: 'It's not only older people that want jobs for money' and 'Some kids enjoy working ... my brother is 9. He enjoys working. I enjoy earning money' (Gasson et al., 2003, pp. 171–72). Many children believed they had a right to work, as the following comment suggests: 'It's because everyone no matter what age they are, has the right to get a job. As long as their work conditions are decent, they should also be allowed to choose when they want to start work' (Gasson et al., 2003, pp. 171–72).

About 27% of young people were in favour of a legislated minimum age for entry into employment. However, about half of these responses were motivated by a concern for possible harm to adults, particularly employers. In the words of one young person: 'I have worked in a dairy for 2 years and if you're too young you waste the boss's money' (Gasson et al., 2003, p. 169). However, some students were concerned that young workers might be exploited and believed that a minimum age for work might prevent younger children from being harmed or being forced to work: 'So you don't get 4 year olds doing complicated or dangerous jobs', 'My parents would make me get a job and I wouldn't be able to ask them for money. I'd have to use my own' (Gasson et al., 2003, p. 169).

The participants who supported a legislated minimum age for employment were asked to suggest one. Most suggested their own age or younger, and it was those who were not working who were more likely to specify a higher age. It was notable that only about 3% of children were working and wanted to legislate themselves out of employment. These children were more likely than other workers to work for a family member, and more likely than other workers to work for over 12 hours a week.

The 2003 study found that some children passed their earnings on to their family to help with living costs, but most said they spent their earnings on things they wanted rather than needed. A more recent study had similar results, with 76% reporting that they worked 'to have money of my own to spend on things I want' (Adolescent Health Research Group, 2008 cited in O'Neill, 2010, p. 28).

Importantly, however, the 2003 study found many young people were uncertain of their pay rates. While rates of pay may vary from week to week according to the hours worked or the number of deliveries made, many of the children surveyed found their pay information difficult to interpret. Furthermore, the survey revealed that young people, in general, know little about their employment rights. They seemed unaware that in theory they have the same rights as older employers to a written contract, holiday pay and sick pay. In line with this, Pugh (2007 cited in O'Neill, 2010, p. 29) found that 'less than half of employees were given information on their employment rights in their current job.'

Parents' concerns about children's working conditions

In a 2009 study of children and work in Aotearoa New Zealand, nine parents of working children were interviewed (Gasson et al., 2009). They told us about the kind of work their children did, and the conditions under which they worked. Some were concerned that in Aotearoa New Zealand people under 16 years of age are not entitled to a minimum wage – this remains the case in 2013, and additionally a former section of the Income Tax Act allowing tax refunds for children has now been repealed (Taxation (Budget Measures) Act 2012) – and one parent described how an employer gave people aged under 16 years longer hours and harder work because they were cheaper to employ. Neither the employee nor her mother complained because the child's school work was not suffering, and they were concerned that a complaint could result in the young worker losing her job. The child used her wages for school and cultural trips that she would otherwise have to forgo. Her mother believed that the consequences for the child of not working and not being able to take part in extracurricular activities would be worse than working the longer hours. Another parent compared the working conditions of her son and daughter who were doing similar work for different companies. The terms and conditions at her daughter's employment were much less favourable than those of her son.

The children were not always treated with respect by their employers. One parent said that in the course of his daughter's delivery work, the contractors changed. He described the impact this had on the child's working environment: 'The first … were pretty casual and quite supportive and understanding of small kids … these new contractors took a terribly hard line … each week there would be statements … "you are not doing this right" … because my wife and I were helping we ensured it was done right … these were general messages to every kid' (Gasson et al., 2009).

The parents of young people involved in delivery work noted the lack of transparency in what their children were paid, and one noted that the child never got a pay statement. The parent of a young person employed in the tourist industry encouraged her son to ask for the contract to which he was entitled. It was provided reluctantly towards the end of the boy's holiday work, but in an apparent move to penalise him for requesting it, his employers stopped providing morning and afternoon tea.

Summary and conclusion

According to the UDHR, all people are born equal with dignity and rights, and all have a right to work and to equal pay for equal work. The UNCRC and the WFCLC require young people to be protected from work that harms them, and the UNCRC requires that the best interests of the child be a primary consideration, while the MAC excludes children under 15 years old from work except under special circumstances. The exclusion of young people from work arguably violates the UDHR and the UNCRC, as such a move would only be legitimate if it were a necessary and effective way of protecting young employees, and there is a lack of evidence for this (Bourdillon et al., 2009). Therefore, we believe the Aotearoa New Zealand government should not ratify the MAC unless it finds reason to believe the MAC will improve young people's lives. Many young people in Aotearoa New Zealand choose to work, and their parents often support them. The children and parents believe that the social, economic, and developmental advantages of appropriate employment can outweigh the disadvantages.

Leonard (2004) argued that British legislation around children and work is based on the assumption that only a small number of children work, primarily because of poverty, and that this does not reflect reality. Many children work in Britain, mainly for reasons other than poverty. However, their conditions of employment are inferior to adults, and they have fewer employment rights. Leonard (2004), therefore, suggested that 'to fully protect children means starting from the premise that employment is now an everyday feature of many children's lives and mov[ing] from this to looking at ways to simultaneously protect and promote their interests. At the very least, this necessitates consulting with working children' (p. 57).

The description of the situation of young workers in Britain and Leonard's advice for protecting children in work both fit the situation in Aotearoa New Zealand. Young employees neither expect nor receive sufficient employment information, and are ignorant of their employment rights. They work in diverse occupations and often experience inadequate working conditions. The lack of union support or other sources of workplace protection leaves them largely at the mercy of employers, and while some are respectful and supportive of young people, others exploit their lack of power. This is compounded by young employees' lack of knowledge of appropriate processes, and a reluctance to complain to or question their employers for fear of losing their jobs.

Given the large number of school-age children in work, children in Aotearoa New Zealand require appropriate working standards and conditions and the right to participate in their implementation. Contact needs to be made with young employees and their employers to facilitate networks to provide young employees with information about workplace rights and conditions, and to enable them to support each other. Beyond this, adults need to listen to young workers and to take their advice seriously. If we are serious about addressing the exploitation of young workers, we need to set up adequately resourced working parties that include them and their employers, to identify harmful practices and to address issues that are raised. An effective system must be developed for national monitoring of child employment. Economic and social measures have to be taken to provide children with genuine employment alternatives. Young people should not be forced into employment because of poverty or an education system that fails to meet their needs; however, excluding children from beneficial work they enjoy would neither do right by children nor uphold Aotearoa New Zealand's commitments to the Universal Declaration of Human Rights or the Convention on the Rights of the Child.

CHAPTER 13

Technology occupies us: Children, media and Aotearoa New Zealand society

Martha Bell & Victoria Farmer

This chapter sets the context for studies of new media in society emerging from concerns about the older medium, television, in the lives of children.[1] It draws on aspects of an empirical study conducted in two urban centres in 2008–2009 which asked children about their uses of television, paying particular attention to their insistence that watching television is less important in their lives than using other screen technologies.[2] Their responses depict everyday uses of screen technologies in combinations of devices, in multiple uses and in relation to other family members' uses. It ends with children's own explanations of how new technologies are central to having 'something to do.'

The electronic media environment

Following overseas research, previous media studies in Aotearoa New Zealand focused on attitudes to radio and television, daily consumption of television, radio and newspapers and the role of the family home as the site of media use (Broadcasting Standards Authority, 2008; Jackson, Low, Gee, Butler, & Hollings, 2007; Lealand, 2001; Lealand & Zanker, 2003; Walters & Zwaga, 2001;

---

1   Children are aged 18 years and under according to the UN Convention on the Rights of the Child (UNCRC). This chapter focuses on children in the pre-teen years, aged 10–13, attending school.
2   A preliminary paper on which this chapter is based was presented to the Annual Conference of the Sociological Association of Aotearoa New Zealand (SAANZ), 26-28 November 2008. The empirical research was led by Rachael Taylor (PI) for a pre-pilot to a feasibility study with research team members Grant Schofield, Oliver Davidson, Jim Lewis, Martha Bell and Victoria Farmer. Funding is gratefully acknowledged from Lottery Health 2008, as is the support of the Edgar National Centre for Diabetes and Obesity Research and the Centre for Research on Children and Families, University of Otago. Thank you to the enthusiastic children and parents who shared stories about their lives with media.

Weatherall & Ramsay, 2006). The idea of children as a 'special' (Zanker, 2001a) television audience located in the home was a particular assumption in this literature, constructing the home environment as the place of parental control of children's activities and familial standards of care.

Television broadcasting is used to represent the society in which its audience lives and, to this end, 'capture' an audience while communicating its culture (Bell, 2001). With the arrival of digital television in 1998, almost 40 years after televised programming was introduced, children born near the turn of the century are the first generation to grow up in a digitised, globalised broadcasting environment. For them, the communication of culture is increasingly mediated through satellite platforms that enable the instant transmission of vast masses of digital data from myriad sources to various objects with screens. The resultant data casting is often referred to as the convergence (Lealand & Zanker, 2003; Livingstone, 2002; Matthewman, 2011) of telecommunications with information technology infrastructure.

Currently, convergence is both a plan and a practice. It is a plan not yet accomplished in terms of infrastructure. At the time of writing, media devices in homes still comprise individual television sets (soon to have universal digital access devices), individual video cassette and/or DVD playing machines, possibly a desktop computer and printer, landline and cellular telephones, possibly an electronic games console, some with a fixed camera and wireless remote control, and a radio. While the convergence of technologies into a single network of compatible screens is a future anticipation, households are limited to the life of their non-networked devices. In practice, convergence is the act of making combinations through mixed and multiple uses. Until full convergence arrives, 'media multitasking' (Watkins, 2009, p. 162) is a formative feature of the contemporary electronic media environment. Social engagement itself is multiply mediated and each person is differently individualised as a technology consumer.

The arrival of 3G digital technologies,[3] which offer the potential for convergence within families and households, shifts the focus from single technologies of communications to their mixture and dispersal. Thus, audience effects can no longer be investigated as if one type of media holds an audience and determines how its users will be influenced. The proliferation of forms of technology leads to a reconsideration of special audiences as well as environments of reception. Children can be seen to be active viewers who

---

3 Technologies comprise objects and devices, but importantly also span their purpose and design and the detachment of things from their processes of activation, through software, for example. The most important invention enabling the proliferation of new media is the digitisation of technologies already spawning a third generation (3G) (Matthewman, 2011).

make choices, not only about what they watch on television, but also about how, as they diversify their reception through club membership, websites and music videos. Children can sustain a more spatial and temporal relation to mediated content, attaining distance, fragmenting consumption and giving temporary – even random – loyalty. It is understood that they are not all-consumed with characters and storylines, but make distinctions between stereotypes, social issues and wider cultural choices in which programming is situated. More fragmented, and mobile, viewing practice allows for the children's contextual and critical perspectives of what they view, according to media researchers (Buckingham, 2009; Zanker, 2001a). 'Children's television', for example, in the designated after-school and dinner-time programming slots, spans adult-style interview formats with local television drama actors, presenter-led sequences and then the actual drama itself before the traditional watershed time of 8.30 p.m. ending children's programming. At the same time, 'imported cartoons' (Zanker, 2001a, p. 271), such as *The Simpsons*, the most popular television programme for 6- to 13-year-olds (Broadcasting Standards Authority, 2008), deliver American popular culture in both 4 p.m. and 7 p.m. time slots. Children switching to these programme channels become part of the globalised 'intergenerational audiences' (Zanker, 2001a, p. 270) targeted by companies such as Nickelodeon. And many children watch televised content until 9.30 p.m. and later on weekends, especially those with a television in their bedroom. Convergence thus constitutes a cultural shift that can be examined in terms of children's everyday lives.

Childhood studies and new media

Childhood Studies has shown that children are both positioned and restrained by the state, especially in relation to structures of schooling (e.g. Jones, 1991; Mitchell & Singh, 1987), and also that they are active participants in civic life (Freeman & Nairn, 2000; Freeman, 1998; Smith, Taylor, & Gollop, 2000). The range of theorising about shifting ideas of 'the child' shows that the emergent space for children as independent individuals within society is aligned with political moves to instigate rights for children, universally recognised by the UNCRC and mandated in Aotearoa New Zealand in the Education Act 1989. Critical perspectives on the repositioning of children within such a liberal humanistic framework and political tradition have brought attention to developmental discourses still isolating children as growing and forming human beings, in terms of biological and psychological development (Morss, 1996; Woodhead, 2009), rather than including children as knowledgeable and choice-making agents acting within the experiential contexts of their own growth. Such perspectives have encouraged research involving children's own views and ideas. In this regard, Childhood Studies has drawn increasingly on more child-centred methods to explore sociological thinking about children's agency and the context of children's cultures (Honig, 2009; James & Prout, 1997).

Children's reflections on their environments have been elicited in written surveys, in focus groups, in drawings and via photographs. Children's views have been solicited on social problems implicating wider social policies and regulatory systems. Children's voices allow children to be represented as children, not adults in formation, from the perspective of what they say and how they participate in the issues of their own lives with competent knowledge (Smith, 2007). In particular, children show competence in naming their own experiences and in changing constructions of childhood itself: children themselves make sense of being children within globalised and transnational influences, of which they may be so much more aware through the proliferation of images and information about other children (Prout, 2005).

Aotearoa New Zealand researchers have argued for the recognition of the ways in which children create meaningful places for themselves. These places 'must be environments that encourage children's and young people's accessibility and exploration, that are welcoming to them and their carers, that allow them to explore and integrate into wider social worlds and which meet their diverse and changing needs' (Freeman & Nairn, 2000, p. 11). The media are part of such environments, while also diversifying children's needs, argued the editor of a special issue of *Childrenz Issues* on children's use of media: 'One way of listening to children's voices is to take the time to understand the cultures of children and young people ... those cultures are mediated by the media children use and the adults who manipulate those media' (Gaffney, 2001, p. 4). Covering digital media, known as 'new media,' as well as electronic and print media (information, journalism and advertising), the collection of articles warns that attempts to categorise 'new' media as better than 'old' media (more active) or worse than 'old' media (dividing children from their elders or families from each other) are cyclic and predictable with the advent of socio-technological change. The articles delved into ways that children's own perspectives are part of how media effects should be analysed. The authors considered children as participants in media uptake, but also in production of content, programming and opinion – in short, capable of 'making media themselves' (Zanker, 2001b, p. 16).

Lealand's (2001) extensive study surveyed 383 children (8–14 years old) in a large urban centre in Aotearoa New Zealand and established a benchmark for media use activities by giving a snapshot of the children's daily activities, electronic media use and computer access. It found, for example, that while half of the sample read a newspaper on 'some days' during the week, almost 100% watched television (TV) 'usually' and 'some days' after school during the week. Almost one-third of the children had a TV in their bedroom (some with pay TV and some without), which was interpreted as 'media ownership'. Four different types of game devices were also reported, with almost one-quarter of the children having the most popular gaming machine (PlayStation) in their room. Almost three-quarters of the children had a bookshelf of personal (non-school) books in their bedroom as well and just under one-third read a personal book 'every day'. However, only half of the 383 students 'phoned someone' on the telephone 'every day'. The survey found that the majority of children said their parents encouraged them to learn about computers, leading the author to conclude that anxiety about bad screen watching habits seemed to be diminishing and that it was no longer sufficient to judge television watching as a bad habit compared to computer use (and 'getting ahead') as good. The study recommended asking children 'how new media complements, supplements or replaces uses of "older" media by children' (Lealand, 2001, p. 11).

This chapter follows the approach of viewing children as social actors and eliciting reflections on their own experiences and the contexts in which they live. Children in this study, outlined in the next section, primarily discussed how, where and when they watched television. While Aotearoa New Zealand is known as a society of 'early adapters' of digitised media (Goode & Littlewood, 2004), it is important to ask how children participate in this trend or experience exclusion. In schools, where critical literacy skills are taught, 'multi-literacies' are now being identified in order to facilitate critical readings of new media texts (Sandretto, 2011). It will be important to know how children participate in, or resist, such new literacies. These two examples of the uses of new media in the everyday home and learning environments for children illustrate that children's lives are increasingly involved with new media and their technologies. How children are engaged in accessing, using, combining and responding to mediated modes of interacting in their social and cultural worlds is a question that has been facing researchers in Aotearoa New Zealand and beyond for at least the last decade (Lealand, 2001; Livingston, 2002).

These two examples illustrate something else, more central to the concerns of this chapter: that is, that children are able to use technology in everyday ways to shape their own lives. As researchers concerned with Aotearoa New Zealand childhoods, 'we do need to pay closer attention to technology and the ways in which it configures the social than we hitherto have done' (Matthewman, 2004, p. xii). Media studies, therefore, stretches the approach of viewing children as central social actors in their own experience to one acknowledging that children act with technologies in social ways that inform their experience. Their personal and public lives are increasingly linked to, and linked by, networks of technologies, their producers and their literacies. Social studies of technologies would argue that any private/public distinctions are blurred by the existence of such networks, their producers and literacies, which are termed assemblages.[4] Social studies of childhood must acknowledge that technical and scientific change is diversifying childhoods even in any one society: 'Children's capacities are extended and supplemented by all kinds of material artefacts and technologies ... hybrids of nature and culture. This shapes the constitution of childhood and the experiences and actions of children' (Prout, 2005, p. 4). Furthermore, childhood itself 'is to be regarded as a collection of diverse assemblages constructed from heterogeneous materials' (Prout, 2005, p. 4).

Convergent media represent assemblages of interests, investments and networks of users that generate interconnecting, while potentially exclusionary, spaces. Television itself is therefore only a small part of 'different assemblages of actors (parents, experts, technologies, children, spaces and so on)' (Oswell, 2002, pp. 18–19). Whereas in the past, television assemblages enacted 'dividing practices' that established 'the idea of childhood' (Oswell, 2002, p. 15) as well as the ideas of 'generation,' 'audience,' 'home' and 'lifestyle,' the extension of television usage to multiple screens, mixed media and spatial experience must be considered. Mobile telephones, for example, may subvert such positioning practices (Osit, 2008; Wajcman et al., 2008). When televisions and telephones both use screens, users' needs shift regarding the use of both. In short, technologies of the everyday and the global are 'actors in social processes rather than merely props for social action' (Prout, 1996, p. 199).

---

4 'Assemblages' (Latour, 2005) are defined as networked relationships between people, places and things. 'Things' are material technologies affecting social life via linkages of interests (Prout, 2005; Wajcman, 2002). In Childhood Studies, attention to the linkages between things and interests produced an analysis of child health technologies, focusing on the asthma inhaler (Prout, 1996). When Science and Technology Studies (STS) emerged as an interdisciplinary field of inquiry in the 1970s, it introduced the study of the way technologies shape 'big' scientific issues; it quickly became a way to study social life and controversial uses of science's material technologies (Matthewman, 2011).

Television and mediated screen technologies

The empirical design for this child-centred study was motivated by public health concerns with sedentarism in children's lives.[5] The rationale was that children are participating in increasingly at-risk behaviours requiring stricter governance in terms of family life and activities. The aim of the investigation was to identify discrete behaviours that could be targeted for intervention. Parents and children were invited to give accounts of family situations, decisions and challenges specifically around television watching. Of interest to the research group were the incentives that could be offered to induce children to 'give up' such entertainment. No such particular behaviours or inducements could be easily identified across the focus group discussions. Children often suggested a Lotto-type prize or a shopping spree – for a replacement television that was bigger and better than their current television set or a television for their bedroom or a computer – as the reward for giving it up. When asked what else they would do if they did not have television, the first suggestion was that they would go on the computer. They could not conceive of wholly living without television, although the discussions raised times in their lives when television had been suspended (as discipline, for example) or absent (at a holiday house, for example). They could conceive of giving it up for a few weeks or a month. If they were to do something else instead of watching television, it would be playing a video game, browsing sites on the internet or instant messaging friends. Since the children thought in temporal terms, the findings were interpreted to mean that a short period without television would offer families a chance to experience everyday life without television and to reflect on it together, as opposed to complete removal. The discussions of television watching in their families, in both children's and parents' groups, however, revealed the beginnings of media convergence in the households of those involved.

Pre-teenage children are allowed some choice about leisure and schoolwork activities by parents, who begin to accord them greater responsibility in and

---

5   The pre-pilot study, Television in our Families, recruited a sample of 80 participants, with 58 children and 22 adults participating in 14 focus groups and three home-based interviews. In all, 21 families were involved: of these, two families self-identified as not having television (no-TV families) and discussed the reasons for their choice. In practice, both families tended to use a screen for viewing a video (on a non-networked television set or on a computer screen) together as a family. Including these two families, there were eight children with a parent also in the study. Seven primary schools were involved with nine separate focus groups: four of children and five of parents. In five focus groups, data were collected by the children interviewing each other. Access to and range of electronic media devices were not quantified; data analysis was interpretive. All quotations are taken from the study's verbatim transcripts and all names are pseudonyms.

contribution to family life. When such expectations extend to taking care of themselves after school and keeping in touch with working parents until they get home, pre-teens often negotiate the use of a range of technologies, from toaster to telephone (Vestby, 1996). They turn to electronic media technologies, some getting together with a friend, taking turns 'having a go' while watching each other. This demographic is passing through 'middle childhood' faster, in part because they aspire to a cultural world in which they are 'less dependent on adults' (Zanker, 2001b, p. 13) and in part because they are quickly appropriating technological skills that access a much more privatised world, with fewer opportunities for interpersonal identity formation, and more opportunities for casual personal interaction than they are ready for (Elliott & Lemert, 2006, p. 25). There were spirited debates about whether a television or a networked computer in one's bedroom was more 'social.'[6] In one group, a computer was thought to be 'way more useful 'cause you can actually do homework on it ... and you can talk to friends and stuff.' In another group, the talk turned to social identity websites: 'We all have Bebo and so we just email each other on Bebo,' said Zoe. Simulation websites (Singing Sims), games websites (Runescape), and auction websites (Trade Me) were also visited.

Just over one-third of the 58 children in the study had a television in their bedroom.[7] When considering the question of whether people should have televisions in their bedrooms, the children's groups' members often agreed that it is good for parents, who like to watch late-night television, but 'bad' for children. The participants with their own television did not think that it was a concern, explaining with animation how important it was to be able to stay in bed on weekend mornings and to watch television in bed in the evening rather than have to go to bed after watching. Lindsay explained, 'Like, I go to bed at 8.30 but I watch TV to 9.30, so I just go to bed and watch it instead of having to stay up and then I'll have to walk to my bedroom.' Philip told his group that it was all right not to have a television in his bedroom because 'I normally sleep in the lounge when I watch the TV and I go to sleep [there].' Notably, boys in the two all-male focus groups had little interest in television in their bedrooms, which they said were too small. These boys wanted to watch their television programmes, usually sport, 'together as a family'. The girls in other focus

---

[6] 'Social' meant virtual textual interaction to these children as compared to its application in media use surveys when it means co-presence with other people in the room (e.g. Walters & Zwaga, 2001).

[7] A similar one-third figure was found in a nationally representative study of American children published in 2004 (Watkins, 2009, p. 162). Likewise, a British survey by ChildWise found one-third of children under age 11 had DVD players in their bedrooms (Elliott & Lemert, 2006, p. 25).

groups often mentioned their preference for, and older sisters' preferences for, a television in a personal space to watch by themselves. Harriet, an only child, said 'I do have a TV in my room, but like I've got boundaries on how much I can watch it.'

Analytical themes explored relate to contemporary concerns around time, faster lifestyles and instant technology. Children's comments on the perceived need to stop and rest after what one child described as 'quite long days' became the focus for discussions of why the television was actually turned on and whether television watching was a choice or a habit.[8] However, comments also showed that television was used frequently as a way to immobilise the participants, children and adults, for short periods of time in the day. How and when this happened became part of parental regulation (such as stipulating an equivalent amount of time outdoors for the time spent watching television) and part of children asserting their needs for 'something to do' when the weather was poor or they were tired. For example, two children explained their reason for watching television:

> You don't really want to be outside when it's pouring with rain, but you just want to kind of relax and just enjoy – I really like to relax and do stuff.

> I don't know, like something to do. 'Cause I usually do have a lot to do, but I can't be bothered doing it. 'Cause we have got these beach motorbikes and I do like to fix them up a bit. But that's only usually in the weekends, not during the weekdays 'cause I am too tired.

The parents of no-TV families had often reached the decision to avoid watching television because of the way they watched when they were too tired to turn it off. Marion, for example, still feels that 'I probably would not have the self-control to turn it off when really I should be doing something else or really I should go to bed.' Her family organises holidays around hotels with Sky broadcasting in their rooms so that they can watch as much television as they want as a treat for themselves. She assured the interviewer: 'So, it's not like we're media deprived.'

The children articulated the positive benefits of television slowing the fast pace of family life; they also felt that the negative effects included stopping a person from doing other things they should be doing. The ambivalence expressed in the discussions of the positive and negative effects of television elicited perceptions of television's agency. For some, it brings people together: Daphna said, 'My dad's working in the [home] office and he like only usually

---

8   See also Bell (2011), which explores conceptual themes of 'time out', 'stopping time', 'mental health', 'doing other things' and faster family lifestyles.

comes around for the news so it kinda brings us all together,' and Ethan said, 'television is more like a uniter for us – it's one room where something is on and people go to ... have a conversation or drink something ... It has a quite decent role in our family.' For others, it acts on them. 'It gives you something to do,' said Rory; but for Kendra, 'it sort of wastes your time'; for Claire, 'it makes me and my brother get into a fight'; and for Jill, 'you don't want to always have a TV in your room, otherwise you just turn them [sic] on'.

The capacity of television to absorb a person's attention was explained as something done by the technology itself. 'You get engulfed by whatever you are watching,' worried Wendy; 'You forget about your homework and other stuff,' said Nan; 'It can make you like lazy and you might like get addicted to it and you won't want to do anything else like exercise and stuff,' echoed Carli. Finally, a grandparent, Anne, expressed frustration with the television: 'Ours never goes on in the morning ... For a short time, it did go on. It was too disruptive. I could never get Lindsay to do anything'.

There are now multiple televisions in households (Walters & Zwaga, 2001). The children responded generally that there were two televisions in their families and if there were three or more, then they were in bedrooms and spare rooms, after the lounge and parents' bedroom. More than one television allows more than one programme to be watched at one time if there were conflicting preferences or if a family member wanted to watch something by themselves. The availability of multiple televisions was a concern for those children who wanted to watch everything 'together as a family' and for parents who wanted to monitor age-appropriate programming and the time spent watching.

In addition to multiple media use, there is mixed media use. The children often commented on their comparative use of various technologies; television has a small role to Kate, 'because, yeah, I'm usually on the computer'. Ethan said he enjoys television when family members get together, but prefers to wait for the boxed set of a programme on DVD which he will burn onto a disc and copy onto his portable devices to watch whenever he chooses. Yash said, 'My mum usually watches *Close Up* and the news and my sister probably watches it the most and I usually go on the computer.' Jason said that after he and his brother 'go to bed, then my mum goes on the computer and my dad watches TV'.

Others commented on the combination of electronic devices in use. The most prominent is the use of a cell phone while watching television. It was mentioned most often in terms of texting and then in terms of conversations with friends. The use of a landline telephone was mentioned once in the negative when, for example, the family had a rule against talking on the telephone while watching TV. The use of computers and televisions in the same space and at the same time was another example. This could be by the same person, such as in Zandra's family: 'We've got the laptop and we normally have it in the lounge because it's the warmest room. And so you kind of find that you watch what's on television while the computer's loading and stuff like that.' All three forms of media could be in use by the same child: 'She'll actually be on the computer and on the phone and have the TV on at the same time,' explained Harriet's mother of the media available in their lounge.

Mixing media use also facilitated compensation. A child would finish watching television at the Adult Only (AO) programming threshold at 8.30 p.m. and a parent, vacating the computer, would come in to watch their choice, so that the child was then able to go onto the computer. In Zandra's family, these two forms of e-media were in use simultaneously in the same room. In another example, a child wanting to go on the computer might leave the television unattended to entice a sibling to 'free up' the computer. In a third example, the television was useful for occupying a toddler so that an older sibling could go on the computer uninterrupted: Anna was frustrated with the way her noisy younger siblings could be 'annoying' when she was using the computer and so she would use TV as a bargaining tool with exchange value for uninterrupted computer time.

The television also comprised a music source that would be turned on while the child did their homework, sometimes on the computer in the same room and sometimes in a bedroom. Background television was something that helped when doing homework:[9] 'I find watching TV helps me do homework … I can't concentrate without a sound, because I am so used to like having the baby screaming or [younger brother] running around the house. So … if everything's quiet, then I just turn on the TV and do homework,' said Karen. The music videos channel offered a retreat from the family dynamics in their bedroom; more than one child across the focus groups felt that the music channel helped when they were feeling angry, upset or sad.

Some child participants talked of switching between types of media easily. For example, when Troy stays with his nana, he will 'play five hours a day on computer and if I am not on computer, I am probably watching TV,' he said. The children explained that if the television was in use, they would go onto the computer and vice versa. They referred to this in the hypothetical as well: if the television was taken away in an intervention, then they would go on the computer. For example, 'I wouldn't mind because I have a computer and an iPod,' said Andrea. 'I'd read and go on my computer and tidy my room and do my homework,' said Seraya.

---

9   One-fifth of all children aged 6–13 do their homework after school on school days with the television on (Broadcasting Standards Authority, 2008, p. 21).

Technology unites two boys in play at Milford Sound.

The children in one focus group insisted that 'kids aren't all into TV any more, it's more the computer now.' They were advocating less of a focus on individual media technologies and more awareness of the convergence of mixed media use. A student explained that her family decided to 'keep' its television so that when someone is using the computer, another person can watch a DVD on the television screen with the recording/playing device attached. Another focus group discussion moved to the way the children see themselves growing up with media: 'I guess we're growing up now in an age where we've got a lot of technology and we kind of depend on that because … that's really the whole thing that occupies us,' said Zoe. 'Like when you're away from like technology you just find that you have to be with your family, otherwise you just get bored,' added Karen.

Reflections on growing up with mediated technologies that transport users into spaces of experience, communication and interaction (Morley, 2000) situate these children in relation to each other in ways that cross-cultural identities, such as nationality and dis/ability, and also situate children in new relations with adults. Technology may cross generational barriers, so that parents no longer supervise all their children's social relationships, which could be monitored more easily when carried out by telephone or face-to-face visiting, but which may now involve private emails to extended family, online buying and selling, instant messages and virtual avatars. While it is to be expected that children between the ages of 10 and 13 widen their social circles, parents in the past could know of – if not be part of – conversations, but now are less so because chat, email and text make such conversations inaccessible. Convergence of media most commonly includes cell phones, although the child participants were still using an adult's cell phone. Adults and children may collaborate in mixing media in contrast to those who do not adopt new technologies. Children use technologies for convergent purposes, for example, and this may be not so different to adults who also use new media.

Convergence is a practice constructing a media culture of immersion in 'multi-layered experience' (Zanker, 2001a, p. 278) such that more than one media device and more than one form of cultural access are in play for any number of family members in the same room. For some, this is a threat and parents are reproached for not being 'in charge' of sequencing and limiting their family's media use (Cowan, 2007). For others, this 'media-centric generation of children' has 'media rights' and participates in constructing family media environments (Zanker, 2001a, p. 279). Furthermore, the milieu of media use is changing to a mobile screen environment in which entertainment, information and communication are often portable, but also individualised, interactive and instantaneous. As much as they are viewers, children of the 2000s use devices that rearrange their uses of screens in turn.

Conclusion

Television watching is an accepted form of media use in children's lives, especially in networked households and in the context of simultaneous media use by family members. This chapter has outlined the ways that groups of 10- to 13-year-olds discussed the diminishing role of television as a way to analyse mediated screen technologies in their families. The children's talk indicated times that they perceived television as acting on them, times that their family members watched televisions dispersed around the house, and ways that they mixed and multiplied the screen devices they used at one time. They gave examples of why these things happened in their own families in regard to the relationships between parents and siblings and themselves. Even the no-TV families were not 'media deprived.' The practices of media use among these children are connected to the interests of the adults around them, from parents and teachers to public health researchers themselves. These children share a keen desire to involve themselves with technology in their private and public lives.

PART THREE

Children's and Young People's Voices

CHAPTER 14

Children's participation and voice in early childhood education

Lyn Foote, Fiona Ellis & Ruth Gasson

Since the early 1990s early childhood teachers in Aotearoa New Zealand have been using the early childhood curriculum framework, *Te Whāriki,* to guide their practice. One of the key principles of this document is empowerment. In the document, empowerment is explained as children being encouraged 'to develop independence and to access the resources necessary to enable them to direct their own lives' (Ministry of Education, 1996, p. 40). Implicit in this is the notion of children as active participants in their learning environment, able to make decisions about their learning pathways. The idea, if not the practice, of giving voice to children has gained prominence internationally (James, 2007).

This chapter describes an aspect of a qualitative research project designed to investigate the transformative potential of children's learning environments. One feature of this investigation was an exploration of how teachers gave children voice in the creation of learning spaces. Teachers were asked how they included children's voice in the setting up of the environment. The environment in action was also observed by tracking four children as they engaged in play to examine their participation.

Background

More than 94% of children in Aotearoa New Zealand have engaged in some form of early childhood education (ECE) prior to starting school. For most children this will have involved at least six hours a week, and more than half of them will have attended ECE between four and 24 hours a week (Ministry of Education, 2012). Thus, a significant number of the interactions that young children have with people and the physical environment take place in ECE settings.

The interactions young children have with adults and peers have long been recognised as formative; more recently, the impact of the physical environment, dubbed 'the third teacher' in the Reggio Emilia philosophy of early childhood education (Pairman & Terrini, 2001), has also received attention. When the physical environment is viewed as an educator, teachers begin to notice how surroundings can take on a life of their own, and how young children perceive and use space to create meaning. It is now widely accepted by ECE teachers that children's experiences can be limited or enhanced by their physical environment (Strong-Wilson & Ellis, 2007). Early childhood environments send messages to children about who holds power, and about learning and learning strategies that are valued, and these messages affect the way children develop both as learners and as social beings. As Pairman and Terreni have said, 'the environment "speaks" to children – about what they can do, how and where they can do it and how they can work together' (2001, p. 1). Much consideration has therefore been given to determining how to design all aspects of early childhood education *for* children.

Until the 1990s, however, at least in practice, less consideration was given to facilitating children's input into the nature and the process of their early childhood education. Children were seldom consulted when decisions were made about their environment, and they were unlikely to be actively involved in designing an education of their choice. Adults designed the learning environment and there were few processes in place to encourage the sharing of such power with children (Strong-Wilson & Ellis, 2007).

Since 1993, when the Aotearoa New Zealand government ratified the Convention on the Rights of the Child (1989) (UNCRC), this lack of involvement by children has increasingly been recognised as problematic. Article 12 of the UNCRC provides for children to be consulted and their views taken account of in matters that affect them, in accordance with their age and maturity. The ECE environment definitely affects children, and there is evidence that with appropriate support, children can constructively participate in making decisions about it (Lancaster, 2006). Therefore, in line with the UNCRC, such participation is considered a child's right. Furthermore, other benefits accrue to children when their participation rights are valued. They are more likely to feel positive about themselves, they have an improved sense of agency, their social learning develops, and their motivation for learning is enhanced (Berthelsen & Brownlee, 2005). The Reggio Emilia recognition of the environment as the third teacher encourages teachers to promote the notion of 'children's places' as opposed to 'places for children', and when attention is directed to children creating their own places, teachers are expected to be mindful of children's inquiry and to be aware of the things that attract children's interest. When children actively control the context there is a need to think about how they can be enabled to participate (Strong-Wilson & Ellis, 2007). In line with these ideas, *Te Whāriki*, the Aotearoa New Zealand early childhood curriculum, gives children increasing responsibility for their own learning and supports them in making their own decisions and judgments (Ministry of Education, 1996, p. 40).

From the 1990s, children's participation in ECE settings has become a focus of research. Participation rights have been examined from a variety of approaches including the principles of participation, good practice, and the implementation of participation rights (Lancaster, 2006; Smith, 2007). A model commonly used to gauge levels of participation and to help practitioners increase children's participation was developed by Roger Hart in 1992. Hart's 'ladder of participation' identifies eight steps leading from non-participation to full participation, whereby children are involved in 'child-initiated shared decisions with adults' (Shier, 2001, p. 109). In 2001, Shier developed a complementary model, which he presented as a tool for practitioners to use to investigate the process of participation. Shier's model excludes the first three levels of Hart's model – those related to non-participation. It includes five levels of participation:

Children are listened to.

Children are supported in expressing their views.

Children's views are taken into account.

Children are involved in decision-making processes.

Children share power and responsibility for decision-making.

At each level of participation .... individuals and organisations may have differing degrees of commitment to the process of empowerment. The model seeks to clarify this by identifying three stages of commitment at each level: openings, opportunities, and obligations. (ibid., p. 110)

Sheir's model seems to be a useful evaluation tool which could be used by teachers as a basis for critically reflecting on the various ways they encourage participation and children's voice in their early childhood context. All levels are important but encourage children's participation in different ways.

In Level 1, Shier included situations in which children initiate conversations and teachers listen, but children's contributions have no real impact on teachers' decisions about learning environments. At Level 2, children are supported to express their own views and ideas. Staff actively elicit children's views and support their expressions, but the teacher decides how the environment will be created. At Level 3, children's views are taken into account in decision-making, and ideas which are deemed appropriate by the adults are incorporated into environmental planning. Level 4 is characterised by children being involved in the decision-making processes and having their ideas help shape the decision-making process. At Level 5 'children share power and responsibility in the decision-making' (Shier, 2001, p. 115). The inclusion of a policy that requires children and adults to share power and decision-making is presented as the ultimate goal.

The increased focus on participation rights is, in part, a response to the fact that of the three kinds of rights provided for in the UNCRC – protection rights, provision rights and participation rights – it is participation rights that have been the 'most violated and disregarded' (Shier, 2001, p. 108). Acknowledgment of the participation rights of young children must not compromise their other rights, because all rights in the UNCRC are equally valued. As Berthelsen and Brownlee have stated, '[r]ecognition of the participation rights of young children involves a balance between acknowledgement of vulnerability and dependence upon adults; appreciation of children's competencies and capabilities; and encouragement, as appropriate, to allow children greater autonomy and independence' (Berthelsen & Brownlee, 2005, p. 52). Berthelsen and Brownlee are concerned that adults commonly underestimate children's capabilities: thus they have argued for a valuing of children's agency and perspectives that is not based on judgments of age-defined capacities.

Te Whāriki (Ministry of Education, 1996), the curriculum framework which guides early childhood settings in Aotearoa New Zealand, reflects contemporary thinking about the benefits that accrue to children and society when children's rights, including participation rights, are fully attended to. Central to *Te Whāriki* is the notion of children as active and empowered learners who learn through their interactions with people, places, and things (Ministry of Education, 1996). Children's interaction with, and engagement in, their learning environment is therefore a key issue for teachers to address as they plan for children's learning. Similarly, the importance of actively listening to children is emphasised in the Ministry of Education early childhood resource, *Kei Tua o te Pae / Assessment for Learning*, which maintains that 'teachers who pay careful attention to children's voices gain windows into their world views and assumptions' (Ministry of Education, 2004, p. 4).

Burgess and Fleet (2009) evaluated ECE curriculum initiatives and found that the role of the environment needs to be reconceptualised. They argued

Listening to and talking to children facilitates shared decision-making.

that fundamental to such a reconceptualisation is a clarification of the kind of teacher that ECE environments are expected to have. Similarly, Smith (2007) challenged ECE teachers to consider how they could capture the language of children so that the ECE environment would engage children's curiosity and interest, and encourage them to take some responsibility for their learning. Arguably, to do this as effectively as possible, teachers would need to facilitate the sharing of power and decision-making with children (Level 5 of Shier's model).

The research

For the research project described below, ethical consent was gained from the University of Otago Ethics Committee (Foote & Ellis, 2008). One sessional centre and one full-day centre were approached and invited to participate in the project. Both agreed. These centres were selected because they were resource rich and their staff were committed to enriching children's learning. The eight teachers from these centres were interviewed about their beliefs and practices in relation to the creation of early childhood centre environments. All were trained ECE teachers, and their teaching experience ranged from three years to more than 20 years.

In addition, four children, a girl and a boy in each of the settings, all aged four, were each observed for a period of four hours on two separate occasions in order to explore the ways in which the environment supported their participation in the programme. Centre staff identified the children to be observed, and made the initial approach to the families for written consent. They knew the children and families and had a trusting relationship with them. They identified children and families who were regular attendees at the centre, were confident and were likely to be comfortable in a research project. They took care to ensure families knew their consent was entirely voluntary and emphasised their right to refuse to participate without adverse repercussions for them or their children. The children were told that the researcher was from the University of Otago's College of Education, and that she was interested in what they did during their time at the centre. They were asked if they would mind if the researcher watched what they did during the morning. All the children agreed. To minimise the extent to which children were disconcerted by the researcher taking notes, the researcher took on the role of participant observer, responding to children when they approached. In line with Carr (2000), by being a participant observer, the researcher attempted to share agency with the children.

The staff and children were familiar with the researchers, who had visited the centres regularly and routinely over a number of years to observe students on their practicums. It was believed that the existing familiar and collegial relationships would help ensure that the teachers and children were comfortable in the presence of the researcher, and would also help ameliorate anxiety or issues of power that could potentially arise. The purposeful selection of centres that were already supportive of children's learning, and were interested in working with the researchers to improve their effectiveness, also helped to affirm collegial relationships. The teachers at the centres understood that they were not being judged, but the researchers were working with them towards a shared goal.

Interview questions were developed by the researchers to encourage discussion. For example, some of the following questions were asked:

What guides decisions when setting up the environment?
How are decisions made about where resources and equipment will be placed?
How is it decided what will be displayed?
How are children included in the setting up of the environment?

The interviews were audio taped, transcribed, and checked by the participants for accuracy. The transcripts were analysed separately by the two researchers for patterns and themes, then coded using Shier's model of the levels of participation. This process was undertaken independently by the two researchers, before being checked for inter-rater reliability to ensure that the codes were being applied consistently and rigorously.

Field notes were taken detailing children's participation during a morning. A record was kept of the dialogue and details of the child's interactions with people, places, and things in the environment. Notes included the contexts in which the children were involved and the resources they utilised. The researchers took care not to be intrusive and to remain, 'constantly "alert for signals of assent and dissent"' (Hedges, 2011, p. 7). The researcher was prepared to leave a child immediately if the child appeared disturbed or restricted by her presence. At times the children engaged with the researcher, asking for stories to be read, telling the researcher how to do a puzzle, or asking for music.

Shier's model (2001) was used as a tool to understand how teachers were facilitating children's journeys towards full participation in centre decision-making. This model was a basis upon which researchers and teachers could identify ways of encouraging children's participation in decisions about their learning environment.

At Level 1 of Shier's model, the key question is whether children are listened to. It was evident that teachers did listen to children. When asked 'what guides decisions in setting up environments?', it was apparent that the teachers felt responsible for creating an appropriate learning environment for children. Fulfilling this responsibility involved teachers identifying children's interests and ensuring the environment was responsive to children and the things that engaged their attention. Teachers described how they listened and responded to children: 'I kind of look around and I think um, we're pretty much up to speed with the children's interests' (Foote & Ellis, 2008). This indicates that teachers were 'listening' to children but not necessarily actively eliciting their views.

The teachers consistently remarked that the learning environment needs to be relevant to the children and that teachers should follow children's ideas. One of the challenges for teachers is to find out children's intentions rather than deciding themselves what is of interest to children. When related to Shier's model, this kind of response fits on Level 1 of the ladder, as it tends to reflect the teachers' perceptions of what interests the children and the teachers' attempts to make the environment interesting for children and provide them with choice about what would be available. As one teacher put it, 'You're changing it [the environment] constantly, giving them variety' (Foote & Ellis, 2008).

Interestingly, it often seemed that although teachers listened to children and made every effort to interpret the interests of children, they rarely asked the children themselves about what interested them. In this sense, the teachers still exerted most control over happenings. Some of that control was linked to teachers' perspectives of an ideal ECE curriculum. For example, one teacher said: 'I think it is important to cover all the curriculum areas as well, like have your puzzle area and your block area ... ' (Foote & Ellis, 2008).

When the environment was observed in action through the play of the children, teachers' listening and engagement was affirmed:

Peter is playing with a medical kit. He gets the stethoscope out.

Teacher: 'And what does that do?'

He gets the 'hammer' out. The teacher asks if he is going to check her reflexes.

Peter, smiling, taps the teacher with the hammer.

Teacher: 'Do they work? Do they work?'

Peter: 'Yes.'

(Foote & Ellis, 2008)

This response conveyed to the children the message that they had a voice and they were being listened to in this context. Listening is seen as an important pedagogical practice used by early childhood teachers to gain insight into children's thinking in early childhood settings (Sandvik, 2009). What teachers do with the messages that they hear has important implications for the environment. Do teachers use what they hear to shape the environment or do they put aside what they hear because it is not part of the learning plan?

Shier defined the next level of participation as episodes when children get support to express their own views and ideas. Examples of this included teachers noting how they enabled or empowered children to choose what resources they wanted to use and where they might use them. Teachers explained, for instance: 'Like they can access everything and can use it however they want to'; 'They know they can go and access whichever puzzles they want to ... they can ask for it and we'll go get it for them' (Foote & Ellis, 2008).

Teachers were also mindful of providing opportunities for the participation of the children: 'Um, I think we've moved a little bit away from placing resources on the table, like table top resources, and ... as long as they're visible to the children somewhere in the environment, we've established a setting where the children can access those resources. Because I think it's quite limiting if you put something on the table and they might think that's what we're doing today' (Foote & Ellis, 2008). This comment suggests that the teacher was reflecting on children's participation by encouraging them to make their own decisions about the direction of their play. The observation data showed that the children were able to move readily throughout the programme, choosing where to play and what resources to use. The context and the interactions with the teachers gave them opportunities to express their own views and ideas, as the following notes describe:

Lucy watches a boy cutting a shape for the screen printing.

Teacher: 'Do you want to cut your shape out?'

Lucy cuts the shape out.

Lucy: 'I'm making a different shape. It is a really interesting shape.'

Lucy moves to the screen printing. She puts paint in and spreads it around. She stops.

Teacher: 'Look how the pattern has come out.'

Lucy puts the shape back onto the picture.

Lucy: 'I'm going to do another one.'

Teacher: 'Will you use the same shape?'

Lucy: 'No, a different shape. I'll cut out another shape. I'll see what else I'm going to do. Look at this, I'm cutting out an interesting shape.'

She shows another child what she was doing, then leaves to wash her hands.
(Foote & Ellis, 2008)

The child was encouraged to share her ideas, but there was no observational evidence to suggest that these ideas were taken further.

At the next level of Shier's model (Level 3), it would be anticipated that children's views would be used explicitly to shape further opportunities within the learning context. The observation data indicated that while children expressed their views, they were not always translated into practice. Sometimes this may be a factor of the pedagogical approaches of the teachers, where they intentionally listen to children to identify their evolving working theories before extending the interaction. (Sandvik, 2009).

On other occasions children's views were not translated into practice because of the way that the structural features of the environment and attention to certain aspects of safety set limits on what teachers believed could be achieved. One teacher stated, 'We also have to guide it in terms of safety, space, and all those issues again. As long as you keep an eye on health and safety factors ... safety is probably the first and foremost, it's the biggest, isn't it?' Another teacher commented, 'I think artwork should be displayed and they should be allowed to put their artwork up as well ... But I'm really um, I'm really ... I don't want too much on the walls ...' (Foote & Ellis, 2008).

The teachers were mindful of providing opportunities for children's participation by facilitating their decision-making in the centre about the learning environment. However, these responses could indicate that the control and the ownership of the learning environment rested more with teachers than the children. It may be that teachers find it difficult to reconcile their responsibility for children's safety and learning with the provision of opportunities for children to participate in decision-making.

There was evidence in the observation data of children's views being taken into account, and as a consequence, they had some impact on the decision-making or actions of the teacher in the organisation of the environment:

Harriet talks to the teacher about music that is playing.

Harriet: 'I like that one.'

The teacher puts the same music back on, and comments that she will try to find violin music for her.

(Foote & Ellis, 2008)

In this example, a child's request impacted on what happened. Although the teachers had commented in the interviews that children could ask for anything they wanted, overall the children played with the equipment and resources which were visible in the environment, making few requests for anything that was not directly available. It appeared that some children did not feel confident enough to ask, or if things were not readily available or visible, they did not think to use them in their play.

The key factor in the fourth level of Shier's model is that decisions are made jointly by children and adults. There were fewer examples of children being actively involved at this level. The fewer instances may have been linked to the age of the children and their perceived level of competency, which was the kind of situation that Berthelsen and Brownlee (2005) tried to avoid by arguing against judging children's agency against age-defined capacities. Nonetheless, teachers in one centre described how they planned curriculum activities with children:

We have a full group meeting time and we have informal discussion with children in small groups. After discussion we might draw a plan ... everyone gets a chance to speak and everyone's voice is heard and that includes any new equipment we buy, any new books, anything at all um, all goes down for the children before it goes out so we all get to see it, all get to look at it, all get to decide, and they talk about how they might play with it and what they might do so, they're completely involved in all of that right from the word go.

(Foote & Ellis, 2008)

Children were consulted about equipment to be purchased and were encouraged to participate in decision-making about what should be part of the centre's environment. However, the process was under the 'control' of the teachers who led the discussion.

Another example of participation at this level was seen where the teacher consulted a child about the placement of equipment. In this case, the teacher's subsequent questioning set the directions in relation to where the equipment would go, rather than enabling the children to make the decision.

Lucy is outside. The teacher asks where she could put the shadow screen, and asks what is needed to make a shadow.

Teacher: 'We are shadows in the light. No light no shadows. Sunshine and light, shadows, so we need to put it in the ...'

Lucy: 'Sun.'

The teacher and Lucy move the shadow screen across the outdoor area to where the sun can shine on it.

(Foote & Ellis, 2008)

This teacher appeared to be using this episode to take the child's learning further. When teachers are focused on engaging children in specific learning, there may be less opportunity for teachers and children to engage in shared decision-making. There were no comments in the interview transcripts that suggested children were able to equally share power and responsibility for the decision-making.

The extent to which children were able to control, or had power to create, their learning space appears to have been shaped by the intentions of the teachers. For example, one teacher said, 'They're beginning to understand the culture of what we were trying to get them to do' (Foote & Ellis, 2008).

There was a sense that the teachers had expectations that children would conform to the environment, and it was the teacher who had defined the purpose for spaces. By their actions, they set the directions for what was happening in spaces, and the children, by their actions, showed that they stayed within that space, not seeking other possibilities. Such an approach limits children's participation and their ability to set the direction of their learning.

Conclusion

Shier's model can be used to analyse teachers' beliefs and practices. It provides a basis upon which teachers can reflect on their practice to evaluate the opportunities afforded to children to engage in decision-making about their learning environment. The teachers in this research were highly committed to providing the very best opportunities for children's learning. They were committed to listening to children and they recognised children's right to be active participants. Ironically, though, there were few opportunities for children to share in decision-making with the teachers. Some of this may have been a consequence of their beliefs about children's levels of competency or their view of the role of the teacher. Perceptions about the physical limitations of environments appeared to impact on practices.

The UNCRC challenges teachers to reflect on their practice, particularly in relation to the nature of participation rights afforded children. Critiquing how children's voices are expressed in an early childhood setting is a key question for teachers implementing *Te Whāriki*, the early childhood curriculum framework. Children are empowered when they are able to make 'an increasing number of their own decisions and judgements' (Ministry of Education, 1996, p. 40).

Shier's model provides a tool which could be used by teachers as an evaluation strategy to understand how they acknowledge children's participation rights. If children are to have opportunities to become confident and competent learners (Ministry of Education, 1996), who can make decisions about their own learning, teachers should think about the nature of the learning environments they provide. As Strong-Wilson and Ellis (2007) have suggested, when children have some control over their own learning spaces they are empowered. In such contexts they are more likely to have a sense of agency. A goal for effective early childhood practice is the development of children's learning places, owned and valued by children, rather than places for children, owned and valued by the teachers, where the children feel they are temporary guests.

The observations of the children showed while the children were actively involved in the centre programme, the environment and the available opportunities were created by the adults. There was little to suggest that teachers enabled the creation of 'children's places' (Strong-Wilson & Ellis, 2007). Children's places are contexts created by the children 'at their own scale in any environment they can manipulate or modify', and such places support 'children's development of community, positive identities and successful learning' (Strong-Wilson, 2007, p. 43). These places empower children.

Teachers listened and responded to children but there was little to suggest that children's ideas shaped what was available in terms of people, places and things. If we are to facilitate increased participation of children in the creation of their places for learning, teachers need to consider how children can be involved in decision-making. With an increased focus on child voice and child agency, it is important that teachers in Aotearoa New Zealand consider whose voice is most evident in the early childhood setting. While listening to children is important, teachers need to go beyond listening and seek to understand children's perspectives more fully. Teachers committed to ensuring participation rights have an obligation to work towards children expressing their views and experiencing a balance of power in decision-making.

Each aspect of the Shier model addresses a component of children's participation. While it can be interpreted as a linear model, implying that the lower levels are less important, it can also be used as a tool to illustrate different levels of participation, each of which is valuable in particular ways. A model such as Shier's could give teachers a conceptual framework to evaluate centre practices in relation to how they encourage children's agency and voice throughout an early childhood programme. Such an approach could encourage teachers to become more intentional in the strategies they use to engage children in decision-making.

Many teachers in Aotearoa New Zealand talk about being committed to the UNCRC and *Te Whāriki* but how often do they use these to critically reflect on their practice? What aspects of the UNCRC do teachers address? Do protection rights gain more privilege than participation rights?

If early childhood environments in Aotearoa New Zealand are going to acknowledge children's participation rights and move from being places for children to being children's places, the challenge will be to give children more opportunities to be involved in decision-making and to share power and control in setting up the early childhood environment.

CHAPTER 15

Children of prisoners

Julie Lawrence

The incarceration rate in Aotearoa New Zealand is high compared to similar countries (such as Australia and the United Kingdom). In the past decade Aotearoa New Zealand has witnessed a significant increase in the numbers of people given a custodial sentence, and as a result, currently has the sixty-fifth highest incarceration rate in the world and sits eleventh among other country members of the Organisation for Economic Co-operation and Development (OECD). Gordon (2011a) has provided an overview of the policy context and estimates that 30,000 children per year in Aotearoa New Zealand experience parental incarceration. With the number of prison inmates set to rise from the current 8790 to around 12,500 in 2018 (Howard League, 2010), it follows that Aotearoa New Zealand children are experiencing parental incarceration at a higher rate than most western countries and the number of children affected is certain to increase.

Parental incarceration is a strong risk factor for multiple adverse outcomes for children through the life course, including antisocial behaviour, criminal offending, mental health problems, school failure, drug abuse and unemployment (Murray et al., 2012; Poehlmann, 2010). Makariev and Shaver (2010) found that children with an incarcerated parent are 'two and a half times as likely to have a serious mental health problem such as anxiety or depression (p. 312). This is concerning in the context of Aotearoa New Zealand's rising statistics on child and adolescent mental health problems, which currently amount to a public health issue affecting up to 17,000 children – a 14% increase since 2004 (The Wesley Community Centre, 2009).

The impact of incarceration has been conceptualised as a form of family crisis leading to demoralisation (Schneller, 1978) and the victimisation of children (Bloom & Steinhart, 1993). But while there is a growing interest in the phenomenon of the children of incarcerated parents, there has been little investigation regarding the actual experiences of the children and other family members. Although there has been a growth in overseas literature, only recently has the issue received any attention in Aotearoa New Zealand. Gordon's recent research (2009; 2010; 2011a; 2011b) has substantially contributed to debates and discussions around the working practices with the children of prisoners, as well as to the national and international literature.

The importance of the issues was brought to the forefront in 2011 with the 'Children of Incarcerated Parents' being the topic for the UN Committee on the Rights of the Child's Day of General Discussion in Geneva.[1] As individuals, children's experiences and reactions to parental incarceration will differ (Robertson, 2012). From the perspective of the United Nations Convention on the Rights of the Child (UNCRC), a number of articles are particularly relevant to children with an incarcerated parent:

- the right to be free from discrimination (Art. 2);
- protection of the best interest of the child (Art. 3);
- the right to have direct and frequent contact with parents from whom the child is separated (Art. 9);
- the right of the child to express his or her views and to be heard in matters affecting their situation (Art. 12);
- the child's right to protection of their family life and their privacy (Art. 16);
- the right of the child to protection from any physical or psychological harm or violence (Art. 19).

This chapter will focus on the right to have direct and frequent contact with parents from whom the child is separated (Art. 9), including the right to be provided with information about the whereabouts of the absent member(s) of the family unless the provision of the information would be detrimental to the well-being of the child (Art. 9.4).

The study

This chapter presents some of the findings from a small mixed-methods research study, which set out to investigate the child's attachment network and the collaborative or antagonistic relationships among the extended family and social network of children who have experienced parental incarceration. The study is exploratory, and as such, is a starting point as opposed to an end point. The children's stories provide a rare in-depth picture of the thoughts and

---

[1] The 51 written submissions can be accessed online at www2.ohchr.org/English/bodies/crc/discussion2011_submissions.htm.

perceptions of some children with an incarcerated parent and the multitude of issues facing them.

Reported in this chapter are findings from the semi-structured interviews with eight children and their caregivers, which explored the children's knowledge and understanding of their fathers' incarceration, their relationship and their experience of contact with him. Also interviewed were the caregiver of a baby aged six months and the mother of a five-year-old boy, who was not interviewed because he was not aware that his father had been in prison. The children who were interviewed (four girls and four boys) ranged in age from six to 17 years. They lived in a range of family situations: five with their biological mothers; one with both his parents; one with his paternal grandmother; one with her maternal cousin; and two with foster parents. For all the children, it was their father whose incarceration they had experienced most recently and

Table 15.1: *The children's demographics. To preserve the children's anonymity, they were each asked to choose a name for use in the research.*

Child	Age*	Ethnicity	Gender	Main caregiver*	Offence that led to most recent incarceration	Father previous incarceration?
Scarlett	17	Pākehā	F	Mother	Alcohol-related offence	Yes
Dave	14	Pākehā	M	Mother	Alcohol-related offence	Yes
Mishron	13	Māori	M	Foster	Attempted murder	Yes
Bob	13	Māori	F	Foster	Attempted murder	Yes
Mr Cool	13	Māori	M	Mother	Poaching	No
Tamatea	11	Māori	M	Mother	Burglary	Yes
Evany	9	Māori	F	Maternal second cousin	Burglary/Drug-related offences	Yes
Melody	6	Māori	F	Mother	Poaching	No
Tane†	5	Māori	M	Mother & father	Aggravated robbery	Yes
Ash§	6 months	Māori	M	Paternal grandmother	Burglary	No

Key: * At time of interview
† Tane's pseudonym was chosen by his mother.
§ Ash's pseudonym was chosen by his grandmother.

who was the main focus of the interview. At the time of the interview, two of the fathers had completed their sentence, while the remainder were incarcerated.

Parental incarceration may lead family dynamics to alter and to the child being looked after by other family or non-family members. The children in this study lived in a range of caregiver situations and the following stories illustrate how some of them came to live with their present families.

Foster care

Siblings Bob and Mishron have lived with their present foster family for eight years. Prior to this placement they were living with their mother; but immediately before, they were staying with their father for the first time since they were three years old. At the time of the interview their father and older brother were both incarcerated for attempted murder and armed robbery respectively, and their mother had been out of prison for four years but was 'still in the paper quite regularly for very minor silly offences' (foster mother).

The twins saw and recalled their father being arrested:

Bob: I remember him getting handcuffed …

Interviewer: So you remember him being handcuffed, how did that feel?

Bob: Well a dog jumped on him, I remember that. They didn't come into my house. I remember why he got arrested though. He smashed his girlfriend's car and put a hose in it …. I was in the front yard and I was on one of my little toy motorbikes.

Interviewer: And how did it feel? Do you remember?

Bob: I didn't really feel anything 'cos that was the first time we'd seen him.

Interviewer: That was the first time you'd seen him arrested or was that the first time you'd met him?

Bob: First time we'd met him.

Mishon: It's kind of weird 'cos he doesn't even feel like my dad.

Bob: 'Cos he left us when we were three, but I only remember [meeting him when I was] five.

Kinship Care

Evany was aged nine when she was interviewed and had been in the care of her maternal second cousin (Evany called her 'stepmum') since she was an infant. Also in the household were her 'stepdad' and three older 'stepbrothers'.

Although Evany's father's incarceration was not why she was initially placed with her stepmother, he went to prison soon after her placement, and had 'been in and out of prison like … always … since we have known him' (in her stepmother's words). Her biological mother committed suicide when Evany was three years old.

Evany's stepmother described how she came to live with her:

> I got a phone call and mum says 'Look, would you be interested in taking care of this little baby maybe for three weeks. She's in hospital, maybe she's a bit undernourished, she's not feeling good, she's got a broken femur' … they couldn't do anything with the femur because it had been gone too long … it was broken at a party. The parents were leaving a party drunk and, of course, someone stepped in to protect the child and when they went to take the child, the child got a broken femur … and that's how [Evany] came into my care.

When asked when her dad first went to prison, Evany's response was, 'Well he's been in there quite a lot, so I don't really know.'

Biological mother

Of the six children in the study who lived with their mothers, four were born while their father was in prison. Tamatea was 11 years old when he was interviewed for the study. He lives with his mother and his seven-year-old half-brother. His mother found out that she was pregnant 'about three days after his father was put in prison':

> It was very strange and very difficult coping with being pregnant as well as having the father of your baby in prison, that was really tough …
>
> So I guess I had a lot of choices about whether to keep the contact going, how much contact to have … if that was going to be healthy for me or … I think one of the worst things was … his court case was just before Christmas.

Scarlett and Dave's father was in prison when they were both born. He was mid-sentence when Dave was born, but was arrested while their mother was in labour with Scarlett.

Paternal grandmother

Like Tamatea, Scarlett, Tane and Melody's little brother, Ash was born while his father was incarcerated. He was six months old at the time of the interview, and living with his paternal grandmother. She described how he came to live with her:

So, [Ash's father] went to prison six months ago and his girlfriend was pregnant with [Ash] at the time ... This is [Ash's father's] first child. So she was directed by CYFS to live with her mother, but they fought and so I offered her a room here to come and live here with [Ash] ... and she was only here a few weeks and went out for lunch one day and didn't come back. So that's how I ended up with [Ash].

Key themes

Three key themes emerging from the data will be explored in the remainder of this chapter. These relate to the children's knowledge and understanding of parental incarceration, their experiences of their contact with their incarcerated father, and their relationship with him.

Children's knowledge and understanding of the parental incarceration

One of the main themes in this research was the different level of information that individual children were given about their incarcerated father and their family situation (where? and why?). Without information, children are less able to formulate their ideas and express their opinions fully.

Where?
The majority of the children had experienced their father's absence through incarceration at multiple time points. Although none of them specified an age, they said that they had been aware that their father was in prison from a young age. However, their caregivers' answers to the question of when they told the children suggested differently. For the mothers of those children who were born or were a baby when their father was incarcerated, there was a general feeling that there was a 'right' age at which their child should be told. None of them reported having had an ongoing conversation with their child over time as their child's understanding developed.

For example, Scarlett's mother told her when she was seven years old: 'Because at first when they were little I used to say, "Dad's away on holiday." I never actually told them. I'd just say "Oh Dad's away or visiting, or working." I just used to say something like that. But then something came up, I was speaking to someone about things and she said "No, you tell them the truth."'

Tamatea's mother also told him when he was seven: 'He used to see someone at [counselling service] and we worked out a wee plan. So he knew that he was away and didn't know where and then, when he got to the stage where he could understand a bit better, I sort of spoke to him about it. So he's probably known since he was about seven or eight ... maybe.'

Tane's father completed his sentence two years ago and Tane was unaware that he had been in prison for the first three years of his life. His parents both felt that while it was very important that he knew that his father had been in prison, he was too young to be told at the moment, and they would tell him when he was older.

Evany did not know with absolute certainty if her father was in or out of prison at the time of interview. According to her caregiver, he was not in prison, but she herself was not aware:

Interviewer: So do you know if he's in or out of prison at the moment?

Evany: I think he's in … probably.

Interviewer: Do you know when he comes out and goes in [to prison]? Does someone usually tell you?

Evany: No, not really.

Mr Cool's stepfather, who is also Melody's father, went to prison for the first time when the children were 13 and six years old. They were aware of the lead-up to the sentencing court appearance and were told 'that night' that he had gone to prison.

Why?

Generally, the children had some idea about why their father was in prison, although often they did not know the full details and some made assumptions. As well as not being sure when to tell the children, sometimes caregivers found it hard to tell them the truth about the offence, and so they told an incomplete or fictional version of events. Often half-truths were told to 'protect' a child, which – while unintentionally – can confuse the child. Also, there is a danger that if the whole story emerges, it could have a negative impact on the child–parent relationships.

Tamatea knew that his father was in prison for burglary at the time of our interview, but his mother was wrestling with her decision not to tell him the full nature of his father's previous high-profile crime because she feared he would seek the information from other sources like the internet or the media:

> … He doesn't know the whole story. And only two months ago it was in the paper that he'd gone back away for burglary and of course they didn't just put that in, they put all this big screed about what he'd done in the past. Tamatea didn't see it and I was so thankful. I was really quite distraught about it, I lost the plot a bit.

The Sensible Sentencing Trust have got information ... on the internet that my son can Google and find out exactly what [his father] did. And I'm really unhappy about it and I can't withdraw it, only [his father] can. And that's one of the forces behind me telling him as well, I mean I've always wanted to be open with him but knowing that he can Google it and it's right there ... I can see their reason for doing it to a certain extent but do they think about the impact on the children?

While Evany did not know the full reason for her father's incarceration(s), she made assumptions: 'Well I think that the reason he's in prison a lot is because he's in a gang. He's in the [gang name].'

In contrast, Melody and Mr Cool both knew the reason that their father/ stepfather was in prison. Their mother had made a decision to tell them because of her own childhood experiences and because of the advice from the children's uncle suggesting that 'keeping things from them isn't actually helping or being honest with them. And telling them would help them cope a lot better':

I told them that night ... So me and mum went in and just explained to the kids that dad done wrong by [offence commited] and because of what he did ... well I had to explain to them that the rule is if you take [details of offence] then you get in trouble and you know what happens when you get in trouble, you have to see the policeman and they will tell you your punishment. Just like mum and dad does for you, you get punished for your naughty behaviour. So that's the way I had to explain it and mum was guiding me through it and was like 'we're strong, we can do this'. And that's just what I had to do. I said 'Dad's done this and for his naughty behaviour ... cos I remembered at kindy they used to lock up their friends in the dungeon and ... so I said 'Dad is now in the dungeon. But the thing with that is that we get to talk to him on the phone every day, and we get to write letters to Dad and that's great 'cos I get some mail from Daddy and we get to visit him every Sunday'. So we get to keep that normality and that's what I said to [father's name], that we need to keep some normality in their lives and in their everyday living. That he's still a part of it. Just because he's not present, he's still part of it. So he still gets to talk to them about their days at school, just like when he was here.

Contact with incarcerated parent

Visits and other contacts with an incarcerated parent allow children to express their emotional reactions to the separation. The contact also helps children to develop a more realistic understanding of their parents' circumstances, preserves important connections, and provides assurances for children that their parents are safe (Allard & Lu, 2006). Prior to Melody visiting her father in prison, she worried about whether he would have basic things, as her mother explained:

> I found [Melody] washing down the walls and she's spent a good half an hour / 45 minutes in there. And then she comes out to me and said 'Does Dad have a bed?' I said 'Yes he has a bed.' She said 'Does he have blankets?' Me: 'Yes he has blankets.' Her: 'Is it nice and warm for him?' Me: 'Yes.' Her: 'Does he get fed? Is there food in there?' Me: 'Yes they make him breakfast, they make him lunch and they make him tea.' Her: 'But what about chips? He likes chips!' Me: 'Because we call those things luxuries, like remember if you have a lolly I say that's a luxury and you just need to enjoy your luxury things, but they come at a cost and they are a luxury treat. And if Daddy wants to get treats like that, then Mummy has to put money into a bank account for Daddy, and then he can use that to go and gets his chips. So Daddy will get his chips. Is there anything else?' Her: 'No, I just wanted to know.'

Of note is the fact that all but Tamatea had experienced some form of contact (i.e. visit, letter, or phone call) with their father at least once whilst he was incarcerated, although at the time of the interview fewer than a quarter of them still had any contact.

Visits

Half of the children in this study had visited their father in prison at least once, but most could not recall the experience because they had visited as a baby. The caregivers often made the decision either never to visit or to stop their child visiting their father in prison in order to protect their children from what they viewed as the negative impact of the visits. A common feeling among caregivers was that the prison environment was not suitable for children.

For example, the father of Scarlett and Dave has been incarcerated numerous times at various prisons and was described as 'institutionalised' by their mother. Dave has never visited him in prison. However, as described by her mother, Scarlett was taken to visit him regularly until she was about three years old.

> Well it wasn't too bad when he was in [local prison], but then we got a van when he was in [prison 175 km distance] … I think I did that a couple of times, but the second time there were some other ladies on the bus and I think one of them actually did some shoplifting on the way there and I just thought 'no, this is not for my child'. I remember them talking about it and I thought 'no'. So that was the last time and as I said she was starting to get a wee bit older and I thought 'no'.

Ash met his father at his first prison visit when he was 10 weeks old, and he had visited twice monthly since. His grandmother believed these visits were important 'so he knows who he is. It's important for both [father] and Ash to bond.' Despite her strong beliefs about the importance of these visits and her willingness to facilitate them, she found them to be logistically difficult and financially draining, and the actual experience of visiting with a baby 'horrendous':

> I'm only allowed to take in one nappy, a bottle, wet wipes that they ripped open so they all dried out ... Everything has to fit in one clear plastic zip-lock bag. They give you a zip-lock bag. He's not allowed any toys. You have to feed the baby away from the prisoners, no prisoners are allowed to feed the baby. You have to change the baby away (which is fine) you have to change the baby out somewhere else.

Tamatea has never had contact with his father in prison (the only contact he has ever had is one phone call). His mother visited Tamatea's father in prison for the first year but she never took Tamatea. She talked about her decision:

> I didn't really want him to meet his dad in prison. I just had this thing about the 'first time meeting your dad' ... I didn't want it to be there. Yeah, and I guess it was probably a lot to do with the fact that *I* was finding it so hard that I thought he would find it like that as well, which he probably wouldn't have had any idea about that. So that was my main reason, I just didn't want them to meet in that environment.

Another influence on her decision not to take Tamatea to visit his father in prison was the actual crime he had committed:

> The charge he went in on was quite a serious ... it did sort of get to that point, when Tamatea was one, when my psychological health went really badly downhill and that's when I stopped the contact. So it probably had a lot to do with that, as well as the distance.

Caregivers had a great deal of influence over the children's perspectives towards their incarcerated father and their situation. There were many examples where caregivers became gatekeepers between the children and their fathers whether they chose to or not. For instance, despite Ash's grandmother facilitating the contact between Ash and his father (her son), she described how she would use contact with Ash to punish her son if he returned to prison in the future:

Because if he comes out and goes back in then he doesn't get visits because that's part of his punishment, it's part of making him realise 'well this is what you're missing out on.' So then I won't take him down to visit. If [Ash] asked to go and see daddy, then I'd explain to him 'well, daddy's in prison and this time we can't go and visit 'cos daddy has to learn that unfortunately if he goes to prison he doesn't get to see any of us, but we'll see him when he gets back out.' 'Cos I don't see that I should have to put [Ash] through all that pain and suffering if [Ash's father]'s going to be selfish, if that's what the case may be.

Children's views on contact

The children in the study had mixed views about visiting their fathers in prison. Melody and Mr Cool visited their father/stepfather in prison, exchanged letters and talked on the phone regularly with him. They talked positively about their visits to the prison:

Interviewer: And what do you do there?

Melody: Play on the playground ... go and give him hugs.

Interviewer: ... and how does that feel?

Melody: Good.

Mr Cool: I thought the prison would be like real yuck and that, but it wasn't that bad. ... Yeah, it was pretty cool going through all the scanners and that ... I imagined it to be like in movies and stuff ... like all run down.

They also exchanged letters and talked on the phone up to three times a day, as Mr Cool said: 'Yeah I've written him a couple of letters. Oh the first time it felt pretty awkward cos I didn't know what to say but after I did, it felt pretty good so ... yeah.'

Tametea and Evany both wanted contact with their fathers but were reliant on their caregivers. Tametea and his mother were making plans for him to meet his father for the first time but he returned to prison before the meeting occurred, as Tamatea's mother reported: 'When I first told Tamatea that he went back to prison he cried and it's like the first time that he's actually showed emotion, so I was like really 'uhhhh' [breath in] but it was also at the same time a positive change that he's actually opened up a bit.' Evany wanted contact in person with her father:

Interviewer: OK, so at the moment would you be able to see your dad if you wanted to?

Evany: Um, probably not because I don't know what prison he's in or anything.

Interviewer: And if he was in prison would you want to go and visit him there?

Evany: Probably ... um ... maybe ... it depends if I could or not.

Interviewer: So if you could, how would you feel about that?

Evany: Probably nervous because I haven't seen him in a long time.

Evany also wanted contact through letters:

Evany: Well I wrote him heaps of Father's Day cards but I haven't had the chance to go and give them to him.

Interviewer: So you keep them?

Evany: Yeah.

Interviewer: Would you like the chance to send your cards or to write to him?

Evany: Yeah I would.

Four of the children said that they did not want contact with their father while he was in prison or when he was released. This was mainly because the children felt that their father had not been in their lives and he had let them down. For example, Mishron and Bob said:

Mishron: I don't feel the need to write letters to dad, cos I don't really know him ...

Bob: He hasn't written to us for like two years.

Mishron: I stopped. I don't know why.

Scarlett said:

I told him I don't want to see him any more ... One New Year's, I spent it with him and I said 'Can you stay out [of prison] for my birthday?' He got in trouble *that day* ... I just haven't talked to him since. I just don't want to ... I don't care if he's in prison or if he's out. I think it's because now I know he's not going to be around ever ...

Despite Dave saying that he did not want to see his father, later in his interview he explained that if his father 'was going to be better,' he would like to have contact.

Discussion and conclusion

While for some children, separation through parental incarceration may be beneficial, such as perhaps when a parent has abused a child or exposed the child to other forms of violence (Eddy & Reid, 2003), for most, maintaining the relationship is crucial. Equally, the children and families of prisoners have varying degrees of expectations of their incarcerated parent.

For the incarcerated parent, their ability to parent, even at the most basic level, is likely to be influenced and shaped by the person caring for their children and the role this caregiver is willing to take in maintaining contact. Caregivers can be influential in paternal involvement because their attitudes and behaviours may facilitate or constrain an incarcerated father's opportunities to parent, develop, and maintain relationships with his children from prison. Roy and Dyson's (2005) study about incarcerated fathers found that in the prison situation 'gatekeeping emerged as a complex and often ambiguous process of negotiation and identity transformation, in which prisoners reworked their identities as fathers' (p. 305).

The research literature has highlighted how heavily dependent the children are on non-imprisoned 'gatekeepers' for contact with their incarcerated father and often for the continuation of their relationship with him (Clarke et. al., 2005). Even in a family where the non-incarcerated caregiver is supportive, the wide-reaching impact of the incarceration on the economic and social structure of a family can limit their ability to be supportive. Several families in this study, as in others (Christian, Mellow & Thomas, 2006), faced difficulties because of the additional financial costs in promoting and maintaining a parent–child relationship from their limited economic resources and transport options. Another by-product of maintaining family relations is the need to provide an incarcerated parent with money for prison provisions from a reduced family income (Hairston, 2002).

A further implication of incarceration is a change in how parents and children communicate and how they navigate the variety of challenges they face in regard to maintaining contact with each other. This key part of parenting is altered dramatically and is reliant on expensive telephone calls, written communication, and prison visits. As Hairston (1998) pointed out, letter writing assumes a willingness and ability on behalf of the child to respond in a mode which is often viewed as an extension of homework. Also, although not explored in this research, low levels of education are common among inmates and poor writing skills may result in a reluctance for a prisoner to write to his child.

The relationship between the caregiver and the incarcerated parent has been found to be a very important influence on whether or not a child has contact with their absent parent (Nurse, 2002). In this study, with the exception of Bob and Mishron, the caregivers all had a prior or current relationship with the child's incarcerated father. It was evident that the emotions and feelings of any historical or current relationship impacted on the child's relationship with the incarcerated parent. Six of the children lacked a close relationship with their father when he was first incarcerated and two-thirds of these had no wish to have any contact with their father.

Separation can impose major obstacles to maintaining family ties and relationships with children. These relationships are dependent not only on personal histories but also on numerous other influences. Among those that did, and continue to, facilitate contact between the children and their fathers, their own mindset, the emotional, practical and financial support that they received from informal support (extended family and friends), and formal support were crucial.

This research, like that of others such as Hairston (1991), found that caregivers' attitudes had an influential role on visitation patterns. Some caregivers resisted the idea of visitation by children because of the unpleasant and inhospitable visiting conditions or because of their belief that visitation would produce negative reactions in the children. For some children, particularly Mr Cool and Melody, the visits alleviated their concerns about their father's well-being.

Many factors influence how a child experiences a prison visit, including the actual correction facility. While in theory correctional facilities make accommodations for visiting and maintenance of family ties, this is not their core purpose or design. The experience of the participating families illustrated that children visiting and interacting with the criminal justice system are often viewed as a possible security risk, which can make facilitating parent and child contact challenging.

Some caregivers found it hard to tell children that their father was in prison and many struggled with deciding when, and what, to tell them. In such cases in this study, the choice not to tell was made not deliberately to deceive the children but in the belief that it would protect the children and minimise the impact of the incarceration on them. Those caregivers that did provide information were sometimes vague. Children need to receive honest, factual information, and they need to have their experience validated (Nolen-Hoeksema & Larson, 1999). The provision of reliable, dependable information allows children to begin to understand their situation, start coping with their new family circumstances, and grieve the loss of their incarcerated parent.

This chapter has shown that often, for the children in this study, the right to have direct and frequent contact with the parent from whom they were separated was not fully met. Sometimes this was due to a lack of developmentally appropriate information about the whereabouts of their absent father or how to contact him; but more often it was due to the lack of support or facilitation to maintain contact by either the caregiver or their father. While this chapter did not set out to make any recommendations that would address this, the findings indicate that the caregivers of these children felt they could have benefited from support to facilitate contact between their children and their incarcerated father in terms of:

- information about the importance of a child maintaining contact with their incarcerated father;
- emotional support to enable them to tell their child in a developmentally appropriate way and maintain ongoing conversations with the child;
- practical support such as transport; and
- financial support to maintain telephone contact where possible.

Likewise changes to the environment in which the visits take place could have led to continued visits at the prison between children and father.

The voices of these 'unseen victims' (Clark, 1995) and their caregivers in this small study offer an insight into the effects of incarceration on their lives and give some hint of directions that can be taken to meet their needs. Aotearoa New Zealand has a growing prison population and information is needed to understand not just the negative impacts that incarceration has for prisoners' children but also the potential alternatives that might alleviate such negative impacts.

CHAPTER 16

Children's understandings of success

Judith Sligo & Karen Nairn

'And will you succeed?
Yes indeed, yes indeed!
Ninety-eight and three-quarters per cent guaranteed!'
    from *Oh, the places you'll go!*, Dr Seuss (1990)

What do children think 'success' means? We investigated what a group of children understood by the term 'success' and what they thought it meant to be 'successful'. To contextualise the study, we discuss the significance of success in Aotearoa New Zealand's education system and society, then present our findings. We conclude with some recommendations for promoting children's success.

Striving for successful citizens

Children's success is a focus for research, policymakers, media and parents in contemporary Aotearoa New Zealand, which has undergone a neo-liberal transformation unparalleled elsewhere (Larner, 1996). The educational environment, which encourages individuals to strive for success from an early age, is prioritised in policy. A discourse of individualism emphasises personal responsibility and agency for choices and decisions, and the role of the state is significantly reduced. Policy attention is focused on children and young people negotiating their future paths. Education becomes the means for individuals to achieve economic success. This rhetoric of education as the conduit to success ignores the unequal distribution of cultural, financial and material resources among families (Nairn, Higgins & Sligo, 2012).

Neo-liberal discourses are so dominant that education is now framed and shaped within its parameters (Davies & Saltmarsh, 2007). Initiated in the

1980s, educational reforms focused on containing the cost of education (New Zealand Department of Education, 1989). Alongside this was the desire to build 'a world-leading education system that equips all New Zealanders with the knowledge, skills and values to be successful citizens in the 21st century' (Ministry of Education, 2012, unpaginated). National Standards reflect Aotearoa New Zealand society's preoccupation with student success and failure (Snook & O'Neil, 2010) and the neo-liberal discourse of individual responsibility for achieving success (Beck & Beck-Gernsheim, 2002). The revised Aotearoa New Zealand education curriculum, introduced in 2007, also addressed concerns with student success, identifying principles and values informing the curriculum. These require students to value excellence and perseverance, with the expectation that they achieve personal excellence regardless of their personal circumstances (Ministry of Education, 2007a).

Numeracy and literacy are considered particularly important in the quest for educational success. The Ministry of Education's two priority outcomes for 2009–10 were that *every* child achieves literacy and numeracy levels that enable their success and that every young person has the skills and qualifications to contribute to their, and Aotearoa New Zealand's, future. Generally speaking, New Zealand children perform well in these foundational skills: many are reading significantly above the international average (Telford & May, 2010) and in 2006 the mean mathematical literacy performance of only five countries was significantly higher than Aotearoa New Zealand's (Telford & Caygill, 2007).

Not *all* Aotearoa New Zealand school students are achieving at these rates, however, and there is concern about the success of particular groups, especially Māori (Marie, Fergusson & Boden, 2008) and Pasifika students (Lai et al., 2009) who have lower numeracy and literacy scores (NEMP, 2008). Students from lower socio-economic families are also more likely to underachieve (Snook & O'Neil, 2010). Attention was also focused on the relative academic success of girls and boys (Gibb & Fergusson, 2009). Improvement in female education outcomes prompted concerns about the comparative educational status of males (for example, Mallard, 2004). This contest evolved into a debate about 'which girls' and 'which boys' succeed and in which subjects (Ministry of Education, 2007).

Neo-liberal education policies expect individuals to take responsibility for their own success; but inequities shaped by uneven distribution of economic resources and unequal gender and race relations heighten anxieties about parents' potential to provide for their children's success (Watson, Hughes & Lauder, 2003).

Contributing to parental panic about success

The media reflects and may contribute to the preoccupation with children's success. Popular magazines provide parents and students with information focusing on success: for example, television programmes dealing with managing difficult children air on prime time television and there is a plethora of 'how-to' books providing advice for parents on raising successful children.

There is growing pressure on parents to keep their children safe and busy (Guldberg, 2009) and increasing numbers of extracurricular activities are available. Parents ferry their offspring to music, sports and drama classes. The proliferation of out-of-school reading and mathematics tuition progammes reflects anxieties about literacy and numeracy. Parents are required to monitor more areas of their children's lives, and health and wealth become equated with 'success'. How do children define and perceive success, within a context where preoccupation with success is taken for granted and success is often measured in economic terms?

What is 'success'?

'Success' is a term that is largely taken at face value, yet it means different things to different people. It is used across settings but is not always defined or clarified. Success broadly refers to doing well, getting good results and achievement.

Academic research about children's success focuses on the influences on children's behaviour and educational outcomes (see, for example Matheson & Banerjee, 2010; Pianta & Stuhlmann, 2004) and the efficacy of programmes designed to improve children's behaviour and learning (such as Gilliam, Ripple, Zigler & Leiter, 2000; Weissberg, Kumpfer & Seligman, 2003). This literature implicitly equates success with the generic definitions in the previous paragraph.

Focusing on children's own definitions and experiences of success provides a new angle to this literature. Below, we present results from a study (Sligo, 2001) about 'success' with a group of primary-age children conducted for a Master's thesis by the first author (JS) and supervised by the other (KN).

The research project

'Identity' is a useful concept for understanding how the children in this study made sense of themselves and viewed success. Identity is complex, dynamic and always in process. It is not an individual process; rather, it takes place in the context of relationships – within families, neighbourhoods and communities, with peers, and within institutions, such as school (Nairn et al., 2012). Gender, ethnicity and socio-economic status, and the intersection of these and other axes of difference, also impact on how children develop their identities. We investigated whether feelings of success were part of identity building and whether children's perspectives of success were influenced by neo-liberal education policies.

The research was an in-depth, qualitative study undertaken within a sociology of childhood framework, which 'takes children seriously in their own right, in acknowledging their constructiveness as actors' (Qvortrup, Bardy, Sgritta & Wintersberger, 1994, foreword) privileging their voices and views. Deploying multiple methods of data collection, we investigated the children's definitions and understandings of 'success' and analysed individual and societal factors that seemed to influence their evolving concepts.

The setting was a high-decile school in a small Aotearoa New Zealand city. A total of 22 children participated in the research. All the children except one (who was Indian) were Aotearoa New Zealand Europeans. The class was a composite of Years 3 and 4 with students aged seven to nine years. The majority came from families with two parents in paid professional work. A minority came from families with single parents or reconstituted families and a small number had parents who were tertiary students or employed in low-paying jobs. All the children were from families where education was valued.

While purposeful recruitment of children from highly motivated, educationally focused families was not the intention, this was the outcome. This group of children, therefore, was not particularly diverse in terms of ethnicity or socio-economic status, although there was a range of academic (and other) abilities. There was a fairly even gender split (10 boys and 12 girls), and in the following analysis we pay particular attention to gender.

Gender is a salient factor in discussions of success because girls' and boys' achievement levels are frequently compared. We conceptualise gender in a post-structuralist sense: socially constructed and intersecting with other differences (Jones, 1991; 1993). Girls and boys are often referred to as separate groups, homogeneous and in opposition to each other. In the process of organising our analysis around gender, we risk doing the same. Nevertheless, gender is a useful starting point for considering how girls' and boys' perceptions of success are different and similar. Young children quickly come to understand that the world is organised around a gender dichotomy (Francis, 2002) and that the 'taking up' of a legitimate gender is important for their sense of social competence. Of course, there are different ways of 'being' male or female and some are more dominant than others. Some individuals position themselves within competing discourses about gender but to go against gender norms risks being understood as 'not normal' (Jones, 1993).

The project involved a range of data collection methods including classroom observations; interviews; a structured language task (completing sentences about abilities); and artistic tasks where the children drew or painted images showing their successes. These tasks gave an overview of the children's understandings of success and all the children participated in these activities. There were also four activities that the children could choose from (puppet shows, role play, drawing and writing or photography), where the children worked in small groups and the focus was on describing success. Eight children also participated in in-depth interviews, individually and together in a focus group.

How did the participants define 'success'?

When asked what success meant to them, all the participants provided a definition. The children offered full definitions, often elucidating with examples and references to their own lives. Their definitions included thoughtful and complex concepts like achieving, overcoming, completing or gaining something.

Over half of the participants (eight girls and five boys) stressed the importance of encountering a challenge or overcoming adversity for something to be considered successful. For example, Harry said:[1] '[Success] is when you finish something and you really want to do it and it takes a long time.' Nicole said that you'd need to finish 'this wonderful thing' which would take 'really long'. Tomi, a female participant, summarised:

> J: So is it important that it's something hard?
>
> Tomi: Yep. And if it's easy and, and it's like a lot of words but it's real easy to do and you don't finish it, that wouldn't be [success].

Seven children also made reference to persevering with a task as a feature of success. Perseverance implies the completion of a task and this was also a characteristic of six participants' definitions. For these people (five boys) finishing was important: 'I think success means ... that you've finished something ... and you do it well' (Brian).

Developing skills and trying hard were also important. Girls were more likely than boys to emphasise the importance of the process of acquiring new skills. The following example is from Sally: 'I think success is what you can get better at and ... um thinking about things, but, um, doing things.'

The children's definitions reflected some prevalent societal discourses. The neo-liberal significance of the individual was apparent in the children's discussion of individual achievements (although the nature of the questions did

---

1 All the children's names are the pseudonyms they chose for themselves.

promote this to some extent). Other societal discourses evident in the children's views included overcoming challenges as a way of becoming a successful independent citizen and the notion that acquiring skills is as important as the outcome. Along with these definitions of success, there was one person who thought success meant luck (giving the example of winning Lotto) and two who talked about saving or spending money as success (perhaps suggesting that success equates with wealth).

How did the participants know they were successful?

The data revealed three themes around how the children knew they were successful.

Competition and winning

The participants said that they knew that they were successful via competition and winning. This was particularly true for the boys. Seven boys (but only three girls) talked about winning as a way of knowing that they were successful:

> J: Yeah. Can you have success in sort of other ways?
>
> Isaac: If you won a game.

The boys' references to competition generally referred to sports but sometimes to board or video games. Competition is often related to participation in sports, which is also an institution for constructing and reconstructing male hegemony (Bryson, 1994). Swain (2000) stated, 'To be manly in sports, traditionally means to be competitive, successful, dominating, aggressive, stoical, goal directed and physically strong' (p. 103). To some extent it is not surprising that the boys felt successful when they were competing in sports because it is one way of 'being' male, of which these boys were developing an understanding.

Alternatively, some of the research participants referred to a different understanding of sport and exercise that also prevails in Aotearoa New Zealand society. This is its link with health and the importance of being active and 'having a go'. In Aotearoa New Zealand primary schools, the development of KiwiSport was intended to encourage skill development and an active lifestyle with a reduction in the emphasis on competitiveness. This discourse was apparent in the words of several participants who downplayed the importance of winning:

> J: How would you know, would you only be successful at the game if you won?
>
> Isaac: Umm, no, not really, um, getting a fair go at it.

Swain (2000) suggested sport has varied rewards for participants: 'Additional to the feeling of enjoyment that it gave them were those of comradeship, competitiveness and physical fitness' (p. 101). This appears to be particularly true for many boys, where these feelings are important for their sense of masculinity.

Getting feedback
External feedback was another way some children knew they were successful. Four girls and three boys said they would know they were successful because they were told they were or because they received a reward. Some children also tested themselves against criteria to determine their success. This excerpt from Joey's interview shows how he makes use of a range of external signs to validate his success:

J: How do you know that you're good at those things?

Joey: Umm, 'cos I've been tested on them and I've got good results with them.

J: Yep. How do you know you're good at your story writing?

Joey: I get some ticks and the teacher tells me that I've done well.

J: What about at soccer?

Joey: Umm, well, the coach saying we've done a good job and that's excellent skills from you.

The children who referred to adults (teachers, coaches, parents) to validate their successes were influenced by adult assumptions of what counted as success. Within the adult–child dualism, children are often understood as without power, and this is reinforced when children are reliant on adults' acknowledgement in order to experience feelings of success.

Feelings of satisfaction
Participants described knowing that they were successful via their feelings of pride and pleasure. Only one boy included emotions within his initial definition of success, but several discussed emotions in their interviews. Four girls defined success with feelings. Sally summarised her thoughts on how to recognise success by saying 'Feeling happy with what you've done ... That's all!'

The children in this study did not indicate that they were exclusively rewarded by internal emotions or external rewards: both were important. The children made sense of discourses of success via their understandings of themselves as individuals, students, sporting participants and gendered beings. The activities in which children participated influenced their understandings. The boys' exposure to competitive sports made competition and winning a logical way for them to understand their successes.

In what areas did the participants feel success?

The children in the study were interviewed about and showed their domains of success via writing, artworks and small group activities. The results are discussed below, first referring to success in and out of school, and then focusing on in-school successes across curriculum areas.

The children had different understandings about their feelings of success at school compared to other settings. 'School-based activities' included core curriculum areas and other school-time activities. 'Out-of-school activities' included activities the children talked about doing out of school, such as playing video games, rugby and ballet, and caring for pets. We acknowledge the artificial binary of these 'in-school' and 'out-of-school' designations, but it is useful in considering children's views on success. Some activities were difficult to categorise because of the breadth of the school curriculum, but were judged from context to allocate them as 'in-' or 'out-of-' school activities.

Children feel more successful out of school

Both genders had more areas of success in their out-of-school than their in-school activities. Given the current neo-liberal emphasis on success in education, it is interesting to note that the children in this study generally felt more successful away from the school environment. For example, the children who took photographs had fewer or no photographs taken at school. Sally said:

J: And you didn't take any photos at school, why was that?

Sally: Because, I feel more successful at home than at school.

J: Why is that?

Sally: Because I have a variety of things to do at home. At school, when we're doing something, sharing pencils or you've got to choose this piece of paper or this colour. At home I've got all different paper, felts and I can choose which one I want to use.

The girls were more likely to feel successful at school than the boys. The 12 girls recorded feeling successful in school-related activities a total of 89 times while the 10 boys recorded feeling successful in school activities only 36 times. Boys mentioned seven different in-school activities where they felt successful, while girls mentioned 14.

Girls also had a greater range of successful experiences in school and discussed their interests with more specific detail, such as 'making up stories' or 'writing poems' rather than more generic descriptions, such as 'maths'. Boys were generally less school-focused than girls. Research suggests that many boys

Success and competency can take many different forms.

conflate schoolwork with femininity (Renold, 2001a). It is not straightforward for girls either. There is pressure on young women to be successful in a range of ways, and negotiating this within the context of differently valued femininities can involve a precarious balancing act (Renold & Allan, 2006).

We grouped the areas of out-of-school successes into nine categories.[2] The children were encouraged to think about all domains of success, and most had several. The 10 boys described, drew or wrote about 59 different areas of success, while the 12 girls recorded 60. However, the high number of sports

---

2   These were: sports; active games; swimming; computer games; home craft; pet care; music and dance; being a caring friend; and other.

mentioned by boys largely accounted for their areas of success. Overall, some girls felt successful in all categories except computer games. The boys' feelings of success fell across a narrower range of activities (primarily sports, active games, and computer games).

Seven boys made 24 references to feeling successful with sports (rugby, cricket, soccer and T-ball[3]). Eight boys also felt successful when playing active games, while only two girls did. When asked why most of the photographs of his successes were of his rugby team, Spike said, 'That's because that's what I feel successful about, mostly.' All of these boys were involved in team sports outside of school hours. Only two girls participated in sports out of school (gymnastics and martial arts).

Including other sporting activities like swimming, however, meant that there were only two girls who did not feel successful engaging in some physical activity. Girls were more likely to feel successful in dance activities, with 88% of the references to music and dance being made by girls. The ways in which girls 'constituted themselves in and through the body' (Wright, 1996, p. 62) were primarily to do with dance. Dance emphasises 'feminine' features such as grace, poise and agility, compared to 'masculine' physical activity where the emphasis is on strength, competition and toughness. Generally, boys played sports, while girls took dance and ballet lessons. In most cases, the active opportunities available to children were limited to traditionally 'gender appropriate' activities (Garrett, 2004).

As noted, identity is formed in relationships. Relationships with peers were important for feelings of success. Social connections impacted on these children's feelings of success. Children had similar domains of success to their friends, and some would regulate friends' participation choices and/or areas of success. Renold (2001b) suggested that friends can confirm each other's behaviour as acceptable, thereby influencing the selection of appropriate domains for success. Social groups can create competing influences: having a supportive peer group seems to help children to acknowledge success but may limit areas of success. The few children in the class who did not have close friendships described feeling success in different spheres compared to the children who had close friendship groups. For example, a boy who was not friends with the boys described feeling success in reading, while this was rarely mentioned by other boys. Those with fewer friends had more trouble isolating their successes, however, and described fewer areas of success than their peers.

---

3   A junior form of softball organised in Aotearoa New Zealand schools.

At school: Curriculum areas

Mathematics was an important subject to the girls in the study. Six girls said they felt successful with maths but five said they would like to be better. Mathematics seemed to be experienced in contradictory ways by girls:

Lisa: I'm not really good at maths, I don't think.

J: Why do you think that?

Lisa: I don't know. I used to think I'm good because I could be way better.

These girls showed a concern for mathematics that was not apparent amongst the boys. Meyer and Koehler (1990) found that 'at both the middle school and high school levels, females reported lower levels of confidence in their ability to learn mathematics than did males' (p. 61). In this study only two boys described mathematics as an area of success and only one wanted to be better at maths. Interestingly, the boys made daily use of mathematical skills in construction activities along with formal classes. This was not echoed in the girls' free choice activities, which were frequently writing and drawing. While these choices are likely to benefit literacy skills, they may compromise the development of confidence in numeracy skills.

Literacy is considered an area of concern for some boys, whose reading and writing abilities tend to lag behind those of girls (Watson, Kehler & Martino, 2010). The children in this study reflected only some of the gendered assumptions around literacy. Girls were more likely to describe feeling successful with reading (nine girls compared to three boys) but the boys who did talk about reading as an area of success mentioned it several times.

Writing was mentioned by both genders (10 girls and seven boys) as an area of success. The children in this classroom wrote frequently on their choice of topics and often the stories followed traditionally gendered patterns. A group of boys worked on illustrated stories involving humour, fantasy and violence. Girls often wrote about friendships and relationships. The children also noticed differences in their interests. For example, one boy said, 'I like to have things like magic and girls don't like things like that. Well, some of them do and some of them don't. I like dangerous things and things like that. Some girls do like things like those things'.

This participant was aware that these generalisations are not true for *all* boys and *all* girls. There was some resistance to dominant ideas of what boys and girls *should* write about: one girl worked simultaneously on a kitten story and an adventure book. Nevertheless, the predominant topics for writing were stereotypical. Perhaps this explains the difference in the boys' acceptance of writing as an area of success compared to reading. In their writing the boys were able to express dominant masculinity and, like the boys in Hallden's (1999) study, 'distance themselves from women and teachers and join the escapist macho world' (p. 477).

The participants' other curricular areas of success were also gendered. Art was an area of success for all of the girls and only two of the boys, despite the large amount of time these children spent on artistic endeavours. The boys participated in frequent illustration and construction work and it appeared to hold status among their peers. Seven boys described feeling successful with their construction work but did not call it 'art'. Construction was viewed as something more appropriately masculine than art. Boys also described feeling successful with technology and computers. Only one girl made one mention of success with computer games. Five boys made multiple references to success with technology and computer games. A range of technology was available in the classroom but success with technology was described primarily by boys, possibly due to their greater use of technology at home, which girls did not mention.

Conclusion

This study found that children develop and express feelings of success from a young age. The children in this study negotiated discourses of appropriate gender and school behaviour, as well as personal understandings, to construct a view of themselves as successful. They recognised that they were successful via a combination of internal and external reinforcers. Sometimes peer groups policed what were considered appropriate activities for success. Children generally felt more successful in out-of-school pursuits and stereotypical pursuits were already internalised by many.

Neo-liberal discourses imply that 'anyone can climb the techno-rationalist ladder to success' (Benjamin, 2003, p. 108). This might be the case for well-resourced children. This study focused on children whose parents were mostly professionals so were more likely to have resources to enable their children's success in a variety of domains. Even so, the children had developed gender-stereotyped ideas, limiting their potential areas of success. Many Aotearoa New Zealand families are not resourced to provide their children with opportunities to try a range of activities out of school. This means that the onus falls on schools to create opportunities for children to find and develop their skills, aptitudes and abilities; and to ideally encourage children to do so outside the limits of stereotypes.

Having friends helps with success.

Reay (2001) stated that learning in classrooms is much wider than test results suggest. Children learn a lot about how to be a 'successful' boy or girl, and gender-delineated skills and perceptions are augmented. Individuals then experience fewer non-stereotypical pursuits, resulting in diminished confidence and potential reluctance to participate (Slater & Tiggemann, 2010). Research suggests that physical fitness may have a positive influence on academic performance (Trudeau & Shephard, 2009) so girls without access to physical activities might have reduced academic and health benefits. Likewise, it is important that all students develop good reading abilities. Having poor reading skills does not bode well for good academic and social outcomes (McGee et al., 2002). Ideally, both girls and boys should have opportunities to use their bodies and minds in active *and* creative ways from an early age so that they can develop feelings of success across a variety of domains.

Our findings take on greater significance with the current emphasis on National Standards, which measure narrow and conventional forms of success. Current policy emphasises numeracy and literacy skills, and secondary and tertiary qualifications, as the key steps in the development of an educated workforce. Yet a wide range of interests and skills is valuable for jobseekers, often ensuring a more seamless transition to work, and contributing to a wider range of skills in the workplace (Rubin, Bommer & Baldwin, 2002).

In addition to career goals, there are important reasons for encouraging all children to try a range of activities at an early age. As we found in this study, children's commitments and feelings of success include other facets of their lives, which in times of rapid change, are likely to be increasingly vital for individuals' well-being and ability to adapt to an uncertain world. Ideally, success should be recognised in a variety of ways and across diverse domains. The Ministry of Education's goal of equipping 'all New Zealanders with the knowledge, skills and values to be successful citizens in the 21st century' (Ministry of Education, 2012) should involve more than education qualifications and academic skills. More than half of the children in this study stressed perseverance and the significance of having a challenge or overcoming adversity before they would consider that they were successful. These children seemed to have a very good sense of what knowledge, skills and values are required in the twenty-first century.

CHAPTER 17

Disrupting heteronormativity: A high-school queer–straight alliance?

Kathleen Quinlivan

The trouble is that, there is this thing which has been going around for a long time, which is called being normal. And that's the problem ... people trying to be normal ... being cool, or fitting in ... I think ... the definition of normal should just be changed to just being unoriginal and having no individual ideas!

(James, Interview 1, 14 March 2007).

This chapter explores how a diverse group of secondary school students in Yes!, a Queer–Straight Alliance (QSA), disrupt normative understandings of sexuality, gender, race, dis/ability and difference within the context of a racially diverse, middle-class, suburban, Aotearoa New Zealand secondary school. I critically engage with the ways in which student members in the group interrupt what James (a Yes! QSA member) refers to as the 'problem' of normalcy amongst his peers; I then discuss both the possibilities and challenges that arise when normative constructions of difference are disrupted within a school context.

I begin by providing some background to the development of Gay–Straight Alliances/Diversity Groups in Aotearoa New Zealand as a response to the predominantly heteronormative culture of secondary schools. I then outline the usefulness of post-structuralist and queer theoretical frameworks in helping to explain and understand the ways in which the Diversity Group interrupts understandings of gender and sexual identities and difference, and works towards contesting the predominantly normative peer culture of their school. Next I outline the methodology of the case study. Following that, I critically explore both the possibilities and the challenges of the ways in which Yes!, as a QSA, is challenging the heteronormative culture of its school.

Background and theoretical frameworks

In the past 10 years or so, there has been an unprecedented explosion in the growth and development of community- and school-based Diversity Groups, or as they are increasingly called, Queer–Straight Alliances, in Aotearoa New Zealand cities and towns. The development of these groups can perhaps be linked to the increased visibility of queer youth through the growth and expansion of local community-based organisations such as Rainbow Youth in Auckland and Q'topia in Christchurch. The development of a national queer youth network, funded by the New Zealand Aids Foundation and Rainbow Youth, has supported local initiatives.

Stemming from the American school-based Gay–Straight Alliance (GSA) model, which emerged as part of the Massachusetts Safe Schools Programme in 1988, Aotearoa New Zealand Queer–Straight Alliances (QSA) tend to be of a less formal nature than their American counterparts, often occurring within community as well as schooling contexts (Quinlivan, Goulter & Caldwell, 2010). The widespread number of QSAs has emerged in response to the ongoing prevalence of homophobic bullying and intolerance that makes many schools unsafe social and academic environments for many gender and sexually diverse youth, both internationally and in Aotearoa New Zealand. (Henriksen, 2007; Martino & Pallotta-Chiarolli, 2005; Nairn & Smith, 2003; Quinlivan, 2006, 2009; Robinson, 2005; Rossen, Lucassen, Denny, & Robinson, 2009; Youdell, 2006).

A recent Aotearoa New Zealand quantitative study (Rossen et al., 2009) reported that 343 same- and both-sex-attracted youth attending secondary school felt less positive about school and were more likely to have truanted than their opposite-sex-attracted peers. Both- and same-sex-attracted youth also felt less safe at school and were more likely to have been bullied because they were gay or thought to be gay.

QSAs work to counteract the predominantly heteronormative cultures of secondary schools by providing peer-supportive spaces for students who might otherwise feel socially isolated. They can also operate as educational sites that acknowledge proactive youth of all genders and sexualities and encourage them to critique and challenge normative understandings of sexuality, gender and difference (Mayo 2009).

Before turning to the specific subject of my case study, the QSA named 'Yes!' at Kereru High School,[1] I want to discuss the theoretical frameworks

---

[1] 'Kereru High School' is a pseudonym.

that underpin my analysis of the ways students both construct and contest understandings of sexual and gender diversity and difference.

Theoretical frameworks

Post-structuralist selves: Identities/subjectivities and discourse

Post-structuralist and queer theoretical ideas problematise the Cartesian idea of a fixed, stable and unitary self, suggesting that this notion of identity fails to acknowledge the extent to which evolving multiple selves, shaped within specific social, historical and cultural sites, exist in an ongoing process of production and contestation. The focus on subjectivity as an interactive process situates a person within a society, rather than understanding the individual as separate from it. This approach recognises that selves are multiple and often intermeshing, in a constant state of 'becoming' rather than 'arrival' (Butler, 1997; Hendriques, Hollway, Urwin, Venn & Walkerdine, 2004). People's embodied, gendered, raced, sexualised and classed subjectivities are a product of the discourses available to them, and intersubjectively shaped and challenged through interaction with others in particular contexts.

Post-structuralist theories problematise not only identity but also language: they call into question the relationship between the meaning of the word (signifier) and the object that the word represents (signified). Rather than seeing discursive understandings as *describing* a reality, post-structuralist theories suggest that language *creates* stories about identities, realities, and social practices (Popkewitz, 1997). Discursive constructions of difference and their reconceptualisation are seen as unstable, contingent, dynamic and socially negotiated (Grbich, 2007). People's conscious and subconscious engagement with the production of intersubjective selves gives rise to the possibility – through agency – of questioning and resisting the dominant discourses that constrain people in particular ways (Butler 1997). Understanding the construction and destabilisation of subjectivities in this way recognises the role played by social and cultural contexts (in this case, the multiple sites within a secondary school) in shaping dominant normative discourses of sexuality, gender and difference that mould what is possible for students to be (Youdell, 2006, 2009). Because subjectivities are socially produced, normative constructions of discourses can also be challenged.

A range of competing discourses about genders, sexualities and difference are produced and challenged in school contexts. Affirmative action and rights discourses often sit uncomfortably alongside deficit 'at risk' discourses of biological essentialism. However, such dissensus can have its productive dimensions (De-Palma & Atkinson, 2009; Nairn & Smith, 2003). There can be a strategic value in drawing on the biological essentialist argument that queer students were 'born that way' in order to inform affirmative action and rights discourses within institutional and schooling contexts (see also Spivak, 1998). Queer theoretical frameworks have been influential in problematising fixed notions of identity and sexuality, arguing that drawing on a biological deficit discourse, which frames queer youth as 'abnormal' and 'at risk' in relation to the dominant heterosexual norm, and therefore as 'abject' and 'other', is problematic. A range of writers note that the notion of homophobia can reiterate deficit discourses which both reinforce heteronormativity and frame queer youth as the problem (Quinlivan, 2002; Marshall, 2010; Rasmussen, Rofes & Talburt, 2004; Talburt & Rasmussen, 2010; Youdell, 2006, 2010). In contrast, Warner's (2003) notion of heteronormativity frames the dominance of the normalising discourses of heterosexuality, rather than the 'abnormality' of same sex desire, as the issue that needs to be problematised and addressed.

A post-structuralist and queer reading provides analyses of the ways in which the students in Yes!, supported by adults within Kereru High School, work towards interrupting normative discourses, offering an alternative peer site of learning about sexualities, genders and difference.[2] It is also able to critically explore the intended and unintended consequences of the ways in which the students worked towards re/signifying such constructions within their school (Talburt & Rasmussen, 2010; Youdell, 2011).

Yes! An ethnographic case study at Kereru High School

Methodology

The data drawn on in the Kereru High School ethnographic case study is part of a wider research project funded by the New Zealand AIDS Foundation and the University of Canterbury, which documents case studies of Queer–Straight Alliances as sites of learning across a range of Aotearoa New Zealand secondary school and community contexts (Quinlivan et. al, 2010). A case study methodology recognises and accounts for the range of school cultures, and the differing communities in which they are situated, as well as attending to the differences of QSAs in school and community contexts.

Kereru High School is a co-educational, middle-class, ethnically diverse decile 6 school in an outer suburb of a large Aotearoa New Zealand metropolitan centre. Over a two-year period, three sets of data were collected within the

---

[2] See also Allan (2009) in relation to reframing constructions of disabilities.

case study. First, face-to-face baseline, mid-term and follow-up individual and group interviews were undertaken with 11 Year 10 to 13 (13- to 17-year-old), queer and straight, racially diverse, and diverse 'ability' students from Yes!. Eight of the students were female and three were male. Some of the students joined Yes! because they had experienced harassment on the basis of difference themselves; others participated because they wanted to support their friends; all of the students involved had a strong sense of social justice.

Face-to-face baseline, mid-term and follow-up individual and group interviews were also undertaken with two mid-career counsellors (one male and one female), one male school principal, a male dean and one male and one female teacher. Participant observations were undertaken in a range of sites within the school, including at Yes! meetings, assemblies, staff meetings and in classrooms. Observational field notes were also written over the course of the two-year case study. Pseudonyms have been used to protect the confidentiality of the participants and the school. The demographic data, identifying each student's multiple identities, were chosen by students themselves. In some cases, they chose not to provide identities.

In the next section, I draw on a range of data from the project to explore the extent to which students in Yes! were able to resignify deficit constructions of gender, sexuality and difference, especially among their peers. I also consider the constraints that they faced in their efforts to challenge normative constructions of difference within the school context.

Yes! as a site of learning at Kereru High School

A highly proactive counselling team drives a school philosophy of total well-being for students and is implementing a range of initiatives to address students' holistic development both in and outside the classroom at the school. As at many schools, however, Yes! students noted the extent to which a range of contexts within Kereru High School and in its wider community reflected predominantly heteronormative cultural norms (Henriksen, 2007; Painter & Keaney, 2009; Quinlivan, 2006, 2009; Rossen, et.al, 2009). Robbie noted that among students themselves, there is a fear of being labelled as gay, describing it as 'homophobia phobia' (Plummer, 1999). Both he and Amanda suggested that many students strongly desire to align themselves with heterosexual masculinities and femininities to avoid being labelled by their peers as being attracted to those of the same sex (Youdell, 2005; Robinson, 2005). These practices produce and reinforce an ongoing cycle of heteronormative and gender-normative utterances and actions: 'I think it's homophobia, the homophobia phobia. They think, "Well, he's gay, I'm fine with that, but my mate's not, and if, if I'm fine with that, and I'm seen to be fine with that, they're gonna think I'm gay." Or, "They're not gonna like me, because I don't care", so ... they act homophobic. It's ... just a never-ending cycle, really'. (Robbie, NZ European/Māori, straight, Interview 1, 14 March 2007)

Amanda noted that the constant instances of subtle and underground heteronormative peer bullying she experienced combined to become overwhelming. These often happened outside the jurisdiction of formal school procedures, and went unnoticed by school leadership:

> ... there's not really that much physical harassment at school ... it's mainly verbal ... quite psychological ... it's like warfare, almost. Just these little, little bits and pieces that don't seem like much at the time, but it all adds, it's all adding up into this giant thing ... Somebody ... wrote an anonymous letter to my parents outlining, just saying, oh, 'she's at school, she's bisexual, she likes chicks, she has a girlfriend at the moment, in case you haven't noticed this' ... it was actually pretty upsetting to see that someone would write that to someone's parents ... It's horrible ... It's out of school, like, school, the ... management of school has no idea what's going on underneath ... (Amanda, 15, NZ European, bisexual/gay, Interview 1, 14 March 2007)

Heteronormative comments in classrooms, uttered by students – and, in some cases, by teachers – were noted by several of the students in Yes!. In some cases students' comments went unheard by teachers; they were also ignored and passed over. As Zoey noted below, sometimes negative connotations of 'gayness' were colluded with by teachers, who Zoey felt should have challenged them: 'One of my teachers the other day, [in response to a student describing a task as gay – "that's so gay"] ... goes "I know this project is so gay, but you have to do it anyway, no matter how gay it is!" And I was like, you're a teacher, you're not supposed to say that!' (Zoey, 16, NZ European, Interview 1, bisexual/gay, 14 March 2007)

Other Yes! students attending the group had also been bullied by their peers on the basis of differences such as race, 'non-normative' masculinities and femininities, aspects of physical appearance, being 'nerds', and perceived intellectual impairments.[3] Ella, a young woman in Yes! who described herself as African and Kenyan, explained how a fellow student drew on normative constructions of race and gender to constitute her as a slave:

---

3   Over the course of the case study the aims of Yes! broadened to address issues of race, gender and dis/ability as well as sexualities.

I had problems with, um, people mocking me and judging me for my colour. I had this one guy who was in class, and he'd always say 'go back to your country, we don't want you here', or 'you're a disgrace to Africa and New Zealand, you should get out of this country', and, you know, some of those things kind of hurt me ... but I think it came to a point that I couldn't handle it one time ... the guy who just hurt me was like 'you black people should just never, go back, you're just slaves, come wipe my shoes', and all that, and he, I've never actually, I never actually told anything, 'cause he's Māori, and I never, um, resented his culture, or said anything about his culture ... (Ella, 14, African/Kenyan, straight, Interview 1, 14 March 2007)

Amanda also noted the cumulative effects of ongoing heteronormative bullying – and its underlying pathologising and deficit assumptions – on her sense of self, to the extent that she began to internalise constructions of 'abnormality': 'Well most of it, it just builds up, it makes you feel really, like, bad, and maybe you're wrong, sort of thing. Yeah, it made me feel like maybe, maybe they are right, and that it is disgusting, and that it's wrong and unnatural.' (Amanda, 15, NZ European, bisexual/gay, Interview 1, 14 March 2007)

While some students in the group were Peer Sexuality Support leaders, many Yes! members joined the group because they had been subjected to peer harassment on the basis of normative constructions of difference. Ella's experiences of racism motivated her to join Yes! in order to challenge her peers' assumptions about race and femininity: 'I think it [what happened to me] kind of fired me up, to show I can actually do something, I'm not a slave, that actually Africans can do something' (Ella, 14, African/Kenyan, straight, Interview 1, 14 March 2007). Other students joined Yes! in order to shift the school culture. Jasmine wanted to enable her peers to feel more comfortable and supported at school than she did: 'I wanna make the school a better place, like, I want people to feel comfortable coming to school. And, um, I just wanna help those students who are going through what I went through, or what I am still going through.' (Jasmine, 14, African American / French Canadian, straight, Interview 1, 14 March 2007)

Next, I want to look at the ways in which Yes! students work towards Jasmine's goal of making the school 'a better place' by interrupting heteronormative understandings of difference within the peer culture; I will then discuss some of the intended and unintended implications of their initiatives and actions in terms of what is possible within schooling contexts.

Students interrupting understandings of normalcy in peer culture

In this section, I explore the ways in which the Yes! students interrupt notions of normalcy in relation to sexualities, genders, races and abilities within their peer culture, the possibilities they opened up, and their sometimes troubling implications.

The Yes! students operated on a range of fronts, both formally and informally, to challenge deficit constructions of sexuality and differences. They educated each other within the group and also challenged both their peers' and their family members' attitudes in private and in more public contexts both within and outside the school. Rachel, a relatively new member of Yes!, suggested that challenging the negative connotations of the word 'gay' has raised awareness of the word's derogatory implications, made students think twice before using it, and drawn attention to the power of language in shaping understandings of difference: 'I know my mates are sick of me saying "don't use 'gay' as a derogatory word, it is a derogatory word", but it definitely has built awareness, I totally agree, because, you know, we haven't done a lot yet, but you can already see a lot of people change, and it challenges people to change what they think, and change the way that they associate words and different things.' (Lisa, Year 11, straight, Interview 1 with Carmen, Pei & Kerry, 14 November 2007)

Yes! is comprised of a diverse group of students and Zoey recognised that having a wide range of differences in the group works against understandings of gayness that conflate it with whiteness, and widens understandings of intersections between race and diverse sexualities. She also noted that this diversity enables Yes! to contest deficit constructions of non-heterosexual students requiring confidential support: 'It helps get us more noticed. Because people with different ethnicities [are] involved, it's not just gay white people. But then the people of different ethnicities will realise that the gay white people are not as bad as they might have thought before. It's [not] like sort of putting them in the same room, rather than having a secret, well not a secret, but like a little place for those people only. You know?' (Zoey, Year 12, bisexual, Interview 2 with Hemi & Robbie, 26 October 2007)

Having heterosexual students in Yes! enables some group members to overtly interrupt the heteronormative and gender-normative assumptions of their peers. Robbie recognised that because he isn't gay himself – and is therefore presumably less threatening – it is easier for him to challenge not only his peers' fear of being labelled as gay, but also deficit constructions of gay male sexuality as insatiable. He explained that he aligns himself with his peers' humour to play on the heteronormative fears of male students: 'For me, they mock me about being gay, and I don't care, because I'm not, and I know I'm not ... I just laugh, and say "no, I'm not." Or, if I don't like them, then I say "yeah, sure, I am" ... Play with their minds ... Freak them out, and start coming on to them. Get them really scared.' (Interview 1 with Robbie, 16, heterosexual, NZ European/Māori, 14 March, 2007)

Through forming friendships with male students who have previously harassed her on the basis of her race and gender, Ella, a Yes! member, interrupted their previously held deficit constructions of gender and race which were based on framing her as different. She explained that one student now has call to question why he would put her down, and noted how ashamed he is of his previous actions:

> ... yesterday I was sitting with a group of friends, guys, and they're terrible, they used to mock me and ... but now we're sitting down like we're friends and we're all laughing and then one of them just said this joke because I mean, we joke a lot and now I've turned it into a game so, I always rate them ... So he said a joke and I started laughing and then one of them said 'I can't mock you any more. It's sad, I can't do it. My heart says no' and I'm like 'really?' 'Yeah, I don't even know why I started. I can't do it any more. It hurts me. It feels like I'm mocking one of my best friends' and I was shocked to hear that, you know. (Ella, 14, African/Kenyan, straight, Interview 1, 14 March 2007)

Being seen to participate in friendship networks by peers played an important role in disrupting heteronormative equations of difference with isolation and 'otherness'. Amanda explained how an old friend validated her worthiness and destabilised a peer's pathologising constructions of heteronormativity by happily sitting next to her in the classroom: 'A new girl ... I've known her for years though, she came to the class, and there's another girl, I won't use her name, she's like "Don't go sit next to her, she's bi." Whatever. And my friend, who I've known years, she's like "I've known her for years, I don't care," and just sat down with me. It's just things like that.' (Amanda, 15, NZ European, bisexual/gay, Interview 1, 14 March 2007)

Members of Yes! also publicised their group's intentions by wearing badges and performing in assembly. The badges often acted as conversation starters among students, which enabled them to publicise the group and its messages. Their assembly items largely consisted of 'skits' that called into question the wide use of deficit constructions of difference which led to exclusion among their peers. Several of the Yes! students noted the challenging nature of performing publicly in front of their peers, but they also spoke of how it had improved their confidence and built their leadership capacities.

In the final section of this chapter I examine the intended and unintended consequences of the ways in which student members of Yes! interrupted normalising constructions of difference within their school.

Intended and unintended consequences

The effects of normative understandings of difference on students, and the discursive resignification that the Yes! students undertook within Kereru High School to disrupt those understandings, draw attention to the ways in which schools are sites where understandings about differences are produced and regulated, and can also be interrupted (Butler, 1997). The students in Yes!, supported by committed staff, worked courageously to draw attention to the damaging effects of deficit understandings of a range of differences and to align themselves cleverly, albeit sometimes problematically, with peer norms in order to disrupt them. Yes! students encouraged and supported each other to identify and challenge discrimination on the basis of difference within a range of formal and informal peer contexts, both at school and in their families. The group enabled the students to reframe their own deficit constructions of difference, albeit within acceptable peer norms. Their activities have also interrupted normative attitudes within the wider school, and provided students with an avenue for addressing discrimination. However, despite both students' and staff's best intentions, their efforts to trouble understandings of difference that privilege normalcy can also misfire and have unintended or unforeseen effects (Talburt & Rasmussen, 2010; Youdell, 2011).

As illustrated by the students to whom I have talked, I suggest that what it is possible to achieve within schools, in terms of interrupting normative understandings of difference, is constrained by schooling practices and cultural norms that powerfully shape who it is possible to be and what it is possible to do in relation to engaging with differences (DePalma & Atkinson, 2009; Youdell, 2006, 2011). The students showed how they interrupted heteronormativity; but this largely occurred in ways that were acceptable to peer norms, and that sometimes had the inadvertent effect of re-pathologising difference.

In the Yes! performances during school assemblies, discussion of 'not being afraid to be different' and the idea that 'we are all different' sounded plausible. At the same time, however, this discussion tended to minimise the fact that exclusion is often based on, and enabled by, understandings of difference. Paradoxically, the assumption that difference needs support also reinforced negative connotations of difference: 'We are NOT afraid to be different and you shouldn't either. Every single one of you sitting here today is different, but we are all the same underneath, and we are here to make you all feel welcomed in this school and offer support' (Fieldnotes, 29 November, 2007).

Juliet, the guidance counsellor who supported the Yes! students, played an important role in valuing and supporting the Yes! students' work in the school, while maintaining the school's reputation. She emphasised the extent to which she had to 'work cleverly', promoting and supporting Yes! in ways that would not threaten the conservative community serving the school:

> I think that (with) sex and sexuality, you are coming into collision with some of these strongly held views of parents about 'poofters', and, you know, disgustingness … you still do have that perception … we've got quite a conservative element in the public forum, there's very differing sort of intakes from very wealthy kids … to … middle income … to very poor … impoverished families … it's recognising those kind of different values, so again it's working cleverly, and so that building of tolerance, that building of acceptance. (Interview with Juliet, 13 March 2009)

On the one hand, such an approach is both strategic and understandable, given the increasing extent to which schools need to protect and maximise their reputation. On the other hand, ideas of building tolerance and building acceptance for a disadvantaged 'other' can have the unfortunate unintended effect of 'misfiring' (Youdell, 2011), inadvertently reinforcing deficit understandings of difference, and reinforcing (heterosexual) normalcy.

The Yes! students' formal and informal work is backed by a strong philosophy of meeting students' holistic needs, resourced and increasingly driven by the school leadership and supported by dedicated staff such as Juliet, who is part of an extensive counselling programme. The aims of Yes! sit comfortably within an increasingly strong philosophical move to cater to, and develop, students' intra- and interpersonal skills within the school, and validate the role of the group. However, despite the best intentions of both staff and students, the fact that Yes! is situated within the counselling programme brings with it some paradoxical challenges. Ella noted the extent to which, in the minds of students, counselling – and by implication, Yes! – is associated with having a 'problem': 'I think the thought of having counselling, the actual word, "counselling", is a really big one 'cause they think [Yes!] it's sitting in a room and somebody listening to your problem and specially for some kids they think, they feel like they're weak, talking about their problem' (Ella, 14, African/Kenyan, straight, Interview 2, 9 November 2007). The school leadership is challenging the traditional secondary school binary that values the formal academic learning sphere of the classroom over the personal and interpersonal knowledge gained in the counselling programme. However, as Ella suggested, there is still the connotation that talking about personal issues is something you do if you have a problem, and having a 'problem' is framed as a weakness (and a subjectivity that students don't want to associate themselves with). Because it is located within the realm of counselling, Yes! runs the risk of being associated with constructions of difference equated with having a 'personal problem'.

A related issue concerns a particular sphere of the school which has traditionally had a higher status as a learning domain in secondary schools: the classroom. While Yes! students worked individually and together to interrupt the normative assumptions of their peers, and also publicised their group on a wider scale in assemblies, their work appeared to be largely contained within the peer 'world' of the school. Situated within the counselling arena, the activities of the group were seen as having little effect within the higher status knowledge domain of the classroom.[4] Some Yes! students suggested that the classroom and its focus on developing students' academic achievements tends to be privileged within the school at the expense of building students' personal and social development:

> *Hemi:* I think, for this school anyway, I think it, the school has a whole focus on what they want you to achieve, they don't focus on what *you* want to achieve. Like, the school's achievement for every student is to pass their grades, but they're only focused on what their achievements are for good students, they don't focus on what the students' achievements are for coming to school.
>
> *Kathleen:* In terms of the whole person?
>
> *Robbie:* You come to school, and you learn this, you need to do your test, you need to pass, and then you can go away. It's not like you need to come here and learn how to live life, and communicate with others, and get friends.
>
> (Hemi, 17, Māori, & Robbie, 16, NZ European,
Interview 2 with Zoey, 26 October 2007)

While the cultural norms of schooling privilege academic development over building intra- and interpersonal skills, groups such as Yes! – and indeed the wider counselling network in which they are situated – are easily dismissed, and even devalued, as sites of learning.

---

4 As part of the case study, a professional development workshop was undertaken with the staff which used student data to speak to the role valuing student differences played in enhancing students' learning outcomes in the classroom. Researching the effect the workshop had on teachers' practice in the classroom was beyond the scope of the case study.

Exploring the unintended as well as the intended consequences of the ways in which the work of Yes! students influences the culture of the school doesn't diminish the gains they have made in interrupting normative understandings of difference among their peers, and the ongoing courage and tenacity they have demonstrated in undertaking such work. The diverse students who comprise Yes! work hard both formally and informally with their peers to challenge deficit constructions of a wide range of differences and their intersections. Such work will always be challenging within school contexts that struggle with reconciling a range of competing purposes. Kereru High School is working hard to challenge the traditional role of secondary schools solely as sites where academic achievement is valued more than personal development. The counselling network's support of Yes! is one example of the direction that the school seeks to move in. However, given the contested purposes of secondary schooling, 'reworking' normative constructions of difference is a complex and often paradoxical process that is strongly and powerfully shaped by the social and cultural norms of students, teachers, school structures and wider society.

Kereru High School is making some interesting inroads into destabilising traditional understandings of the roles of schools in preparing students for life, and endeavouring to provide them with a more holistic education. In referring to Yes! as a 'work in progress' in her final interview, Juliet realistically acknowledged the challenging ongoing discursive work that that such a project entails in order to produce wider philosophical shifts within the school. Understanding the possibilities and potential of such initiatives as Yes!, as well as some of the challenges, and (often unintended) limitations, informs both the group's ongoing development and the wider philosophical direction of Kereru High School. Other schools could learn much from the ways in which students in Yes! engage with issues of difference among their peers in the school. The group members' actions show that understanding how difference and identities are discursively produced provides proactive opportunities for both students and teachers to explore ways of challenging deficit constructions of difference. As the agentic actions of Yes! students and the adults who support them have shown, they are working hard to make a difference about difference in their school.

CHAPTER 18

Stories from the margins: Rangatahi Māori experiences of transition to work

Moana Mitchell & Hazel Phillips

Transition from school in Aotearoa New Zealand is fraught for many young people, especially rangatahi Māori (indigenous youth). Not only do rangatahi face historical educational inequalities, but also when they leave school they face disadvantage in the labour market. Their (often early) trajectories beyond school are set by their experiences *in* school. Yet despite education policies and practices to address the historical disparities that they face, many rangatahi continue to leave school early with few or no qualifications. As part of being marginalised, rangatahi are constructed as different and at risk. Deficit thinking is one of the primary ways through which marginalisation takes place. Ironically, the marginalisation that rangatahi experience creates an alternate identity, whereby actions of resistance and agency are employed as they position themselves into post-school opportunities. The choices that rangatahi make and the actions that they take are not a result of the support they get from schools and post-school organisations, but rather a consequence of the lack of support. In contrast, it is the support of whānau and the communities in which they live that create the spaces for, and forms of, their agency. This chapter is interested in highlighting how rangatahi have had to negotiate education and post-school systems while still maintaining their own integrity as rangatahi.

The content of this chapter comes out of Moana Mitchell's (2009) research, and follows the narrated experiences of two urban rangatahi Māori, Josh and Ben, talking about their transition from school. Both stories offer compelling insight into the power of schools and teachers, and the impact that they have on shaping the experiences and trajectories of rangatahi Māori, as well as the way in which both young men 'talked back' to their experiences.

Given the multiple and complex experiences and locations of rangatahi, there were – and continue to be – many different ways that rangatahi experienced this transition. To fully appreciate the complexity involved in transition, we begin by discussing the theoretical contexts in which rangatahi are constructed and construct their selves, and the impact that this has on their educational and transition experiences. We employ the often interconnected concepts of marginalisation, deficit theorising, silencing and stereotyping in order to understand Josh and Ben's experiences at the hands of an education system intent on marking them as different and inferior. To conclude this section we outline the way in which being on the margins opens spaces for critical engagement and resistance, and note the culturally embedded nature of that resistance. Finally, Josh's and Ben's stories are told.

Theoretical context

Marginalisation

Marginalisation is an experience with which many Māori students struggle throughout their schooling. It impacts on the way rangatahi are viewed or constructed and how they view themselves. In relation to the marginalisation of rangatahi Māori, Māori academic Adreanne Ormond touched on the Māori reality of being marginalised by the dominant 'narrative of the outsiders' (2006, p. 121). Ormond highlighted 'the relationship between the Pākehā dominant and Māori minority social groups' (p. 120) and related this to the experiences of young Māori from the Māhia Peninsula on the East Coast. She argued that the 'outsider' narrative is dualistic in function, helping the dominant Pākehā social group to reinterpret their connectedness to Aotearoa New Zealand while also framing Māori into the margins of belonging.

Deficit thinking

An explicit way in which marginalisation is perpetuated and experienced is through deficit thinking. One of the ways this is done is by 'blaming the victim', in this case rangatahi, for their perceived differences. In education, the students' 'problems' are pinpointed by identifying the differences between the disadvantaged or failing student and those who are advantaged. The outcome is that disadvantaged students are blamed for those differences. While 'race', ethnicity, and socio-economic status go on to 'define life chances', it is the 'impact of "failure"', within the context of school, that results in these experiences 'being constructed in terms of personal deficit' (Wright, Standen and Patel, 2010 p. 28). Deficit thinking refers to 'the notion that students (particularly of low-income, racial/ethnic minority background) fail in school (e.g., perform poorly on standardised tests) because such students and their families have internal defects or deficits, that thwart the learning process ... Deficit thinking is founded on racial and class bias that "blames the victim", rather than examining how schools are structured to prevent students from learning' (San Miguel & Valencia, 2002, p. 368).

Bishop and Berryman (2006) have contended that the deficit thinking of teachers contributes to a negative schooling experience for Māori students. They argued that the relationships developed between Māori students and their teachers are compromised if teachers believe that their students have 'deficiencies'. In the current schooling context for Māori, one of the foremost programmes aimed at rejecting deficit thinking is Te Kotahitanga. This school-based research and professional development programme challenges teachers to 'remain focused on the goal of raising Māori students' achievement within a community that rejects deficit theorising of Māori students and actively seeks to maintain agency' (Forgie, cited in Black, 2008, unpaginated).

Deficit thinking has had a considerable impact on the perceptions not only of the 'educability' of Māori students but also of school practices. Valencia and Black (2002) argued that deficit thinking is a pseudoscientific idea because it uses a fusion of ideology and science, first to understand the perceived cognitive, motivational and cultural differences of students of colour, and second to advance interventions to alleviate those differences. For example, the testing and consequent streaming of students according to their 'academic ability' at high school is one of the ways indigenous, minority and working class youth across the world have been marginalised. Streaming and tracking students, according to Lehmann (2009), socialises students towards particular transition pathways, and in the process creates 'powerful dispositions' regarding their educational and career goals as well as their trajectories. In doing so, it influences the internalisation of equally powerful public discourses about education, knowledge and the knowledge economy. It is in this way that Māori, and marginalised youth in general, can value education yet at the same time resist their schooling.

Silencing

Another explicit way in which marginalisation of rangatahi occurs is through invisibility. Fine (1991) introduced the idea of silencing in her 1990s analysis of high school dropouts in America. Silencing occurs when students' lived experiences are denied in schools because they do not conform to the culture of schools. As a consequence they are rendered either passive or resistant to their marginalisation (Piazza, 2003, para. 2). One of the ways that silencing infiltrates itself into an educational setting is through teachers – either consciously or unconsciously – overlooking students that seem to be failing and preferring those who look like they want to learn (Abu El-Haj, 2005). In relation to rangatahi experiences, this highlights how Māori students are forced to the margins, to the back of classrooms and eventually to leaving school early.

Stereotyping

In an ironic way silencing also works to highlight or emphasise the negative. This is revealed in the stereotype of the 'at risk' label, which describes young people who do not conform or do not fit the 'norm'. This pathologising of young people as 'at risk' is problematic and buys into the rhetoric that young people require intervention (Valencia, 1997). In a school setting, the label of 'at risk' is almost always associated with being a poor learner (Zyngier, 2004). Zyngier suggested that it 'is at the messy point of teachers and students responding to each other in relation to classroom discourse and assessment practices where we are truly going to see whether school is really for them' (2004, p.12). Youdell (2012) argued that the discursive practices of teachers (and students) contribute to the construction of young people's 'intelligible' selves. Her study found that the African-Caribbean students' identities as learners came to be considered as undesirable and in opposition to the notion of the ideal student. As a consequence, the school saw these young people and their culturally embedded learner identities as trouble and a challenge to authority, and thus kept them under 'closer surveillance in order to be subjected to greater control' (Youdell, 2012, p. 15).

The idea that stereotypes can potentially represent divisions of power and control is proposed by Ungar, who contended that adult labels for young people, such as 'deviant', contribute to the 'discursive power and definitional certainty one group imposes on another' (2004, p. 107). Social constructionist theory argues that 'knowledge communities' define what knowledge is and maintain this knowledge discursively through language and its associated practices. This aligns to the pervasive use of deficit-based language that permeates school transitions for rangatahi Māori.

Spaces for resistance

Silencing is also a strategy of resistance and self-determination, challenging the thinking that silence is a negative space for students (Weis, 2007). Weis and Fine proposed that 'within the very centres of structured silence can be heard the most critical and powerful' voices (1993, p. 1). Silence provides the discursive space for students to reflect and 'talk back' to those who legitimise the dominant discourse within secondary schools and promote the deficit perceptions of indigenous peoples and ethnic minorities. In rethinking marginality, hooks

(1992) considers it as a means of resistance and a conscious move away from a common deficit-based definition. Her placing of marginality into a holistic framework proposes a two-way relationship between the margin and the centre that implies both need each other to exist. She represents the centre as the authority and the status quo, and alludes to this being a place where African Americans exist in subordinate roles. Being confined to the fringes essentially allowed hooks to redefine these people as critically conscious, bicultural by nature and competent to live in both the margin and centre. In her view living on the fringes helps feed the 'fire' of resistance.

Yosso (2005), in challenging deficit thinking, posited that marginalised black communities in America are rich communities rather than deficient ones, and it is their culturally embedded locations that feed the 'fire' of resistance. Drawing on a range of critical literature, she identified six forms of community cultural wealth, from which communities draw to survive and resist oppression. These forms of capital are neither mutually exclusive nor static; rather, they work in dynamic ways to contribute to community wealth.

While Yosso's work was with black communities in the US, her analysis has resonance for Māori communities and is particularly pertinent to understanding the way rangatahi maintain their integrity in the face of powerful influences that undermine and marginalise them. For Yosso, these six forms of capital are embedded within the cultural life worlds of the communities in which she worked. Similarly, we consider that, in the Aotearoa New Zealand context, specifically Māori cultural knowledge, values and practices are at the heart of Māori understandings and aspirations. Thus, the overarching notion of cultural capital in which the six forms of capital are expressed and realised in a Māori community context can be understood as both historical and contemporary expressions of cultural knowledge, values and practices, which not only mediate rangatahi experiences and identity, but also make them uniquely Māori. The notion of collective memory has relevance here because it is a way of drawing on the experiences of tūpuna (ancestors) and their cultural knowledge, values and practices to enable not only positive identity, but also culturally embedded future strategies and actions (Wexler, 2009).

Adapting Yosso's (2005) six forms of community capital, we outline below the wealth that is manifested in Māori communities and which rangatahi have drawn on to resist, affirm and make decisions about their lives within the context of their transitions:

- Aspirational capital: the ability of rangatahi 'to maintain hopes and dreams for the future, even in the face of real and perceived barriers' and without 'the objective means to obtain those goals' (pp. 77–78).

- Linguistic capital: the culturally mediated repertoires of communication that exist in Māori communities. Bilingualism, oral histories, pepeha and whakapapa are examples of linguistic capital.
- Familial capital: not only the way rangatahi learn the importance of maintaining healthy relationships and community networks but also the 'lessons of caring, coping, and providing education, which informs [their] emotional, moral, educational and occupational consciousness' within the context of whānau (p. 79).
- Social capital: the networks of people and the community resources in which rangatahi are embedded and which they are able to draw on.
- Navigational capital: the ability of rangatahi to strategically manoeuvre through 'structures of inequality'. Thus, navigational capital 'acknowledges individual agency within institutional constraints' at the same time that it facilitates navigation through 'places and spaces including schools, the job market and the health care and judicial systems' (p. 80).
- Resistant capital: refers to 'those knowledges and skills fostered through oppositional behaviour that challenges inequality' (p. 80).

Urban rangatahi narratives

Below are Josh's and Ben's stories about their experiences of urban high schools and the impact of those experiences on their post-school opportunities. Josh grew up in Auckland, while Ben grew up in Porirua in a predominantly Māori and Pacific Island neighbourhood. Both went to co-educational state high schools. Josh attended, in his own words, a 'white' school while Ben, on the other hand, went to a school that had a high Māori and Pacific Island student roll. While their experiences were diverse, their narratives speak to a 'commonality of experiences' at the hands of an education system and broader society that viewed them through deficit lenses, that silenced and placed them under surveillance, and that constrained not only the kind of decisions that they made around their learning but also their trajectories beyond school. Both rangatahi also 'talked back' to their experiences of marginalisation to forge alternate identities, which were rooted in their cultural life worlds.

Josh's story

Josh's eventual exit out of secondary school was not typical of either Māori or non-Māori students. In his final year Josh was a chronic truant. His mother was a factory shift worker and for several months he intercepted school correspondence about his truancy. In this way he remained 'lost' in the school system. However, due to a rugby scholarship, which meant that his end-of-year exam fees had already been paid, Josh went on to sit and pass three of five exams that year. From there, he left school, only to be contacted by a former Māori teacher who had helped him considerably. This teacher informed Josh that a scholarship had become available for a university bridging course: after being interviewed, he was selected for the scholarship that began his university career.

Reflecting on school, Josh recalled how strategies of punishment and control (Youdell, 2004), which had nothing to do with learning, devalued the education that he expected. In talking back to the school system that failed him, Josh felt such strategies left students like him with very little choice. It signalled a disengagement from education, which was sanctioned by the secondary school he attended:

> Nobody asks you why you're not doing your homework; they just go if you don't do your homework you're on detention, so you don't do your detentions. Why have you got so many detentions? You can get an after school detention, oh yeah sweet I don't mind after school detentions. So you get a few more after school detentions. Why are you not doing your after school detentions? Oh we're gonna suspend you. Oh sweet I don't mind, suspend me I'm off school. I don't have to do homework oh you know too many suspensions, next thing probably gone, don't have to worry about it.

A significant limitation for rangatahi in school is the grouping of students into two broad categories according to their abilities: academic and practically focused. However, studies have found that streaming reflects social class rather than ability or intelligence (Pinto, 2006). It is precisely the playing out of this assumption about the educability of students that Māori students have been disadvantaged, and their educational and work opportunities limited:

> If the kids want to be lawyers and doctors and think they have what it takes to do that, let them go. That's what schools have been doing anyway, but then let the others have an option as well, don't just close them off, don't let them sit in schools till they're 18 and have nothing. That ruins their spirit and everything.

It became clear to Josh that equal opportunity for all students at his secondary school was a myth:

> It was a white school, and then it was streamed which made it worse because they put all the dumb people in the dumb area, they kept them all together. If you couldn't write a story you weren't normal at college, well at the college that I went. So you knew who were all the brainy people and you knew who were all the dumb people.

'Hyper aware' of negative stereotyping and low expectation (Aronson, 2004), Josh was highly critical of the hierarchical education system and the transitions structure that inevitably left many of his friends feeling marginalised:

> By the time they get to 18 they leave as failures, and they don't want to go back into a class, into learning again because they've already failed. So when you're 18 and everyone's going off to university, you're 18 and got nowhere to go, you don't want to go to polytech because you look like a dumb dude and you're 18, and you have to start learning again and you've just failed college.

Josh came from a home that did not have a lot of money. He regularly went to school with pie sandwiches (a pie inside two slices of bread) and a big bag of chips to share. Josh felt strongly that it was harder for families like his own to realistically make the leap from poverty into education and well-paying jobs, because of the lack of family experience in, and connection to, higher education and high status well-paying professions. His reflection mirrors what other studies have shown about the influence parents' own education has on their children's participation in higher education (Lee, Sax, Kim & Hagedorn, 2004):

> They can see that their dad's a lawyer. Well it's pretty hard to see what a lawyer does, what kind of business they have to do if your dad's a factory worker, your grandfather was a farmhand or something like that. It's pretty hard to see what lawyers do. Those kids whose parents are lawyers, or even teachers, they get to see all that. They get to see what their parents do.

Josh identified parents as unknowingly getting themselves caught up in the rhetoric of education, encouraging their children to buy into a dream that inevitably came down to two choices, achievement or failure:

> Parents have been brought by that dream of their sons and daughters being doctors, they buy into it as well, just as much as students and just as much as teachers who think it's the right thing to do. They just think it because they were probably told the same thing at school as well, but because they're so brainwashed into wanting to be a lawyer, into wanting to be a doctor, wanting to be a scientist, mathematician, whatever, all those flash jobs, everybody's into it, everybody wants to do it, but when there's failure, nobody knows what to do next, what else is there to do?

Josh talked at length about rangatahi dreams and the need for these aspirations to be tempered with what it takes for them to be realised. He explained that to realise post-school aspirations not only required hard work, it also took time, which meant the deferment of income. However, these aspects of realising career goals were not talked about in school; rather, the focus had been on the 'end game':

> Yeah, it's just like a coach saying you're at college and you're playing first 15 and the coach saying you can be an All Black, but the coach needs to also say, look you have to make the secondary schools, you've got to make the 21s, you've got to make NPC, you've got to make Super 14s, then you might become an All Black. Whereas if they tell you at school, if you don't do your homework, you won't be a lawyer, or if you do your homework, you can be a doctor, not knowing that you have to go to university, spend three years there, then be a junior doctor for another three years before you can even get paid properly.

The reality of post-school experiences is that they do not always correspond with the school-to-work transition rhetoric, 'work hard at school and you will get a good job'. The meritocratic discourse that Josh is referring to has been an effective smokescreen to hide the locus of educational disparities by blaming underachievement and consequent labour outcomes on young people. Historically, schools have been deeply implicated in perpetuating this meritocratic discourse (Themelis, 2008). The reality, as reiterated by Josh, was that the inherent competition and volatility of the labour market meant that jobs were not always there for transitioning secondary school students:

> I just don't think college teaches you anything about leaving college and finding a job. They don't tell you anything about finding a job or how to get a job or what kind of jobs there are. Pretty much it's just the high profile jobs that are talked about. It's just like an All Black, not everyone can be an All Black, yeah but they don't tell you that. They just keep pushing and saying oh if you keep training every day, you'll be an All Black. There are five hundred thousand people being told the same story! There aren't five hundred thousand jerseys. It's so small, so if you widen it and just say, you could be a Super 14 player. Why not Super 14? They make money, and there's way more jerseys to grab.

Reflecting on his post-school opportunities, Josh pinpointed the fact that good luck was the only reason he was given a university scholarship; however, as he noted, that same luck was not present for other family members and friends. Being told to have faith when reality is tough does not necessarily materialise into successful transitions:

> They always say have hope but when everything's gone and you have nothing left, hope doesn't give you much, doesn't give you any security, doesn't give you a job.

Ben's story

Ben, the youngest of four children, considered himself a somewhat 'cheeky' and naturally inquisitive person who gravitated towards likeminded Māori and Pacific Island friends while at his local secondary school. This did not bode well with the school hierarchy, and subsequently Ben found himself regularly in trouble. It was put to him that he should take up a pre-trades course. Ultimately, Ben felt that he was being forced to accept a vocation and a transition out of secondary school. Although this seemed a logical trajectory because his father and older brother were both in the building industry, Ben was not interested in following them. Ben enjoyed mathematics and had excelled in this for most of his schooling. He imagined that he could have taken mathematics to university level, had he been given the chance. Despite showing promise for mathematics, Ben was nevertheless considered a 'poor learner' and 'trouble' (Youdell, 2012), and consequently he was asked to leave school at 15. It took him about six months to find his own job, which he did and was proud of.

Ben's experience of being asked to leave school reflects the embedded nature of power and control in Aotearoa New Zealand schools, and in particular, the way deficit thinking and stereotyping of students is put into practice. Like many rangatahi, Ben felt like there was nothing he could do to challenge the stereotypical perceptions that teachers had of him. Through his continued experience of school, Ben became resigned to the fact that whatever he did or aspired to, his pathway had already been set:

> I felt the teachers kind of pushed me away from secondary school and wanted me to do a pre-trades course to get me out into the workforce as soon as possible.

At the time of the interview, Ben had just become a first-time father. As he talked about his little boy, he had the same sparkle in his eye as when he talked about his love of mathematics. This gleam of excitement slowly faded away as he began to speak about his teachers and their conviction that they knew a better pathway for him (Zyngier, 2004). The deficit-based assumption that Māori are only good for manual labour not only changed secondary schooling for Ben, it also set him on a particular post-school path:

> Yeah, they said I'd be good out there in the workforce and on building sites and that I could use my mathematics but that's not what I really wanted to be. I mean I'd give anything up for maths back in the day. I would have given everything up.

Ben's mother was concerned for her son's well-being and wanted him to leave school because of the way he was treated by teachers. She saw the damage that they had wrought on her son, and in doing so, drew on her own culturally embedded moral concerns to ensure Ben survived and resisted his marginalisation (Yosso, 2005):

> My mum wanted me to get out of school because she didn't think what they were teaching me was the right thing, so she didn't want them to torment me in any way and that, and for me to do the wrong thing so I thought it'd just be easier if I moved on.

In 'talking back' to his experience later, Ben reflected on the reason he did not challenge the school's decision to ask him to leave; the way that this decision was based solely on the opinion of a single teacher is a reflection of Ben's time at school: 'I felt there was no point in fighting if they didn't want me there anyway.'

While Ben's experience of not challenging the school when he was asked to leave helped 're-create the oppressive conditions from which it originated' (Solarzano and Delgado Bernal, 2001 p. 317), his reflection of his experience speaks to his strategic manoeuvring through 'structures of inequality'. Having to leave school because of teachers imposing their own ideas on his transition became a positive learning experience for Ben. He mused over the opportunities lost and the insight gained through talking back:

> Well it taught me in terms of not letting anyone run you over or run your dreams out the way or run what you want to be out the way, because they did that to me. I knew that I let them win in the end by giving them what they wanted.

When considering how he felt at school, Ben reflected on what could have made a real difference at secondary school:

> You have to be given the chance at school you know. You've got to have someone that listens to you, just as much as you listen to them.

The motivation to improve his life in his current circumstances really encouraged Ben to think about his baby boy and what he needed to do in his role as a dad. Whereas hope for Josh held little promise, hope for Ben has become a driving force as he determines the kind of life he wants for himself and his child. Reflecting on the way he perceived people on the dole before he had a child, Ben was determined to work, no matter what:

> Now it's my boy. He pulls me forward all the time, even those down times, depressing times. Got a kid to support so decided to keep pushing forward.

And before, I just think it was the dole really. I don't think I liked the dole, I just thought it was for bludgers. And I used to always give everyone heaps about being bludgers, so I don't want to be a hypocrite about it. So it was anything to stay away from the benefit.

Conclusion

Josh and Ben were viewed through deficit eyes, which influenced both their school and post-school experiences. It is not surprising then that they challenged and resisted the identities that were imposed on them and that limited their opportunities. It is in this context that they occupied parallel discursive spheres where counter-narratives and identities were constructed and enacted (Wright, Standen & Patel, 2010). This parallel or alternate sphere is also the place from which their Māori cultural and urban identities shaped their resistance, their aspirations and ultimately their destinations. In resisting the futures that were constructed for them, they drew on the knowledge and experience within the communities where they lived (Yosso, 2005). Despite their experiences of school, the rangatahi who were interviewed expressed positive views about the value of education for getting ahead, as well as aspirations for themselves and their whānau both in the present and the future. Their agency, rather than being articulated through individual actions, was 'reflected through cultural practices, outlook and lifestyle' (Wright et al., p. 131).

So what of Ben and Josh and their continuing journeys? At the time of writing this chapter, Ben had become a professional rugby player in Australia and Josh was at the end of his studies towards a qualification in sports science.

CHAPTER 19

Conclusion: Where are we going?

Nancy Higgins & Claire Freeman

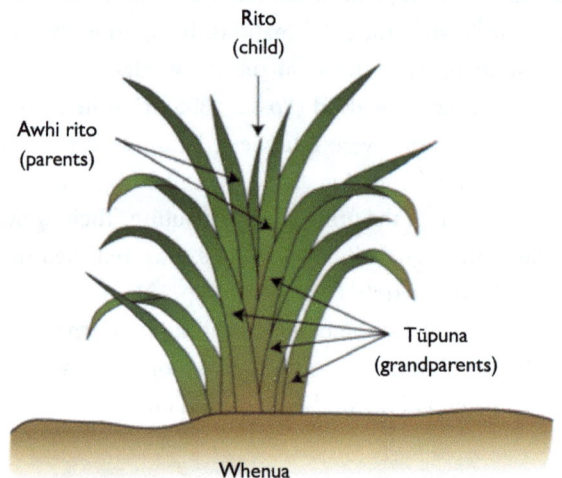

Acknowledging the tangata and the whenua[1]

What is it that holds and brings this book together? We believe it is the people and the land, the tangata and the whenua. The people of Aotearoa New Zealand are charged with kaitiaki – taking care of the land and its people, with tamariki at the centre, and this is no simple task. The challenges are immense – not least of which are the economic, social and environmental challenges facing our tamariki and rangatahi (children and youth).

---

1 www.paharakeke.co.nz/index.php/about/harakeke-folklore-rituals/. Flax graphic redrawn by Tracy Connolly.

The economic challenge

At present there are many economic worries for Aotearoa New Zealand. Rising poverty has seen the gap between the rich and the poor grow larger and larger. In 2011, 40,000 children (mostly from Māori and Pacific Island families) were being fed by charitable programmes; in 2012 the Catholic Church produced a pamphlet for social justice week entitled, *Our daily bread: Putting food on the table* (Beech, 2012); and the government is currently considering creating different types of 'food in schools' programmes. A government-appointed Expert Advisory Group on Solutions to Child Poverty has been formed to consider how to improve the lives of children in poverty over the next 10 years. In this group's consultation seminars, participants have said that families and whānau in poverty should learn how to grow vegetables, should budget better, should learn more about nutrition, and should not spend their money on non-essentials like alcohol (Boston, 2012). However, a 2010 University of Otago study found that such claims about the inadequacies of poor people are not supported by research. Rather, evidence shows that income was the main factor in ensuring food security in families (Smith, Parnell, & Brown, 2010).

Essentially, the most effective solution to the problem of child poverty is simply to eliminate it. This means increasing the income of poor families, which in turn requires that the government raise employment levels, wages, and, for those not in employment, government financial benefits. The present government has stated that they will not consider raising benefits. The real level of financial help given to families, who depend on government assistance, has not been raised since Ruth Richardson's 'mother of all budgets', which was implemented by a National-led government in 1990 (Wynd, 2012). Subsequently, governments under both Labour and National have declined to restore benefits to the equivalent of pre-1990 levels. The impacts of poverty on children are not just financial. Children in poor families exhibit higher rates of psychosomatic symptoms, chronic illness and low well-being, and young people may be more likely to be depressed, show signs of anxiety, have low self-esteem and have high levels of alcohol and drug use (Children's Social Health Monitor, 2011; Dale, O'Brien, & St. John, 2011; Experts Advisory Group on Solutions to Child Poverty, 2012). While the government considers these issues, it is heartening to see that youth themselves are taking active measures to reduce child poverty. In Christchurch, two young people are now leading the Christchurch Branch of the Child Poverty Action Group (Christchurch Child Poverty Action Group, 2012).

New Zealanders are well aware of the need to provide for their families despite the difficult economic situation many find themselves in. For those able to find work, a number of approaches are being taken, including having both parents in the workforce, working multiple jobs and working longer hours. A 2009 Families Commission Report noted these trends as follows: 'In 2006, 98,466 dual-earner couples with dependent children worked 80 or more combined hours, while 27,063 dual-earner couples with dependent children worked more than 100 combined hours ... Nearly a third of dual-earner couples with one child worked more than 80 combined hours a week while a quarter of those with three children worked these long hours' (Families Commission, 2009, p. 8).

Not only do parents seek work but also many young people themselves are working, or trying to find work, as a response to the economic pressures on their families as well as for personal and other reasons. Young people are thus similarly vulnerable to the fallout arising from the weak national and global economic situation, and moreover, are often in jobs that lack the protection measures given to 'adult' employees.

The young people of today have grown up 'during economic and social reforms that [have] transformed New Zealand's economy and society' (Nairn, Higgins & Sligo, 2012, p. 11). This transformation has seen Aotearoa New Zealand become a neo-liberal nation whose ideology is primarily individualistic and market driven, so that the pressure is on for young people and their families to take responsibility for their own education and careers, without the kind of support that the state provided when their parents were young. The young people in Nairn, Sligo & Higgins' 2012 study *Children of Rogernomics* recognised that dealing with, and responding to, market forces is an inevitable part of their future – a future in which not all young people and their families will be equally privileged in their ability to succeed.

The social challenge

Children today have grown up in a complex social world, which comprises the worlds of their family/hāpu, their extended family/whānau, their peers, their neighbourhood, their school, their culture, and, for some, their religion. These are worlds that may or may not intersect, and may even be contradictory in their expectations. The family is also increasingly complex. Children live in blended families, in multiple-family units, in gay and lesbian families, in shared accommodation with other adults and families, and in single-parent families. The nuclear family is not the 'norm' for many Aotearoa New Zealand children and young people.

Children are also growing up in diverse communities, and thus need to accept, respect and respond appropriately to difference – a challenge children and young people are meeting. Children and young people throughout Aotearoa New Zealand are forming alliances to create change. They also have greater fluency in Te Reo (Māori language) and better cultural competency, partly because of educators' commitment to the Treaty of Waitangi, and the Kōhanga Reo (early childhood language nests) and Kura Kaupapa (Māori immersion schools) movements. Aotearoa New Zealand is part of a global social and political economy in which being able to negotiate across societal and even nation boundaries is an essential life skill. Children's and young people's abilities to respond positively to change position them well for the diverse and exciting society that Aotearoa New Zealand now has become.

The environmental challenge

In Aotearoa New Zealand, as elsewhere around our planet, children are growing up in a rapidly changing world where there is no room for complacency. Children and their families face an uncertain environmental future, in which thought and innovation will be the essential criteria for survival, but where an ethos of caring and environmental responsibility must prevail if any type of future is to be secured. There is little doubt that climate change is here, and despite many attempts through the promulgation of international conventions, global agreements have not yet been signed that will stop a dangerous two-degree warming of the planet and the consequent growth of unprecedented 'weather events' and food shortages. Instead of trying to cure the 'disease' itself, nations around the planet – including Aotearoa New Zealand – are focusing their attention on coping with its symptoms. They are planning for the massive migration of people from Pacific Island nations whose land could be lost to rising tides and to food shortages because of droughts. Some believe Aotearoa New Zealand will be able to help the world get through climate change by increasing its dairy industry; yet as a by-product of this, Aotearoa New Zealand has also increased its carbon emission, the use of its water in irrigation schemes, and the pollution of its waterways.

For example, recently in Darfield, a dairy farming area on the Canterbury plains not far from where we are writing this chapter, about 10% of the population sought medical attention for gastroenteritis and the water was reported as unsafe to drink because of animal effluent entering the water supply (Canterbury District Health Board, 2013; Styliano, 2012). It is also of concern that government documents have stated that one of the reasons why the elected Canterbury regional council, Environment Canterbury, was 'discharged' and is now managed by appointees of the national government is because the government wished to encourage the dairy industry and the irrigation of the Canterbury plains (Young, 2012). This loss of regional democracy has resulted in the limitation of New Zealanders' right to object to such environmental changes. The Aotearoa New Zealand government has also opened up its oceans to oil companies who are searching for oil off the country's coasts. Solid Energy, a state-owned company, exports coal to nations who have coal-generated electricity plants, while energy in Aotearoa New Zealand is mostly from renewable and non-carbon-emitting sources. Some argue that in the short term, such moves are a logical response to the need to sustain the Aotearoa New Zealand economy while the global economy is in a downturn.

What is more heartening to see, though, is that children and young people are taking initiatives to meet our environmental challenges. For example, at the time of writing this chapter, five young people were cycling the length of Aotearoa New Zealand to attend the *Power Shift Youth Climate Summit* (Power Shift, 2012b). One of the riders, Lyndsey Horne, said 'cycling is an action that we can take today to address what is essentially the defining issue of our generation. Having cycled for 10 days already through Aotearoa New Zealand's beautiful landscape we can see how much there is to lose if climate change isn't addressed' (Power Shift, 2012b, para. 7). Billed as 'the biggest youth climate summit Aotearoa New Zealand has ever seen', Power Shift's purpose was to 'launch a massive campaign to push for climate solutions' (Power Shift, 2012a, para. 3). Governments around the world have so far made little progress in agreeing to solutions that will slow down climate change. This is despite promises made in 1992 at the Earth Summit in Brazil (aka United Nations Conference on Environment and Development), despite annual meetings of the 198 nations who have signed the 1992 *United Nations Framework Convention on Climate Change* (UNFCCC or FCCC), and despite follow-up UNNCED meetings (Tollefson & Gilbert, 2012).

Aotearoa New Zealand youth are also forming organisations to respond to the environmental challenge. For example, Generation Zero is a youth-driven organisation focused on creating a 'zero carbon' world (Generation Zero, 2012a). It recognises that 'while every other generation has inherited a world with a promise for greater prosperity and a brighter future – our generation of young New Zealanders are facing a potential inheritance of ecological, environmental and economic debt' (Generation Zero, 2012c). Generation Zero has stated that it is youth who now have the 'opportunity to rewrite, reinvent, and redesign' New Zealand, and as a consequence are 'building a huge, influential movement of young people who are standing up for our rights to a positive future'. (Generation Zero, 2012b). The positive actions of young people in this regard are commendable. However, it is also essential that adults take responsibility for the environmental damage that they are inflicting on the earth, and to initiate progress to redress this damage.

Addressing environmental disasters

Currently, the people and the government of Aotearoa New Zealand are coping with the aftermath of the Christchurch earthquake. More than 10,000 homes need to be rebuilt and about another 105,000 need to be repaired with funds from the government's Earthquake Commission, which insures Aotearoa New Zealand houses against natural disasters. A whole city seems to be waiting for builders. People are still living in their cars, their garages, their caravans, their friends' places, and their damaged homes. The government has focused on planning for and rebuilding the 'houses for businesses', including a new rugby stadium and a conference centre, to boost the economy. Meanwhile, Christchurch, in the past often referred to as the 'Garden City', is becoming 'Protest City' as thousands of people march to ask for a plan for social housing, and a plan for their own housing. Schools in Christchurch are being closed and merged as families leave the city and school rolls fall. This is having a severe impact on local communities, which have already experienced extensive disruption and instability.

Christchurch youth have responded to the earthquake with positive action. A 'youth hub' has sprung up in the city. Services and youth organisations who lost their premises 'got together to be together' and created their own neighborhood in order to coordinate services and move away from a fragmented approach to service delivery (Youth Hub, 2012). Those at Canterbury University formed the Student Volunteer Army as a result of the September 4, 2010 earthquake: 2500 students communicated and rallied through social networking sites, such as Facebook, to clear 65,000 tons of liquefaction from streets and homes all around the city, and then after the February 22, 2011 earthquake, they cleared another 360,000 tons (Student Volunteer Army, 2012). The Student Volunteer Army is continuing its work, and seeking to develop further involvement of youth in natural disaster recovery. In fact, the Volunteer Army has helped to create and dispatch communication systems in Japan after the 2011 tsunami and in New York after the 2012 Hurricane Sandy (Scott, 2012).

In conclusion, it appears that adults can learn a lot from children and youth. They are offering us some solutions to enable us to take care of the people and the land in Aotearoa New Zealand. In the long term, it is mostly our children who will feel the effects of adults' decisions. The authors in this book have dedicated much of their working and personal lives to improving the lives of children and youth in Aotearoa New Zealand. They, and we, see the possibility of a different future: a fun, safe, and rewarding future. This book is less about whether Aotearoa New Zealand is a good place to grow up, but really about whether it *can be*. We think it can: in the course of our research we have seen children laugh and play in difficult and in beautiful circumstances, and youth themselves try to fill the gaps that have been found in our kaitiaki of the people and land. A common thread which runs through the collection of chapters in this book is that they all include elements of hope, and so we leave you with a picture of some Christchurch children and youth moving forward into the future.

Moving forward into the future: Punting down the Avon River in Christchurch.

About the contributors

Nicola Atwool, PhD: Senior Lecturer, Department of Sociology, Gender and Social Work, University of Otago, *nicola.atwool@otago.ac.nz*. Nicola has worked in the social services for 35 years as a practitioner, educator, and advocate, including working as a Principal Adviser in the Office of the Children's Commissioner. Nicola has a long-standing interest in advocacy for children and young people. Her research interests include the social construction of childhood, attachment and resilience, and effective intervention with children and families. The goal of her research is to influence policy and practice to improve outcomes for children and young people exposed to adversity.

Martha Bell, PhD: Research Fellow, Department of Anthropology & Archaelogy, University of Otago, *martha.bell@otago.ac.nz*. Martha has a background in the sociology of the body, physicality and embodied experience. She has a particular interest in dis/abilities and mobilities as they relate to extreme sport. She is currently part of a multidisciplinary research team investigating reproductive technologies, genetics and disability.

James Calder, BSc: Contract Research Assistant, University of Otago, *james-90@orcon.net.nz*. James has been employed as a research assistant in projects involving young people's work and rights.

Fiona Ellis, MEd Teaching: Senior Lecturer, Early Childhood, University of Otago College of Education, *fiona.ellis@otago.ac.nz*. Fiona has been actively involved in advocating for children's rights. She has been engaged in research, which has explored how children's rights are addressed in early childhood environments.

Christina Ergler, PhD: School of Environment, The University of Otago, c.ergler@otago.ac.nz. Christina is a lecturer in geography at the University of Otago. She recently completed her PhD, *A Bourdieusian analysis of children's seasonal play practices*, at Auckland University. Her research interests span across social, cultural and health geography. She is interested in methodologies for accessing children's expertise, an approach she calls 'beyond passive participation'.

Victoria Farmer, MSc: Edgar National Centre for Diabetes and Obesity Research, Department of Medicine, University of Otago, victoria.farmer@otago.ac.nz. Victoria is currently a PhD candidate, who is co-ordinating a large, multi-centre randomised controlled trial investigating activity in primary school-aged children. She is interested in paediatric and early childhood health and the prevention of overweight in early childhood.

Lyn Foote, MEd: Coordinator of Early Childhood Programmes, University of Otago College of Education, lyn.foote@otago.ac.nz. Lyn has been actively involved in researching aspects of quality early childhood education. She has an interest in children's rights – particularly participation rights and how these are reflected in early childhood practice.

Claire Freeman, PhD: Associate Professor, Director of the Master of Planning Programme, Department of Geography, University of Otago, cf@geography.otago.ac.nz. Claire's interests are in environmental planning, including sustainable communities, planning for children and young people and planning with nature. In 2011 Claire and Paul Tranter published their book, *Children and their Urban Environment: Changing Worlds* (Earthscan), which provides a comprehensive account of how the urban environment impacts on children's lives.

N. Ruth Gasson, PhD: Senior Lecturer, University of Otago College of Education, ruth.gasson@otago.ac.nz. Ruth's research is in the area of social justice, rights and policy. Her most recent research adopts a children's rights perspective to explore the work carried out by young New Zealanders. She is particularly interested in promoting participation rights for young people.

Megan Gollop, MEd: Senior Research Fellow, Centre for Research on Children and Families, University of Otago, megan.gollop@otago.ac.nz. Megan's research focuses on the rights and well-being of children and families as relevant to policy and practice, predominantly in the following areas: children's perspectives; sociolegal research regarding family law matters, particularly separation and divorce; parenting and parental discipline; mobility and transition; and children and young people's participation in research. Megan is completing a PhD at the University of Otago.

Anita Gibbs, PhD: Associate Professor, Department of Sociology, Gender and Social Work, University of Otago, *anita.gibbs@otago.ac.nz*. Anita teaches in sociology and social work, having trained as a social worker in Britain. Her research interests include parenting pathways, adoption and caring for children, applied and autoethnographic research methods. She is also an adoptive parent of two Russian-born children and is actively involved in support networks for adoptive families.

Karen Guo, PhD: Senior Lecturer, Faculty of Education, The University of Waikato, *kguo@waikato.ac.nz*. Karen teaches in the early childhood programme. Karen's research interests include immigrant children and families, cultural diversity and multiculturalism. Her current research is focused on early childhood teachers' professional development in China.

Nancy Higgins, PhD: Independent Researcher and Director, Coprosma & Associates, Inc., Christchurch, *n.higgins@clear.net.nz*. Nancy's research work is in the areas of social justice, inclusive education, and disabled children and youth. Most recently, Nancy has completed a project with Ngāti Kāpo o Aotearoa about access to health and education services for kāpo (blind) tamariki (children) and rangatahi (youth), and their whānau. She is currently actively involved in The Collaborative for Research and Training in Youth Development and in the Inclusive Education Action Group.

Robin Kearns, PhD: Professor of Geography, School of Environment, University of Auckland, *r.kearns@auckland.ac.nz*. Robin's research spans a range of themes within social and cultural geography, with a particular interest in the links between identity, place and well-being. Curiosity about the spaces of children's health care led him to investigate child-friendly hospitals and involvement in a local primary school was the beginning of research on children's preferences for school travel, which was influential in the development of Auckland's walking school bus programme. Latterly he has worked with Karen Witten and colleagues on HRC-funded projects related to children's opportunities for independent mobility within intensifying urban settings.

Julie Lawrence, PhD: Research Fellow, Department of Women's & Children's Health, University of Otago, *julie.lawrence@otago.ac.nz*. Julie's professional background in nursing and social work has shaped her research interests, and she has been involved in social research with children and families since the early 1990s. Her research focus has been on topics such as the children and families of prisoners, parenting behaviours and, in particular, family discipline.

Jude MacArthur, PhD: Senior Lecturer, School of Education, Massey University (Albany), *j.a.macarthur@massey.ac.nz*. Jude has led research projects for the Ministry of Education and the New Zealand Royal Society's Marsden Fund, focusing primarily on the school experiences of children and young people with disabilities. These projects fostered her interest in disabled children's and young people's rights, participation and perspectives in both research and education, inclusive education, and in the ethical implications of including children and young people as active participants in research.

Helen May, PhD: Professor of Education, University of Otago College of Education, Dunedin, *helen.may@otago.ac.nz*. Helen May is a past junior school teacher and childcare worker and has spent 25 years working in university teacher education contexts. She has written books on the history, policy and curriculum of early years education.

Margaret McKenzie, MA: Senior Lecturer, School of Social Services, Otago Polytechnic, *margaret.mckenzie@op.ac.nz*. Margaret's research interests are in family social work practice and child welfare programmes and policy. She has written and published on various aspects of this, including work on Family Group Conferences, supervised access, research with vulnerable groups, and the role of community development in child protection from a cross-national perspective. The chapter that she and Jude MacArthur have contributed to this book arose from a working group that was established while she was co-convenor of the Children and Young People as Social Actors Research Cluster at the University of Otago.

Moana Mitchell (Ngāti Kahungunu, Ngā Ruahinerangi, Ngāti Porou), MA: PhD student, Te Kura Māori, Faculty of Education, Victoria University of Wellington, *moana.mitchell@vuw.ac.nz*. Moana's Master's thesis, 'All we got to see were factories': Scoping Māori transitions from secondary school, will be further extended in her PhD study. She has been a research assistant as part of the Māori and Pacific component of a national research project about innovative education employment linkages for young people. Moana has a real interest in community issues for Māori whanau and has managed Te Korowai Aroha Whanau Services in Porirua and Awhina Wahine Inc. in Tawa. She is currently teaching in the social work programme at Te Wānanga o Aotearoa – Porirua campus. Moana has a daughter, Waimirirangi, and is passionate about Māori education and Māori school-to-work transition.

Karen Nairn, PhD: Senior Lecturer, University of Otago College of Education, *karen.nairn@otago.ac.nz*. *Children of Rogernomics: A neoliberal generation leaves school* is Karen's most recent publication, written with co-authors Jane Higgins and Judith Sligo. The book is about 93 young New Zealanders who grew up during the economic and social reforms of the 1980s and 1990s (often referred to as Rogernomics). The book's focus is the identity work of these young people. The book connects the stories of young people with the wider social and economic story of Aotearoa New Zealand during the last three decades.

Hazel Phillips (Ngāti Mutunga), PhD: Independent Indigenous Researcher, Kotuku Aotearoa Wellington, *kotuku@me.com*. Hazel is an indigenous researcher who works with and in Māori communities. She has a background in Māori education and development and is passionate about social justice for Māori as well as for all marginalised people and especially for tamariki/rangatahi. Her aspiration is for a just and equitable society.

Kathleen Quinlivan, PhD: Senior Lecturer, School of Educational Studies and Human Development, University of Canterbury, *kathleen.quinlivan@canterbury.ac.nz*. Kathleen works across theory and practice contexts to explore ways of learning that engage with genders, sexualities and difference across a range of formal and informal educational sites with young people. She has published widely in the area of genders, sexualities and schooling both nationally and internationally. She is currently co-editing a forthcoming Routledge text, *Pleasure Bound: Interrogating the politics of pleasure in sexuality education*. Kathleen directs a New Zealand AIDS Foundation research project exploring the role that gay–straight alliances play as sites of learning across a range of Aotearoa New Zealand secondary schooling contexts.

Judith Sligo, MA: Dunedin Multidisciplinary Health and Development Research Unit, University of Otago, *judith.sligo@dmhdru.otago.ac.nz*. Judith has been researching a range of topics, including parenting and intergenerational behaviours and health, over the past 16 years. In that time, she has also been involved in several other research projects with children and young people, including the project described in this book. Others have included studies focused on young people's participation in public life and socialising without alcohol. She is currently working on her PhD, in which she is looking at the transition from school to the workplace for three generations of young people.

Anne Smith, PhD: Professor Emeritus at the University of Otago and Adjunct Professor at Southern Cross University, New South Wales, *anneb.smith@otago.ac.nz*. Anne was formerly Director of the Children's Issues Centre, a research, education and advocacy centre for children's rights. Anne has published many research articles and several books, including *Understanding children's development* and (with colleagues) *Children's voices: Learning in the making* and *Global pathways to abolishing physical punishment*. She has a particular interest in young children's learning; links between research, policy and practice for children; family discipline, and children's citizenship.

Nicola Taylor, PhD: Professor, Alexander McMillan Chair in Childhood Studies, and Director of the Centre for Research on Children and Families, University of Otago, *nicola.taylor@otago.ac.nz*. Nicola has a particular interest in sociolegal research with children, parents and professionals on a broad range of child and family law, welfare and parenting issues – particularly those concerning separation, divorce, relocation, care and protection, children's views, and international law and human rights issues.

Karen Witten, PhD: Associate Director of the Social and Health Outcomes Research and Evaluation (SHORE) and Whāriki Research Centre in the School of Public Health at Massey University, *k.witten@massey.ac.nz*. Karen's primary research interests centre on interactions between the physical characteristics of cities and neighbourhoods and the social relationships, transport choices and well-being of the people living in them. Much of her current research concerns children's independent mobility and physical activity in urban and suburban neighbourhoods. She is a social scientist and Professor of Public Health.

Photographers

The editors wish to acknowledge and thank the following contributors, who kindly provided photographs for inclusion in the book: Mere Courtis, Rosalind Day, Claire Freeman, Anita Gibbs, Nancy Higgins, Mark McGuire, Rosemary Soryl and Karen Witten.

References

Foreword

Brash, D. (2004). Nationhood: Address to the Orewa Rotary Club, 27 January: www.donbrash.com/orewa-2004-nationhood (retrieved 3/12/12).

Editorial (2004). The NZ race card. *Sydney Morning Herald*, 8 March, p. 12: www.smh.com.au/articles/2004/03/07/1078594232381.html?from=storyrhs

Freire, P. (1998). *Teachers as cultural workers: Letters to those who dare to teach*. Boulder, Colorado: Westview Press.

Ministry of Health and University of Otago (2006). *Decades of disparity III: Ethnic and socio-economic inequalities in mortality, New Zealand 1981–1999*. Wellington.

Hager, N. (2006). *The hollow men: A study in the politics of deception*. Nelson: Craig Potton Publishing.

Hansen, J. (2011). *Storms of my grandchildren: The truth about the coming climate catastrophe and our last chance to save humanity*. London: Bloomsbury.

Chapter 1: Introduction

Auckland City Council (2010). *Auckland state of the city report 2010*: www.aucklandcity.govt.nz/council/documents/stateofcity/docs/chapter4.pdf

Ballard, K.K. (1994) (ed.). *Disability, family, whānau and society*, Palmerston North: Dunmore Press.

Carrington, S. & MacArthur, J. (2012) (eds). *Teaching in inclusive school communities*. Brisbane: Wiley Publishers.

Children's Social Health Monitor (2011). *The children's social health monitor 2011 update*. Dunedin: NZ Child and Youth Epidemiology Service: www.nzchildren.co.nz

Child Youth Family (2012). *Who we are and what we do*: www.cyf.govt.nz/about-us/who-we-are-what-we-do/index.html

Duncan, J. & Te One, S. (2012). *Comparative Early Childhood Education Services: International Perspectives (Critical Cultural Studies of Childhood)*. NewYork: Palgrave Macmillan.

Families Commission (2012). *Home*: www.familiescommission.org.nz

Frazer, D., Motzen, R. & Ryba, K. (2005) (eds). *Learners with special needs in Aotearoa, New Zealand*. Palmerston North: Dunmore Press.

Gollop, M. (2012, September). *Children and young people's post disaster relocation experiences*. Paper presented at the Second International Conference of the International Childhood and Youth Research Network, Children, Young People and Adults: Extending the Conversation, Preston, Lancashire.

Hayward, B. (2012). *Children, citizenship and environment: Nurturing a democratic imagination in a changing world*. Routledge: London.

Higgins, N., MacArthur, J. & Morton, M. (2008). Winding back the clock: The retreat of New Zealand inclusive education policy. *New Zealand Annual Review of Education*, 17 (2007), 145–167.

Higgins, N., Phillips, H., Cowan, C., Tikao, K. & Wakefield, B. (2010). *Growing up kāpo Māori: Whānau, identity, cultural well-being and health: Final report*. Dunedin: Donald Beasley Institute & Hastings: Ngāti Kāpo o Aotearoa Inc.

Hodgson, M. O'Brien, Mre. (2010). *Child poverty and child well-being: New Zealand in an international context*. Auckland: Social Policy and Social Work Programme, School of Health and Social Services, Albany Campus, Massey University.

May, H. (2005). *School beginnings: A nineteenth century colonial story*. Wellington: New Zealand Council for Educational Research.

May, H. (2011). *'I am five and I go to school': Early years schooling in New Zealand, 1900-2010*. Dunedin: Otago University Press.

Ministry of Education (2012). *Success for all: Every school, every child*: www.minedu.govt.nz/NZEducation/EducationPolicies/SpecialEducation/OurWorkProgramme/SuccessForAll.aspx

Nairn, K, Higgins, J. & Sligo, J. (2012). *Children of Rogernomics: A neoliberal generation leaves school*. Dunedin: Otago University Press.

NZ Government. (2010). *Cultural identity*: www.socialreport.msd.govt.nz/cultural-identity/maori-language-speakers.html

NZ Government & Statistics New Zealand (2010). *Population and sustainable development*: www.population.govt.nz/myth-busters/myth-10.aspx

OECD (2009). *Doing better for children*: www.oecd.org/els/social/childwellbeing

Office of the Children's Commissioner (2012). *About us*: www.occ.org.nz/about us

Ritchie, J.B. & Ritchie, J.E. (1978). *Growing up in New Zealand*. Hornsby NSW and Boston: Allen & Unwin.

Save the Children (2011). *13th state of the world's mothers report*: www.savethechildren.org/site/c.8rKLIXMGIpI4E/b.8076153/k.B2B6/Chronic_Malnutrition_and_Child_Survival_Facts_and_Stats.htm

Smith, A.B. (2000). *Advocating for children: International perspectives on children's rights*. Dunedin: University of Otago Press.

Smith, A.B. with Keith Ballard (2005). *Understanding children's development*. Wellington: Bridget Williams Books.

Statistics New Zealand (2006). *QuickStats about culture and identity*: www.stats.govt.nz/Census/2006CensusHomePage/QuickStats/quickstats-about-a-subject/culture-and-identity/asian.aspx

Statistics New Zealand (2002). *Census snapshot: children*: www.stats.govt.nz/browse_for_stats/people_and_communities/Children/census-snapshot-children.aspx

Statistics New Zealand (2011). *Population statistics stock take*: www.stats.govt.nz/browse_for_stats/population.aspx

Survival [for tribal peoples] (2010). *New Zealand finally supports UN declaration on indigenous rights*, April 20: www.survivalinternational.org/news/5846

Sutton-Smith, B. (1981). *A history of children's play: New Zealand, 1840-1950*. Philadelphia: University of Pennsylvania Press.

Te Roopu Waiora Trust (n.d.). *About us*: www.teroopuwaiora.org.nz/12/contact

Waitangi Tribunal (n.d.). *The Treaty of Waitangi*: www.waitangi-tribunal.govt.nz/treaty

United Nations (2013). *United Nations Human Development Report 2013: The rise of the south: Human progress in a diverse world*: http://hdr.undp.org/en/media/HDR2013_EN_Summary.pdf

Chapter 2

Alanen, L. (2011). Critical childhood studies? *Childhood, 18* (2), 147–150.

Alderson, P. (2001). Life and death: Agency and dependency in young children's health care. *Childrenz Issues, 5* (1), 23–27.

Bennett, P. (2011). Introduction. Green Paper for vulnerable children: Every child thrives, belongs, achieves. Wellington: Ministry for Social Development (p. v).

Bluebond-Langner, M. & Korbin, J. (2007). Challenges and opportunities in the anthropology of childhoods: An introduction to children, childhoods, and Childhood Studies. *American Anthropologist, 109* (2), 241–246.

Carr, M., Smith, A.B., Duncan, J., Jones, C., Lee, W. & Marshall, K. (2010). *Learning in the making: Disposition and design in early education*. Rotterdam: Sense Publishers.

Dobbs, T., Smith, A.B. & Taylor, N. (2006). 'No, we don't get a say, children just suffer the consequences': Children talk about family discipline. *International Journal of Children's Rights, 14* (2), 137–156.

Durrant, J. (2011). The empirical rationale for eliminating physical punishment. In J. E. Durrant & A.B. Smith (eds), *Global pathways to abolishing physical punishment: Realising children's rights* (pp. 42–66). New York: Routledge.

Flowerdew, J. & Neale, B. (2003). Trying to stay apace: Children with multiple challenges in their post-divorce family lives. *Childhood, 10* (2), 147-161.

Freeman, M. (1998). The sociology of childhood and children's rights, *International Journal of Children's Rights, 6*, 433-444.

Furedi, F. (2001). *Paranoid parenting: Abandon your anxieties and be a good parent.* London: Penguin.

González, N., Moll, L.C. & Amanti, C. (2005). *Funds of knowledge: Theorizing practices in households, communities and classrooms.* Mahwah, N.J.: Lawrence Erlbaum Associates.

James, A. (2007). Giving voice to children's voices: Practices and problems, pitfalls and potentials. *American Anthropologist, 109* (2), 261-272.

James, A. (2009). Agency. In J. Qvortrup, W. Corsaro & M.-S. Honig (eds), *The Palgrave handbook of childhood studies* (pp. 1-18). Basingstoke, UK: Palgrave Macmillan.

James, A. (2010). Competition or integration? The next step in childhood studies? *Childhood, 17* (4), 485-499.

James, A. & James, A. (2008). *Key concepts in childhood studies.* Los Angeles: Sage.

James, A. & Prout, A. (eds) (1997). *Constructing and reconstructing childhood: Contemporary issues in the sociological study of childhood* (2nd edn). London: Falmer Press.

Jenks, C. (1996). *Childhood.* London: Routledge.

Johnston, P. (2004). *Choice words: How our language affects children's learning.* Portland, Maine: Stenhouse Publishers.

Karp, J. (2008). Matching human dignity with the UN Convention on the Rights of the Child. In Y. Ronen & C.W. Greenbaum (eds), *The case for the child: Towards a new agenda* (pp. 89-135). Antwerp and Oxford: Intersentia.

Kennedy, A. (2010). Children and the notion of risk: The nanny state? In D. Kassem, L. Murphy & E. Taylor (eds), *Key issues in childhood and youth studies* (pp. 75-85). Abingdon, Oxon: Routledge.

Lansdown, G. (1994). Children's rights. In B. Mayall (ed.), *Children's childhoods: Observed and experienced* (pp. 33-44). London: Falmer Press.

Mayall, B. (2002). *Towards a sociology for childhood: Thinking from children's lives.* Buckingham: Open University Press.

Melton, G. (2008). Beyond balancing: Toward an integrated approach to children's rights. *Journal of Social Issues, 64* (4), 903-920.

McNaughton, G. & Smith, K. (2009). Children's rights in early childhood. In M.J. Kehily (ed.), *An introduction to childhood studies* (2nd edn) (pp. 161-176). Maidenhead and New York: Open University Press.

Oakley, A. (1994). Women and children first and last: Parallels and differences between children's and women's studies. In B. Mayall (ed.), *Children's childhoods: Observed and experienced* (pp. 11-32). London: Falmer Press.

Prout, A. (2005). *The future of childhood.* London and New York: Routledge Falmer.

Prout, A. & James, A. (1997). A new paradigm for the sociology of childhood? Provenance, promise and problems. In A. James & A. Prout (eds), *Constructing and reconstructing childhood: Contemporary issues in the sociological study of childhood* (2nd edn) (pp. 7-33). London: Falmer Press.

Pufall, P.B. & Unsworth, R.P. (eds) (2004). *Rethinking childhood.* New Jersey: Rutgers University Press.

Qvortrup, J. (2005, June). *2005: The little 's' and the prospects for generational childhood studies.* A paper presented at the international conference, Childhoods 2005, Oslo, 29 June – 3 July.

Qvortrup, J. (2009). Childhood as a structural form. In J. Qvortrup, W. Corsaro & M.-S. Honig (eds), *The Palgrave handbook of childhood studies* (pp. 21-33). Basingstoke, UK: Palgrave Macmillan.

Qvortrup, J., Corsaro, W. & Honig, M.-S. (2009). Introduction: Why social studies of childhood? In J. Qvortrup, W. Corsaro & M.-S.. Honig (eds), *The Palgrave handbook of childhood studies* (pp. 1-18). Basingstoke, UK: Palgrave Macmillan.

Rogoff, B. (1990). *Apprenticeship in thinking: Cognitive development in social context.* New York and Oxford: Oxford University Press.

Smith, A.B. (2002). Interpreting and supporting participation rights: Contributions from sociocultural theory. *International Journal of Children's Rights, 10*, 73–88.
Smith, A.B. (2007). Children's rights and early childhood education: Links to theory and advocacy. *Australian Journal of Early Childhood, 32* (3).
Smith, A.B., Taylor, N.J. & Gollop, M.M. (eds) (2000). *Children's voices: Research, policy and practice.* Auckland: Pearson Education.
Smith, A.B., Taylor, N.J. & Tapp, P. (2003). Rethinking children's involvement in decision-making after parental separation. *Childhood, 10* (2), 203–218.
Stainton-Rogers, W. (2004). Promoting better childhoods: Constructions of child concern. In M.J. Kehily (ed.), *An introduction to childhood studies* (pp. 125–144). Maidenhead and New York: Open University Press.
United Nations Committee on the Rights of the Child (UNCRC) (2011). *Consideration of reports submitted to states parties under Article 44 of the Convention.* Paris: United Nations.
Waller, T. (2009). Modern childhood: Contemporary theories and children's lives. In T. Waller (ed.), *An introduction to early childhood: An interdisciplinary approach* (2nd edn) (pp. 2–11). Los Angeles and London: Sage.
Woodhead, M. (2004). Foreword. In M.J. Kehily (ed.), *An introduction to childhood studies* (1st edn) (pp. x–xi). Maidenhead and New York: Open University Press.
Woodhead, M. (2005). Early childhood development: A question of rights. *International Journal of Early Childhood, 37* (3), 79–98.
Woodhead, M. (2009). Chapter 3: Child development and the development of childhood. In J. Qvortrup, W.A. Corsaro & M.-S. Honig (eds), *The Palgrave handbook of childhood studies* (pp. 46–61). Basingstoke, UK: Palgrave Macmillan.

Chapter 3

Allen, G. & Smith, I.D. (2008). *Early intervention: Good parents, great kids, better citizens.* London: Centre for Social Justice/Smith Institute.
Atwool, N.R. (2003). If it's such a good idea, how come it doesn't work? Theory and practice of integrated service delivery. *Childrenz Issues, 7* (2), 31–35.
Bennett, P. (2012). Social workers in schools expansion under way: www.beehive.govt.nz/release/social-workers-schools-expansion-underway
Boyden, J. & Mann, G. (2005). Children's risk, resilience and coping in extreme situations. In M. Ungar (ed.), *Handbook for working with children and youth* (pp. 3–25). Thousand Oaks, CA: Sage.
Brown, W.K. & Rhodes, W.A. (1991). Factors that promote invulnerability and resiliency in at-risk children. In W.K. Brown & W.A. Rhodes (eds), *Why some children succeed despite the odds* (pp. 171–177). New York: Praeger.
Buchanan, A. (2006). Including the socially excluded: The impact of government policy on vulnerable families and children in need. *British Journal of Social Work, 37*, 187–207.
Callan, S. (2008). *The next generation.* London: Centre for Social Justice.
Carroll-Lind, J., Chapman, J. & Rauskausas, J. (2011). Children's perceptions of violence: The nature, extent and impact of their experiences. *Social Policy Journal, 37*, 1–13.
Centre on the Developing Child at Harvard University (2007). *A science-based framework for early childhood policy: Using evidence to improve outcomes in learning behavior and health for vulnerable children:* www.developingchild.harvard.edu
Child Poverty Action Group (2011). *Left further behind: How policies fail the poorest children in New Zealand.* Auckland.
Child, Youth & Family (2009). *Differential response information for community providers:* www.cyf.govt.nz
Children's Social Health Monitor (2011). *The children's social health monitor 2011 update.* Dunedin: NZ Child and Youth Epidemiology Service: www.nzchildren.co.nz
Cicchetti, D. & Toth, S.L. (1995). A developmental and psychopathology perspective on child abuse and neglect. *Journal of the American Academy of Child and Adolescent Psychiatry, 34*, 541–564.

Compas, B. (1987). Coping with stress during childhood and adolescence. *Psychological Bulletin*, 101, 392-403.
Connolly, M. & Doolan, M. (2007). *Lives cut short.* Wellington: Dunmore Publishing.
Connolly, M., Wells, P. & Field, J. (2007). Working with vulnerable infants. *Social Work Now*, 38, 5-10.
Cortis, N., Katz, I. & Patulny, R. (2009). *Engaging hard-to-reach families and children.* Occasional Paper no. 26, Stronger Families and Communities Strategy 2004-2009. Canberra: Department of Families, Housing, Community Services and Indigenous Affairs.
Duncanson, M., Smith, D. & Davies, E. (2009). Death and serious injury from assault of children under five years in Aotearoa New Zealand: A review of international literature and recent findings. Unpublished paper available from www.occ.org.nz
Families Commission (2008). *The kiwi nest: 60 years of change in New Zealand families.* Research report no. 3/08. Wellington: www.nzfamilies.org.nz
Families Commission (2009). *Finding time: Parents' long working hours and time impact on family life.* Research report no. 2/09. Wellington: www.nzfamilies.org.nz
Fergusson, D. & Boden, J. (2011). Alcohol use in adolescence. In the report of the Prime Minister's Chief Science Advisor, *Improving the transition: Reducing social and psychological morbidity during adolescence* (pp. 59-78). Auckland: Office of the Prime Minister's Science Advisory Committee: www.pmcsa.org.nz
Fergusson, D. Boden, J. & Hayne, H. (2011). Childhood conduct problems. In the report of the Prime Minister's Chief Science Advisor, *Improving the transition: Reducing social and psychological morbidity during adolescence* (pp. 235-256). Auckland: Office of the Prime Minister's Science Advisory Committee: www.pmcsa.org.nz
Fonagy, P. (2003). Psychopathology from infancy to adulthood: The mystery of unfolding of disturbance in time. *Infant Mental Health Journal*, 24 (3), 212-239.
Fraser, M.W. (2004). The ecology of childhood: A multisystems perspective. In M.W. Fraser (ed.), *Risk and resilience in childhood* (pp. 1-12). Washington DC: NASW Press.
Gilbert, R., Kemp, A., Thoburn, J., Sidebotham, P., Radford, L., Glaser, D. & MacMillan, H.L. (2009). Recognising and responding to child maltreatment. *Lancet*, 373, 167-180.
Girling, M., Huakau, J., Casswell, S. & Conway, K. (2006). *Families and heavy drinking: Impacts on children's wellbeing. Systematic Review.* Blue Skies Report no. 6/06. Wellington: Families Commission: www.nzfamilies.org.nz
Gray, A. (n.d.). *Early-intervention support and vulnerable families and whānau.* Wellington: Families Commission.
Harold, G. (2011). Families and children: A focus on parental separation, domestic violence and child maltreatment. In T=the Prime Minister's Chief Science Advisor's Report, *Improving the transition: Reducing social and psychological morbidity during adolescence* (pp. 177-190). Auckland: Office of the Prime Minister's Science Advisory Committee: www.pmcsa.org.nz
Hibbard, R.A., Desch, L.W., Committee on Child Abuse and Neglect & Council on Children with Disabilities (2007). Maltreatment of children with disabilities. *Pediatrics*, 119, 1018-1026.
Infometrics (2011). *1000 days to get it right for every child: The effectiveness of public investment in New Zealand children.* Wellington: Every Child Counts: www.everychildcounts.org.nz
Jack, G. (2000). Ecological influences on parenting and child development. *British Journal of Social Work*, 30, 703-720.
Kalil, A. (2003). *Family resilience and good child outcomes: A review of the literature.* Wellington: Ministry of Social Development.
Maluccio, A.N. Canali, C., Vecchiato, T., Lightburn, A., Aldgate, J. & Rose, W. (2011). *Improving outcomes for children and families: Finding and using international evidence.* London and Philadelphia PA: Jessica Kingsley.
Mardani, J. (2010). *Preventing child neglect in New Zealand.* Wellington: Office of the Children's Commissioner.
Masten, A.S. & Coatsworth, J.D. (1998). The development of competence in favorable and unfavorable environments. *American Psychologist*, 53 (2), 205-220.
McLoyd, V.C. (1998). Socioeconomic disadvantage and child development. *American Psychologist*, 53 (2), 185-204.

Ministry of Social Development. (2011a). *Vulnerable children: Numbers and risk factors.* Wellington: Ministry of Social Development: www.childrensactionplan.govt.nz/references/data

Ministry of Social Development (2011b). *Statistical report.* Wellington: www.msd.govt.nz/about-msd-and-our-work/publications-resources

Moffit, T. (1993). Adolescence-limited and life-course-persistent antisocial behavior: A developmental taxonomy. *Psychological Review, 100,* 674–701.

Morton, S.M.B., Atatoa Carr, P.E., Bandara, D.K., Grant, C.C., Ivory, V.C., Kingi, T.R., Liang, R., Perese, L.M., Peterson, E., Pryor, J.E., Reese, E., Robinson, E.M., Schmidt, J.M. & Waldie, K.E. (2010). *Growing up in New Zealand: A longitudinal study of New Zealand children and their families. Report 1: Before we are born.* Auckland: Growing up in New Zealand.

Munro, M. (2011). *The Munro review of child protection: Final report.* Department for Education: www.education.gov.uk/publications

New South Wales Commission for Children and Young People and Commission for Children and Young People (Queensland) (2004). *A head start for Australia: An early years framework:* www.kids.nsw.gov.au and www.childcomm.qld.gov.au

New Zealand Government (2011). Green paper for vulnerable children: Every child, thrives, belongs, achieves : www.childrensaction plan.govt.nz

O'Brien, M., Dale, M. & St John, S. (2011). Child poverty and inequality. In Child Poverty Action Group (2011), *Left further behind: How policies fail the poorest children in New Zealand* (pp. 11–25). Auckland.

O'Dougherty Wright, M. & Masten, A.S. (2006). Resilience processes in development. In S. Goldstein & R.B. Brooks (eds), *Handbook of resilience in children* (pp. 17–37). New York: Springer Sciences & Business Media.

Office of the Children's Commissioner (2011a). Every child thrives, belongs, achieves: Children's voices on the Green Paper. A submission on the Green Paper for vulnerable children from primary school children in years 7 and 8 as told to staff from the Office of the Children's Commissioner during October and November 2011: www.occ.org.nz/media_speeches_and_submissions/submissions?result_3607_result_page=2

Office of the Children's Commissioner (2011b). We all need TLC – tender loving care: Collective youth voices. Submission on the Green Paper for Vulnerable Children from the collective voices of five youth groups from throughout New Zealand as told to staff at the Office of the Children's Commissioner during December 2011 and February 2012: www.occ.org.nz/media_speeches_and_submissions/submissions?result_3607_result_page=1

Perry, B. (2009). *Non-income measures of material wellbeing and hardship: First results from the 2008 New Zealand Living Standards Survey with international comparisons.* Wellington: Ministry of Social Development: www.msd.govt.nz

Perry, B. (2011). *Household incomes in New Zealand: Trends in indicators of inequality and hardship 1982 to 2010.* Wellington: Ministry of Social Development: www.msd.govt.nz

Poland, M., Cameron, A., Wong, K. & Fletcher, M. (n.d.). *Moving on: Changes in a year in family living arrangements.* Wellington: Families Commission: www.nzfamilies.org.nz

Prime Minister's Chief Science Advisor (2011). *Improving the transition: Reducing social and psychological morbidity during adolescence.* Auckland: Office of the Prime Minister's Science Advisory Committee: www.pmcsa.org.nz

Quilgars, D. (2001). The environment. In J. Bradshaw (ed.), *Poverty: The outcomes for children* (pp. 91–101). London: Family Policy Studies Centre.

Reading, R., Bissell, S., Goldhagen, J., Harwin, J., Masson, J., Moynihan, S., Parton, N., Santos-Pais, M., Thoburn, J. & Webb, E. (2009). Promotion of children's rights and prevention of child maltreatment. *Lancet, 373,* 332–343.

Scott, D. (2006). Towards a public health model of child protection in Australia. *Communities, Families and Children Australia, 1* (1), 9–16.

Scott, D. (2009). Think child, think family. *Family Matters, 81,* 37–42.

Smith, M. (2011). Report to Hon Paula Bennett, Minister for Social Development and Employment, following an inquiry into the serious abuse of a nine year old girl and other matters relating to the welfare, safety and protection of children in New Zealand: www.beehive.govt.nz/release/safety-and-protection-children-must-come-first

Sroufe, L.A., Cooper, R.G., De Hart, G.B. & Marshall, M.E., (1992). *Child development: Its nature and course* (2nd edn). New York: McGraw-Hill.

Ungar, M. (2003). Methodological and contextual challenges researching childhood resilience: An international collaboration to develop a mixed-method design to investigate health-related phenomena in at-risk child populations. Summary report on year one activities and the first Halifax meeting: www.irp.edu.ca (accessed 10 June 2005).

Ungar, M. (2005). Introduction: Resilience across cultures and contexts. In M. Ungar (ed.), *Handbook for working with children and youth* (pp. xv–xxxix). Thousand Oaks, CA: Sage.

Wood, B., Hassall, I. & Hook, G. (2008). *Unreasonable force: New Zealand's journey towards banning physical punishment of children.* Wellington: Save the Children New Zealand.

Whitaker, D.J., Lutzker, J.R. & Shelley, G.A. (2005). Child maltreatment prevention piroritues at the Centers for Disease Control and Prevention. *Child Maltreatment, 10*, 245–259.

Wyman, P.A., Cowen, E.L., Work, W.C., Hoyt-Meyers, L., Magnus, K.B. & Fagan, D.B. (1999). Caregiving and developmental factors differentiating young at-risk urban children showing resilient versus stress-affected outcomes: A replication and extension. *Child Development, 70* (3), 645–659.

Yates, T.M., Egeland, B. & Sroufe, L.A. (2003). Rethinking resilience. In S. Luthar (ed.), *Resilience and vulnerability* (pp. 243–266). Cambridge: Cambridge University Press.

Chapter 4

Archbishop of Canterbury (2006). Archbishop warns of 'crisis' in modern childhood: www.independent.co.uk/news/uk/this-britain/archbishop-warns-of-crisis-in-modern-childhood-416548.html

Auckland Regional Council, (2009). Residential intensification: www.arc.govt.nz/auckland/aucklands-growth/residential-intensification.cfm

Baker, M., Barnard, L., Kvalsvig, A., Verral, A., Zhang, J., Keall, M., Wilson, N., Wall, T. & Howden-Chapman, P. (2012). Increasing incidence of serious infectious diseases and inequalities in New Zealand: A national epidemiological study. *Lancet, 379* (9821), 112–119.

Buckingham, D. (2000). *After the death of childhood: Growing up in the age of electronic media.* UK: Polity Press.

Carroll, P., Witten, K. & Kearns, R. (2011). Housing intensification in Auckland: Implications for children and families. *Housing Studies, 26* (3), 353–367.

Cook, V.A. (2011). The teachers seemed a bit obsessive with health and safety: Fieldwork risk and the social construction of childhood. In L. Holt (ed.), *Geographies of children, youth and families* (pp. 279–290). London: Routledge.

Department of Conservation (2006). Review of camping opportunities in New Zealand: Report to the Minister of Conservation. Wellington.

Dixon, J. & DuPuis, A. (2003). Urban intensification in Auckland, New Zealand: A challenge for new urbanism. *Housing Studies, 18* (3), 353–368.

European Commission (2002). *Kids on the move.* Luxembourg.

Families Commission (2008). *The kiwi nest: 60 years of change in New Zealand Families.* Research Report no. 3. Wellington.

Families Commission (2009). *Why families matter: A collection of personal essays.* Wellington.

Freeman, C. (2010). Children's neighbourhoods, social centres to 'terra incognita'. *Children's Geographies, 8* (2) 157–176.

Freeman, C. & Quigg, R. (2008). Commuting lives: Children's mobility and energy use. *Journal of Environmental Planning and Management, 52* (3), 393–412.

Freeman, C. & Vass, E. (2010). Maps and children's lives: A cautionary tale. *Planning Theory and Practice, 11*, 65–88.

Gifkins, M. (1988). *Through the looking glass: Recollections of childhood from 20 prominent New Zealanders.* Auckland: Century Hutchinson.

Gill, T. (2007). *No fear: Growing up in a risk averse society.* London: Calouste Gulbenkian Society.

Gleeson, B. (2006). Australia's toxic cities: Modernity's paradox. In B. Gleeson & N. Sipe (eds), *Creating child friendly cities: Reinstating kids in the city* (pp. 33–47). Routledge, London.

Hall, T. (2010). Goodbye to the backyard? The minimisation of private open space in the Australian outer-suburban estate. *Urban Policy and and Research* (4), 411–433.

Johansson, M. (2006). Environmental and parental factors as determinants of mode for children's leisure travel. *Journal of Environmental Psychology,* 26, 156–169.

Karsten, L. & van Vliet, W. (2006). Children in the city: Reclaiming the street. *Children, Youth Environments,* 16 (1), 151–167.

Kearns, R.A., Collins, D.C.A. & Neuwelt, P.M. (2003). The walking school bus: Extending children's geographies? *Area 35* (3) 285–292.

Louv, R. (2005). *Last child in the woods: Saving our children from nature-deficit disorder.* Carolina, USA: Algonquin Books.

McDonald, N. (2012). Is there a gender gap in school travel? An examination of US children and adolescents, *Journal of Transport Geography,* 20 (1), 80–86.

McGee, R. O. & Ketchel, J. (2003). Pedestrian/bicycle injuries among Dunedin schoolchildren: 1980–2002. A report to the Otago Primary Principals' Association, October. (Presented to the Dunedin City Council Planning and Environment Standing Committee as part of the submission 'Child safety around Dunedin schools, University of Otago, Dunedin.)

McMillan, T.E., (2007). The relative influence of urban from on a child's travel mode to school. *Transport Research, Part A, 41,* 69–79.

Milo Team (2011). *The New Zealand state of play report commissioned by the MILO team:* http://fb.milo.com.au/wp-content/uploads/play_movement_whitepaper_NZ.pdf

Ministry for the Environment (2006). *Gentle footprints: Boots 'n' all.* Wellington

Ministry of Health (2008). *A portrait of health: Key results of the 2006/07 New Zealand health survey.* Wellington.

Ministry of Social Development (2010). *Social report: Housing affordability:* http://socialreport.msd.govt.nz/economic-standard-living/housing-affordability.html

Ministry of Transport (2005). *Annual statistics: Section 6 pedestrian casualties and crashes.* Wellington.

Mizrachi, D. & Whitzman, C. (2009). Vertical living kids: creating supportive environments for children in Melbourne's central city highrises. In P. Maginn, P. et al. (eds), *City growth, sustainability, vitality and vulnerability: Proceedings of the State of Australian Cities conference,* Perth.

New Zealand Productivity Commission (2012). *Housing affordability: Inquiry 2012:* www.productivity.govt.nz

New Zealand Tourism Research Institute (2010). *The influence of perceived risk on participation in outdoor education by pre-teen age school children in New Zealand.* Auckland: NZTRI/AUT.

Palmer, S., (2006). *Toxic childhood: How the modern world is damaging our children and what we can do about it.* London: Orion.

Pooley, C., Turnbull, J. & Adams, M. (2006). The impact of new transport technologies on intraurban mobility: A view from the past. *Environment and Planning A,* 38, 253–267.

Pooley, C., Turnbull, T. & Adams, M. (2005). 'Everywhere she went I had to tag long beside her': Family life course and everyday mobility in England since the 1940s. *History of the Family,* 10, 119–136.

Public Health Advisory Committee. (2007). *An idea whose time has come: New opportunities for health impact assessment in New Zealand policy and planning:* www.nhc.health.govt.nz

Regional Public Health Wellington (2010). *Healthy open spaces: A study of the impact of open spaces on health and well being.* Regional public health information paper: www.wrs.govt.nz/open-spaces-information-hub

Ritchie, J. & Richtie, J (1978). *Growing up in New Zealand.* Allen & Unwin Australia.

SPARC & NZ Tourism Research Institute/Auckland University of Technology (2010). *The influence of perceived risk on participation in outdoor education by pre-teen age schoolchildren in New Zealand:* www.nztri.org

Stanley, F. Richardson, S. & Prior, M. (2005). *Children of the Lucky Country: How Australian society has turned its back on children and why children matter.* Sydney: Macmillan.

Statistics New Zealand (2006). *Urban rural migration*: www.stats.govt.nz/browse_for_stats/population/Migration/internal-migration/urban-rural-migration.aspx

Statistics New Zealand (2010). *Historical context*: www.stats.govt.nz/browse_for_stats/people_and_communities/geographic-areas/urban-rural-profile/historical-context.aspx

Statistics New Zealand (2010a). *Sub-national population estimates*: www.stats.govt.nz/browse_for_stats/population/estimates_and_projections/SubnationalPopulationEstimates_HOTP30Jun10.aspx

Te Ara Encyclopedia of New Zealand (2012). *Childhood*: www.teara.govt.nz/en/childhood/1/1 (accessed 6 July 2012)

Tranter, P. & Pawson, E.P. (2001). Children's access to local environments: A case study of Christchurch, New Zealand. *Local Environment*, 6 (1), 27–48.

Tranter, P. (2006). Overcoming social traps: A key to creating child friendly cities. In B. Gleeson & N. Sipe (eds), *Creating child friendly cities: Reinstating kids in the city* (pp. 121–135). New York: Routledge.

Valentine, G. (2004). *Public space and the culture of childhood.* London: Ashgate.

Chapter 5

Alderson, P. (1995). *Listening to children: Children, ethics and social research.* London: Barnardos.

Alderson, P. (2001). Research by children. *International Journal of Social Research Methodology*, 4 (2), 139–153.

Alderson P. (2008). 'Ten topics for consideration in carrying out social research with children and young people'. *Children's Geographies*, 6, 98–101.

Alderson, P. & Morrow, V. (2004). *Ethics, social research and consulting with children and young people* (2nd edn). Ilford, Essex: Barnardos.

Beazley, H., Bessell, S., Ennew, J. & Waterson, R. (2009). The right to be properly researched: research with children in a messy, real world, *Children's Geographies*, 7 (4), 365–378.

Birbeck, D. & Drummond, M. (2007). Research with young children: Contemplating methods and ethics. *Journal of Educational Enquiry*, 7 (2), 21–31.

Cameron, L. & Murphy, J. (2006). Obtaining consent to participate in research: The issues involved in including people with a range of learning and communication disabilities. *British Journal of Learning Disabilities*, 35, 113–120.

Campbell, A. (2008). For their own good: Recruiting children for research. *Childhood*, 15 (1), 30–49.

Centre for Children and Young People (2005). *Researching with children: Code of ethical practice.* Lismore: Southern Cross University: www.ccyp.scu.edu.au

Cheney, K. (2011). Children as ethnographers: Reflections on the importance of participatory research in assessing orphans' needs. *Childhood*, 18 (2), 166–179.

Clark, P., MacArthur, J., McDonald, T., Simmons-Carlsson, C. & Caswell, P. (2007). *Integrated effective practice in education for students with physical disabilities: A two-part research project.* Wellington: Ministry of Education.

Clavering, E. & McLaughlin, J. (2010). Children's participation in health research: From objects to agents. *Child: Care, Health and Development*, 36 (5), 603–611.

Fargas-Malet, M., McSherry, D., Larkin, E. & Robinson, E. (2010). Research with children: Methodological issues and innovative techniques. *Journal of Early Childhood Research*, 8, 175–192.

Frankel, S. (2007). Researching children's morality: Developing research methods that allow children's involvement in discourses relevant to their everyday lives. *Childhoods Today*, 1 (1), 1–25 (online journal).

Greene, S. & Hill, M. (2005). Researching children's experience: Methods and methodological issues. In S. Greene & D. Hogan (eds), *Researching children's experiences: Methods and approaches* (pp. 1–21). London: Sage Publications.

Harcourt, D. & Sargeant, J. (2011). The challenges of conducting ethical research with children. *Education Enquiry*, 2 (3), 421–436.

Hill, M. (2005). Ethical considerations in researching children's experiences. In S. Greene & D. Hogan (eds), *Researching children's experiences: Methods and approaches* (pp. 61-86). London: Sage.

James, A., Jenks, C. & Prout, A. (1998). *Theorizing childhood*. Cambridge: Polity.

Kelly, B. (2005). 'Chocolate ... makes you autism': Impairment, disability and childhood identities. *Disability and Society, 20* (3), 261-275.

MacArthur, J. Sharp, S., Kelly, B. & Gaffney, M. (2007). Disabled children negotiating school life: Agency, difference and teaching practice. *International Journal of Children's Rights, 15*, 99-120.

McGuire, M. (2005). What if you talked to me? I could be interesting! Ethical research considerations in engaging with bilingual/multilingual child participants in human inquiry. *Forum: Qualitative Social Research, 6* (1), Art. 4: www.qualitative-research.net/fqs

Morrow, V. & Richards, M. (1996). The ethics of social research with children: An overview. *Children and Society, 10* (2), 90-105.

Munford, R. & Sanders, J. (2001). Interviewing children and their parents. In M. Tollich (ed.), *Research ethics in Aotearoa New Zealand: Concepts, practice, critiques* (pp. 99-111). Auckland: Longman.

Nairn, K., Higgins, J. & Sligo, J. (2007). Youth researching youth: 'Trading on' subcultural capital in peer research methodologies. *Teachers' College Record, June 09* (online journal).

Powell, M. & Smith, A. (2006). Ethical guidelines for research with children: A review of current research ethics documentation in New Zealand. *Kotuitui: New Zealand Journal of Social Sciences Online, 1*, 125-138.

Powell, M. & Smith, A. (2009). Children's participation rights in research, *Childhood, 16*, 124-142.

Powell, M.A., Fitzgerald, R., Taylor, N.J. & Graham, A. (March 2012). *Ethical issues in undertaking research with children and young people* (Literature review for the Childwatch International Research Network). Lismore: Southern Cross University, Centre for Children and Young People/Dunedin: University of Otago, Centre for Research on Children and Families.

Quennerstedt, A. (2011). The political construction of children's rights in education: A comparative analysis of Sweden and NZ. *Education Enquiry, 2* (3) 453-371.

Skanvors, I. (2009). Ethics in child research: Children's agency and researchers' 'ethical radar'. *Childhoods Today, 3* (1), 1-22 (online journal).

Skelton, T. (2008). Research with children and young people: Exploring the tensions between ethics, competence and participation. *Children's Geographies, 6* (1), 21-36.

Smith, A.B. (2011). Respecting children's rights and agency: Theoretical insights into ethical research procedures. In B. Perry, D. Harcourt & T. Waller (eds), *Young children's perspectives: Ethics, theory and research* (pp. 11-25). London: Routledge.

Tangen, R. (2008). Listening to children's voices in educational research: Some theoretical and methodological problems. *European Journal of Special Needs Education, 23*, 157-166.

Thomas, N. & O'Kane, C. (1998). The ethics of participatory research with children. *Children and Society, 12*, 336-348.

United Nations. (1989). *Convention on the Rights of the Child*. Geneva.

Wright, K. (2008). Researching the views of pupils with multiple and complex needs. Is it worth doing and whose needs are served by it? *Support for Learning, 23* (1), 32-40.

Chapter 6

Alley, R. (1986). *Rewi Alley: An autobiography*. Beijing: New World Press.

Barrington, J. & Beaglehole, T.H. (1974). *Māori schools in a changing society*. Wellington: New Zealand Council for Educational Research.

Bird, W.W. (1906). Report of the Inspector of Native Schools to the Inspector General of Schools, *Appendices to the Journal of the House of Representatives*, E-2, pp. 2-18. Wellington: Government Printer.

Boyd, W. & Rawson, W. (1965). *The story of the new education*. London: Heinemann.

Beeby, C.E. (1991). Interview with author.

Beeby, C.E. (1992). *The biography of an idea: Beeby on education*. Wellington: NZ Council for Educational Research.

Dewey, J. (1900a). *School and society*. Chicago: University of Chicago Press.

Dewey, J. (1900b). Froebel's educational principles. *Elementary School Record*, 1.

Dewey, J. (1916). *Democracy and education*. New York: Macmillan.

Ewing, J.L. (1970). *Development of the New Zealand primary school curriculum 1877–1970*. Wellington: NZ Council for Educational Research.

Freud, S. (1905). Three essays on the theory of sexuality. In J. Strachey (trans. and ed., 1966), *The standard edition of the complete psychological works of Sigmund Freud*, vol. 17. London: Hogarth Press.

Hall, G.S. (1901). The ideal school as based on child study. *Addresses and proceedings of the National Education Association*, US.

Hall, G.S. (1907). *Aspects of child life and education*. Boston: Athenaeum Press.

Hendry, J. & Braik, G. (1900). Report of the Inspector of Schools: Southland, *AJHR*, E-1B, pp. 41–43. Wellington: Government Printer.

Hogben, G. (1904). Conference of Inspectors of Schools and Teachers' Representatives, *AJHR*, E-1C, pp. 1–23. Wellington: Government Printer.

Isaacs, S. (1929). *The nursery years*. London: Routledge & Kegan Paul.

King, M. (2006). John Money: Scientist, eccentric, patron of the arts. In M. King (ed.), *Splendours of civilisation* (pp. 23–47). Gore: Eastern Southland Gallery/Longacre Press.

May, H. (2005). *School beginnings: A nineteenth-century colonial story*. Wellington: NZ Council for Educational Research.

May, H. (2011). *'I am five and I go to school': Early years schooling in New Zealand, 1900–2010*. Dunedin: Otago University Press.

May, M. (1973). *Freshly remembered: Half a century of school*. Christchurch: Whitcombe & Tombs.

Mayhew, K.C. & Edwards, A.C. (1936). *The Dewey School: The Laboratory School of the University of Chicago 1896–1903*. New York: D. Appleton-Century.

McCahon, C. (1981). Tales out of school. *Education*, 30 (3), 32.

Menzies, A. (March 1952). Reminiscences by the first infant mistress of the Main School, *Phillipstown School Official souvenir of 75th anniversary celebrations*. Christchurch.

Middleton, S. & May, H. (1997). *Teachers talk teaching: Early childhood, schools teachers' colleges 1915–1995*. Palmerston North: Dunmore Press.

Montessori, M. (1915). *The Montessori method*. London: Heinemann.

Piaget, J. (1926). *The language and thought of the child*. London: Kegan Paul.

Somerset, G. (1988). *Sunshine and shadow*. Wellington: NZ Playcentre Federation.

Simon, J. (ed.) (1998). *Nga kura Māori: The native school system 1867–1869*. Auckland: Auckland University Press.

Simon, J. & Tuhiwai Smith, L. (2001). *A civilising mission? Perceptions and representations of the New Zealand native school system*. Auckland: Auckland University Press.

Stirling, E. & Salmond, A. (1980). *Eruera: The teachings of a Māori elder*. Auckland: Oxford University Press.

Strong, T.B. (1923). Report of the Chief Inspector of Primary Schools. *AJHR*, E-2, Appendix A, pp. ii–iv. Wellington: Government Printer.

Chapter 7

Barrington, J. (2004). *A voice for children: The Office of the Commissioner for Children in New Zealand 1984–2003*. Palmerston North: Dunmore Press.

Beagle, J. (1975). Children of the state: A study of the New Zealand industrial school system 1880–1925. Master's thesis, University of Auckland, Auckland.

Beck, U. (1992). *Risk society: Towards a new modernity*. London: Sage.

Bell, M. (2011). The feel of mobility: How children use sedentary lifestyles as a site of resistance. *Sport, Education and Society*, 16 (3), 385–397.

Bryder, L. (1991). *A healthy country: Essays on the social history of medicine in New Zealand*. Wellington: Bridget Williams Books.

Buckingham, D. (2011). *The material child: Growing up in consumer culture*. Cambridge: Polity.
Burrows, L. (2010). 'Kiwi kids are Weet-bix™ kids': Body matters in childhood. *Sport, Education and Society, 15* (2), 235–251.
Bush, G. (1971). *Decently and in order: The government of the city of Auckland 1840–1971: The centennial history of the Auckland City Council*. Auckland: Collins.
Bush, G. & Scott, C. (eds) (1977). *Auckland at full stretch: Issues to the seventies*. Auckland: Auckland City Council/University of Auckland Board of Urban Studies.
Byrnes, G. (2009). *The new Oxford history of New Zealand*. Melbourne: Oxford University Press.
Cavallo, D. (1981). *Muscles and morals: Organized playgrounds and urban reform 1880–1920*. Philadelphia: University of Pennsylvania Press.
Collins, D. & Kearns, R.A. (2007). Ambiguous landscapes: Sun, risk and recreation on New Zealand beaches. In A. Williams (ed.), *Therapeutic landscapes* (pp. 15–31). London: Ashgate Publishers.
Collins, D. & Kearns, R.A. (2010). Walking school buses in the Auckland region: A longitudinal assessment. *Transport Policy, 17* (1), 1–8. doi: 10.1016/j.tranpol.2009.06.003
Collins, D., Kearns, R.A. & Mitchell, H. (2006). 'An integral part of the children's education': Placing sun protection in Auckland primary schools. *Health & Place, 12*, 436–448.
Cusins-Lewer, A. & Gatley, J. (2008). The 'Myers Park Experiment' in Auckland, New Zealand, 1913–1916. In M. Gutman & N. de Coninck-Smith (eds), *Designing modern childhoods: History, space and the material culture of children* (pp. 82–103). New Brunswick: Rutgers University Press.
Daley, C. (2003). *Leisure & pleasure: Reshaping and revealing the New Zealand body 1900–1960*. Auckland: Auckland University Press.
Daley, C. (2009). Modernity, consumption, and leisure. In G. Byrnes (ed.), *The new Oxford history of New Zealand* (pp. 423–445). Melbourne: Oxford University Press.
Dalley, B. (1998). *Family matters: Child welfare in twentieth-century New Zealand*. Auckland: Auckland University Press.
Duhn, I. (2009). Early childhood education. In E. Rata & R. Sullivan (eds), *Introduction to the history of New Zealand education* (pp. 31–43). Auckland: Pearson.
Fairburn, M. (1975). The rural myth and the new urban frontier: An approach to New Zealand social history, 1870–1940. *NZ Journal of History, 9* (1), 3–21.
Freeman, C. & Tranter, P. (2011). *Children and their urban environment: Changing worlds*. London: Earthscan.
Frost, G. (2009). *Victorian childhoods*. Westport: Praeger Publishers.
Gregory, S. (1997). Consuming the 'cool': Children's popular consumption culture. MA thesis, University of Auckland, Auckland.
Husbands, P. (1992). The people of Freeman's Bay 1880–1914. Master's thesis, University of Auckland, Auckland.
Jenks, C. (1996). *Childhood*. London: Routledge.
Kearns, R.A. & Barnett, J. (2000). 'Happy Meals' in the Starship Enterprise: Interpreting a moral geography of health care consumption. *Health & Place, 6* (2), 81–93.
Kearns, R.A. & Collins, D. (2000). New Zealand children's health camps: Therapeutic landscapes meet the contract state. *Social Science & Medicine, 51*, 1047–1059.
Kearns, R.A., Collins, D. & Neuwelt, P. (2003). The walking school bus: Extending children's geographies? *Area, 35* (3), 285–292.
Kindergartens Inc. (2009). *History of kindergartens in Aotearoa* (accessed online 10 July 2012).
Labrum, B. (2000). Persistent needs and expanding desires: Pakeha families and state welfare in the years of prosperity. In B. Dalley & B. Labrum (eds), *Fragment: New Zealand social and cultural history* (pp. 188–210). Auckland: Auckland University Press.
Lynch, P. (2006). *Camping in the curriculum: A history of outdoor education in New Zealand schools*. Lincoln: PML Publications.
Macpherson, C., Spoonley, P. & Anae, M. (2001). *Tangata o te moana nui: The evolving identities of Pacific peoples in Aotearoa/New Zealand*. Palmerston North: Dunmore Press.

Malone, K. (2007). The bubble-wrap generation: Children growing up in walled gardens. *Environmental Education Research, 13* (4), 513–527.

May, H. (1992). *Minding children, managing men: Conflict and compromise in the lives of postwar Pakeha women*. Wellington: Bridget Williams Books.

May, H. (1997). *The discovery of early childhood: The development of services for the care and education of very young children, mid eighteenth century Europe to mid twentieth century New Zealand*. Auckland: Auckland University Press/Bridget Williams Books/NZ Council for Educational Research.

McDonald, D. (1978). Children and young persons in the New Zealand society. In P. Koopman-Boyden (ed.), *Families in New Zealand society* (pp. 44–56). Wellington: Methuen.

MILO (2012). *The New Zealand state of play report*. Auckland: MILO.

Morris, B. (2005). Play: A personal history. *First years: NZ Journal of Infant and Toddler Education, 7* (1), 5–10.

NZNCIYC, Lewis, B. & Lockhart, P. (1980). *The IYC report: A resource for the future: the history, activities, and future recommendations of the New Zealand National Commission for the International Year of the Child*. Wellington: Committee for Children.

Parr, C.J. (1919). Parks, playgrounds, and open spaces. Paper presented at the New Zealand town-planning conference and exhibition, Wellington.

Phillips, J. (1983). *Mothers matter too: A book for New Zealand women at home*. Auckland: Reed Methuen.

Public Health Advisory Committee. (2010). *Healthy places, healthy lives: Urban environments and well-being*. Wellington: Ministry of Health.

Ritchie, J. & Ritchie, J. (1970). *Childrearing patterns in New Zealand*. Wellington: A.H. & A.W. Reed.

Schwartzman, H.B. (1980). *Play and culture: 1978 proceedings of the Association for the Anthropological Study of Play*. West Point: Leisure Press.

Shallcrass, J. (1973). Changing attitudes to children in the past 30 years. In *New Zealand children yesterday, today and tomorrow: The 1972 lectures delivered to the Association for the Study of Childhood, Wellington, New Zealand* (pp. 1–6). Wellington: Association for the Study of Childhood.

Somerset, G. (1976). *Vital play in early childhood*. Auckland: Playcentre Publications.

Stephenson, M. (2009). Thinking historically: Maori and settler education. In E. Rata & R. Sullivan (eds), *Introduction to the history of New Zealand education* (pp. 1–15). North Shore: Pearson.

Stover, S. & New Zealand Playcentre Federation. (1998). *Good clean fun: New Zealand's Playcentre movement: in celebration of the 50th anniversary of the New Zealand Playcentre Federation*. Auckland: Playcentre Publications.

Sullivan, R. (2009). Towards total safety. In E. Rata & R. Sullivan (eds), *Introduction to the history of New Zealand education* (pp. 44–56). Auckland: Pearson.

Sutton-Smith, B. (1953). Traditional Games of New Zealand Children. *Folklore, 64* (3), 411–423.

Sutton-Smith, B. (1981). *A history of children's play: The New Zealand playground 1840–1950*: University of Pennsylvania Press.

Taylor, N. & Smith, A. (2008). Repealing a defence for the physical punishment of children: Changing the law in New Zealand. *Childrenz Issues: Journal of the Children's Issues Centre, 12* (2), 7–12.

Tennant, M. (1994). *Children's health, the nation's wealth: A history of children's health camps*. Wellington: Bridget Williams Books/Historical Branch, Dept of Internal Affairs.

Trewby, M. (1995). *The best years of your life: A history of New Zealand childhood*. Auckland: Viking.

Wills, D. (1973). The child's body and his recreation. In *New Zealand children yesterday, today and tomorrow: The 1972 lectures delivered to the Association for the Study of Childhood, Wellington, New Zealand* (pp. 7–17). Wellington: Association for the Study of Childhood.

Chapter 8

Anaya, J. (2011). *Report of the Special Rapporteur on the Rights of Indigenous peoples, James Anya, Addendum: The situation of Māori people in New Zealand*. UN Doc A/HRC/18/35/Add.4.

Baker, M., Barnard, L., Kvalsvig, A., Verral, A., Zhang, J., Keall, M., Wilson, N., Wall, T. & Howden-Chapman, P. (2012). Increasing incidence of serious infectious diseases and inequalities in New Zealand: A national epidemiological study. *Lancet, 379* (9821), 112–119.

Barnes, C. & Mercer, G. (2003). *Disability*. Cambridge: Polity Press.

Berryman, M. (2008). Repositioning within indigenous discourse of transformation and self-determination. Unpublished PhD thesis, University of Waikato, Hamilton.

Bevan-Brown, J. (1989). Intellectual disability: A Māori perspective. Unpublished Master's thesis, Massey University, Palmerston North.

Bevan-Brown, J. (1994). Intellectual disability. In K. Ballard (ed.), *Disability, family, whānau and society* (pp. 205–230). Palmerston North: Dunmore Press.

Bevan-Brown, J. (2000). Why are learners with special needs from ethnically diverse groups missing out on effective, culturally appropriate services and what can be done about it? A paper presented at the Including the Excluded, International Special Education Congress 2000, July 24–28, University of Manchester, England.

Bishop, R. (2002). De-pathologizing the lived experiences of children: Māori children's experiences of schooling: A work in progress. A paper presented at An Interactive Symposium, Annual AERA Conference April 1–5, New Orleans, Louisiana.

Butler, A & Butler, P. (2005). *The New Zealand Bill of Rights Act: A commentary*. Wellington: LexisNexis.

Collins, A. & Hickey, H. (2006). *The role of whānau in the lives of Māori with physical disabilities*. Blueskies Report no. 12/06. Wellington: Families Commission.

Dale, M., O'Brien, M., and St John, S. (eds) (2011). *Left further behind: How policies fail the poorest children in New Zealand*. Auckland: Child Poverty Action Group.

Durie, A. (1997). Whānau, whānaungatanga, and healthy Māori. In P. Waititi, M. McCarthy & A. Durie (eds), *Mai i rangiatea: Māori well-being and development* (pp. 9–12). Auckland: Auckland University Press/Bridget Williams Books.

Higgins, N., Phillips, H. & Cowan, C. (2011). 80 years of growing up kāpo (blind) Māori: What can we learn about inclusive education in New Zealand? *International Journal of Inclusive Education*: www.tandfonline.com/doi/abs/10.1080/13603116.2011.602519

Higgins, N., Phillips, H., Cowan, C., Wakefield, B. & Tikao, K. (2010). Growing up kāpo Māori: Whānau, identity, cultural well-being and health/ E tipu kāpo Māori nei: Whānaungatanga, Māramatanga, Māoritanga, Hauoratanga: www.kāpoMāori.com/Reports__Plans_41.aspx

Higgins, N., Phillips, H., Stobbs, K., Wilson, G. & Pascoe, H. (2012). *Growing up kāpo Māori: Accessing paediatric ophthalmology services: Summary of findings for the Health Research Council*. Hastings: Ngāti Kāpo o Aotearoa.

Johnson, M.R.D. & Morjaria-Keval, M. (2007). Ethnicity, sight loss and invisibility. *British Journal of Visual Impairment, 25* (1), 21–30.

Kingi, J. & Bray, A. (2000). *Māori concepts of disability*. Dunedin: Donald Beasley Institute.

Kliewer, C. & Fitzgerald, L. (2001). Disability, schooling, and the artefacts of colonialism. *Teachers College Record, 103* (3), 450–470.

Macfarlane, A. (2005). Inclusion and Māori ecologies: An educultural approach. In D. Fraser, R. Moltzen & K. Ryba (eds), *Learners with special needs in Aotearoa New Zealand* (pp. 99–116). Palmerston North: Dunmore Press.

Miles, C. (2002). Special, multicultural and invisible? *International Journal of Disability, Impairment, and Education, 49* (3), 323–328.

Ministry of Health (2001). *The New Zealand Disability Strategy: Making the world of difference: Whakanui Oranga*. Wellington.

Ministry of Health (2002). *He Korowai Oranga*. Wellington.

Ministry of Social Development (2010). *2010 The social report: Te pūrongo oranga tangata*: http://socialreport.msd.govt.nz

Moeke-Pickering, T. (1996). Māori identity within whānau: A review of literature. Unpublished paper, University of Waikato.
O'Brien, M., Dale, M. and St John, S. (2011). Child poverty and inequality. In M. Dale, M. O'Brien & S. St John (eds) (2011), *Left further behind: How policies fail the poorest children in New Zealand* (pp. 11–25). Auckland: Child Poverty Action Group.
Phillips, H. (2005). Te ata hapara: Educational provision for Māori students with moderate to high needs. In J. McCarthur, B. Kelly, N. Higgins, H. Phillips, T. McDonald, M. Morton & S. Jackman (eds), *Building capability in education for students with moderate to high needs: A literature review commissioned by the Ministry of Education from the Donald Beasley Institute* (pp. 81–156). Wellington: Ministry of Education.
Rodriguez-Piñero Royo, L. (2009). 'Where appropriate': Monitoring/implementing of indigenous peoples' rights under the declaration. In C. Charters and R. Stavenhagen (eds), *Making the declaration work: The United Nations Declaration on the Rights of Indigenous Peoples* (pp. 314–43). Copenhagen: International Work Group for Indigenous Affairs.
Singham, M. (2006). Multiculturalism in New Zealand: The need for a new paradigm. *Aotearoa Ethnic Network Journal*, 1 (1), 33–37.
St John, S. & Wynd, D. (eds) (2008). *Left behind: How social and income inequalities damage New Zealand children*. Auckland: Child Poverty Action Group.
Statistics New Zealand (2006). *New Zealand Census*: www.statisticsnz.govt.nz
Statistics New Zealand (2010). *Subnational family and household projections 2006 (base)-2031 update*: www.statisticsnz.govt.nz
Tikao, K., Higgins, N., Phillips, H. & Cowan, C. (2009). Kāpo Māori in the ancient world. *MAI Review Journal*, 2, article 4: www.review.mai.ac.nz/index.php/MR/article/view/237/271
United Nations Committee on Economic, Social and Cultural Rights (2012). *Consideration of reports submitted by states parties under articles 16 and 17 of the covenant, concluding observations of the Committee on Economic, Social and Cultural Rights, New Zealand* (E/C.12/NZL/CO/3): www.converge.org.nz/pma/E-C.12-NZL-CO-3.pdf
Wilkie, M. (2000). Matauranga motuhake: Special education for Māori: Kaupapa Māori research. Paper presented at the Surviving Paradox: Education in the new millennium NZARE conference.

Chapter 9

Banerjee, S. & Linstead, S. (2001). Globalization, multiculturalism and other fictions: Colonism for the new millennium. *Organization*, 8 (4), 683–722.
Blackmore, J. (1999). Localization/globalization and the midwife state: Strategic dilemmas for state feminism in education? *Journal of Education Policy* 14 (1), 33–55.
Brown, D. (2010). Cooperative learning. In V. Green & S. Cherrington (eds), *Delivering into diversity: An international exploration of issues of diversity in education* (pp. 21–33). New York: Nova Science Publishers.
Chan, A. (2006). 'The teachers said my child is different'. *The First Years: New Zealand Journal of Infant and Toddler Education*, 8 (1), 34–38.
Chan, A. (2009). Critical multiculturalism: The challenge of multiculturalism within a New Zealand bicultural context: A Chinese perspective. *International Journal of Equity and Innovation in Early Childhood*, 7 (1), 29–40.
Claiborne, L. & Cornforth. S. (2010). Supporting diversity, difference and inclusion in higher education. In V. Green & S. Cherrington (eds), *Delving into diversity: An international exploration of issues of diversity in education* (pp. 255–263). New York: Nova Science Publishers.
Dijkstra, S., Geuijen, K. & de Ruijter, A. (2001). Multiculturalism and social integration in Europe. *International Political Science Review*, 22 (1), 55–83.
Duhn, I. (2008). Globalising childhood: Assembling the bicultural child in the New Zealand early childhood curriculum, Te Whāriki. *International Critical Childhood Policy Studies*, 1 (1), 82–105.

Grey, A. (2010). Developmental theories in early childhood education. In B. Clark & A. Grey (eds), *Scanning the horizon: Perspectives on early childhood education* (pp. 46–57). Auckland: Pearson.

Goodwin. L., Cheruvu. R. & Genish, C. (2008). Responding to multiple diversities in early childhood education. In C. Genishi & A.L. Goodwin (eds), *Diversities in early childhood education: Rethinking and doing* (pp. 3–11). New York: Routledge.

Gonzalez-Mena, J. (2003). Bridging cultures with understanding and sensitivity. Keynote presentation at the 8th Early Childhood Convention. Palmerston North, New Zealand, 22–25 September.

Guo, K. (2005). Asian Immigrant parents' and New Zealand early childhood teachers' views of parent–teacher relationships. *NZ Research in Early Childhood Education, 8*, 125–135.

Guo, K. (2010). Chinese immigrant children in New Zealand early childhood centres. Unpublished PhD thesis, Victoria University of Wellington.

Hall, S. (1992). New ethnicities. In J. Donald & A. Rattansi (eds), *Race, culture, and difference* (pp. 252–259). London: Sage.

Kassimeris, C. & Vryonides, M. (2012). Conclusion. In C. Kassimeris & M. Vryonides (eds), *The politics of education: Challenging multiculturalism* (pp. 169–182). New York: Routledge.

Kassimeris, C. & Vryonides, M. (2012). Politics and education. In C. Kassimeris & M. Vryonides (eds), *The politics of education: Challenging multiculturalism* (pp. 5–16). New York: Routledge.

Kincheloe, J. & Steinberg, S. (1997). *Changing multiculturalism*. Buckingham: Open University Press.

Larner, W. (2006). Brokering citizenship claims: Neo-liberalism, biculturalism and multiculturalism in Aotearoa New Zealand. In E. Tastsoglou & A. Dobrowolsky (eds), *Women, migration and citizenship: Making local, national and transnational connections*. England: Ashgate Publishing.

Larner, W., Le Heron, R. & Lewis, N. (2008). Co-constituting 'After neoliberalism': Political projects and globalizing governmentalities in Aotearoa/New Zealand. In K. England & K. Ward (eds), *Neoliberalization: States, networks, peoples* (pp. 223–247). Oxford: Blackwell Publishing.

Lock, T. (2010). Critical multiculturalism and subject English. In S. May & C. Sleeter (eds), *Critical multiculturalism: Theory and praxis* (pp. 87–98). New York: Routledge.

May, S. (1999). Critical multiculturalism and cultural difference: Avoiding essentialism. In S. May (ed.), *Critical multiculturalism: Rethinking multicultural and antiracist education* (pp. 11–41). London: Falmer Press.

May, S. & Sleeter, C. (2010). Introduction. Critical multiculturalism: Theory and praxis. In S. May & C. Sleeter (eds), *Critical multiculturalism: Theory and praxis* (pp. 1–18). New York: Routledge.

McLaren, P. & Torres, R. (1999). Racism and multicultural education: Rethinking 'race' and 'whiteness'. In S. May (ed.), *Critical multiculturalism: Rethinking multicultural and antiracist education* (pp. 42–76). London: Falmer Press.

Ministry of Education (1996). *Te Whāriki: He whāriki matauranga mo nga mokopuna o Aotearoa: Early childhood curriculum*. Wellington: Learning Media.

Moss, P. (2008). Toward a new public education: Making globalization work for us all. *Child Development Perspectives, 2* (2), 114–119.

Penn, H. (2005). *Understanding early childhood: Issues and controversies*. Maidenhead, England: Open University Press.

Pieterse, J. (2007). Global multiculture, flexible acculturation. *Globalizations, 4* (1), 65–79.

Rhedding-Jones, J. (2005). Questioning diversity. In N. Yelland (ed.), *Critical issues in early childhood education* (pp. 131–145). Berkshire: Open University Press.

Ritchie, J. (2010). Being 'sociocultultural' in early childhood education practice in Aotearoa. *Early Childhood Folio, 14* (2), 2–6.

Robinson, K. & Diaz, C. (2006). *Diversity and difference in early childhood education: Issues for theory and practice*. Berkshire: Open University Press.

Ryan, J. (1999). *Race and ethnicity in multi-ethnic schools: A critical case study*. Clevedon: Multilingual Matters.

Sanders, B. (2004). Childhood in different cultures. In T. Maynard & N. Thomas (eds), *An introduction to early childhood studies* (pp. 53–64). London: Sage.

Sarsona, M., Goo, S., Kawakami, A. & Au, K. (2008). Keiki steps: Equity issues in a parent-participation preschool program for native Hawaiian children. In C. Genishi & A.L. Goodwin (eds), *Diversities in early childhood education: Rethinking and doing* (pp. 151–165). New York: Routledge.

Scholte, J. (2008). Defining globalization. *The World Economy*, *31* (11), 1471–1502.

Sharma, S. (2010). Critical multiculturalism and cultural and media studies. In S. May & C. Sleeter (eds), *Critical multiculturalism: Theory and praxis* (pp. 113–126). New York: Routledge.

Singham, M. (2006). Multiculturalism in New Zealand: The need for a new paradigm. *Aoteroa Ethnic Network Journal*, *1* (1), 33–37.

Smith, A. (1998). *Understanding children's development* (4th edn). Wellington: Bridget Williams Books.

Smith, P. (2012). *A concise history of New Zealand* (2nd edn). Cambridge: Cambridge University Press.

Statistics New Zealand (2009). *Review of the official ethnicity statistical standard 2009*: www.stats.govt.nz/browse_for_stats/people_and_communities/Households/review-of-the-official-ethnicity-statistical-standard-2009/final-report.aspx (accessed 20 March 2012)

Sutherland, O. (1973). *Justice and race: A monocultural system in a multicultural society*. A report on the first year of comprehensive legal aid scheme for Māori offenders appearing before the Nelson Magistrate's Court. Wellington: NZ Race Relations Council.

Yang, Y. (2008). Observing the world from the perspective of multi-culture in Canada. *Journal of Politics and Law*, *1* (3), 79–83.

Chapter 10

Boshier, P. (2005). The Care of Children Act 2004: Does it enhance children's participation and protection rights? *Childrenz Issues*, *9* (2), 7–19.

Boshier, P. (2009, May). *The child's voice in process: Which way is forward?* Presentation by the Principal Family Court Judge to the Association of Family and Conciliation Courts 46th Annual Conference, New Orleans.

Boshier, P., Taylor, N.J. & Seymour, F. (2011). Early intervention in New Zealand Family Court cases. *Family Court Review*, *49* (4), 818–830.

Cashmore, J. & Parkinson, P. (2008). Children's and parents' perceptions on children's participation in decision making after parental separation and divorce. *Family Court Review*, *46*, 91–104.

Fitzgerald, R. (2009). Children having a say: A study on children's participation in family law decision making. Unpublished doctoral dissertation, Southern Cross University, Lismore, Australia.

Goldson, J. (2006). *'Hello, I'm a voice, let me talk': Child-inclusive mediation in family separation*. Wellington: Families Commission Innovative Practice Report no. 1/06.

Goldson, J. & Taylor, N.J. (2009). Child-inclusion in dispute resolution in the New Zealand Family Court. *New Zealand Family Law Journal*, *6* (7), 201–209.

Gollop, M., Smith, A.B. & Taylor, N.J. (2000). Children's involvement in custody and access arrangements after parental separation. *Child and Family Law Quarterly*, *12* (4), 383–399.

Gollop, M. & Taylor, N. (2005). *Supervised contact centres: The perspectives of children, parents and staff*. Report to Ministry of Social Development. Dunedin: Children's Issues Centre, University of Otago.

Gollop, M. & Taylor, N.J. (2012). New Zealand children and young people's perspectives on relocation after parental separation. In M. Freeman (ed.), *Law and Childhood Studies: Current legal issues* (vol. 14, pp. 219–242). London: Oxford University Press.

Gollop, M.M., Taylor, N.J. & Smith, A.B. (2000). Children's perspectives on their parents' separation. In A.B. Smith, N.J. Taylor & M. Gollop (eds), *Children's voices: Research, policy and practice* (pp. 134–156). Auckland: Pearson Education.

Henaghan, R.M. (2012). Why judges need to know and understand Childhood Studies. In M. Freeman (ed.), *Law and Childhood Studies: Current legal issues* (vol. 14, pp. 39–54). London: Oxford University Press.

Honig, M. (2009). How is the child constituted in Childhood Studies? In J. Qvortrup, W. Corsaro & M. Honig (eds), *The Palgrave handbook of Childhood Studies* (pp. 62–77). New York: Palgrave Macmillan.

James, A.L. (2010). Competition or integration? The next step in Childhood Studies? *Childhood, 17* (4), 485–499.

Lansdown, G. (2005). *The evolving capacities of the child*. Florence: UNICEF Innocenti Centre.

Lansdown, G. (2010). The realisation of children's participation rights: Critical reflections. In B. Percy-Smith & N. Thomas (eds), *A handbook of children and young people's participation: Perspectives from theory and practice* (pp. 11–23). London: Routledge.

McIntosh, J., Long, C. & Wells, Y. (2009). *Children beyond dispute: A four year follow up study of outcomes from child focused and child inclusive post-separation family dispute resolution*. Australia: Family Transitions, Attorney-General's Department and La Trobe University.

Melton, G. (2006, September). *Background for a general comment on the right to participate: Article 12 and related provisions of the Convention on the Rights of the Child* (prepared for use by the UN Committee on the Rights of the Child).

Mill, I. (2008). Conversations with children: A judge's perspective on meeting the patient before operating on the family. *NZ Family Law Journal, 6* (3), 72–79.

Monk, D. (2009). Children and the law. In M.J. Kehily (ed.), *An introduction to Childhood Studies* (2nd edn, pp. 177–197). Berkshire: Open University Press.

Parkinson, P. & Cashmore, J. (2008). *The voice of a child in family law disputes*. London: Oxford University Press.

Percy-Smith, B. & Thomas, N. (eds) (2010). *A handbook of children and young people's participation*. London: Routledge.

Practice Note: *Lawyer for the child: Code of conduct* (issued by the New Zealand Principal Family Court Judge, 24 March 2011).

Robinson, A. & Henaghan, R.M. (2011). Children: Heard but not listened to? An analysis of children's views under s 6 of the Care of Children Act 2004. *NZ Family Law Journal, 7* (2), 39–52.

Smart, C., Neale, B. & Wade, A. (2001). *The changing experience of childhood: Families and divorce*. Cambridge: Polity Press.

Smith, A.B. (2002). Interpreting and supporting participation rights: Contributions from sociocultural theory. *International Journal of Children's Rights, 10* (1), 73–88.

Smith, A. & Gollop, M. (2001a). Children's perspectives on access visits. *Butterworths Family Law Journal, June*, 259–266.

Smith, A. & Gollop, M. (2001b). What children think separating parents should know. *NZ Journal of Psychology, 30*, 23–31.

Smith, A.B., Gollop, M.M. & Taylor, N.J. (2000). Children in foster and kinship care. In A.B. Smith, N.J. Taylor & M.M. Gollop (eds), *Children's voices: Research, policy and practice* (pp. 72–90). Auckland: Pearson Education.

Smith, A.B., Gollop, M.M., Taylor, N.J. & Atwool, N.R. (1999a). *Children in kinship and foster care*. Dunedin: Children's Issues Centre, University of Otago.

Smith, A.B., Gollop, M.M., Taylor, N.J. & Atwool, N.R. (1999b). Children's voices in foster or kinship care: Knowledge, understanding and participation. *Journal of Child Centred Practice, 6* (1), 9–37.

Smith, A.B., Taylor, N.J. & Gollop, M.M. (eds) (2000). *Children's voices: Research, policy and practice*. Auckland: Pearson Education.

Smith, A.B., Taylor, N.J., Gollop, M., Gaffney, M., Gold, M. & Henaghan, R.M. (1997). *Access and other post-separation issues: A qualitative study of children's, parents' and lawyers' views*. Dunedin: Children's Issues Centre, University of Otago.

Smith, A.B., Taylor, N.J. & Tapp, P. (2003). Rethinking children's involvement in decision-making after parental separation. *Childhood, 10* (2), 201–216.

Taylor, N.J. (1998). The voice of children in family law. *Children's Legal Rights Journal*, 18 (1), 2–14.

Taylor, N.J. (2005). Care of children: Families, dispute resolution and the Family Court. Unpublished doctoral dissertation, University of Otago, Dunedin.

Taylor, N.J. (2006). What do we know about involving children and young people in family law decision making? A research update. *Australian Journal of Family Law*, 20 (2), 154–178.

Taylor, N.J., Fitzgerald, R., Morag, T., Bajpai, A. & Graham, A. (2012). International models of child participation in family law proceedings following parental separation/divorce. *International Journal of Children's Rights*, 20 (4), 645–673.

Taylor, N.J., Gollop, M. & Henaghan, M. (2010a). *Relocation following parental separation: The welfare and best interests of children*. Dunedin: Centre for Research on Children and Families, University of Otago.

Taylor, N.J., Gollop, M. & Henaghan, M. (2010b). Relocation following parental separation in New Zealand: Complexity and diversity. *International Family Law Journal*, March, 97–105.

Taylor, N.J., Gollop, M.M. & Smith, A.B. (2000). Children's views on Counsel for the Child. In A.B. Smith, N.J. Taylor & M. Gollop (eds), *Children's voices: Research, policy and practice* (pp. 110–133). Auckland: Pearson Education.

Taylor, N.J., Gollop, M., Smith, A.B. & Tapp, P.F. (1999). *The role of Counsel for the Child: Perspectives of children, young people and their lawyers*. Wellington: Department for Courts.

Taylor, N., Gollop, M., Tapp, P., Gaffney, M., Smith, A. & Henaghan, M. (2000). *Children's rights in New Zealand family law judgements*. Dunedin: Children's Issues Centre, University of Otago.

Taylor, N., Smith A., Gollop M. & Tapp P. (2001). Child–parent contact following separation and divorce: The implications for family law of NZ and international research. In *Proceedings of the New Zealand Family Law Conference*. Wellington: New Zealand Law Society.

Taylor, N.J., Tapp, P. & Henaghan, R.M. (2007). Respecting children's participation in family law proceedings. *International Journal of Children's Rights*, 15 (1), 61–82.

Tisdall, E.K.M., Bray, R., Marshall, K. & Cleland, A. (2004). Children's participation in family law proceedings: A step too far or a step too small? *Journal of Social Welfare & Family Law*, 26 (1), 17–33.

United Nations Committee on the Rights of the Child (2009). *General comment number 12: The right of the child to be heard*. Geneva: CRC/C/GC/12.

UNICEF (2008). Fact sheet: The right to participation: www.unicef.org/crc/files/Right-to-Participation.pdf (accessed 18 June 2012).

UNICEF (n.d.). Rights under the Convention on the Rights of the Child: Guiding principles: www.unicef.org/crc/index_30177.html (accessed 18 June 2012).

Woodhead, M. (2009). Childhood Studies: Past, present and future. In M. Kehily (ed.), *An introduction to Childhood Studies* (2nd edn, pp. 17–31). London: Open University Press.

Chapter 11

Barth, R. & Miller, J. (2000). Building effective post-adoption services: What is the empirical foundation? *Family Relations*, 49 (4), 447–455.

Berridge, D. (2007). Theory and explanation in child welfare: Education and looked-after children. *Child and Family Social Work*, 12, 1–10.

Biehal, N., Ellison, S. Baker, C. & Sinclair, I. (2010). *Belonging and permanence: Outcomes in long-term foster care and adoption*. London: BAAF.

Child, Youth and Family (2010). Why you should care: www.cyf.govt.nz/about-us/news/2010/why-you-should-care.html

Connolly, M. (2004). *Child and family welfare: Statutory responses to children at risk*. Christchurch: Te Awatea Press.

Dance, C., Ouwejan, D,. Beecham, J. & Farmer, E. (2010). *Linking and matching*. London: BAAF.

Else, A. (1991). *A question of adoption*. Wellington: Bridget Williams Books.

Frengley, S. (2007). Kinship care: Roots or grafts? Unpublished MSW thesis, University of Otago, Dunedin.

Gibbs, A. (2010). Parenting adopted children and supporting adoptive parents: Messages from research. *Aotearoa New Zealand Social Work,* 22 (2), 44-52.

Gibbs, A. (2011). Going to the courts twice: A critical appraisal of the UK's policy of re-adoption for intercountry adoptions. *Children and Society,* 25 (4), 1-10.

Goldson, J. (2003). Adoption in New Zealand: An international perspective. In A. Douglas and T. Philpot (eds), *Adoption: Changing families, changing times* (pp. 246-250). London: Routledge.

HCCH (2011). Country profile for intercountry adoption: Receiving state New Zealand: www.hcch.net

Johnstone, J. & Gibbs, A. (2012). 'Love them to bits; spend time with them; have fun with them': New Zealand parents' views of building attachments with their newly adopted Russian children. *Journal of Social Work,* 12 (3), 225-245.

Luckock, B. & Hart, A. (2005). Adoptive family life and adoption support: Policy ambivalence and the development of effective services. *Child and Family Social Work,* 10, 125-134.

Ludbrook, R. (1990). *Adoption: Guide to law and practice.* Christchurch: Government Printing Office.

Macdonald, G. & Turner, W. (2008). Treatment foster care for improving outcomes in children and young people: www2.cochrane.org/reviews/en/ab005649.html

Neil, E., Cossar, J., Jones, C., Lorgelly, P. & Young, J. (2011). *Supporting direct contact after adoption.* London: BAAF.

New Zealand official yearbook (2010). Wellington: Statistics New Zealand.

Pringle, M.K. (1986). *The needs of children* (3rd edn). London: Hutchinson Education.

Scherman, R. (2010). Does adopted mean different? The developmental impact of adoption on children. In J. Low and P. Jose (eds), *Lifespan Development New Zealand perspectives* (2nd edn) (pp. 196-205). Auckland: Pearson.

Select Committee on Health Third Report (1998). The welfare of former child migrants: www.publications.parliament.uk/pa/cm199798/cmselect/cmhealth/755/75504.htm

Sellick, C., Thoburn, J. & Philpot, T. (2004). *What works in adoption and foster care.* Ilford, UK: Barnardos.

Selwyn, J. & Quinton, D. (2004). Stability, permanence, outcomes and support: Foster care and adoption compared. *Adoption & Fostering,* 28 (4): 6-15.

Selwyn, J., Saunders, H. & Farmer, E. (2010). The views of children and young people on being cared for by an independent foster-care provider. *British Journal of Social Work,* 40, 696-713.

Sinclair, I. (2005). *Fostering now: Key messages from research.* London: Jessica Kingsley.

Shannon, D. (2001). Adoption reunion practice model. Unpublished Master's of Social Work dissertation, University of Otago, Dunedin.

Staines, J., Farmer, E. & Selwyn, J. (2011). Implementing a therapeutic team parenting approach to fostering: The experiences of one independent foster-care agency. *British Journal of Social Work,* 41, 314-332.

Walker, S. (2001). The Maatua Whangai Programme o Otepoti from a caregiver perspective. Unpublished MCApSc thesis, University of Otago, Dunedin.

Chapter 12

Adolescent Health Research Group. (2008). *Youth '07: The health and wellbeing of secondary school students in New Zealand.* Auckland: University of Auckland.

Bourdillon, M., Levison, D., Myers, W. & White, B. (2010). *Rights and wrongs of children's work.* New Brunswick/New Jersey/London: Rutgers University Press.

Bourdillon, M., White, B. & Myers, W. E. (2009). Re-assessing minimum-age standards for children's work. *International Journal of Sociology and Social Policy,* 29 (3/4), 106-117.

Boyden, J. (1997). Childhood and the policy makers: A comparative perspective on the globalization of childhood. In A. James & A. Prout (eds), *Constructing and reconstructing childhood* (pp. 190-222). London: Falmer Press.

Caritas NZ. (2006). *Delivering the goods.* Wellington: Caritas Aotearoa New Zealand.

Frederiksen, L. (1999). Child and youth employment in Denmark: Comments on children's work from their own perspective. *Childhood,* 6 (1), 101-112.

Gasson, N.R., Diorio, J. & Stigter, J. (2009). Young workers, their employers and parents (unpublished). University of Otago College of Education, Dunedin.

Gasson, N.R. & Linsell, C. (2011). Young workers: A New Zealand perspective. *International Journal of Children's Rights, 19* (4), 641–659.

Gasson, N.R., Linsell, C., Gasson, J. & Mundy-McPherson, S. (2003). *Young people and work.* Dunedin: Dunedin College of Education.

Hobbs, S., McKechnie, J. & Anderson, S. (2007). Making child employment in Britain more visible. *Critical Social Policy, 27* (3), 415–425.

International Labour Organisation (1973). *Minimum age convention.* Geneva.

International Labour Organisation (1999). *Worst forms of child labour convention.* Geneva.

International Labour Organisation (n.d.). ILO conventions and recommendations on child labour: www.ilo.org/ipec/facts/ILOconventionsonchildlabour/lang--en/index.htm

Leonard, M. (2002). Working on your doorstep: Child newspaper deliverers in Belfast. *Childhood, 9* (2), 190–204.

Leonard, M. (2004). Children's views on children's right to work: Reflections from Belfast. *Childhood, 11* (1), 45–61. doi: 10.1177/0907568204040184

Morrow, V. (1994). Responsible children? Aspects of children's work and employment outside school in contemporary UK. In B. Mayall (ed.), *Children's childhoods: Observed and experienced* (pp. 128–143). London: Falmer Press.

Myers, W. (2001). The right rights? Child labour in a globalising world. *Annals of the American Academy of Political and Social Science, 575* (38), 38–55. doi: 10.1177/0002716201575001003

NZ Government (2003). *Second periodic reports of states parties due in 2000: New Zealand.* Geneva: United Nations.

NZ Government (2008). *Third and fourth periodic reports of states parties due in 2008: New Zealand.* Geneva: United Nations.

O'Neill, D. (2010). *School children in paid employment: A summary of research findings.* Wellington: Department of Labour.

Pugh, J. (2007). *Health and safety knowledge of young workers: A study of school-aged, part-time workers in the Taranaki region.* Wellington: Department of Labour.Punch, S. (2003). Childhoods in the majority world: Miniature adults or tribal children. *Sociology, 37* (2), 277–295.

Rogoff, B. (2003). *The cultural nature of human development.* Oxford: Oxford University Press.

Shuttleworth, P. (2010). *Employment of children.* Auckland: Action for Children and Youth Aotearoa.

Taylor, N., Smith, A.B. & Nairn, K. (2001). Rights important to young people: Secondary student and staff perspectives. *International Journal of Children's Rights, 9,* 137–156.

United Nations. (n.d.). Status of treaties IV-11: www.treaties.un.org/Pages/ViewDetails. aspx?src=TREATY&mtdsg_no=IV-11&chapter=4&lang=en

White, B. (1996). Globalisation and the child labour problem. *Journal of International Development, 8* (6), 829–839.

Wilkinson, R. & Pickett, K. (2009). *The spirit level.* London: Penguin Books.

Woodhead, M. (1998). *Children's perspectives of their working lives: A participatory study in Bangladesh, Ethiopia, the Philippines, Guatemala, El Salvador, and Nicaragua.* Stockholm: Save the Children.

Woodhead, M. (2004). Psychosocial impacts of child work: A framework for research, monitoring and intervention. *International Journal of Children's Rights, 12* (4), 321–378. doi: 10.1163/1571818043603607

Chapter 13

Bell, C. (2001). All we need to know because TV tells us so. In J. Farnsworth & I. Hutchison (eds), *New Zealand television: A reader* (pp. 21–30). Palmerston North: Dunmore Press.

Bell, M. (2011). The feel of mobility: How children use sedentary lifestyles as a site of resistance. *Sport, Education and Society, 16* (3), 385–397.

Broadcasting Standards Authority (2008). *Seen and heard: Children's media use, exposure, and response.* Wellington.

Buckingham, D. (2009). Children and television. In J. Qvortrup, W.A. Corsaro & M.-S. Honig (eds), *The Palgrave handbook of Childhood Studies* (pp. 347–359). Houndmills/New York: Palgrave Macmillan.

Cowan, J. (2007). Are you in charge of your kids' media diet? *Parenting*, summer issue, 10–14.

Elliott, A. & Lemert, C. (2006). *The new individualism: The emotional costs of globalization.* London/New York: Routledge.

Freeman, C. & Nairn, K. (2000). Children, young people and their environments: Changing themes. *Childrenz Issues, 4* (3), 7–12.

Freeman, M. (1998). The sociology of childhood and children's rights. *International Journal of Children's Rights,* 6, 433–444.

Gaffney, M. (2001). Editorial. *Childrenz Issues,* 5 (2), 3–4.

Goode, L. (2004). Keeping in (and out of) touch: Telecommunications and mobile technocultures. In C. Bell & S. Matthewman (eds), *Cultural Studies in Aotearoa New Zealand* (pp. 268–284). Auckland: Oxford University Press.

Goode, L. & Littlewood, J. (2004). Digitising the Land of the Long White Cloud: The future of television in Aotearoa New Zealand. In R. Horrocks & N. Perry (eds), *Television in New Zealand: Programming the nation* (pp. 302–319). Melbourne: Oxford University Press.

Honig, M.-S. (2009). How is the child constituted in Childhood Studies? In J. Qvortrup, W.A. Corsaro & M.-S. Honig (eds), *The Palgrave handbook of Childhood Studies* (pp. 62–77). Houndmills/New York: Palgrave Macmillan.

Jackson, S., Low, J., Gee, S., Butler, C. & Hollings, J. (2007). *Children's media use and responses: A review of the literature.* Wellington: NZ Broadcasting Standards Authority.

James, A. & Prout, A. (eds) (1997). *Constructing and reconstructing childhood: Contemporary issues in the sociological study of childhood* (2nd edn). London/Washington: Falmer Press.

Jones, A. (1991). *'At school I've got a chance': Culture/privilege: Pacific Islands and Pakeha girls at school.* Palmerston North: Dunmore Press.

Latour, B. (2005). *Reassembling the social: An introduction to actor-network-theory.* Oxford: Oxford University Press.

Lealand, G. (2001). Some things change, some things remain the same: New Zealand children and media use. *Childrenz Issues,* 5 (2), 6–11.

Livingston, S.M. (2002). *Young people and new media: Childhood and the changing media environment.* London: Sage.

Matthewman, S. (2004). Introduction. In C. Bell & S. Matthewman (eds), *Cultural studies in Aotearoa New Zealand: Identity, space and place* (pp. vii–xiv). Melbourne: Oxford University Press.

Matthewman, S. (2011). *Technology & social theory.* Basingstoke: Palgrave Macmillan.

Mitchell, D.R. & Singh, N.N. (eds) (1987). *Exceptional children in New Zealand.* Palmerston North: Dunmore Press.

Morley, D. (2000). *Home territories: Media, mobility and identity.* London/New York: Routledge.

Morss, J.R. (1996). *Growing critical: Alternatives to developmental psychology.* London: Routledge.

Osit, M. (2008). *Generation text: Raising well-adjusted kids in an age of instant everything.* New York: American Management Association.

Oswell, D. (2002). *Television, childhood and the home: A history of the making of the child television audience in Britain.* Oxford: Oxford University Press.

Prout, A. (1996). Actor-network theory, technology and medical sociology: An illustrative analysis of the metered dose inhaler. *Sociology of Health & Illness, 18* (2), 198–219.

Prout, A. (2005). *The future of childhood: Towards the interdisciplinary study of children.* London and New York: Routledge Falmer.

Sandretto, S. with Scott Klenner (2011). *Planting seeds: Embedding critical literacy into your classroom programme.* Wellington: NZCER Press.

Smith, A.B. (2007). Children as social actors: An introduction. *International Journal of Children's Rights, 15* (1), 1–4.

Smith, A.B., Taylor, N.J. & Gollop, M.M. (eds) (2000). *Children's voices: Research, policy and practice.* Auckland: Pearson Education.

Statistics New Zealand (2009). *Household use of information and communications technology 2009*: www.stats.govt.nz/browse_for_stats/industry_sectors/information_technology_and_communications/HouseholdUseofICT_HOTP2009.aspx

Vestby, G.M. (1996). Technologies of autonomy? Parenthood in contemporary 'modern times'. In M. Lie & K.H. Sorensen (eds), *Making technology our own? Domesticating technology into everyday life* (pp. 65–90). Oslo: Scandinavian University Press.

Wajcman, J. (2002). Addressing technological change: The challenge to social theory. *Current Sociology, 50* (3), 347–363.

Wajcman, J., Bittman, M. & Brown, J.E. (2008). Families without borders: Mobile phones, connectedness and work-home divisions. *Sociology, 42* (4), 635–652.

Walters, R. & Zwaga, W. (2001). *The younger audience: Children and broadcasting in New Zealand.* Palmerston North: Dunmore Press.

Watkins, S.C. (2009). *The young and the digital: What the migration to social-network sites, games, and anytime, anywhere media means for our future.* Boston: Beacon Press.

Weatherall, A. & Ramsay, A. (2006). *New communication technologies and family life.* Blue Skies Report no. 5/06. Wellington: Families Commission.

Woodhead, M. (2009). Child development and the development of childhood. In J. Qvortrup, W.A. Corsaro & M.-S. Honig (eds), *The Palgrave handbook of Childhood Studies* (pp. 46–61). Houndmills/New York: Palgrave Macmillan.

Zanker, R. (2001a). Kumara kai or the Big Mac Pac? Television for six to 12-year-olds in New Zealand. In J. Farnsworth & I. Hutchison (eds), *New Zealand television: A reader* (pp. 270–279). Palmerston North: Dunmore Press.

Zanker, R. (2001b). The problem with 'tweens'. *Childrenz Issues, 5* (1), 12–17.

Chapter 14

Berthelsen, D. & Brownlee, J. (2005). Respecting children's agency for learning and rights to participation in child care programs. *International Journal of Early Childhood, 37* (3), 49–60.

Burgess, J. & Fleet, A. (2009). Frameworks for change: Four recurrent themes for quality in early childhood curriculum initiatives. *Asia–Pacific Journal of Teacher Education, 37* (1), 45–61.

Carr, M. (2000). Seeking children's perspectives about their learning. In A. Smith, N. Taylor & M. Gollop (eds), *Children's voices: Research, policy and practice* (pp. 37–55). Auckland: Pearson Education.

Foote, L. & Ellis, F. (2008). *Investigating the transformative potential of the early childhood education environment: What do teachers think?* University of Otago College of Education.

Hedges, H. (2011). Firsthand learning through intent participation: Aidan's morning in an early childhood setting. *The First Years: Nga Tau Tuatahi, 13* (2), 5–10.

James, A. (2007). Giving voice to children's voices: Practices and problems, pitfalls and potentials. *American Anthropologist, 109* (2), 261–272.

Lancaster, Y.P. (2006). Listening to young children: Respecting the voice of the child. In G. Pugh & B. Duffy (eds), *Contemporary issues in the early years* (4th edn) (pp. 63–76). London: Sage.

Ministry of Education (1996). *Te Whāriki: He whāriki mātauranga mō ngā mokopuna o Aotearoa: Early childhood curriculum.* Wellington, New Zealand: Learning Media.

Ministry of Education (2004). *Kei tua o te pae/ Assessment for learning: Early childhood exemplars.* Wellington: Learning Media.

Ministry of Education (2012). *Annual ECE Census Summary Report 2011.* Wellington: www.educationcounts.govt.nz/__data/assets/word_doc/0016/103390/Annual-ECE-Summary-Report-2011_final.doc

Pairman, A. & Terreni, L. (2001). *If the environment is the third teacher what languages does she speak?* Wellington: Early Childhood Development.

Sandvik, N. (2009). A pedagogy of listening: Following different and unknown pathways. *The First Years: Nga Tau Tuatahi, 11* (1), 21–26.

Shier, H. (2001). Pathways to participation: Openings, opportunities and obligations. *Children and Society, 15,* 107–117.

Smith, A.B. (2007). Children's rights and early childhood education: Links to theory and advocacy. *Australian Journal of Early Childhood*, *32* (3), 1–8.

Strong-Wilson, T. & Ellis, J. (2007). Children and place: Reggio Emilia's environment as third teacher. *Theory into Practice*, *46* (1), 40–47.

Chapter 15

Allard, P. & Lu, L. (2006). *Rebuilding families, reclaiming lives: State obligations to children in foster care and their incarcerated parents.* Brennan: Center for Justice.

Arditti, J.A. (2003). Locked doors and glass walls: Family visiting at the local jail. *Journal of Loss and Trauma*, *8*, 115–138.

Arditti, J.A., Smock, S.A. & Parkman, T. (2005). 'It's been hard to be a father': A qualitative exploration of incarcerated fatherhood. *Fathering*, *3*, 267–288.

Bloom, B. & Steinhart, D. (1993). *Why punish the children? A reappraisal of the children of incarcerated mothers of America.* San Francisco: National Council on Crime and Delinquency.

Christian, J., Mellow, J. & Thomas, S. (2006). Social and economic implications of family connections to prisoners, *Journal of Criminal Justice*, *34*, 443–452.

Clark, J. (1995). The impact of the prison environment on mothers, *Prison Journal*, *75* (3), 306–329.

Clarke, L., O'Brien, M., Day, R., Godwin, H., Connolly, J., Hemmings, J. & Van Leeson, T. (2005). Fathering behind bars in English prisons: Imprisoned fathers' identity and contact with their children. *Fathering*, *3* (3), 221–241.

Eddy, J. & Reid, J. (2003). The adolescent children of incarcerated parents: A developmental perspective. In J. Travis and M. Waul (eds), *Prisoners once removed: The impact of incarcerated and reentry on children, families, and communities.* Washington DC: Urban Institute Press.

Eddy, J.M. & Poehlmann, J. (2010). *Children of incarcerated parents: A handbook for researchers and practitioners.* Washington, DC: Urban Institute.

Gordon, L. (2009). *Invisible children.* Christchurch: PILLARS.

Gordon, L. (2010). *Working with the families and children of prisoners in Aotearoa/New Zealand: A guide to effective practice to ensure good outcomes for the children.* Christchurch: PILLARS.

Gordon, L. (2011a). *Causes of and solutions to inter-generational crime: The final report of the study of the children of prisoners.* Christchurch: PILLARS.

Gordon, L. (2011b). *A study of the children of prisoners: Findings from Māori data.* Te Puni Kōkiri: Wellington.

Hairston, C.F. (1998). The forgotten parent: Understanding the forces that influence incarcerated fathers' relationships with their children. *Child Welfare Journal*, *77*, 617–639.

Hairston, C.F. (1991). Family ties during imprisonment: Important for whom and for what? *Journal of Sociology and Social Welfare*, *19*, 87–104.

Hairston, C.F. (2002). Fathers in prison: Responsible fatherhood and responsible public policies. *Marriage and Family Review*, *32*, 111–135.

Howard League for Penal Reform (2010). Personal communication, 23 August 2010.

Makariev, D.W. & Shaver, P.R. (2010). Attachment, parental incarceration and possibilities for intervention: An overview. *Attachment & Human Development*, *12* (4), 311–331.

Murray, J., Farrington, D., Sekol, I. & Olsen, R. (2009). Effects of parental imprisonment on child antisocial behaviour and mental health: A systematic review. *Campbell Systematic Reviews*, *4*.

Murray, J., Farrington, D. & Sekol, I. (2012). Children's antisocial behaviour, mental health, drug use, and educational performance after parental incarceration: A systematic review and meta-analysis, *Psychological Bulletin*, *1* (38(2)), 175–210.

National Health Committee (2010). *Health in justice: Kia piki te ora, kia tika! Improving the health of prisoners and their families and whānau: He whakapiki i te ora o ngā mauhere me ō rātou whānau.* Wellington: Ministry of Health.

Nolen-Hoeksema, S. & Larson, J. (1999). *Coping with loss.* Hillsdale, NJ: Lawrence Erlbaum.

Nurse, A.M. (2002). *Fatherhood arrested: Parenting from within the juvenile justice system.* Nashville: Vanderbilt University Press.

Poehlmann, J. (2010). Attachment in children of incarcerated parents. In J.M. Eddy and J. Poehlmann (eds), *Children of incarcerated parents: A handbook for researchers and practitioners* (pp. 75-100). Washington, DC: Urban Institute.

Robertson, O. (2002). *Collateral convicts: Children of incarcerated parents: Recommendations and good practice from the UN Committee on the Rights of the Child Day of General Discussion 2011*. Switzerland: Quaker United Nations Office.

Roy, K.M. & Dyson, O.L. (2005). Gatekeeping in context: Baby mama drama and the involvement of incarcerated fathers. *Fathering, 3* (3), 289-310.

Sack, W.H. (1977). Children of imprisoned fathers. *Psychiatry, 40,* 163-174.

Schneller, D.P. (1978). *The prisoner's family: A study of the effects of imprisonment on the families of prisoners.* San Fransisco: R&E Research Associates.

Wesley Community Action (2009). *The Health of prisoners' families: A qualitative research project examining the effects that a family member being in prison has on the health of prisoners' families in New Zealand.* Wellington.

Chapter 16

Beck, U. & Beck-Gernsheim, E. (2002). *Individualization.* Translated by P. Camiller. London: Sage.

Benjamin, S. (2003). What counts as 'success'? Hierarchical discourses in a girls' comprehensive school. *Discourse: Studies in the Cultural Politics of Education, 24* (1), 105-118.

Bryson, L. (1994). Sport and the maintenance of masculine hegemony. Chapter 3 in S. Birrell & C. Cole (eds), *Women, sport and culture* (pp. 47-64). Champaign, Illinois: Human Kinetics.

Davies, B. & Saltmarsh, S. (2007) Gender economies: Literacy and the gendered production of neo-liberal subjectivities. *Gender and Education, 19* (1), 1-20.

Department of Education Implementation Unit (1989). *Tomorrow's schools.* Wellington.

Francis, B. (2002). Relativism, realism, and feminism: An analysis of some theoretical tensions in research on gender identity. *Journal of Gender Studies, 11* (1): 39-54.

Garrett, R. (2004). Negotiating a physical identity: Girls, bodies and physical education. *Sport, Education and Society, 9* (2), 223-237.

Gibb, S.J. & Fergusson, D.M. (2009). Gender differences in educational participation and achievement across subject areas. *NZ Journal of Educational Studies, 44* (1), 83-90.

Gilliam, W.S., Ripple, C.H., Zigler, E.F & Leiter, V. (2000). Evaluating child and family demonstration initiatives: Lessons from the comprehensive child development program. *Early Childhood Research Quarterly, 15* (1), 41-59.

Guldberg, H. (2009). *Reclaiming childhood: Freedom and play in an age of fear.* Abingdon: Routledge.

Hallden, G. (1999). 'To be or not to be': Absurd and humoristic descriptions as a strategy to avoid idyllic life stories – boys write about family life. *Gender and Education,* 11 (4), 469-479.

Jones, A. (1991). Is Madonna a feminist folk-hero, is Ruth Richardson a woman? Postmodern feminism and dilemmas of difference. *Sites, 23,* 84-100.

Jones, A. (1993). Becoming a 'girl': Post-structuralist suggestions for educational research. *Gender and Education, 5* (2), 157-166.

Kingfisher, C. & Goldsmith, M. (2001). Reforming women in the United States and Aotearoa/New Zealand. *American Anthropologist, 103* (3), 714-732.

Lai, M.K., McNaughton, S., Amituanai-Toloa, M., Turner, R. & Hsaio, S. (2009). Sustained acceleration of achievement in reading comprehension: The New Zealand experience. *Reading Research Quarterly, 44* (1), 30-56.

Larner, W. (1996). The 'new boys': Restructuring in New Zealand, 1984-94. *Social Politics, 3* (1), 32-56.

McGee, R., Prior, M., Williams, S., Smart, D. & Sanson, A. (2002). The long term significance of teacher-rated hyperactivity and reading ability in childhood: Findings from two longitudinal studies. *Journal of Child Psychology and Psychiatry, 43* (8), 1004-1017.

Mallard, T. (2004). Boys' achievement investigation under way. Speech given to NZ Principals and Leadership Centre Conference on Boys' Education, Massey University, Albany, Auckland: www.beehive.govt.nz/node/20243

Marie, D., Fergusson, D. & Boden, J. (2008). Educational achievement in Maori: The roles of cultural identity and social disadvantage. *Australian Journal of Education, 52* (2), 183–196.

Matheson, K. & Banerjee, R. (2010) Pre-school peer play: The beginnings of social competence. *Educational and Child Psychology, 27* (1), 9–20.

Meyer, M. & Koehler, M. (1990). Internal influences on gender differences in mathematics. Chapter 4 in E. Fennema & G. Leder (eds), *Mathematics and gender* (pp. 60–95). New York: Teachers College Press.

Ministry of Education (2007). *Boys' achievement: A synthesis of the data.* Wellington.

Ministry of Education (2007a). *The New Zealand curriculum.* Wellington: Learning Media.

Ministry of Education (2012). *New Zealand Education:* www.minedu.govt.nz

Nairn, K., Higgins, J. & Sligo, J. (2012). *Children of Rogernomics: New Zealand's neo-liberal generation leaves school.* Dunedin: Otago University Press.

National Education Monitoring Project (2008). Reading and speaking: http://nemp.otago.ac.nz/read_speak/2008/index.htm

Pianta, R.C. & Stuhlmann, M.W. (2004). Teacher–child relationships and children's success in the first years of school. *School Psychological Review, 33* (3), 444–458.

Qvortrup, J., Bardy, M., Sgritta, G. & Wintersberger, H. (1994). *Childhood matters: Social theory, practice and politics.* Foreword. Vienna: Avebury.

Reay, D. (2001). 'Spice girls', 'nice girls', 'girlies', and 'tomboys': Gender discourses, girls' cultures and femininities in the primary classroom. *Gender and Education, 13* (2), 153–166.

Renold, E. (2001a), Learning the 'hard' way: Boys, hegemonic masculinity and the negotiation of learner identities in the primary school. *British Journal of the Sociology of Education, 22* (3), 369–385.

Renold, E. (2001b). 'Square-girls', femininity and the negotiation of academic success in the primary school. *British Educational Research Journal, 27* (5), 577–588.

Renold, E. & Allan, A. (2006). Bright and beautiful: High achieving girls, ambivalent femininities, and the feminization of success in the primary school. *Discourse: Studies in the Cultural Politics of Education, 27* (4), 457–473.

Rubin, R.S., Bommer, W.H. & Baldwin, T.T. (2002). Using extracurricular activity as an indicator of interpersonal skill: Prudent evaluation or recruiting malpractice? *Human Resource Management, 41* (4), 441–454.

Slater, A. & Tiggemann, M. (2010). 'Uncool to do sport': A focus group of adolescent girls' reasons for withdrawing from physical activity. *Psychology of Sport and Exercise, 11*, 619–626.

Snook, I. & O'Neill, J. (2010). Social class and educational achievement: Beyond ideology. *NZ Journal of Educational Studies, 45* (2), 3–18.

Swain, J. (2000). 'The money's good, the fame's good, the girls are good': The role of playground football in the construction of young boys' masculinity in a junior school. *British Journal of Sociology of Education, 21* (1), 95–109.

Telford, M. with May, S. (2010). PISA 2009: Our 21st century learners at age 15: www.educationcounts.govt.nz/publications/series/2543/pisa-2009/pisa-2009-our-21st-century-learners-at-age-15/3

Telford, M. & Caygill, R. (2006). PISA 2006: How ready are our 15-year-olds for tomorrow's world? Wellington: Ministry of Education: www.educationcounts.govt.nz/publications/series/2543/pisa_2006/16616

Trudeau, F. & Shephard, R. J. (2009). Relationships of physical activity to brain health and academic performance of school children. *American Journal of Lifestyle Medicine, 4*, 138–150.

Watson, S., Hughes, D. & Lauder, H. (2003). 'Success' and 'failure' in the education marketplace: An example from New Zealand. *Journal of Educational Change, 4*, 1–24.

Watson, A., Kehler, M. & Martino, W. (2010). The problem of boys' literacy underachievement: Raising some questions. *Journal of Adolescent and Adult Literacy, 53* (5), 356–361.

Weissberg, R.P., Kumpfer, K.L. & Seligman, M.E.P. (2003). Prevention that works for children and youth: An introduction. *American Psychologist, 58* (6/7), 425–432.

Wright, J. (1996). The construction of complementarity in physical education. *Gender and Education, 8* (1), 61–79.

Chapter 17

Allan, J. (2009). Provocations: Putting philosophy to work on inclusion. In K. Quinlivan, R. Boyask & B. Kaur (eds), *Educational enactments in a globalised world: Intercultural conversations* (pp. 1-12). Rotterdam: Sense Publications.

Butler, J. (1997). *Excitable speech: A politics of the performative*. London: Routledge.

De Palma, R. & Atkinson, E. (eds) (2009). Outing queer into practice: Problems and possibilities. In *Interrogating heteronormativity in primary schools: The work of the 'no-outsiders' project* (pp. 1-6). Stoke on Trent.

Grbich, C. (2007). *Qualitative data analysis: An introduction*. London: Sage.

Hendriques, J., Hollway, W., Urwin, C., Venn, C. & Walkerdine, V. (2004). Constructing the subject. In J. Hendriques, W. Hollway, C. Urwin, C. Venn & V. Walkerdine (eds), *Changing the subject: Psychology, social relation and subjectivity* (pp. 92-118). London: Methuen.

Henrickson, M. (2007). 'You have to be strong to be gay': Bullying and educational attainment in LGB New Zealanders. *Journal of Gay and Lesbian Social Services, 19* (3/4), 67-85.

Marshall, D. (2010). Popular culture, the 'victim' trope and queer youth analytics. *International Journal of Qualitative Studies in Education, 23* (1), 65-85.

Martino, W. & Pallotta-Chiarolli, M. (2005). *Being normal is the only way to be: Adolescent perspectives on gender and school*. Sydney: University of New South Wales Press.

Mayo, C. (2009). Access and obstacles: Gay-straight alliances attempt to alter school communities. In W. Ayers, T. Quinn & D. Stovall (eds), *Handbook of Social Justice in Education* (pp. 319-331). New York: Routledge.

Nairn, K. & A. Smith (2003). Taking students seriously: Their rights to be safe at school. *Gender and Education, 15* (2), 133-149.

Popkewitz, T. (1997). The production of reason and power: Curriculum history and intellectual traditions. *Journal of Curriculum Studies, 29* (2), 131-164.

Painter, H. & Keaney, P. (2009). *How safe and inclusive are Otago schools? A report on the implementation of recommendations from 'Safety in our school - Ko te haumaru I o tatou kura' action kit*. Dunedin: Otago University Students' Association Queer Support.

Plummer, D. (1999). *One of the boys: Masculinity, homophobia and modern manhood*. New York: Harrington Park Press.

Quinlivan, K. (2002). Whose problem is this?: Queerying the framing of lesbian and gay secondary school students within 'at risk' discourses. In K.H. Robinson, J. Irwin & T. Ferfolja (eds), *From here to diversity: The social impact of lesbian and gay issues in education in Australia and New Zealand* (pp. 17-31). New York: Harrington Park Press.

Quinlivan, K. (2006). Affirming sexual diversity in two New Zealand secondary schools: Challenges, constraints and shifting ground in the research process. *Journal of Lesbian and Gay Studies in Education, 3* (2-3) 5-33.

Quinlivan, K. (2009). When 'everything collides in a big boom!' Attending to emotionality and discomfort as sites of learning in the high school health classroom. In K. Quinlivan, R. Boyask & B. Kaur (eds), *Educational enactments: Intercultural conversations in a globalised world* (pp. 77-90). Rotterdam: Sense Publishers.

Quinlivan, K., Goulter, M. & Caldwell, F. (2010). *Diversity groups as sites of learning in New Zealand school and community contexts*. New Zealand Aids Foundation.

Rasmussen, M.L., Rofes, E. & Talburt, S. (2004). Introduction. In M. Rasmussen, E. Rofes & S. Talburt (eds), *Youth and sexualities: Pleasure, subversion and insubordination in and out of schools* (pp. 17- 39). New York: Palgrave Macmillan.

Robinson, K. (2005). Reinforcing hegemonic masculinities through sexual harassment: Issues of identity, power and popularity in secondary schools, *Gender and Education, 17* (1), 19-37.

Rossen, F.V., Lucassen, M.F.G., Denny, S. & Robinson, E. (2009). *Youth '07: The health and wellbeing of secondary school students in New Zealand: Results for young people attracted to the same sex or both sexes*. Auckland: University of Auckland.

Spivak, G. (1988). Subaltern studies: Deconstructing historiography. In R. Guha & G. Spivak (eds), *Selected subaltern studies* (pp. 337-38). Oxford: Oxford University Press.

Talburt, S. & Rasmussen, M. (2010). 'After queer' tendencies in queer research. *International Journal of Qualitative Studies in Education, 23* (1), 1–14.

Warner, M. (1993). Introduction. In M. Warner (ed.), *Fear of a queer planet: Queer politics and social theory* (pp. vii–xxxi). Minneapolis: University of Minnesota Press.

Youdell, D. (2005). Sex-gender-sexuality: How sex, gender, and sexuality constellations are constituted in secondary schools, *Gender and Education 17* (3), 249–270.

Youdell, D. (2006). *Impossible bodies, impossible selves: Exclusions and student subjectivities.* Springer: Dordrecht.

Youdell, D. (2009). Lessons in praxis: Thinking about knowledge, subjectivity and politics in education. In R. De Palma & E. Atkinson (eds), *Interrogating heteronormativity* (pp. 35–49). Stoke on Trent: Trentham Books.

Youdell, D. (2011). *School trouble: Identity, power and politics in education.* New York: Routledge.

Chapter 18

Abu El-Haj, T. (2005). Global politics, dissent and Palestinian–American identities: Engaging conflict to reinvigorate democratic education. In L. Weis and M. Fine (eds), *Beyond silenced voices: Class, race and gender in US schools* (rev. edn). Albany: SUNY Press.

Aronson, J. (2004). The threat of stereotype. *Educational Leadership*, 14–19 November.

Black. J., (2008). The racial divide. *NZ Listener, 214* (3574).

Bishop, R. & Berryman, M. (2006). *Culture speaks: Cultural relationships and classroom learning.* Wellington: Huia Publishers.

Fine, M. (1991). *Framing dropouts: Notes on the politics of an urban high school.* Albany: SUNY Press.

Hooks, B. (1992). Marginality as site of resistance. In R. Fergusson, M. Geverk, T. Minti-ha & C. West (eds), *Out there: Marginalisation and contemporary cultures* (pp. 341–343). Cambridge, Massachusetts: MIT Press.

Johnston, P. & Pihama, L. (1995). What counts as difference and what differences count: Gender, race and the politics of difference. In K. Irwin, I. Ramsden & R. Kahukiwa (eds), *Toi wāhine: The worlds of Māori women* (pp. 75–86). Auckland: Penguin Books.

Lee, J., Sax, L., Kim, K. & Hagedorn, L. (2004). Understanding students' parental education beyond first-generation status. *Community College Review, 32* (1), 1–17.

Lehman, W. (2009). University as vocational education: Working-class students' expectations for university. *British Journal of Sociology of Education, 30* (2), 137–149.

Mitchell, M. (2009). All we got to see were factories.' Scoping Māori transitions from secondary school. Unpublished Master's thesis, Victoria University of Wellington.

Ormond, A. (2006). Who determines what story is told? Narratives of marginalisation. *AlterNative, Special Supplement*, 118–143.

Penetito, W. (2002). Personal reflections on developments in Maori education 1970–2001. In F. Pene, A. Taufe'ulungaki & C. Benso (eds), *Tree of opportunity: Rethinking Pacific education* (p. 130). Suva: Instititute of Education, University of the South Pacific.

Pinto, L. (2006). The streaming of working class and minority students in Ontario. *Our Schools, Our Selves, 15* (2), 79–89.

San Miguel, G. & Valencia, R. (1998). From the treaty of Guadalupe Hidalgo to Hopwood: The educational plight and struggle of Mexican Americans in the Southwest. *Harvard Educational Review, 68* (3), 353–412.

Solorzano, D. & Delgado Bernal, D. (2001) Critical race theory, transformational resistance and social justice: Chicana and Chicano students in an urban context, *Urban Education, 36*, 308–342.

Themelis, S. (2008). Meritocracy through education and social mobility in post-war Britain: A critical examination. *British Journal of Sociology of Education, 29* (5), 427–438.

Ungar, M. (2004). *Nurturing hidden resilience in troubled youth.* Toronto: University of Toronto Press.

Valencia, R. (1997). *Evolution of deficit thinking: Educational thought and practice.* London/Washington: Falmer Press.

Valencia, R. & Black, M. (2002). 'Mexican Americans don't value education!' On the basis of the myth, mythmaking, and debunking. *Journal of Latinos and Education, 1* (2), 81–103.
Walker, R. (1991). *Liberating Maori from educational subjection*. Auckland: University of Auckland.
Weis, L. (2007). Toward an agenda for the critical study of social class and schooling. *Comparative minds, critical visions*, vol. 1 (working paper series), Buffalo, NY: Center for Comparative and Global Studies in Education, State University of New York at Buffalo.
Weis, L. & Fine, M. (1993). *Beyond silenced voices: Class, race and gender in United States schools*. Albany: State University of New York Press.
Wexler, L. (2009). The importance of identity, history, and culture in the wellbeing of indigenous youth. *Journal of History of Childhood and Youth, 2* (2), 267–299.
Wright, C., Standen, P. & Patel, T. (2010). *Black youth matters: Transitions from school to success*. New York and London: Routledge.
Yosso, T. (2005). Whose culture has capital? A critical race theory discussion of community cultural wealth. *Race, Ethnicity and Education, 8* (1), 69–91.
Youdell, D. (2012). Identity traps or how black students fail: The interactions between biographical, sub-cultural, and learner identities. *British Journal of Sociology of Education, 24* (1), 3–20.
Zyngier, D. (2004). Improving the pathways for young people who are early school leavers and/or require alternate education. *International Journal of Learning, 11,* 55–69.

Chapter 19

Beech, L. (2012). Our daily bread: Putting food on the table. *Caritas Social Justice Series, 17,* 1–28.
Boston, J. (2012). Experts Advisory Group nationwide workshops on solutions to child poverty in New Zealand. A presentation to the Christchurch workshop, 25 September, University of Canterbury, Christchurch.
Canterbury District Health Board (2013). Report on 2012 Darfield gastroenteritis outbreak, 19 February: www.scoop.co.nz/stories/GE1302/S00054/report-on-2012-darfield-gastroenteritis-outbreak-released.htm
Children's Social Health MonitorChildren's Social Health Monitor (2011). *The children's social health monitor 2011 update*. Dunedin: NZ Child and Youth Epidemiology Service: www.nzchildren.co.nz
Christchurch Child Poverty Action Group (2012). Notes from the inaugural meeting on 28 August 2012. Available from Nathalie Blakely, co-convenor, Christchurch branch of CPAG.
Dale, M.C., O'Brien, M. & St John, S. (eds) (2011). *Left further behind: How policies fail the poorest children in New Zealand*. Auckland: Child Poverty Action Group: www.cpag.org.nz/assets/sm/upload/d4/ei/sg/g4/LFBDec2011.pdf
Expert Advisory Group on Solutions to Child Poverty (2012). Lifecourse effects on childhood poverty: www.occ.org.nz/__data/assets/pdf_file/0010/9838/No_2_-_Lifecourse_effects.pdf
Families Commission (2009). *Finding time: Parents' long working hours and time impact on family life*. Research report no. 2/20. Wellington: www.familiescommission.org.nz/sites/default/files/downloads/finding-time.pdf
Families Commission (2012). *New Zealand families today: A brief demographic profile*. Wellington.
Generation Zero (2012a). Our vision: http://generationzero.org.nz/solutions
Generation Zero (2012b). Get involved: Join us: http://generationzero.org.nz/volunteer
Generation Zero (2012c). Who are we?: www.ecoevents.org.nz/member-organisations/generation-zero
Nairn, K. Higgins, J. & Sligo, J. (2012). *Children of Rogernomics: A neoliberal generation leaves school*. Dunedin: Otago University Press.
Power Shift (2012a). *What is Power Shift? Power Shift NZ–Pacific 2012: The biggest youth climate summit NZ has ever seen*: http://powershift.org.nz/about-power-shift
Power Shift (2012b). Five young Wellington cyclists riding to climate conference in Auckland: http://wellington.scoop.co.nz/?p=50553

Scott, D. (2012). Quake volunteers help with Sandy cleanup: www.stuff.co.nz/the-press/news/7955146/Quake-volunteers-help-with-Sandy-cleanup

Smith, C., Parnell, W. & Brown, R. (2010). *Family food environment: Barriers to acquiring affordable and nutritious food in New Zealand households*. Wellington: Families Commission, Blue Skies Fund: http://socialjusticeweek.org.nz/wp-content/uploads/2012/09/family-food-environment.pdf

Shuttleworth, K. (2012). Key dismisses proposal as 'dopey', *New Zealand Herald*, 28 August 2012: www.nzherald.co.nz/nz/news/article.cfm?c_id=1&objectid=10830083

Student Volunteer Army (2012). History: www.sva.org.nz/index.php/svatheclub

Styliano, G. (2012). Apology for Darfield gastro outbreak, 29 August 2011: www.stuff.co.nz/the-press/news/7571455/Apology-for-Darfield-gastro-outbreak

Tollefson, J. & Gilbert, N. (2012). Earth Summit: Rio report card: The world has failed to deliver on many of the promises it made 20 years ago at the Earth summit in Brazil. *Nature International Weekly Journal of Science*, 486 (7401): www.nature.com/news/earth-summit-rio-report-card-1.10764#unfccc

Wynd, D. (2012). Solutions to child poverty, submission, Office of the Commissioner for Children's Expert Advisory Group: www.cpag.org.nz/assets/Submissions/OCC_EAG%20Submission%20FINAL.pdf

Young, R. (2012). Race to irrigate behind ECan move: www.stuff.co.nz/the-press/news/7874996/Race-to-irrigate-behind-ECan-move

Youth Hub (2012). About Us: Youth Hub Barbadoes: www.youthhub.org.nz/index.php?option=com_content&view=article&id=1&Itemid=3

Index

Page numbers in **bold** refer to illustrations.

abuse and neglect *see* child abuse and neglect
accidents: playgrounds 120; traffic 66
adolescents *see* queer youth; rangatahi Māori; teenagers
adopted and fostered children 167–68; adoption rates 169; birth families 168, 169–70, 171, 172, 173, 174–75, 177, 178; British child migrants 170; extended family kin-based care 170, 171; foster care of prisoners' children 222, 223; fostering rates 170; historical, legal and practice perspectives 168–71; intercountry adoptions 169, 171, 172, 175, 177; key messages from research 178; needs of children and their families 173–78; Pacific nation kin 169; parental selection, preparation and training 171–73; stranger-based adoptions 169, 171; supporting adopted and fostered children in the future 178–79; 'treatment foster care' 178
Adoption Act 1955 169
Adult Information Act 1985 169–70
Africa, immigrants from 142, 151
agency and voice *see* children's agency and voice
alcohol 45, 49, 275
Alley, Fredric 101–02
Alley, Gwen (later Somerset) 101, 121
Alley, Rewi 101
Alternative Dispute Resolution (ADR) 165
Amberley School 101
Anglican Family Care 23
Asia 18
Asian peoples 18, 142, 151; *see also* Chinese people
assemblages 197
Auckland: children's play and playgrounds 116, **117**, 118; housing 62; Pacific population 18; population 16, 18, 20, 60, 62; suburbanisation 118
Australia: children 59, 65, 66; housing 61, 62; New Zealanders in 16
Awakeri School 18, 20

Barnardos 23
beaches 114, **115**
Beeby, Clarence (C.E.) 109

behaviour, adults 49; impact on children 50–51
behaviour, children: adopted and fostered children 174; and physical education 114; prisoners' children 220; and vulnerability 45, 47, 49, 52
benefits 24, 54, 135–36, 177, 275
bicultural society 14, 20, 128, 142, 144, 150, 151
Bill of Rights Act 1990 131
biological essentialism 251, 252
Bird, William W. 106, 107
Bradwell, Cyril 108
Braik, George 99
Britain 18, 65, 66, 95, 99, 112–13, 142, 170, 178, 190, 220
Buckingham, David 65
bullying 82–83, 250, 254–55

camping **55**, 68, 70, 76
cannabis 47
car ownership and use 66–67, 70, 118, **119**, 124
Care of Children Act 2004 35, 156, 163–65, 170
Chief Science Advisor to the Prime Minister 47, 49, 50, 51, 55
child abuse and neglect 22, 31, 45, 53–54, 133, 168; adopted and fostered children 167, 171, 172–73, 174, 175, 178; and confidentiality 90; interventions 50, 52; protection from abuse at expense of other needs 31; reports of concern 50; research protocols 82; socioeconomic factors 48; statistics 48; *see also* sexual abuse
child employment 180–82, 190–91, 276; benefits of work 181, 182, 184, 188, 189, 190; and education 183, 184, 185, 186; government policies 181, 182; international agreements 183–87; minimum ages 182, 186, 188, 190; non-Western countries 181, 184; parents' concerns 189–90; profile of young workers 187–89; protection of children *from* work 181, 182, 183–85, 186–87, 189; protection of children *in* work 181, 182, 185–87, 191; remuneration 182, 188, 189; rights 180, 182, 183–87, 189, 190, 191; statistics 182; time restrictions 182; types

of work 182; working conditions 182, 189–90, 191
Child Poverty Action Group 23, 275
child psychology 99
Child Welfare Bill 1925 118
Child, Youth and Family 22, 23, 48–49, 225; and adoptive parents 171, 177, 179; children in custody of 170; Partnered Response initiative 50; threshold for intervention 50
childhood: being and becoming 40–41; constructions of 30–33, 78; deficit-based understanding of 32; diversity of childhoods 14, 78–79; literature about 14
Childhood Studies 29, 30, 32, 33, 34, 36, 37–38, 39, 40, 78, 81; critical 41–42; ethics 77; and family law developments 153, 155, 165–66; key features 155; macro and micro levels of children's experiences 42–43; and new education movement 96, 108, 209; and new media 194–97; pluralistic and singularistic perspectives 42
children: rights 21, 23, 36–38, 57, 77, 78, 91, 121–22, 154, 157, 183–87; as social actors 29, 33, 81–82, 85, 91, 121, 122, 155, 196, 197; UNCRC definition of child 180; *see also* children in Aotearoa New Zealand
Children and Young People as Social Actors Research Cluster, University of Otago 77–78, 79, 80, 82–83, 85, 88, 89, 90, 91
children in Aotearoa New Zealand: mobility 13, 63, 112, 125; pressures 13; rights 121–22, 157, 183–87; services for 22–25; as social actors 121, 122, 155, 196, 197; statistics 13, 62; *see also* adopted and fostered children; and specific subjects, e.g. education; disabled children; participation; Pasifika children; prisoners' children; tamariki Māori; vulnerable children
Children, Young Persons and their Families Act 1989 22, 170
children's agency and voice 33–36, 39, 40, 42, 86, 155; in learning and development 96, 99, 108, 109, 145, 207–11; and participant observation 212; *see also* participation
Children's Commissioner 22–23, 122
Children's Issues Centre 153
children's knowledge and understanding of parental incarceration 225–27
Children's Social Health Monitor 16, 48
Chinese people: Auckland 18; children, in early childhood settings 144, 145, 146, 149–50; Dunedin 143; fathers working away from Aotearoa New Zealand 149; ideas about learning and play 145; population 18
Christchurch 18, 26–27, **27**, 49, 60, 279
Christchurch longitudinal study 46, 47
climate change 9, 10, 25, 277, 278
clubs 114, 121
collectivism 99, 146; Māori 64, 128, 129, 130, 131
colonial heritage 18
colonisation 46, 127–29
community capital 266–67
computer games 123, 193, 196, 199, 240, 242, 243, 244, 246
computer use by children 196, 198, 199, 201–02, 203
counselling 155, 156, 165, 176, 177, 179, 225, 253, 259–60
Crimes Act, Section 59 53
cultural and subcultural capital 80, 149, 266
cultural boundary 146–47
cultural bridging 144
cultural converging 144, 148, 149
cultural diversity 9, 14, 18, 20, 128, 141, 142, 143–44, 145–46
cultural togetherness 144
culture: adopted and fostered children 175–76; communication through electronic media 193, 194; definition 143, 145, 152; Māori 8, 20, 128, 132, 134–35, 142, 266–67, 277; Pākehā 14, 129; vulnerability and cultural belonging 46; Western 149–50, 151; *see also* bicultural society; multicultural society

Dansey's Pass Holiday Park **71**
Darfield, Canterbury 277–78
deficit thinking: about childhood 32; and Māori kāpo (blind) children 134, 138; rangatahi Māori 262, 263, 265, 271, 272; social and political context 128
dental services 24
developmental psychology 29, 32–33, 42
Dewey, John 96, 99
diet, international influences 20
digital media *see* electronic media
Disability Commissioner 23
disability paradigms 129–30
disabled children 21; educational achievement 23; health services 24; Māori children 24, 127 (*see also* Māori kāpo (blind) tamariki and rangatahi); medical model 32, 129; research participation 83, 84; school experiences 79–80; vulnerability 45, 47

318 ❀ CHILDHOODS

discourses influencing childhood 30–33
Diversity Groups *see* Queer–Straight Alliances
drug abuse *see* substance abuse
Dunedin: Chinese community 143, **143**; relationship of children to city and home neighbourhoods 70, **71**, 72–75
Dunedin longitudinal study 46, 48

early childhood education 23, 207; children's agency and voice 35–36, 39–40, 145, 207–19; children's views translated into practice 215–16, 218–19; Chinese children 144, 145, 146; identification and interventions for vulnerable children 52–53; joint decisions by teachers and children 216–17, 218–19; Māori children 20, 52, 131, 136, 277; multicultural 150–51, 152; Pasifika children 52; physical environment 207–08, 210–19; *Te Whāriki* 35–36, 150–51, 207, 209, 210, 218, 219; teachers' listening and engagement 213–14; teachers' support for children to express views 214–15; *see also* education, early years schooling; kindergartens; Play Centre movement
early intervention 50
earthquakes, Christchurch 18, 26–27, **27**, 49, 279
economic challenges facing children and youth 275–76
education 23–24; academic achievement at expense of personal and social development 260, 261; achievement levels 23, 47, 49, 220, 236, 264; adopted and fostered children 175, 176; and child employment 183, 184, 185, 187; compulsory schooling 23, 105, 111, 112, 113, 118; costs 23; global connections 18; impact of failure 263, 269; Māori 20, 32, 52, 105–07, **106**, **107**, 128–29, 130, 131, 132, 136–37, 267–73; National Standards 236, 247; new education methods 95–96, 99–100, 106, 107–08, 109; policies of testing, streaming and tracking 32, 43, 264, 268; relative achievement of boys and girls 236, 238; and success 235–36, 242, 245–46, 247–8; and vulnerability 45, 46, 49, 52–53; and working hours 54; *see also* early childhood education; education, early years schooling; schools
Education Act 1877 23

Education Act 1989 194
education, early years schooling, 1900-1920s: adult memories 95, 96–97, 101–06, 108, 109; crowded classrooms **98**, 101; data sources 97–98; discipline and punishment 101–02, 103, 105, 106–07; gallery lessons 108, 109; gendered classroom 102–03, **103**; Māori children 105–07, **106**, **107**; playground land wars 103–05; slow pace of change 107–09
Edwards, Dorothy 97
electronic media 192–94; and 3G digital technologies 193; and Childhood Studies 194–97; and children's contribution to family life 198–99, 204; and children's friendships 199; children's use to shape own lives 196–97, 203–04; and generational barriers 203–04; 'media multitasking' 193; multimedia 201–04; television and mediated screen technologies 194, 197, 198–204
Elmwood School 101
employment: responses to economic pressures 275–76; *see also* child employment; rangatahi Māori – experience of transition to work
environment 14, 17, 25–26, 59–60; challenges for New Zealand children 75–76; domestic 60–63; Dunedin case study 70, **71**, 72–75; early childhood education physical environment 207–08, 210–19; environments today 65–66; outdoor 63–65, 67–70
Environment Canterbury 277–78
environmental challenges facing children and youth 277–79
environmental disasters 279–80
equity and inequity 10, 17, 25, 48, 57, 185, 275; education 236; housing 62–63; Māori 9, 130–31, 132–33; multicultural issues 147, 148
'ethical radar' 86, 89
ethics: emerging questions 77–78; informed consent 87–90; as a process 86; research involving children 78, 79, 81–85, 90–91
ethics committees 78, 84, 211
ethnicity 14, 18, 142; Auckland population 18, 20; and poverty 130; and risk 46
Europe 95, 99, 151, 178
evaluation of programmes and services 56, 58
evidence-based programmes 55–56

Fagan, Andrew 63–64
families: assumption that all families may need support at times 56, 58; 'astronaut families' 149; benefit-dependent 48; at the centre of children's lives 27–28; and child vulnerability 45, 46, 52, 53; diversity of structures 14, 276; in private sphere 54; services for 50–52, 53, 55–58; suburban nuclear family 118–20, 276; supporting children's knowledge and understanding 40; *see also* parents
Families Commission 22, 23, 54, 276
Family Court 155–56; children's participation 35, 153, 156, 163–65, 166; Counsel (Lawyer) for the Child 156, 157, 158, 161, 162, 163, 164; judges 155, 156, 164–65
Family Court Matters Bill 165
family group conferences 171
family law 34–35
family law decision-making, children's participation 153, 165–66; Care of Children Act 2004 35, 156, 163–65; children's concerns 162–63; children's knowledge and understanding 160–61; consultation within the family 158–60; influences on 154–55; mediation 165; role of professionals 161–62; socio-legal research programme 156–63; statutory context 155–56
family violence 22, 45, 48–49; socioeconomic factors 48
fathers 120; incarcerated 220, 221, 222–37
feminist movement 120–22, 123
fertility rates 18
festivals 20
financial assistance, government 24, 54, 135–36, 177, 275
Foetal Alcohol Spectrum Disorder 49
fostered children *see* adopted and fostered children
Freud, Sigmund 99
Froebel, Friedrich 99–100
futurity 40, 41

gambling 45
gay youth *see* queer youth
Gay-Straight Alliance 250
gender 238, 251; and success 236, 238, 239, 240, 241, 242–44, 245–46, 247; and Yes! Queer-Straight Alliance 253, 254, 256, 257
Generation Zero 278
Gleeson, Brendan 65

global connections 18, 20, 149, 277
global economic downturn 18
globalisation: and children's sense of childhood 195; and multiculturalism 148–49, 151, 152; of play 123
Green Paper for Vulnerable Children 31, 34, 37, 44, 46, 47, 49, 51, 53
Growing Up in New Zealand: longitudual study (2010) 49; Ritchie and Ritchie (1978) 14, 64–65
Guardianship Act 1968 156, 163, 165
guided participation 38–40

Hague Convention on Private International Law 169, 171
haka **21**
Hall, Stanley 96
Hart's 'ladder of participation' 209
Hayward, Bronwyn 25
health: infectious diseases, and housing 62–63; Māori 128, 130, 131, 133; socioeconomic factors 48; and vulnerability 45, 47
health services 24; adopted and fostered children 175, 176; and child vulnerability 52; disabled children 24, 132–33; and Māori 130–33, 135, 136–37
health status 16
Hendry, James 99
heteronormativity 249, 250, 252, 253, 254–55, 256–57, 258
High Street Kindergarten, Dunedin 102, **102**
High Street School, Dunedin 102–03
Hogben, George 100
holidays 17, 55, **55**, 68
'home for life' scheme 171, 177
homophobia 250, 252, 253–54
Horne, Lyndsey 278
housing 14; effects of inadequate housing 62–63; government-supported accommodation 24; inner-city apartments 62; Māori 63, 132; medium-density **61**, 62; Pasifika peoples 62, 63; stand-alone houses, with gardens 17, 60–61, 112, 118; and vulnerability 45, 48
human rights 21–22, 31, 131, 180–81, 183–87, 190, 191
Human Rights Commission 23

I am five and I go to school (May) 95, 96, 97, 99, 107
identity 9, 15, 21, 22, 147, 199, 237–38, 244; adopted/fostered children 174,

175, 178; incarcerated fathers 232; Māori 8, 64, 127–28, 129, 132, 139; and marginalisation of rangatahi Māori 262, 267, 273; and multiple selves 251, 252; and power 148; *see also* sexual identity
immigration 46, 141, 142, 151
Immigration Act 1987 142
Inclusive Education Action Group 23
income gap 14
Incredible Years programme 55
independence: and car use 66–67, 72–73; and neighbourhoods 75
indigenous people 22
individualism 24, 99, 122–24, 129, 146, 235; individual responsibility for success 235, 236, 239–40
inequity *see* equity and inequity
information 36, 154; access to 31, 36, 39, 40, 154
information technology 149, 193; convergence with telecommunications 193–94, 197, 198, 203, 204; *see also* electronic media
informed consent 87; active and genuinely informed over time 89–90; children's competence to consent 87; difference from assent 89; how sought and who can give 89; parental 89; privacy and confidentiality 90; processes relevant to age, ability, experience and culture 88–89; researcher competence to gain consent 87–88
Intercountry Adoption New Zealand (ICANZ) 177
International Labour Organization 181; Minimum Age Convention (MAC) 180, 181, 182, 183–84, 190; Worst Forms of Child Labour Convention (WFCLC) 180, 187, 190
International Year of the Child, 1979 121
internet 20
Isaacs, Susan 99

kāpo Māori 139
Kei Tua o te Pae/Assessment for Learning 210
Kereru High School 252–61
kindergartens 99–100, 121, 136; High Street Kindergarten, Dunedin 102, **102**
King, Michael 103–04
KiwiSport 240
Koea, Shonagh 64
Kōhanga Reo 20, 277
He Korowai Oranga 131
Kura Kaupapa Māori 20, 277

languages: Auckland 20; Māori 20, 105–07, 129, 277; New Zealand Sign Language 20; post-structuralist theories and language 251; Samoan 20
Le Race 2000 incident 68
life chances 17
literacy 236, 237, 245, 247
Living Standards Survey 2008 47–48
local government 58
Louv, Richard 65

Maatua Whangai 170
Māori: collective identity 64, 128, 129, 130, 131; community capital 266–67; culture 8, 20, 128, 132, 134–35, 142, 266–67, 277; education 20, 32, 52, 105–07, **106**, **107**, 128–29, 130, 131, 132, 136–37, 263–64, 267–73; fertility rates 18; haka **21**; health 128, 130, 131; housing 63, 132; identity 8, 64, 127–28, 129, 132, 139; inequality 9, 130–31, 132–33; life expectancy 9; naming of North and South Islands 59, 127; population 16, 18, 19; poverty 14, 47–48, 129, 130, 269, 275; renaissance 123; socio-economic status 9, 14, 47–48, 63, 129, 130–32, 135–36; urbanisation 118, 128; whakapapa 127, 128, 170, 267; whānaungatanga 64, 128, 130, 139; *see also* bicultural society; rangatahi Māori; tamariki Māori; Te Reo Māori; Treaty of Waitangi
Māori kāpo (blind) tamariki and rangatahi 126–27, 138–40; colonial discourse 127–29; culturally unresponsive services 134–35; deficit thinking 134, 138; and disability paradigms 129–30; discrimination and stereotyping practices 133; exclusionary practices based on impairment and/or age 136–37, 138; Māori traditional world view 127; multiple identities and oppressions 132; socio-economic issues 130–32, 135–36; whānau resistance and agency 137–38, 139, 140
marginalisation: Māori 128; in a multicultural society 152; rangatahi Māori 262, 263, 267, 269, 272; and resistance 265–66; and social and economic policies 42; and social models of disability 127; tamariki and rangatahi Māori with a disability 126, 130, 138, 139; and targeted services 51; vulnerable children 45
maternity care 24

Mathletics 18
Maui 127
May, Muriel 102-03
McCahon, Colin 95, 96
McDonald's restaurants 123
'McMansions' 61
media 20, 192-93; focus on success 237; *see also* electronic media; social media; television
mental health 45, 49, 174, 220
mobile telephones 197, 201, **203**, 204
modernity 113-18
Money, John 103-04
Montessori, Maria 99
'moral panics' 31
Morrinsville School 103-04
mothers 16, 120
multicultural society 18, 20, 128, 141, 143-45; early childhood education 150-51, 152; positioning multicultural childhood within discourses of multicultural relations 145-50; reconceptualising multicultural childhood 151-52
Muri-ranga-whenua 127
music 119, 202
Myers Park **117**, 118

National Safety Association 120
National Standards 236, 247
nationalist movements 113
Native Schools 105, 106
neglect *see* child abuse and neglect
neighbourhoods 66, 73-75, 114
neo-liberalism 9, 10, 24, 25, 122-24, 235-36, 238, 239-40, 242, 246, 276
Netherlands 66, 70
New Brighton School 109
New Zealand AIDS Foundation 250, 252
The New Zealand Disability Strategy 131
Ngāti Kāpo o Aotearoa 24, 132, 133
North East Valley School, Dunedin **103**
numeracy 236, 237, 245, 247

obesity 66, 114-15
OE 16
OECD 130, 220; *Measuring Child Poverty* 16
Office of Disability Issues 23
Ohuru railway camp school **104**
outdoor education 68, 69

Pacific Island countries: and Aotearoa New Zealand 18; and climate change 277; size of population in Aotearoa New Zealand compared to home country 19; *see also* Pasifika children; Pasifika peoples

Pākehā/European domination in Aotearoa New Zealand 14, 123, 128, 129, 147-48, 151
Palmer, Sue 65
parental leave 24
parenting: and child vulnerability 45, 46, 53-54; diverse beliefs and practices 145; evidence-based programmes 55-56; therapeutic team parenting model 177-78
parents: access to children following separation and divorce 156, 157, 158-60; and agency of children 39; and child vulnerability 45, 48-49, 52, 53, 54-55; and children's use of electronic media 198-99, 200, 201, 203-04; concerns about children's working conditions 189-90; education, influence on children's participation in higher education 269; employment 54-55; and play/outdoor activities 68, 69; re-partnering 34; and research involving children 82, 89; rights 78; risk aversion 68, 123-24; separation and divorce 34-35, 49, 122, 153, 154. 157, 160-61; and success of children 237; time spent with children 54-55; *see also* adopted and fostered children; families; family law decision-making, children's participation; fathers; mothers; sole parents
Parr, James 114
participation: children's rights 36-38, 78, 79, 81-82, 84, 154, 187, 208, 209-10; early childhood education 35-36, 39-40, 145, 207-19; in education 96, 99, 108, 109; guided 38-40; Hart's 'ladder of participation' 209; Shier's levels of participation 209-10, 212, 213, 214, 215, 216, 218, 219; *see also* children's agency and voice; family law decision-making, children's participation
Partnered Response initiative 50
Pasifika children: adopted 169; early childhood education 52; educational achievement 23; health 16, 24; statistics 18; vulnerability 46
Pasifika peoples: fertility rates 18; housing 62, 63; move to Aotearoa New Zealand for work opportunities 142; population 18, 19; poverty 47-48, 267; size of population in Aotearoa New Zealand compared to home country 19; and suburbanisation in Auckland 118; *see also* Pasifika children; Samoan people
peer pressure 47
peer research methodology 80

perseverance, and success 239, 248
Pestalozzi, Johann 99–100, 102
Phillipstown School 108
physical education 113–14
physical fitness, and academic performance 121, 240, 247
Piaget, Jean 99
play 38; to 1900 111–13; 1900–1940s 113–18, **115, 117**; 1950s–1970s 118–20; 1970s–1980s 120–22; 1980s to present 122–24; domestic play space 61, **61**, 62; economic and political context 110, 111, 113–14, 116, 118–19, 125; equipment 119, **122**; explorational 121; and extracurricular activities 119, 121, 124–25, 237; and feminist movement 120–22, 123; free play 111, **111**, 113, 114, 121, 125; and globalisation 123; and learning 99, 100, 119; and neo-liberalism 122–24; at school 113; spaces with and without adult supervision 73; on streets 30, 66, 73, 75, 112, 116, 118, 119, 124; and structured entertainment 119, 121, 124–25; toys 112, 116, 118–19, 123, 124; and transport 66, 67
Play Centre movement 120, 121, 136
playgrounds 116, **117**, 118; safety 120
Plunket Society 23, 24, 121
pluralism, multicultural 147–48
policy, and research 77, 78, 79
population: Asian groups 18; Māori 16, 18, 19; Pacific peoples 18, 19; statistics 16, 18, 60
post-structuralist theories 251–52
poverty 14, 25, 47, 275; and child employment 185, 190, 191; and educational underachievement 47; impacts 275; international comparisons 16, 130; Māori 14, 47–48, 129, 130, 269; policies to eliminate 58; statistics 47; and vulnerability 45, 47
power: adult–child imbalance 33, 78, 85, 87–88, 241; early childhood environments 208, 211, 212, 216, 217, 219; and globalisation 149; and multicultural pluralism 147, 148; and poverty 130; researchers 81, 87–88, 212; in schools 271; and stereotypes 265; struggles between cultural groups 148; and urban design 116; and working children 190
Power Shift Youth Climate Summit 278
Presbyterian Support 23

Prime, Kevin 64
prisoners' children 220–23, 231–34; contact with incarcerated parent 227–31, 232–34; foster care 223; kinship care 223–24; knowledge and understanding of parental incarceration 225–27, 233; living with biological mothers 224; living with paternal grandmother 224–25; statistics 220, 222
privacy 90
protection rights 210
provision rights 210
punishment: early years schooling, 1900–1920s 101–02, 103, 105, 106–07; physical 32–33; smacking 122; strategies of punishment and control in school 268

Q'topia 250
queer theoretical frameworks 251–52
queer youth 32, 250, 253–54, 256–57, 259
Queer–Straight Alliances 250–51, 252; see also Yes! Queer–Straight Alliance

racism 8–9, 129, 132; and Yes! Queer–Straight Alliance 253, 254–55, 257
Rainbow Youth 250
rangatahi Māori: deficit thinking 263–64, 265, 272; experience of transition to work 262–63, 269–73; marginalisation 262, 263, 267, 269, 272; silencing 264–65; spaces for resistance 265–67, 273; stereotyping 265, 271; see also Māori kāpo (blind) tamariki and rangatahi; tamariki Māori
Raukokore School 105–06
reading 196, 236, 237, 245, 247
recreational activities 13
refugees 22
Reggio Emilia philosophy of early childhood education 208–09
relationships see social relationships
relocation of children after parental separation 157, 158, 160, 161, 162
research: children's participation 78, 79, 80, 81–85, 90–91; confidentiality 82, 85, 90; importance of research including children 78–80; informed consent 87–90; issues of age and competence 83–84; peer research methodology 80; and policy 77, 78, 79; primary accountability to the child 82–83; respect and consideration for children 85; see also ethics
resilience 45, 174; factors contributing to 46
respiratory disease 14

risk and vulnerability discourses 31–32
role models 47
rural areas: environment 63; Māori migration from 118, 128; population 60; rural myth 112; schools 13
rural–urban shift 60

safety 31, 32, 67–68, 118, 120, 123–24, 215
Salmond, Anne 105
Samoan people: Auckland 20; language 20; population in Aotearoa New Zealand compared to Samoa 19
Schofield, Grant 67–68
School beginnings (May) 99
schools: access and choice 13; children attending non-local schools 72, 73, 75; engagement with communities 52–53; Native Schools 105, 106–07, **107**; outdoor education 68, 69; risk aversion 68; role, compared to mothers 120; rural areas 13; special needs children 23–24; traffic accidents around schools 66; transport to and from school 66, 72; *see also* education; education, early years schooling; Kura Kaupapa Māori; and names of individual schools
Sensible Sentencing Trust 227
sexual abuse 31
sexual identity 9, 32, 250, 253–54, 255, 256–57, 259
Shelly Beach, Auckland **115**
Shier's levels of participation 209–10, 212, 213, 214, 215, 216, 218, 219
shopping 123
silencing 264–65
social actors, children as 29, 33, 81–82, 85, 91, 121, 122, 155, 196, 197
social capital 48, 58, 267
social challenges facing children and youth 276–77
Social Darwinism 113
social media 47
social relationships: and agency 39–40; and disruption of heteronormative equations of difference 257; and learning 39; and success 244; and vulnerability 46, 47
Social Report 2010 (Ministry of Social Development) 130
social services 50–53; for children 22–25; evidence-based 55–56; targeted 51, 57; universal 51–52; whole child/whole family, inter-agency approach 56–58; *see also* health services
social welfare 24, 31, 54, 135–36, 177, 275

social workers 32, 37, 53, 88, 134, 157, 161; and adoption/fostering of children 167, 171, 172, 176, 177
sociocultural theory 39, 84
socio-economic status: and educational achievement 236; and life chances 263; Māori 9, 14, 47–48, 63, 129, 130–32, 135–36; *see also* poverty
sole parents 54
Somerset, Gwen (née Alley) 101, 121
sports 66, 67, 114, 115, 116, 121, 240–41, 243–44
State of the World's Mothers report 16
Stephenson, Hannah 63
stereotyping: Māori kāpo (blind) tamariki and rangatahi 133; racial 128; rangatahi Māori 265, 266; and success 246, 247; in television programmes 194
Stirling, Eruera 105–06
'stranger danger' 67
Strong, T.B. 108
Student Volunteer Army, Christchurch 279
substance abuse 45, 47, 49, 220, 275; *see also* alcohol; cannabis
success: areas of success 242; children's perceptions 237–48; competition and winning 240–41; and curriculum areas 245–46, 247; and education 235–36, 242, 247–8; feedback about 241; and gender 236, 238, 239, 240, 241, 242–44, 245–46, 247; meaning 237, 239–40; out of school 242–44, 246; and overcoming challenges 239, 240, 248; parental anxieties 237; policy priorities 235–36; pressure on children to achieve 13; satisfaction about 241
suicide 16, 47, 130, 224
swimming 114, **115**

tamariki Māori: and deficit thinking of teachers 263–64; with disabilities 24, 127; early childhood education 52, 131, 136; early years school classes 105–07, **106**, **107**; health 16, 24, 133; living with extended kin or foster carers 170; numeracy and literacy 236; statistics 18; vulnerability 46; *see also* Māori kāpo (blind) tamariki and rangatahi; rangatakai Māori
tangata whenua 274
targeted services 51, 58
Te Aro School, Wellington **97**
Te Kotahitanga 264
Te Reo Māori 20, 129, 277; children punished for speaking Te Reo 105–07

Te Roopu Waiora Trust 24
Te Whāriki 35–36, 150–51, 207, 209, 210, 218, 219
Teachers talk teaching (Middleton & May) 97
teenagers: need for parental support 55; pregnancy 16, 49; research participation 83; social and psychological morbidity 49, 50; teenage birth rate 16; *see also* queer youth; rangatahi Māori
telecommunications 13, 20; convergence with information technology 193–94, 197, 198, 203, 204; *see also* electronic media
telephones 196, 201, 202; *see also* mobile telephones
television 20, 119, 192–94; in children's bedrooms 194, 196, 198, 199–200; children's television 194; children's use 193–94, 196, 198–204; children's views on positive and negative effects 200–01; digital 193; and homework 202; intergenerational audiences 194; and mediated screen technologies 194, 197, 198–204; multiple household TV sets 201; music channel 202; no-TV families 200, 204
therapeutic team parenting model 177–78
time compression, and car use 67
transport: and access to wider spatial area 66–67, 70; and independence 66–67
Treaty of Waitangi 20, 131–32, 142, 277
Triple P programme 55
truancy 47
Turner movement 114

unemployment 54
UNICEF 181
United Nations: Committee on the Rights of the Child 221; Conference on Environment and Development 278; Convention on the Rights of Persons with Disabilities 21, 131; Convention on the Status of Refugees 22; Declaration of the Rights of Indigenous People 22, 131; Framework Convention on Climate Change 278; *Human Development Report 2013* 16; Universal Declaration of Human Rights (UDHR) 180, 183, 190, 191
United Nations Convention on the Rights of the Child (UNCRC) 21, 23, 36–37, 194; and child employment 185–87, 190, 191; and children with an incarcerated parents 221; and children's participation in family law disputes 153, 154, 165–66; and early childhood education 208, 210, 218, 219; and informed consent 87; and research involving children 78, 79, 82, 83, 91; and services for vulnerable children 56, 57
United States 17, 65, 66, 95, 99, 178, 194, 250
universal services 51–52; *see also* education; health services
urban areas 60; inner-city living 62; Māori migration to 118, 128; section sizes and housing density 60–62
urban planning, and children 121

Victory Village 53
vulnerable children 31–32, 34; adopted and fostered children 171, 172–73, 174, 178; barriers to delivery of services 53–56; costs of failure to protect children 50; definition and description 44–46; prevalence 46–50; prevention and intervention strategies 50–53; protective factors 46, 50; research participation 84; risk factors 45, 46, 47–49; whole child/whole family, inter-agency approach 56–58; *see also* child abuse and neglect; marginalisation; poverty; prisoners' children; socio-economic status

Waimea School 107
Wellington 60, 63–64
Western culture 32, 141, 146–47, 149–50, 151, 184
Whānau-a-Apanui tribe 105
Whānau Ora initiative 51, 52
whānaungatanga 64, 128, 130, 139
Whirinaki Native School **107**
WINZ (Work and Income New Zealand) 135–36
working children *see* child employment
working hours, New Zealand 54–55, 276
World Kids' Literature Quiz Competition 18
writing 245–46

Yes! Queer–Straight Alliance 40, 249, 252–53; and counselling 259–60; intended and unintended consequences 258–61; interrupting understandings of normalcy in peer culture 256–58; as a site of learning at Kereru High School 253–55
youth *see* queer youth; rangatahi Māori; teenagers